The Politics of Scientific A

Controversies over issues such as genetically engineered food, foot-and-mouth disease and the failure of risk models in the global financial crisis have raised concerns about the quality of expert scientific advice. The legitimacy of experts, and of the political decision-makers and policy-makers whom they advise, essentially depends on the quality of the advice. But what does quality mean in this context, and how can it be achieved? This volume argues that the quality of scientific advice can be ensured by an appropriate institutional design of advisory organisations. Using examples from a wide range of international case studies, including think tanks, governmental research institutes, agencies and academies, the authors provide a systematic guide to the major problems and pitfalls encountered in scientific advice and the means by which organisations around the world have solved these problems.

JUSTUS LENTSCH is Department Head of the Doctoral Programme, at the Heinrich Böll Foundation, a green think tank and an international policy network.

PETER WEINGART is Director Emeritus of the Institute for Science and Technology Studies (IWT), Professor Emeritus of Sociology (of Science) at Bielefeld University and Visiting Professor at the Center for Research on Science and Technology, Stellenbosch University, South Africa.

The Politics of Scientific Advice

Institutional Design for Quality Assurance

Justus Lentsch and Peter Weingart (eds.)

CAMBRIDGE
UNIVERSITY PRESS

CAMBRIDGE UNIVERSITY PRESS
Cambridge, New York, Melbourne, Madrid, Cape Town,
Singapore, São Paulo, Delhi, Tokyo, Mexico City

Cambridge University Press
The Edinburgh Building, Cambridge CB2 8RU, UK

Published in the United States of America by
Cambridge University Press, New York

www.cambridge.org
Information on this title: www.cambridge.org/9780521177153

© Cambridge University Press 2011

First published 2011

Printed in the United Kingdom at the University Press, Cambridge

A catalogue record for this publication is available from the British Library

Library of Congress Cataloging-in-Publication Data

The politics of scientific advice : institutional design for quality assurance /
[edited by] Justus Lentsch, Peter Weingart.
    p.   cm.
    ISBN 978-1-107-00370-5 (Hardback) – ISBN 978-0-521-17715-3 (pbk.)
    1. Science news.   2. Scientific bureaus.   3. Science and state.
I. Lentsch, Justus.   II. Weingart, Peter.   III. Title.
    Q225.P65 2011
    338.9'26–dc22
                                                                    2010050338

ISBN 978-1-107-00370-5 Hardback
ISBN 978-0-521-17715-3 Paperback

Contents

Figures

Tables

Acknowledgements

As the editors of such a collaborative effort we are indebted to numerous people and organisations. Foremost we thank the chapter authors for their contributions and their endurance throughout the lengthy process of bringing this project to completion. All chapters have been commissioned for this volume and were presented and discussed at an international symposium in Berlin. We particularly thank the Fritz Thyssen Stiftung for providing generous funding for this event.

The volume grew out of a larger collaborative effort of the interdisciplinary research group Scientific Advice to Policy in Democracies of the Berlin-Brandenburg Academy of Sciences and Humanities. We therefore would like to thank the members of this group and the president of the Academy, Günter Stock, for his encouragement and support. Without the organisational backing of the Academy's science administration, most notably its director, Wolf-Hagen Krauth, and his team, Regina Reimann and Renate Neumann, this project would have never materialised.

Many of the ideas have been developed in lively intellectual exchange with numerous colleagues. In particular, we would like to thank Sheila Jasanoff, Sabine Maasen, and Mary Morgan and her group How Well Do Facts Travel at the London School of Economics and Political Science (LSE) for personal encouragement, advice and for sharing their ideas with us.

John Haslam at Cambridge University Press was supportive of the project right from the beginning. We gratefully acknowledge the criticism of two anonymous reviewers that greatly helped improve the quality and consistency of the volume.

Finally, thanks goes to Lilo Jegerlehner for her careful typesetting and to Marc Weingart for language editing. We are most grateful to all of them for helping to make the book finally become a reality.

Biographical notes

PETER D. BLAIR is Executive Director of the Division for Engineering and Physical Sciences, US National Academy of Science. From 1983 to 1996 he served in several capacities at the Congressional Office of Technology Assessment, concluding as Assistant Director of the agency and Director of the Division of Industry, Commerce and International Security. Prior to his government service, Dr Blair served on the faculty of the University of Pennsylvania and was co-founder and principal of Technecon Consulting Group, Inc., an engineering-economic consulting firm in Philadelphia. He is the author or co-author of three books and over a hundred technical articles in areas of energy and environmental policy, regional science and input-output analysis.

FRANK A.G. DEN BUTTER is Head of Department of Economics, Free University Amsterdam. Before that he was Director of the Tinbergen Institute. He is Chairman of the Supervisory Committee Economic Institute for the Building Industry, the Central Statistical Committee and serves on various other governmental and scientific committees such as the Scientific Council for Government Policy (1998–2002), Social Economic Policy Committee of Social Economic Council, Consultant for OECD and Dutch Ministries of Finance and Economic Affairs. Moreover, Frank den Butter was chairman of the Royal Netherlands Economic Association (the oldest economists' association in the world) from 1997 to 2003 and member of the Central Statistical Committee (the supervisory committee of the Central Bureau of Statistics, CBS) from 1998 to 2004. He has authored numerous books and articles in econometrics, monetary economics, applied statistics and empirical economics; amongst them *Empirical Models and Policy Making: Interaction and Institutions* (2000, with Mary S. Morgan (eds.)).

PETER COLLINS is the Director of the Royal Society Centre for the History of Science since 2008. He studied chemistry at Oxford

University and gained his Ph.D. in the social history of science in 1978 at Leeds University. Peter Collins joined the Royal Society in 1981 as the first member of staff in the Society's history to work full-time on science policy. From 1985 to 1994 he ran the Science and Engineering Policy Studies Unit (SEPSU). He then was made Head of Science Advice in 1995 and Director of Science Policy in 1999. In this role he was responsible for shaping and promoting the Society's position on a wide range of issues across policy for science and the scientific aspects of public policy, at both national and international levels. Peter has also directed the work of the Council and Fellowship Office since 1999. The CFO deals with all matters relating to the Fellowship, including the election process, and supports the main corporate decision-making bodies such as the Council, the Board and the Audit Committee. In June 2001, Peter Collins oversaw the launch of the European Academies Science Advisory Council (EASAC).

SVEN DAMMANN works as an Administrator at the European Commission, Directorate General for Energy. He previously worked as a civil servant in the Transport, Energy, Infrastructure and the Information Society Section of the European Economic and Social Committee (EESC) and in the European Environment's Strategic Knowledge and Innovation Programme as project officer for emerging issues and research. He holds a Ph.D. from the TU Denmark and the Danish Building Research Institute, and a Diploma in architecture from the University of Hannover. He has special experience in training social movement groups in Western and Eastern Europe in nonviolent conflict and empowerment techniques and participatory decision-making.

ROBIN FEARS is a freelance consultant in research and development policy and strategies. At the secretariat of the European Academies Science Advisory Council (EASAC) he is responsible for the biosciences portfolio. He also did consultancy work for the Academy of Medical Sciences, the Royal Society, and the Food and Agriculture Organisation (FAO), United Nations, in fields such as plant genomics and infectious diseases. Before that he was Director, Science Policy, for SmithKline Beecham.

SILVIO FUNTOWICZ is Head of the Knowledge Assessment Methodologies Sector, Institute for the Protection and Security of the Citizen (IPSC), European Commission – Joint Research Centre (EC-JRC). He previously taught mathematics, logic and research methodology in Buenos Aires, Argentina. In the 1980s he was a Research Fellow at the

University of Leeds. He is the author of *Uncertainty and Quality in Science for Policy* (1990) in collaboration with Jerry Ravetz, where they have invented the concept of 'extended peer review'. Silvio Funtowicz is author of numerous papers in the field of environmental and technological risks and policy-related research.

DAVID GEE is group leader of Emerging Issues and Scientific Liaison of the European Environment Agency's Strategic Knowledge and Innovation Programme. In this capacity he is principal EEA-Editor of the EEA reports *Late Lessons from Early Warnings* on the precautionary principle. He previously worked for over two decades on occupational and environmental risk reduction with UK Trade Unions and with Friends of the Earth, UK, where he was Director. He has specialised on risks and uncertainties arising from chemicals, radiation and asbestos, on green taxes and ecological tax reform and on communicating scientific complexity and uncertainty to non-specialists.

SUSANNE GLASMACHER is Press Spokeswoman and Head of Public Relations at the Robert Koch Institute. Formerly Press Spokeswoman of the Berlin Association of Statutory Health Insurance Physicians, Editor of the *Journal of the Federal Ministry of Education and Research* and the *Journal of the German Cancer Research Centre* and a freelancing science journalist for print and radio. She is a biologist with journalistic training.

SHEILA JASANOFF is Pforzheimer Professor of Science and Technology Studies at Harvard University's John F. Kennedy School of Government. She has held faculty appointments or visiting positions at several universities, including Cornell, Yale, Oxford and Kyoto. At Cornell she founded and chaired the Department of Science and Technology Studies. She has been a Fellow at the Berlin Institute for Advanced Study (Wissenschaftskolleg) and Resident Scholar at the Rockefeller Foundation's study centre in Bellagio. Her research centres on the use of science in legal and political decision-making with a particular focus on regulatory science and peer review. Her books on these topics include *Risk Management and Political Culture* (1986), *The Fifth Branch* (1990), *Science at the Bar* (1995) and only recently *Designs on Nature* (2005). Jasanoff has served on the Board of Directors of the American Association for the Advancement of Science and as President of the Society for Social Studies of Science.

REINHARD KURTH is Professor Emeritus at Humboldt University and Director Emeritus of the Robert Koch Institute (RKI), Berlin. Between 1986 and 2008 he was Director of the three leading

Federal Research Institutes in his field in Germany. He is member of several advisory and governing boards. Amongst others, he is President of the council of the board of trustees of the German Centre for Rheumatism Research, Deutsches Rheumaforschungszentrum, and member of the councils of the Universities of Giessen and Münster. He has received several high-ranking honours for his scientific achievements that are reflected in more than 300 publications. For his outstanding achievements he was honoured in 2005 with the Grand Cross of the Order of Merit of the Federal Republic of Germany. He is elected member of the Berlin-Brandenburg Academy of Sciences and Humanities, the German Academy of Natural Scientists Leopoldina, the American Philosophical Society and the New York Academy of Sciences.

JUSTUS LENTSCH is Head of the Department, Doctoral Programme, at the Heinrich Böll Foundation, a Green Think Tank and an International Policy Network. He previously worked at the Institute for Science and Technology Studies (IWT), Bielefeld University, and in the science and research management of the Berlin-Brandenburg Academy of Sciences and Humanities, where he has contributed to the *Leitlinien Politikberatung* (2008). Having studied mathematics, physics and philosophy he holds a doctorate in philosophy. His fields of interest are science, technology, and innovation studies and science policy. His current work focuses on regulatory science and the role of scientific advice in public policymaking.

NAOMI ORESKES is Professor of History and Science Studies at the University of California, San Diego. Her research focuses on the historical development of scientific knowledge, methods, and practices in the earth and environmental sciences, and on understanding scientific consensus and dissent. Having started her professional career as a field geologist, her research now focuses on the historical development of scientific knowledge, methods and practices in the earth and environmental sciences. Her 2004 essay 'The scientific consensus on climate change' (*Science* 306: 1686) has been widely cited in the mass media, including National Public Radio (Fresh Air), *The New Yorker, USA Today, Parade*, as well as in the Royal Society's publication, *A Guide to Facts and Fictions about Climate Change*, and, most recently, in Al Gore's movie *An Inconvenient Truth*. Together with Erik M. Conway she recently published *Merchants of Doubt: How a Handful of Scientists Obscured the Truth on Issues from Tobacco Smoke to Global Warming* (2010). A 1994 recipient of the NSF Young Investigator Award, she has served as a consultant to the US Environmental

Protection Agency and the US Nuclear Waste Technical Review
Board on the use and evaluation of computer models and has taught
at Stanford, Dartmouth, Harvard and NYU.

SUSAN OWENS is Professor of Environment and Policy and Fellow of
Newnham College, University of Cambridge. She has researched and
published widely on environmental issues and policy processes and
on interpretations of sustainable development in theory and practice,
particularly in the context of land use and environmental planning.
Her work has also made a substantial contribution to public policy.
She has been a member of the standing Royal Commission on
Environmental Pollution since 1998 and has served on a number of
other public bodies. She is currently a member of the Strategic
Research Board of the Economic and Social Research Council. Professor Owens was awarded an OBE for services to sustainable development in 1998 and in 2000 received the Royal Geographical
Society's 'Back' Award for contributions to research and policy formulation in this field. She was made an Honorary Member of the
Royal Town Planning Institute in 2006 and an Honorary Professor of
the University of Copenhagen in 2008. For the academic year 2008–
09 she held the King Carl XVI Gustaf Professorship of Environmental Science, hosted by the Stockholm Resilience Centre and the Royal
Institute of Technology, Stockholm.

VOLKER PERTHES is Chairman of the Stiftung Wissenschaft und
Politik (SWP), Director of the German Institute for International
and Security Affairs, and teaches as Professor of Political Science/
International Relations at Humboldt University Berlin and Free
University of Berlin. Before he became director of the institute, he
was Head of the SWP Research Group Middle East and Africa for
several years. He was Assistant Professor at the American University of Beirut (1991–93) and has also taught at the Universities of
Duisburg, Münster and Munich. He serves as a member of several
scientific boards such as the Shanghai Institute for International
Studies (SIIS) or the Finnish Institute of International Affairs
(FIIA, UPI). He is editor and author of numerous books and
articles on foreign politics and security.

ARTHUR PETERSEN is Professor of Science and Environmental Public
Policy at the VU University Amsterdam and Chief Scientist of the PBL
Netherlands Environmental Assessment Agency. Visiting Professor in
the Centre for the Analysis of Time Series and the Grantham Research
Institute on Climate Change and the Environment at the London

School of Economics and Political Science (LSE) and Research Affiliate in the Political Economy & Technology Policy Program of the Center for International Studies at the Massachusetts Institute of Technology (MIT). He leads the Netherlands Environmental Assessment Agency's efforts in the development and use of methodology for sustainability assessment and methodology for uncertainty assessment and communication and is responsible for the agency's quality assurance. Besides his professional jobs, he has been active within Pugwash, an organisation that brings together, from around the world, influential scholars and public figures concerned with reducing the danger of armed conflict and seeking cooperative solutions for global problems such as those related to poverty alleviation and protection of the environment.

GEOFFREY PODGER has been Chief Executive of the Health and Safety Executive since November 2005. Since graduating from Oxford University in 1974, he has worked for three government departments, two international organisations and three British agencies. In particular he worked extensively on a range of issues for the Department of Health in London. He was chosen in 2000 to be the first Chief Executive of the UK Food Standards Agency and in 2003 as the first Director of the European Food Safety Authority. He became a Companion of the Order of the Bath (a British decoration for public services) in January 2003.

MICHAEL D. ROGERS is a senior research associate at King's College London's Centre for Risk Management and a former science and ethics adviser, Bureau of European Policy Advisers (BEPA), European Commission. He was head of the secretariat of the European Group on Ethics in Science and New Technologies. In the academic year 1999–2000 he was on detached duty at Duke University as the European Union Fellow. In 1989, he became a founding member of the European Commission's technological think tank, the Institute for Prospective Technological Studies. He joined the Forward Studies Unit in 1992. He is now responsible for providing advice on scientific subjects relating to contemporary policy debates such as biotechnology and risk analysis.

DANIEL SAREWITZ is Director of the Consortium for Science, Policy and Outcomes, Associate Director, Center for Nanotechnology in Society; and Professor of Science and Society, School of Life Sciences and School of Sustainability at Arizona State University, Tempe. Prior to taking up his current position, he was the Director of the Geological Society of America's Institute for Environmental Education. From 1989 to 1993 he worked on Capitol Hill, first as a Congressional Science

Fellow, and then as science consultant to the House of Representatives Committee on Science, Space, and Technology, where he was also principal speech writer for Committee Chairman George E. Brown, Jr. Before moving into the policy arena he was a research associate in the Department of Geological Sciences at Cornell University; he received his Ph.D. in geological sciences from Cornell University. His work focuses on understanding the connections between scientific research and social benefit, and on developing methods and policies to strengthen such connections. He is co-editor of *Prediction: Science, Decision-Making, and the Future of Nature* (2000) and author of *Frontiers of Illusion: Science, Technology, and the Politics of Progress* (1996) as well as of numerous articles, speeches and reports about the relationship between science and social progress.

JEROEN P. VAN DER SLUIJS is Assistant Professor and Senior Researcher at the Division Science, Technology and Society (STS), Copernicus Institute for Sustainable Development and Innovation, Utrecht University, and Invited Professor at Centre d'Economie et d'Ethique pour l'Environnement et le Développement, Université de Versailles Saint-Quentin-en-Yvelines. He coordinates the Research Cluster Energy and Global Change: Dealing with Risks and Uncertainties at the University of Utrecht. He is author of numerous articles in the fields of uncertainty management, knowledge quality assessment and NUSAP-uncertainty methods, stakeholder elicitation and Participatory Integrated Assessment.

CHRISTIAN STREFFER is an Emeritus Member of the Main Commission of the International Commission on Radiological Protection (ICRP) (until 2007) and Chairman of the ICRP Committee on Doses from Radiation Exposure. He is Professor Emeritus of Medical Radiobiology at the University of Essen (where he was also President from 1988 to 1992) and Honorary Director of the Institute for Science and Ethics, Essen. He is author of numerous publications in the fields of radiation protection and risk management.

ANDREAS STUCKE is Head of the Department Evaluation and Quantitative Analysis, German Science Council. He previously worked at Bielefeld University and the Max-Planck-Institute for the Study of Societies, Cologne. He holds a Dr. rer. soc. from Bielefeld University. He is author of several publications on science and research politics and the German science system.

VOLKER TER MEULEN is President Emeritus of the German Academy of Natural Scientists Leopoldina that became Germany's National

Academy in 2008. He previously was Professor and Director of the Institute of Clinical Virology and Immunology at the Julius-Maximilians University at Würzburg. In 2007, he was elected Chairman of the European Academies Science Advisory Council (EASAC), which represents the national science academies of the EU member states and conducts policy consulting at European level. From 1992 to 1998 he was a member of the German Science Council. He is one of the leading founders of molecular biology virus research and a pioneer of neurovirology. His scientific achievements are reflected in several hundred publications. He has received several high-ranking academic honours such as the Max Planck Research Prize 1992, the Pioneer Award of the International Society of Neurovirology 2000 and the Robert-Koch-Gold-Medal (2009); in 2008, he became Honorary Doctor of the Medical Faculty at Freiburg University. He is member of several national and international committees, including committees of the World Health Organisation (WHO) and of a wide range of State and Federal Ministries. He has been honoured for his social activities with the Cross of Merit on Ribbon of the Order of Merit of the Federal Republic of Germany in 1992 and the Bavarian Order of Merit 2000, the highest Order of Merit of the Free State of Bavaria.

GERT G. WAGNER is Professor of Economics at the Berlin University of Technology and Research Director at the German Institute for Economic Research (DIW) Berlin where he directs the German Socio-Economic Panel Study (SOEP). He is Chairman of the German Council for Social and Economic Data, member of the German Science Council and serves on the Advisory Board to Statistics Germany; he was a member of the Rürup-Commission. He is a member of the Steering Group on Social Sciences and Humanities of the European Strategy Forum for Research Infrastructures (ESFRI) and member of the BHPS Scientific Steering Committee (British Household Panel Study). He is also a member of the Council for Engineering Sciences at the Union of the German Academies of Science and Humanities and the German Academy of Natural Scientists Leopoldina.

PETER WEINGART is Director Emeritus of the Institute for Science & Technology Studies (IWT), Professor Emeritus of Sociology (of Science) at Bielefeld University and Guest Professor at CREST, University of Stellenbosch, South Africa. He studied economics and sociology at the Universities of Freiburg, Berlin and Princeton. He was Director of the Center for Interdisciplinary Research (ZiF) 1989–94, Fellow of the Wissenschaftskolleg 1983–84, Visiting Scholar at

Harvard University 1984–85, Research Scholar at the Getty Research Institute 2000, since 1996 he is Guest Professor at CREST, University of Stellenbosch (South Africa), member of the Berlin-Brandenburg Academy of Sciences and Humanities and the German Academy of Engineering Sciences (acatech). He was spokesperson of the interdisciplinary research group Scientific Advice to Policy in Democracy of the BBAW. He is editor of the journal *Minerva* as well as managing editor of the *International Yearbook Sociology of the Sciences* and has published numerous books and articles in the sociology of science and science policy.

BERT DE WIT is a Senior Scientist at the Netherlands Environmental Assessment Agency (PBL) in The Hague. Before 2010, he was Programme Manager at The Advisory Council for Research on Spatial Planning, Nature and the Environment (RMNO) in the Netherlands. A biologist by training, his special expertise lies in the field of boundary work between science, policy and society.

Part I

Methodological issues: quality control
and assurance in scientific policy advice

1 Introduction: the quest for quality as a challenge to scientific policy advice: an overdue debate?

Justus Lentsch and Peter Weingart[1]

How can science best be harnessed to support political decision-making? How should scientific advice to policymakers be institutionalised in government to be more accountable to academic science and public concerns at the same time? Concerns about the quality of scientific expert advice to policymakers have been raised for years, particularly in the UK and on the European level. Public debates such as the BSE case, the controversy about genetically engineered food, the foot-and-mouth disease (FMD) or the failure of experts and their risk models in the global financial crisis, have demonstrated that the legitimacy of experts and of the policymakers whom they advise essentially depends on the reliability and transparency of scientific advice. They have highlighted the absence of clear rules to follow as well as the lack of a legal framework and organisational structures for obtaining advice from academics. This lacuna has been further highlighted by the recent call for an institutional reform of the Intergovernmental Panel on Climate Change (IPCC) in reaction to allegations of shortcomings in its most recent assessment report.[2] Thus, the issue of quality control and assurance in scientific expert advising is of vital importance for both decision-makers and the academic community.

In fact, under the guise of evaluation, quality control and assurance have become 'a mantra of modernity' (Pawson and Tilley 1997: 2). In many other spheres of government, formalised procedures of quality control and assurance have become the norm, most notably through the standard-setting procedures of the International Organisation for Standardisation (ISO). In academia as well as in science-based policy

---

[1] The views expressed are those of the authors and strictly personal.
[2] The debate about the IPCC highlighted at least three requirements for a quality management of scientific advisory bodies: First, being able to deal with conflicts of interest, second, having formal procedures to deal with allegations of error, mistakes or bias and, finally, making sure that the body sticks to its mandate (Pielke 2010; see also Tol, Pielke and von Storch 2010).

advice, methods for quality assurance, however, are to a large extent informal, with self-assessment and peer review being the gold standard. But this situation is about to change. Accountability measures, performance indicators, etc. have become central to the new professionalism that increasingly takes hold of the sphere of scientific policy advice as well. Science's jurisdictional claim for defining the 'quality' of research and research-based services such as policy advice is no longer uncontested. In a sense, quality management has become a new mode of the governance of expertise. Michael Power (1997) has diagnosed a trend towards an 'audit society', where not the performance but rather an organisation's proxies of performance are being monitored and measured (Nightingale and Scott 2007: 546). As a consequence, organisations tend to adjust their behaviour to audit goals rather than to their initial social function. Such 'inadvertent consequences' of the audit culture increasingly pose a challenge for the quality of scientific policy advice as well (see Weingart 2005).

Hence, quality control and assurance have become the fundamental commitment in scientific policy advice. The objective is not only scientific robustness, but also to achieve results that are 'fit for function' and enhance the legitimacy of political or regulatory decisions based upon the advice (Funtowicz 2001). However, controlling and assuring the quality of scientific advice for public policymaking is neither a straightforward nor a uniform and well-defined task.

The growing importance of policy-related modes of knowledge production described by concepts like regulatory science (Irwin *et al.*, 1997), mode-2 science (Gibbons *et al.* 1994; Nowotny 2001) or post-normal science (Funtowicz and Ravetz 1990) comes with a shift from a narrow notion of quality towards broader questions of relevance and reliability.

In addition, in policy issues involving science and technology advocates from both sides, politics and science, selectively use science to pursue an agenda driven by their respective partial interests. Thus, the question arises whether there is anything one can do to institutionalise advisory processes in such a way that they advance the public interest.

Amazingly, the question of the *appropriate institutional design* of scientific advisory bodies and how this affects the *quality* of the advice they offer, i.e. their capacity to bridge between science and politics, is largely unexplored.[3]

---

[3] For one of the very few exceptions, see Guston's case study on the US National Toxicology Program (Guston 2005). Bijker, Bal and Hendriks (2009) recently conducted an ethnographical study of the practices of scientific advising in the Netherlands' *Gezondheidsraad*, focusing on what they call 'coordination work', a further development of the concept of 'boundary work' (Gieryn 1983; Jasanoff 1990). Drawing on this case study, Bijker *et al.* try to make a case against the 'democratisation' of scientific advisory bodies.

In order to close this gap, this volume assembles the perspectives from expert advisers and practitioners from organisations that serve as role models or points of reference in the debate: various kinds of advisory bodies, covering a spectrum from think tanks, governmental policy-oriented research institutes to agencies and academies.

The guiding idea of this volume is that the question of quality has to be answered on the level of organisations. The focus of the book is therefore on fundamental principles of quality control and on the institutional mechanisms and practices implementing them. Each chapter is organised around a structured set of guiding questions to ensure that the overview is as coherent as possible. These questions concern the normative commitments; informal and codified criteria; treatment of uncertainty; complexity and value-ladenness; institutions and routines of quality control and the political dimensions. The effort to assemble different organisational practices is long overdue. Whereas much has been written about expertise and many case studies have been produced, the question of organisational design has not yet been dealt with systematically. Exactly this is attempted here.

The problem of quality in scientific advice to policymaking

Although the topic of the 'nature of expertise' is not a new one, up to the present there is no well-developed theory of scientific policy advice available (see Owens, Chapter 5). In one sense, this is a surprising and disturbing circumstance as governments, more than ever before, seek advice from a myriad of different sources, expert committees, councils, think tanks and agencies, etc. But policymaking is a complex process. Moreover, advice can take a multiplicity of different organisational forms – depending on the intended function, its relation to government or the time horizon. Finally, recent developments in the relationship between science and politics are also affecting the system of quality control (see, e.g., Maasen and Weingart 2005; Hemlin and Rasmussen 2006).

Thus, the institutionalisation of scientific advice to policymaking on an unprecedented scale has raised the issue of quality control. The problem appears on several levels. First of all, there is the question of what has caused a dramatic increase, not to say inflation, of supply of advice. It is due to a confluence of several developments. The expansion of state functions has led to an increasing complexity and technical content of policy- and decision-making in political administrations. This development has gradually exceeded the expertise that was typically assembled in ministries and specialised agencies, although the extent to which governments retain such in-house expertise differs according to political culture. In France, for example, the government bureaucracy still commands the largest share of expertise, supported by a highly professionalised education of public servants, while in the US think tanks and other research institutions have a much stronger role in providing expert advice.

A second development related to the first is the impact of neoliberalism and its derivatives such as the paradigm of lean government and new public management. Many governments have actively cut staff in their administrations, outsourcing the needed expertise to independent bodies and to industry. Especially in the broad field of regulation, which makes up a large share of policymaking, relying on the expertise of stakeholders obviously poses problems of differentiating interested from neutral advice and, thus, raises one of the crucial quality issues.[4]

A third development is a direct outcome of the other two. As governments have increasingly cut their in-house expertise, they have helped to create an advisory market. The more money governments invest in expert reports, the design of events and campaigns, special assessments and the like, the larger this market becomes as think tanks, NGOs, independent research institutes, commercial consulting and PR firms, and corporate or individual lobbyists acting as advisers are drawn into it. Only a fraction of these is committed to serious academic research. The larger part either uses the label of being scientific or does not even lay claim to the authority of science. These players on the advisory market are often dependent on the income from their activities and operate under the constraints of having to keep the chain of commissions uninterrupted.

Obviously, quality of advice is a serious problem on this market, not least because it is virtually impossible to convince the actors to accept best practice standards of giving advice. At the same time it is evident that the lack of reliable expertise and the abundance of conflicting information is a burden rather than helpful assistance for policymakers. Thus, the availability of advice says nothing about its quality, and quality of advice appears to be the problem. It is not only a problem because

---

[4] On the particular problem of the role of academic scientists in quality control and assessment of scientific advice in the regulation of drugs, toxic chemicals, etc. see, e.g., Krimsky 2003: 228f.; Wagner and Steinzor 2006. The dimensions of the problem become clear considering the future impact of the new EU guideline on the registration, evaluation and authorisation of chemicals (REACH) that delegates the assessment of chemicals to companies. For a recent historical study of how ideology and corporate interests have distorted the public understanding of some of the most pressing policy issues see Oreskes and Conway 2010.

unreliable expertise could misguide policy decisions. Such knowledge, because of its dual function with respect to politics, may also pose problems of legitimacy. Although democratic governments are legitimated by public consent, they also have to act in accordance with the state of knowledge, i.e. they cannot act completely irrationally (even if there is considerable room for interpretation). This mandate of rationality explains why governments are keen to have their policies supported by expert opinion. But it also has a dark side to it. Since new knowledge is communicated via the media, it can have a de-legitimating function to governments if it contradicts their policies. Announcements by the IPCC that the mean temperature keeps rising and indicates an unabated global warming are communicated via the mass media and have an immediate effect on governments. Whether justified or not, they will create the expectation on their part that, unless they demonstrate an active role in implementing measures to curb emissions of CO_2, popular support may erode. Thus, any communication of knowledge, be it utopian promises of future advances or dystopian scenarios of impending catastrophes which enunciate pressures to act, may undermine the authority and the legitimacy of governments.

This implies that governments have a genuine interest in controlling the kind of advice given to them and, if possible, the individuals or organisations where it is generated. On the other hand, this control may not be conspicuous because only if the expert advice given to them appears independent and objective does it carry the authority to add to the legitimacy of policy. Partisan advice does not count. This constitutes the interest of scientific advisers, in particular, not to become too involved in the politics of their clients. Politicisation undermines their authority.

Quality as a question of organisational design

The particular connection between scientific advisers and policymakers has been identified as an institutional layer between science and politics with its own rules. Expert knowledge communicated by advisers has to meet standards that are not sufficiently identified by epistemic criteria of validity and reliability.[5] Rather, it has to have a dual reference. It must be

---

[5] In a seminal paper William C. Clark and Giandomenico Majone (1985) already advise against overvaluing the importance of the credibility of knowledge or expertise at the cost of two other attributes, namely 'salience' (or relevance of expertise to decision-making) and 'legitimacy' (whether a knowledge generating procedure fairly considers the values, concerns and perspectives of those affected by the decisions or actions based on the very advice).

scientifically sound, *and* it must be politically useful and acceptable. In short, it must be epistemically *and* politically robust.

Epistemic robustness refers to the quality of knowledge in the sense of its validity. As the knowledge generated in advisory contexts responds to political problems and, thus, usually transcends purely disciplinary knowledge it has to meet different requirements of exactness and validity than academic research. Ideally, epistemically robust knowledge claims do not leave any room for interpretation, cannot be disputed by competing evidence, and, thus, cannot be abused. But even knowledge that is characterised by uncertainty and ambivalence may be robust if the probabilities of the postulated functional and causal relations are reliable. Most advice to politics is given in areas of uncertain knowledge which is particularly susceptible to ideological interpretations.

In light of this insight, Oreskes (Chapter 3) suggests an alternative rationale for organising *robust* advisory processes that does not deny uncertainties but rather enables us to live and work with them. The *unitisation model* she advances stems from the world of business. The idea is the same used by oil companies to divide the shares from an oil field amongst the different owners: use mid-course corrections instead of waiting for perfect knowledge at the outset. In this way it is possible to design advisory processes that can cope with uncertainty and indeterminacy even when stakes are high – an idea that is also central to adaptive management. This idea is further illustrated in the chapter by Sluijs, Petersen and Funtowicz (Chapter 14), who describe a structured approach to quality assessment used at the Netherlands National Institute for Public Health and the Environment (RIVM).

Political robustness of knowledge refers to the acceptability and the feasibility to implement recommendations based on it. An advice is robust if it can be politically implemented and meets the needs of the policymakers. Political robustness normally implies that the knowledge and the preferences of those who can be considered stakeholders are taken into account.

Distinguishing between the two dimensions of quality throws new light on two common assumptions underlying most advisory arrangements: first, that *good* or sound scientific knowledge alone provides the best possible foundation for public policy, and second, that the freedom to mutually monitor and criticise each other's contribution (i.e. peer review) is the best possible way to secure inputs of highest quality to public policy (Jasanoff, Chapter 2). Jasanoff argues in her chapter that we have to fundamentally rethink these assumptions in the light of recent scholarship in science studies: Not only is knowledge-making inevitably intertwined with social practices guided by non-epistemic norms and values, but it also has to proceed in the mode of expertise – not academic science – in order to inform political decision-making. The task of an expert body is thus to translate scientific knowledge into 'serviceable truth' (Jasanoff 1990). Quality controls on science for policy, she concludes, will have to be responsive to normative as well as to cognitive demands. At the same time they will have to be concerned with legitimacy as well as with questions of truths. This is the rationale of what Jasanoff calls the *virtuous reason* model – a model that situates the quality question within the more complex framework of public reason and legitimacy.

The last paper in the first part by Sarewitz (Chapter 4) functions as a provocative counterpoint to the first two by Jasanoff and Oreskes: Sarewitz argues that it may sometimes be better to disentangle science and politics. It can be much more promising to look for effective technological interventions to cope with complex and contested challenges to human well-being than to generate and deploy scientific knowledge aimed at improving decision-making and public policies. What makes certain *technological fixes*[6] such remarkably reliable cause-and-effect machines is that their problem-solving capacity is localised in a particular technology whose performance is largely insensitive to the surrounding context and background conditions. Insensitivity against unexpected disturbances and surprises from the context and background conditions is one of the core ideas of the concept of robustness as well. However, technological fixes not only solve problems technically, but in reducing contextual complexity they also reduce uncertainty and disagreement about certain policy goals.

The quality of scientific advice to politics thus depends on the degree to which these two requirements of robustness are being met. It is obvious that they cannot be met equally at the same time. There is not one ideal advisory arrangement but many, all of which are suboptimal. The overall question is: which form must expert advice have, and in which institutional arrangements must it be generated and communicated to meet the dual requirements of political acceptability and scientific validity? Phrasing the problem in this way means that the quality of expert advice to governments is primarily an issue of organisational design. The focus is on organisational conditions because they influence the quality of advice and, at the same time, they can be shaped by scientists and policymakers. Any attempt to influence and improve the

---

[6] The term as such is not new. It was probably Alvin Weinberg who first used it (Weinberg 1967).

quality of advice has to take recourse to organisational measures, including, of course, general principles and rules of law.

The advisory organisations in any political system reveal a great variety due to the historical contexts in which they were established and the functions they are supposed to perform. As legitimacy and credibility of expert claims are, to a large extent, bound to national contexts and governance regimes, some authors speak of 'national styles' (Renn 1995). Others allude to the 'civic epistemology', meaning the institutionalised practices by which expert claims are constructed, validated or challenged within a given society (Jasanoff 2005; Miller 2008). On the other hand, comparative analysis shows that such differences may as well be due to sectoral differences as to national ones (see, e.g., Bijker, Bal and Hendriks, 2009: 42). Beyond all national differences, particularly after World War II, certain prototypes of advisory organisations based on the very same general principles are copied from neighbouring regimes – a phenomenon that sometimes is described as a process of mimetic institutional isomorphism (DiMaggio and Powell 1983). In general, the formal and informal rules and mechanisms that structure the internal processes within advisory organisations function quite similarly across sectors and national styles of science advising.[7]

Both variability and convergence can be seen as an expression of the potential threat that any advice poses to the legitimacy of governments and, likewise, that politicisation poses to the authority of scientists, i.e. the reciprocal interest to control the advisory process and outcome described above.[8] With some simplification it could be said that the shaping of any organisation of scientific advice reflects the conflict between independent and dependent advice. All advisory bodies and their procedural rules are situated somewhere on a continuum whose endpoints are dominated by one or the other: dependence of the advisers and their politicisation on one end, and independence or autonomy of the advisers and the technocratic shaping of politics on the other. This conflict constitutes an inherent instability of any advisory arrangement. In particular, it implies that the *intended functions* of

---

[7] Sectoral and/or national differences come into play when it comes to the wider issues of governance and *policy outcomes*, i.e. the actual 'impact' advisory organisations may have on the policy process. See also Bijker *et al.* 2009.

[8] Pielke has a similar thought when he normatively claims that the design of advisory organisations should reflect the exigencies of the 'issue context' (i.e. degrees of consensus about political values and of the uncertainty in the knowledge base) and its role in the policy process (i.e. broadening or narrowing the spectrum of political choices) (Pielke 2007).

procedural rules may be and typically are altered and factually assume different functions in the process.

Model organisations for scientific policy advice

What are the implications for the organisation of advisory processes? The chapters in the second and main section of this volume focus each on a particular model or reference organisation for scientific policy advice. By this we mean organisations that serve as blueprints or points of reference for the institutionalisation of policy advice across countries (and sometimes even across policy fields). Considered from a very general perspective, roughly three basic kinds of advisory organisations can be distinguished: collegial bodies (such as various forms of councils, committees, etc.), hierarchical, research-based organisations (ranging from policy-oriented think tanks to intermediary agencies) and academies.[9]

Parts II and III on collegial bodies illustrates the broad range of differences. On one end of the spectrum, there are purely scientific advisory bodies like the International Commission on Radiation Protection (ICRP) (see Streffer, Chapter 6). Established as early as 1928, its parent body is still the International Society of Radiology, a cooperation of about eighty national societies (Clarke and Valentin 2005). Registered as an independent charity in the UK, its recommendations provide the basis for regulation in the field of radiation protection all over the world. The ICRP is a paradigm example of a genuine scientific advisory committee operating according to rules under the auspices of a scholarly society. Its mission is to provide recommendations on appropriate standards of protection without unduly limiting beneficial practices giving rise to radiation exposure. Hence, as Streffer illustrates, a transparent risk-benefit communication is essential for the credibility of the organisation.

A different kind of collegial body is described in Owens' chapter on the Royal Commission on Environmental Pollution in the UK (see Chapter 5). In terms of long-term impact on policy formation, the Royal Commission presents a remarkable success story. Owens' case narrative reveals that the success is firstly due to its character as a 'committee of experts' (versus 'expert committee') that combines specialist expertise, alternative disciplinary perspectives and what she calls an 'intelligent lay perspective'. The body as a whole deliberates and in this way constitutes

---

[9] Due to the particular focus of this book, one important institution of science advice is not covered in this book, namely the presidential or chief scientific adviser. For the US American presidential adviser see Pielke and Klein (2009; 2010).

an arena for the constant testing of ideas. Crucial to the success is the normative commitment underlying the organisational and administrative practices that is characterised by Owens as the 'independence thing'.

In his chapter on the Bureau of European Policy Advisers (BEPA) and the European Group on Ethics in Science and New Technologies, Rogers (see Chapter 7) provides an insider's view on the advisory regime at the European Commission. Based on the separation of the advisory function from the policy function, the advisory committees at the European Commission are committed to the quality criteria already formulated in the White Paper on European Governance (COM (2001) 428 final): quality, openness and effectiveness. Whether this 'master narrative' actually comes close to the complexity of contemporary science and governance is the subject of a current debate (Wynne *et al.*, 2007).

At the other side of the spectrum there are collegial bodies that are more like deliberative forums, typically found in a field like science policy. One example is the model of the Netherlands' *sector councils* that is described in De Wit's chapter (see Chapter 8). It has a tripartite composition and advises on strategic aspects of science policy. In this context, good advising means to function as an independent *knowledge intermediary*, focusing on expertise in the mid-long term to address societal problems. At the very end of the spectrum is the German Science Council, dealt with by Stucke (see Chapter 9). Founded in 1957 as one of the first science policy advisory organisations in Europe, unlike a genuine scientific advisory body, the Science Council is more like an arena for science policy in which representatives from science and policy meet and reach robust solutions through bargaining. Good advice in this context means to reach solutions 'that work' in the sense that they satisfy the criteria of intersubjectivity, political connectivity and practicability. This is reflected in the organisational design – its composition (two-chamber model) and its mode of operation (multi-level procedure that strongly forces consensual decisions).

Chapters in Part IV are on different kinds of research-based organisations. It is essential to consider those organisations as part of an advisory regime. Den Butter illustrates this in his chapter (see Chapter 10) on the *industrial organisation of economic policy preparation* – the aim being to ensure the scientific quality of the advice on the one hand and its public acceptance on the other. The Dutch 'polder model', as it is called, goes back to Nobel laureate Jan Tinbergen and relies on a clear separation of different lines of accountability in policy preparation. First, an independent and uncontroversial collection of data by an autonomous agency, the Central Bureau of Statistics (CBS); second, a consensus on the mechanisms of the economy as formalised in econometric models developed by the Central Planning Bureau (CPB); and, finally, a consensus on policy goals between the different parties achieved by deliberation in a corporatist style advisory committee, the Social Economic Council (SER), the main advisory board to the government on socioeconomic issues. Another model of economic policy advice is presented by Gerd G. Wagner (Chapter 11), namely the German system of think tanks on economic research financed by the federal and state governments, the so-called 'leading institutes' for economic research. Perthes, in his chapter (Chapter 16), describes a more traditional think tank, namely the German Institute for International and Security Affairs (SWP). As an independent scientific institute it advises the German parliament (the Bundestag) and the federal government on foreign and security policy issues.[10] The SWP not only functions as a supplier of ideas but also as a 'sparring partner' to put the policymakers' own ideas to an intellectually demanding test.

Advisory organisations of a very different kind are described by Kurth and Glasmacher in their chapter on the German Federal Governmental Research Institutes (see Chapter 15). Those institutes have a longstanding history dating back to the nineteenth century such as the famous institute named after its founder, the Nobel laureate Robert Koch, or the Physikalisch-technische Bundesanstalt. The advisory activities are successful, they argue, if they permit the policymakers a 'view through the telescope'.

Another model is that of the European Agencies, which is dealt with in the chapter by Podger (Chapter 12) on his experience at the UK Food Standards Agency, the European Food Safety Agency and the British Health and Safety Executive and by Dammann and Gee on the European Environment Agency (see Chapter 13). The agencies have been established as a model for institutionalising information-based modes of regulation (Majone 1997). Crucial to the agencies is their independence and their role as *boundary organisations*, i.e. organisations that translate and mediate between science and politics.

The chapters in Part V explore the advisory function of a type of organisation that, since its inception in the seventeenth century, has paved the way for the development of modern science, namely the academies.[11] The advisory mission of the academies covered in this volume arose very

---

[10] The model of the American RAND Corporation (where RAND stands for research and development) has informed the SWP. But contrary to RAND, the SWP is not a contract research organisation, but follows its own research agenda.

[11] For a comment about the chances and limitations of National academies of science and humanities in advising policymaking, see Lentsch (2010).

differently. Established as early as 1660, the Royal Society has a long-standing history of providing advice on science issues. Collins, in his chapter (Chapter 18), makes clear that quality management is essentially a matter of process management. Good advice in this sense is not just the output of a project, but rather a matter of ensuring that all aspects of the process are targeted on delivering the ultimate goal: bringing scientific issues to bear on policy and thereby making an impact on the development of that policy. This is ensured at the Royal Society by a well-developed multi-level review process and the division of labour between professional staff and the fellows and boards of the Society.

Blair (Chapter 17) provides us with insights from quite a different type of academy, namely the US National Academy of Sciences founded in 1863. Unlike the Royal Society, the advisory role of the National Academy provided the rationale for its role as an honorary society. Blair compares the National Academy Complex, now comprising the National Academy of Sciences (NAS), the National Academy of Engineering (NAE), the Institute of Medicine (IOM) and their collective operating arms, the National Research Council with the model of the former Office of Technology Assessment (OTA) of the American Congress (1972–95). Whereas the NAS is committed to providing objective, unbalanced and consented recommendations, the OTA assembled all relevant stakeholder perspectives with the aim of exploring the trade-offs associated with different policy options. Beyond the different concepts of good advice, crucial organisational differences purport to the relations between staff and volunteering experts. Whereas staff at the NAS have only a supporting function and experts author the reports, experts at the OTA have an advisory function, supervising and steering the work done by the professional staff. Ter Meulen and Fears deal with one of the youngest bodies in the landscape of academies, the European Academies Science Advisory Council (EASAC), formed by twenty-six individual members. (Each national academy of the EU member states nominates one of them.) As they explain, EASAC considers science advice not so much as a product but rather as a continuing process. Quality criteria are thus embedded at every stage in the working process, from choice and framing of the project to dissemination activities and continuous exchange between scientists and policymakers.

Principles of good advice

Even though it is impossible to create an advisory arrangement that is not subject to the instability between the intended and the factual functions, the chapters in this volume illustrate, beyond all contrasts and differences, that there are some fundamental principles of quality control that have become universal during the last decades, such as transparency and openness or freedom of information (see Jasanoff, Chapter 2). Turning the focus of attention to these 'domains of convergence' (ibid.), this collection wants to highlight the indispensable values and procedural mechanisms without which the outcome of expert deliberation would not be robust, neither epistemically nor politically.

A number of countries have made the effort to make these principles explicit in the form of guidelines in order to improve the quality of advice to their governments, and it is remarkable that they differ only in some details, or in their foci, but not in their overarching logic. Of these general principles the following four appear to be a good base for securing the quality of advice by meeting the conditions explicated above.

Distance and independence between advisers and the advised

Distance is a relational concept and means mutual independence in order to avoid the mixing of particularistic interests and scientific judgements. If the independence of advice is not secured, it will lose its credibility and, thus, its authority and the legitimating function that it confers.

Plurality refers to forms of advice, the range of disciplines and advisers

Different disciplines and advisers must be represented in the advisory process, adequately reflecting the topics in question. A plurality of perspectives, theories and methods safeguard the adequacy of the knowledge and the trust in it.

Transparency of advice and decision-making processes helps to establish trust in them and in the arguments that inform them

Lack of transparency creates distrust. However, although the principle of transparency is widely employed to make organisations more trustworthy and trusted, it has, in a sense, a Janus face: the mere requirement of disclosure and dissemination of information does not necessarily increase the trustworthiness of an organisation. Hence, in certain cases, it may make sense if advisory bodies meet behind closed doors. In order to increase the trustworthiness of an advisory organisation, it is essential that transparency requirements are linked to a proactive communication that meets the epistemic and ethical standards needed to empower those to whom information is disclosed to actually appraise the performance of the organisation (O'Neill 2006).

> *Publicity and openness secure equal access to all relevant information and are the preconditions of trust*

They refer to, both, the advisory bodies and the results of their deliberations and the use made of them. However, the shift to broader questions of quality and robustness forces us to rethink also the pitfalls of openness and publicity. Hence, it is of utmost importance not only to ensure that scientific information is disclosed, but also that it is actually at the disposal of the right audience at the right moment. In the same way as the principle of transparency, the requirements for openness have to be balanced against institutionally reasonable needs for confidentiality.

While acknowledging the multiple facets of the issue of quality control in scientific policy advice, the chapters in this volume carve out the 'domain of convergence' (Jasanoff, Chapter 2). The present synopsis allows us to identify the basic aspects distinctive to the organisational design of scientific advisory organisations.

REFERENCES

Bijker, Wiebe E., Bal, Roland and Hendriks, Ruud 2009. *The Paradox of Scientific Authority: The Role of Scientific Advice in Democracies*, Cambridge, MA: MIT Press.

Clark, William C. and Majone, Giandomenico 1985. 'The critical appraisal of scientific inquiries with policy implications', *Science, Technologies, & Human Values* 10/3: 6–19.

Clarke, Roger and Valentin, Jack 2005. 'A history of the international commission on radiological protection', *Health Physics* 88/5: 407–22.

DiMaggio, Paul J. and Powell, Walter 1983. 'The iron cage revisited: Institutional isomorphism and collective rationality in organisational fields', *American Sociological Review* 48: 147–60.

Funtowicz, Silvio O. 2001. 'Peer review and quality control', in Neil J. Smelser and Paul B. Baltes (eds.), *International Encyclopedia of the Social & Behavioral Sciences*, Oxford: Pergamon, pp. 11179–83.

Funtowicz, Silvio O. and Ravetz, Jerome R. 1990. *Uncertainty and Quality in Science for Policy*, Dordrecht: Kluwer.

Gibbons, Michael, Limoges, Camille, Nowotny, Helga, Schwartzman, Simon, Scott, Peter and Trow, Martin 1994. *The New Production of Knowledge. The Dynamics of Science and Research in Contemporary Societies*, London, Thousand Oaks, New Delhi: SAGE Publications.

Gieryn, Thomas F. 1983. 'Boundary-work and the demarcation of science from non-science: Strains and interests in professional ideologies of scientists', *American Sociological Review* 48: 781–95.

Guston, David H. 2005. 'Institutional design for socially robust knowledge: The national toxicology program's report on carcinogens', in Sabine Maasen and Peter Weingart (eds.), *Democratization of Expertise? Exploring Novel Forms of Scientific Advice in Political Decision-Making*, Dordrecht: Springer, pp. 63–80.

Hemlin, Sven and Rasmussen, Søren Barlebo 2006. 'The shift in academic quality control', *Science, Technology, & Human Values* 31/2: 173–98.

Irwin, Alan, Rothstein, Henry, Yearley, Steven and McCarthy, Elaine 1997. 'Regulatory science – towards a sociological framework', *Futures* 29/1: 17–31.

Jasanoff, Sheila 1990. *The Fifth Branch: Science Advisers as Policymakers*, Cambridge, MA: Harvard University Press.

Jasanoff, Sheila 2005. *Designs on Nature: Science and Democracy in Europe and the United States*, Princeton University Press.

Krimsky, Sheldon 2003. *Science in the Private Interest: Has the Lure of Profits Corrupted Biomedical Research?*, Lanham: Rowman & Littlefield Publishers.

Lentsch, Justus 2010. ' "Knowledge brokers" in a pluralist world: The new function of (national) academies of science, technology, and humanities', *GAIA – Ecological Perspectives for Science and Society* 19/2: 110–13.

Maasen, Sabine and Weingart, Peter 2005. 'What's new in scientific advice to politics?', in Sabine Maasen and Peter Weingart (eds.), *Democratization of Expertise? Exploring Novel Forms of Scientific Advice in Political Decision-Making*, Dordrecht: Springer, pp. 1–20.

Majone, Giandomenico 1997. 'The new European agencies: Regulation by information', *Journal of European Public Policy* 4/2: 262–75.

Miller, Clark A. 2008. 'Civic epistemologies: constituting knowledge and order in political communities', *Sociological Compass* 2/6: 1896–919.

Nightingale, Paul and Scott, Alister 2007. 'Peer review and the relevance gap: Ten suggestions for policy-makers', *Science and Public Policy* 34/8: 543–53.

Nowotny, Helga, Scott, Peter and Gibbons, Michael 2001. *Re-Thinking Science. Knowledge and the Public in an Age of Uncertainty*, Cambridge: Polity Press.

O'Neill, Onora 2006. 'Transparency and the ethics of communication', *Proceedings of the British Academy* 135: 75–90.

Oreskes, Naomi and Conway, Erik M. 2010. *Merchants of Doubt: How a Handful of Scientists Obscured the Truth on Issues from Tobacco Smoke to Global Warming*. New York: Bloomsbury Press.

Pawson, Ray and Tilley, Nick 1997. *Realistic Evaluation*, London: Sage.

Pielke, Roger Jr. 2007. *The Honest Broker: Making Sense of Science in Policy and Politics*, Cambridge University Press.

Pielke, Roger Jr. and Klein, Roberta 2009. 'The rise and fall of the science advisor to the president of the United States', *Minerva* 47/1: 7–29.

Pielke, Roger Jr. 2010. 'Major change is needed if the IPCC hopes to survive', *Yale Environment* 360, available at: http://e360.yale.edu (last accessed 10 March 2010).

Pielke, Roger Jr. and Klein, Roberta (eds.) 2010. *Presidential Science Advisors: Perspectives and Reflections on Science, Policy and Politics*, Dordrecht: Springer.

Power, Michael 1997. *The Audit Society: Rituals of Verification*, Oxford University Press.

Renn, Ortwin 1995. 'Styles of using scientific expertise: A comparative framework', *Science and Public Policy* 22/3: 147–56.

Tol, Richard, Pielke, Roger and von Storch, Hans 2010. 'Save the panel on climate change', *Spiegel-Online*, 25 January 2010, available at: www.spiegel. de/international/world/0,1518,673944,00.html (last accessed 10 March 2010).

Wagner, Wendy and Steinzor, Rena (eds.) 2006. *Rescuing Science from Politics: Regulation and the Distortion of Scientific Research*, New York: Cambridge University Press.

Weinberg, Alvin M. 1967. *Reflections on Big Science*, Cambridge, MA: The MIT Press.

Weingart, Peter 2005. 'The impact of bibliometrics upon the science system: Inadvertent consequences?', *Scientometrics* 62/1: 117–31.

Wynne, Brian, Felt, Ulrike, Gonçalves, Maria Eduarda, Jasanoff, Sheila, Jepsen, Maria, Joly, Pierre-Benoît, Konopasek, Zdenek, *et al.* 2007. *Taking European Knowledge Society Seriously*, Brussels: European Commission.

2 Quality control and peer review in advisory science

Sheila Jasanoff

For the most part of a century, two almost axiomatic beliefs guided democratic societies in their attempts to incorporate science into public policy. The first is that good scientific knowledge is the best possible foundation for public decisions across ever-widening policy domains. The second is that the best way to secure scientific inputs of high quality is to allow scientists the freedom to monitor and criticise each other's contributions, through procedures conventionally grouped under the heading of peer review. In this way, science comes closest to an ideal described as 'speaking truth to power'. Scientists, in this view, should independently establish the facts of the matter as well as they can be established; politicians can then decide how to act upon those facts, taking other social values into consideration. We can think of this as the *linearity-autonomy* model of science for policy. In it, scientific fact-finding is seen as standing apart from and prior to politics, as decisions move in linear fashion from facts to values. Science is entitled to establish the quality and integrity of its findings on its own terms before political judgements come into play. Deviation from this ideal threatens to convert science into an instrument of politics. With loss of autonomy, science, it is thought, cannot deliver objective information about the functioning of nature or society.

Several episodes from twentieth and even twenty-first century politics account for the power of this model. In the former Soviet Union, Joseph Stalin's embrace of T.D. Lysenko's renegade ideas on agricultural science not only stifled and killed off a generation of geneticists but also produced spectacular failures for Soviet agricultural policy. In Nazi Germany, an equally disastrous alliance between biological sciences and the totalitarian state employed race theories to justify the mass murder of Jews and others deemed deficient according to the prevalent ideology. Fast-forwarding to the present, the administration of President George W. Bush in the United States refused for years to heed mounting scientific evidence that human-generated carbon in the earth's atmosphere has caused sharp temperature increases that may bring catastrophic consequences to much of the planet (Mooney 2005; Gore 2007). In South Africa, President Thabo Mbeki's personal scepticism towards the almost universally accepted viral theory of HIV-AIDS slowed the delivery of anti-retroviral drugs to the country's more than 5 million AIDS-infected persons. These examples offer painful reminders of what can happen to human lives and welfare when science, instead of serving as a check on the exercise of power, allows itself to be enrolled or perverted by political authorities.

That science is necessary for making sound policy decisions in modern societies cannot be questioned; and that science used for policy must be subject to quality controls is likewise beyond doubt. But how should the demand for quality be met? What does *quality* mean in this context, and can it be achieved by treating the goodness of science separately from other aspects of good decision-making? These are not simple questions, nor can they be answered in purely formal terms. Policy-relevant science comes into being in a territory of its own that is subject to neither purely scientific nor wholly political rules of the game (Jasanoff 1990). That territory has to be mapped, explored, and better understood as a prelude to solving the problem of quality control.

It has long been recognised that most scientific and technical questions germane to policy cannot be answered by the paradigm-driven practices of normal disciplinary science. Distinctive issues of credibility, legitimacy, risk and benefit arise in policy contexts, where the knowledge needed for action is rarely definitive and the safety and well-being of many lives may hang on acting in time and acting well. Policy focuses on different end-points from science, marches to different temporal rhythms, is answerable to different audiences, and confronts at the end of the day normative rather than cognitive choices (Weinberg 1972; Jasanoff 1987). Policy issues typically arise from events in the world rather than from findings in the lab. Even when science sends early warning signs that something needs correcting in the world – as in the cases of stratospheric ozone depletion and climate change (for additional examples and discussion, see Gee and Stirling 2003) – the interpretation of those signals, and judgements concerning how and when to respond to them, immediately shift the debate to a plane outside of normal science. The sciences on their own are neither interested in nor capable of answering questions like how best to contain the spread of an epidemic disease, how high to build levees in a hurricane-prone region, whether to allow new forms of expert evidence into court proceedings, or when evidence of adverse effects is sufficient to pull a popular pharmaceutical drug from the market.

The alleged neutrality of science also needs to be reconsidered. In recent years, the linearity-autonomy model for science in policy has come under fire from scholars in several social science fields, including science and technology studies, history of science, science policy, and political theory. All view the production, validation and use of science as intensely social activities, especially when the results are translated into policy. Given the thick embedding of science in culture and society, neither element of the linearity-autonomy dyad can claim to be empirically well grounded. That descriptive inadequacy renders the model itself unsuitable for producing good normative results. We need a substantially different framework for thinking about science in policy, actively drawing on scholarship about the nature of knowledge-making as a social practice. Divorced from foundational insights on that subject, policymakers and societies run the risks of too easy acceptance of science or too ready dismissal of it. Neither is consistent with a mature relationship between democratic politics and rational policymaking.

To rethink the problem of scientific quality in policy settings, it is important to get back to basics. I begin with the relationship between science and politics, interrogating the notion that science is by its nature apolitical. Rather, the perceived boundary between science and the ends it hopes to serve is itself a social achievement. All experience indicates that there can be no perfectly apolitical, or pre-political, knowledge in the service of policy. A second, closely related observation is that it is not science per se that speaks unmediated to power, but that the bridge between science and politics is built by experts, a cadre of knowledgeable professionals with their own social relations, ethical commitments, and connections to power.

These two considerations frame this chapter's central argument: that quality controls on science for policy must be responsive to normative as well as cognitive demands; that is, they must be simultaneously concerned with legitimacy as well as truth under what I term the *virtuous reason* model. From this perspective, the object is not to separate science entirely from political considerations but rather to see how the integration of science with politics can best advance desired public ends. The aim is not to instrumentalise science but to conform its practices to wider social values, especially in the treatment of uncertainty and ignorance. Any reform efforts, moreover, must recognise that processes of validating knowledge for policy are inevitably tied to institutional histories and cultures, making universal panaceas both infeasible and undesirable. Quality control measures have to respect and respond to these underlying social, political and cultural realities.

In the chapter's concluding sections, I briefly review how three nations – United States, Britain and Germany – have approached the validation of policy-relevant science and suggest how their experiences can be used to translate the abstract ideal of virtuous reason into concrete policy proposals.

Science and politics: a question of boundaries

Science, we know, is not simply a mirror of nature. Even in areas where scientific knowledge seems least subjective, such as mathematics or particle physics, what we know is conditioned by prior social commitments about what is important to know and how to go about knowing it; similarly, social choice is implicated in defining what we do not know or have chosen to ignore. Sometimes, quite foundational ways of constructing the world have to be revised in what the philosopher Thomas Kuhn influentially termed *paradigm shifts* (Kuhn 1962). The Copernican revolution is the classic example from the physical sciences, but paradigm shifts also occur in the life sciences. Evelyn Fox Keller's exploration of the concept of the gene shows how one of modern biology's most crucial anchoring devices changed in meaning and consequences over a century of elaboration (Fox Keller 2000). Fundamental shifts in understanding nature often entail responses and readjustments that go beyond the perimeters of the sciences themselves (Jasanoff 2004). An example is the displacement of the term global warming, implying a relatively smooth and evenly distributed increase in the earth's mean surface temperature, by the subsequently preferred notion of climate change, which connotes unpredictable, uneven and potentially extreme occurrences at different locations around the world. The shift from global warming to climate change projects an altered image of the future for both nature and society, with important public policy implications. For example, the prediction of differential climate impacts focused greater attention on the adaptive capacity of populations and ecosystems situated in different parts of the world; in turn, that shift prompted deeper investigation of vulnerability and global social justice. A change in scientists' understanding of how the world works thus became tightly bound up with other global actors' re-evaluation of their needs and priorities – leading, in turn, to further demands on science itself (Jasanoff 2010).

If basic science incorporates social choices, regulatory science, or science made to serve policy goals, is even more deeply enmeshed in cultural understandings of the human condition – from its contexts of production to its circumstances of use. Historians of the social sciences,

for example, have argued that the rise of the social sciences of classification, quantification and prediction accompanied the emergence of the
nation state as the dominant form of government in the nineteenth
century (see, for example, Foucault 1979; Desrosières 1991; Porter
1995). To wield power, and to do so with conviction, states – and
empires – needed to know their populations in a deep-going sense,
separating normal (or safe) from pathological (or risky) behaviours,
and identifying phenomena that required corrective action by the state.
Those pressures have, if anything, intensified as both nation states and
supranational actors confront novel economic, social and environmental
challenges. Most notably, the now omnipresent paradigm of *risk* (Beck
1992) and its intensified manifestations of crisis and emergency, are
engaging the sciences and technologies of modelling, simulation and
surveillance on unprecedented scales. The visual technologies of the
late-twentieth century have added their power to the earlier achievements of quantification in rendering both natural and social phenomena
more tangible and manipulable. All these techniques, moreover, have
benefited from the revolution in computer technologies that permits
data to be amassed, stored, searched and processed at once unimagin-
able speeds and volumes.

Current anxieties over the quality of scientific advice suggest that
policy-relevant science has to some extent fallen victim to its own
large ambitions. The very weight of sociopolitical demands placed on
knowledge-making pulls the sciences towards exploring areas where
uncertainty and ignorance are endemic. The problems that science plays
a part in solving have become ever more daunting. Can we, for instance,
predict how humans will deal with high-level radioactive wastes ten
thousand years from today? Can we say what land cover will obtain
across the northern hemisphere in a hundred years under current best
guesses concerning climate change? Do we know how thousands upon
thousands of hardy, ecologically untested, genetically modified plant
species will affect the robustness of ecosystems a few generations from
now? And what about the cumulative impact of chemicals in a world of
rising incomes and population growth? The further we stretch our
imaginations in time and space, the more these sorts of questions and
their associated zones of uncertainty and ignorance multiply. Moreover,
as knowledge-making capacities accumulate and diffuse throughout
society, the opportunity for social actors to question others' claims also
increases, feeding the pervasive scepticism that Beck refers to as 'reflexive modernization' (1992). Under these conditions, science's ability to
present publics and policymakers with definitive truths (or even 'serviceable truths', as I have called them (Jasanoff 1990: 250)) is severely

weakened and stressed. The idea that scientific quality can be validated by objective, externally given standards, insulated from politics and secured through peer review, becomes correspondingly untenable.

In the policy world, then, it is anachronistic to hold on too tightly to the linearity-autonomy model, with its presumptively sharp boundary between science and politics. Instead, we find ourselves squarely in the so-called Mode 2 world of scientific production, where the old image of science as answerable only to nature is discarded in favour of a view that foregrounds the social aspects of scientific production. As discussed by Michael Gibbons, Helga Nowotny and others (Gibbons *et al.* 1994), we have to recognise, beside the classical processes of curiosity-driven disciplinary science, another form of knowledge-making that openly takes its marching orders from social needs rather than nature's puzzles. Mode 2 science presents the following defining characteristics:

- knowledge is produced in contexts of application (e.g. for purposes of regulation);
- science is transdisciplinary – that is, it draws on and integrates empirical and theoretical elements from a variety of fields;
- knowledge is generated in a wide variety of sites, academic and non-academic, public and private;
- scientific actors are aware of the social implications of their work, and hence are not disinterested;
- publics are conscious of the ways in which science and technology affect their interests and values.

In this mode of production, science's traditional means of judging quality break down. There is no overarching theory against which the rightness of scientific observations can be measured or tested. Likewise, there are no established disciplinary conventions that scientific peers can apply to ensure that work meets rigorous methodological standards. Nor do technological applications offer material evidence that scientific understandings of nature are proceeding on the right track. Instead, assurances of the relative merit of claims and the robustness of conclusions derive from primarily social and normative considerations: that the work was done in the best possible way, by the people in the best position to know how, that is, by those possessing the best available expertise. Put differently, it is not so much scientists as *experts* who govern the production and evaluation of policy-relevant science. And unlike scientists, whose primary mission is fact-making, experts are by definition boundary-crossers whose job it is to link scientific knowledge to matters of social significance: they are the diagnosticians of public problems, the explorers of solutions and the providers of remedies. Scientists may see themselves as engaged in an honest search for truth,[1] and monitor each other accordingly, but it is experts who translate the claims of often inadequate science to serve the immediate agendas of policy and politics. The legitimacy of expertise is thus a crucial element in any regime of quality assurance for science in policy domains.

Expertise and the public trust

As far back as we look in history, experts have been involved in the business of running society. Their connections to power stretch back through time. Daedalus, the archetypal engineering expert of Greek mythology, was hired by King Minos of Crete to contain the monstrous Minotaur; the solution Daedalus devised was an architectural wonder, the labyrinth. The fourth century BC Indian figure of Chanakya was prime minister and chief military and economic adviser to the first Mauryan emperor, Chandragupta, whose rise to power Chanakya is said to have masterminded. Machiavelli, the key political philosopher of the Italian Renaissance, was also military adviser to the Florentine republic. Since the scientific revolution, countless experts with scientific and technical backgrounds have been retained by states to aid in weapons development, mapping and exploration, classification of populations, plants and animals, recording languages and cultures in colonised territories, and developing measures for water supply, sanitation and public health. Experts are so ubiquitous and their functions and qualifications so diverse that, with few exceptions, their individual names are scarcely recorded or remembered.

The role of experts in running political systems attracted the attention of political analysts throughout the twentieth century. Turn of the century convictions about the progressive role of expertise gave way, after World War I, to a disenchantment articulated by such intellectual leaders as Harold Laski at the London School of Economics. His 1930 article on *The Limitations of Expertise* strongly cautioned against problem-solving by experts, whom he saw as confusing their limited technical insights with broader social needs. Experts, in Laski's opinion, cannot be counted on for political judgement: 'The wisdom that is needed for the direction of affairs is not an expert technic but a balanced equilibrium.

---

[1] The picture of science as a disinterested search for truth has long since been set aside by scholars of science and technology in favour of a view that looks at science as an intensely social activity. Nevertheless, distinctions can be made between scientific activity whose primary impetus comes from within fields of inquiry as opposed to activity primarily driven by social needs and demands. For readings on the social nature of science, see Jasanoff *et al.* 1995.

It is a knowledge of how to use men, a faculty of judgment about the practicability of principles. It consists not in the possession of specialized knowledge, but in a power to utilize its results at the right moment, and in the right direction' (Laski 1930: 101).

According to Laski, it takes a mediating statesman to ensure the proper application of the specialist's knowledge to collective ends. In most modern societies, however, that mediating role is performed not by wise politicians but by expert regulatory agencies, which are supposed in the ideal case to act on the advice of technical experts but not to be directed by them.[2] Yet the tendency of government agencies to defer to expert opinion, and the parallel habit of experts to deny that *they* are making the decisions, threaten to leave democracies in a perpetual state of organized irresponsibility, in which no one can be assigned full and final accountability for informed action. The intense worries about a democratic deficit and lack of sufficient citizen participation in the affairs of the European Union (EU) in the early years of the twenty-first century mirror these sorts of concerns.

The theme of narrow expertise acting as a hindrance to the public good is not limited to European contexts but has also resonated with US analysts. Nearly fifty years before Laski, Justice Oliver Wendell Holmes distinguished between two possible sources of legal authority in his famous dictum about the common law: 'The life of the law has not been logic; it has been experience' (Holmes 1881). Without experience (or what Laski referred to as 'a faculty of judgment about the practicability of principles'), Holmes believed that the law could not adapt to changes, and thus remain a vibrant ordering instrument for society. A century later, fuelled by the debacle of the Vietnam War, scepticism towards expertise was again on the rise in American politics, expressed in such works as *The Best and the Brightest*, the journalist David Halberstam's best-selling indictment of the advisers to Presidents John F. Kennedy and Lyndon B. Johnson (Halberstam 1972). The narrowness of US Defense Secretary Robert S. McNamara's policy vision, and its tragic consequences, were brilliantly displayed in Errol Morris's 2004 documentary *The Fog of War*. In a similar vein, the commission investigating the terrorist attacks of September 11, 2001 faulted the US security services for a lack of imagination that prevented effective foresight.[3]

---

[2] In the United States, the ideal of the experienced regulator has been eroded in recent years, raising calls for more active supervision of agency judgement by external scientific peer reviewers. See Jasanoff 1992.

[3] National Commission on Terrorist Attacks Upon the United States (9/11 Commission).

Another persistent source of discomfort, especially in the United States, is the perception that expertise can be bought. The American legal system, with its daily spectacles of duelling expert witnesses, reinforces the widespread belief that technical support can be purchased to back any claim, no matter how far-fetched. Perhaps the most notorious twentieth-century example of expertise for hire is the body of *tobacco science* produced by paid experts to debunk claims that smoking causes cancer and other diseases. But non-corporate litigants have also been accused of manufacturing questionable scientific findings in defence of claims that did not merit support. An example that drew considerable attention in the 1980s was a series of lawsuits by mothers who claimed that their children had suffered birth defects as a result of their taking an anti-nausea drug named Bendectin. Another well-publicised case was a class action by women who claimed to have suffered immune system disorders from wearing silicone gel breast implants. Epidemiological evidence failed to support either set of complaints (Angell 1996; Sanders 1998), leading many to speculate that emotion rather than sound science had prompted jurors to compensate the victims. That analysis provided fodder for the polemical and largely unfounded charge that the US courts had become breeding grounds for 'junk science' (Huber 1991). The Supreme Court responded to those anxieties with a 1993 decision that encouraged judges to scrutinise and exclude evidence that did not comport with scientific standards of quality.[4]

Yet scepticism towards the wisdom and honesty of experts coexists in contemporary societies with massive reliance on expert knowledge as a foundation for policy in proliferating domains: health, safety, environment, labour and economy, agriculture, transportation, defence, and, most recently, state support for science and technology. No citizen of modern times could pass through an ordinary day without depending on the judgements of experts at every step. Technical advice and know-how are built into the designs of the technologies we use, the quality and safety of the food we eat and the environments we live in, the choices we make about how to save or spend money, and the means with which we safeguard our health or treat our illnesses. It would be unthinkable for any human being to look behind all of the products, services and environments of modernity, and second-guess the technical judgements that designed or approved them. As a practical matter, we must take on faith most of the expertise that animates our world. It is therefore imperative,

---

[4] *Daubert v. Merrell Dow Pharmaceuticals, Inc.*, 509 U.S. 579 (1993).

as a policy matter, to think hard about the efficacy of the processes by which expertise is harnessed to serve societal needs.

Peer review of experts by other experts is not the only answer to concerns about the legitimacy of expertise. As we have seen, the principle of autonomy that allows science to monitor its own quality and integrity without significant external supervision cannot be applied unquestioningly to expert advice. Government of experts, by experts, and for experts is in any case no formula for democracy. Experts act as society's agents in the fulfilment of particular goals, and hence are never even in principle disinterested; they also lack the claims to disciplinary coherence and impartiality that justify demands for autonomy in normal research science. Ultimately, it is not truth (or even its nearest approximation) that we ask from experts, but rather the judicious use of available knowledge for the public good. Once we set aside the linearity-autonomy model as too simplistic, how can we re-conceptualise the practices of expert advising so as to ensure the effective performance of this delegated responsibility?

Virtuous reason: a cultural perspective

Starting from the premise that science does not make its way unmediated into policy domains, but that linking knowledge to action is a deeply social undertaking, it follows that quality control measures have to take sociality and cultural specificity into account. For this purpose, the production of expert advice can usefully be broken down into three components, each calling for its own distinct strategy of legitimation. Each component can be characterised as a *body*, but a body in a different sense of the term: first, the body of relevant knowledge; second, the body of the individual expert; and third (since expert advice is rarely the prerogative of single individuals), the collective body or group that advises governments on most significant policy matters. A look at diverse state practices in enrolling each of these bodies into the advisory system illuminates both the problems and the opportunities for quality control of science for policy. States, we see, have tacitly acknowledged the hybrid normative-cognitive character of policy-relevant science, but legitimation practices operate without a reflexive understanding of the assumptions underlying particular national policy choices and emphases.

As Table 2.1 illustrates, nation states differ in their constructions of the three bodies involved in knowledge-making; less easily captured in tabular form, but no less significant for policy, national political cultures also differ in the relative weight they attach to these bodies. Not only is

Table 2.1 *Bodies of expertise – national constructions of expert legitimacy*

	United States	United Kingdom	Germany
Bodies of knowledge	Formal (*sound*) science	Empirical common knowledge	Collectively reasoned knowledge
Embodied experts	Technically most qualified experts	Experienced *safe hands*	Authorised institutional representatives
Advisory bodies	Pluralistic, interested, but fairly balanced (*stakeholder*)	Members capable of discerning public good (*civil service*)	Representative and inclusive of all relevant views (*public sphere*)

each body's function somewhat differently conceived, but more attention is devoted to cultivating virtue in some bodies than in others.

Thus, in the American regulatory system the quality and integrity of scientific knowledge has been the primary concern for more than thirty years, with critics constantly challenging federal agencies for their real or imagined failure to generate good science for decision-making (see Jasanoff 1990). Since the discourse of (pure) science is more or less uncritically extended to policy contexts, it is but a short step to insist that the integrity of science for policy – just like that of science in research settings – should be secured through peer review. The commitment to peer review as a cure-all resonates through these debates. A 2003 policy proposal of the US Office of Management and Budget illustrates the point:

A *peer review*, as used in this document for scientific and technical information relevant to regulatory policies, is a scientifically rigorous review and critique of a study's methods, results, and findings by others in the field with requisite training and expertise. Independent, objective peer review has long been regarded as a critical element in ensuring the reliability of scientific analyses. For decades, the American academic and scientific communities have withheld acknowledgement of scientific studies that have not been subject to rigorous independent peer review. Peer review *has been an essential part of the American science scene and one of the reasons why American science has done so well.* (United States Office of Management and Budget 2003) (emphasis added)

In this passage, the linearity-autonomy model prevails unchallenged. Science is taken as an undifferentiated activity whose success can be measured and secured through the same sorts of criteria and practices regardless of context. Peer review, represented as one reason why 'American science has done so well', is seen as equally applicable to policy-relevant science and with as high expectations of success. Missing from the quoted language is any appreciation of the complexity of producing policy-relevant knowledge, accounting for its insufficiencies, or safeguarding quality and objectivity in situations that are irreducibly political and value-laden.

Focusing mainly on the purity of knowledge, American quality control policies have been less concerned with the qualifications of individual experts and the mix of perspectives in expert committees. An important law governing expert advice, the Federal Advisory Committee Act (FACA), does address the latter issue, but it does so in a way that focuses attention back upon the technical knowledge of committee members. Thus, the act insists on a 'fair balance' among relevant viewpoints, a provision that refers more to epistemological than to social or cultural balance (although the two cannot, of course, be entirely disaggregated). The act also emphasises the need for openness and transparency in committee operations. This typically American demand ensures that external critics can look behind the backdrop of expert deliberations and hold experts to high levels of intellectual rigour. Inconsistencies can be challenged and defects in explanations or reasons be spotlighted. The overall goal, as I have argued elsewhere, is to secure the kind of objectivity that can be described as a 'view from nowhere': a position of transcendental truth shorn of all recognisable human biases (Jasanoff 2005a).

By contrast, the emphasis in Britain's policy culture has been pre-eminently on the body of the individual expert. The advisory system seeks to identify and cultivate persons whose capacity to exercise judgement on the public's behalf is beyond question. As in the United States, British expert panels can and do represent both technical specialties and social interests, as for example in the *long-standing tripartite* Health and Safety Executive comprising labour, industry and government. Ultimately, however, it is the excellence of each person's individual discernment that the state most crucially relies on. To a remarkable extent the legitimacy of British expertise remains tied to the persons of experts who have individually achieved trust not only through knowledge and competence, but through a demonstrated record of selfless service to society. It is as if the expert should function as much as a diagnostician of the public's needs and definer of the public good as a gatherer of scientific and technical information for resolving matters at hand. Instructively, shortly after New Labour took office, the Nolan Committee, also known as the Committee on Standards in Public Life, identified seven principles of public life that constitute, in effect, character tests for being a good public servant: selflessness, integrity, accountability, objectivity, openness, honesty and leadership.[5]

---

[5] Summary of the Nolan Committee's First Report on Standards in Public Life, 1 October 2001.

British faith in individuals' power to see *for* the people is tied to a cultural tradition in which the possibility of common knowledge is taken for granted. Rarely in British policy circles does one encounter the visible and protracted scientific and technical controversies that so frequently mark US policymaking. Instead, expert processes aim to establish communally recognised facts through rituals of official certification. The great advantage of this approach is that it potentially guards against the narrowness of vision that Laski warned against some eighty years ago. The cost, however, can also be considerable. In producing empirical knowledge as they see it, experts can with the best will in the world background their own uncertainty and ignorance, while shielding the presumption of common vision from critical examination. Gaps in what experts know can thus pass unchallenged, leading to serious errors of judgement. Britain's infamous *mad cow* disaster of the 1990s painfully demonstrated the hazards of relying on embodied expertise at the expense of more systematic inquiry into what experts know or do not know.[6] This was a case in which the nation's vaunted capacity to muddle through, with commonsensical accommodations between knowledge and norms, spectacularly failed.

In Germany, to continue the comparison, policy energy has been devoted first and foremost to ensuring the representativeness of the collective expert bodies that advise the state. As discussed elsewhere in this volume, German committees may take a number of forms, depending on their precise relationship to political institutions. But as a general principle expert committees are conceived as microcosms of the potentially interested and affected segments of society. Judgements produced by such groups are seen as unbiased not only by virtue of the participants' individual qualifications, but even more through the incorporation of all relevant viewpoints into an inclusive whole. Not surprisingly, then, the personal credentials that matter most in Germany relate to the expert's position in society. To be an acknowledged expert, one should ideally stand for a field of experience larger than one's own particular domain of technical competence. The most reliable experts do not act on their own: they represent an institution such as a political party, a labour union, a trade association, a religious body, a professional society or a citizen group. In committees, experts work with representatives of other institutions. And it is ultimately the collective vision produced by such multipartite bodies that crucially legitimates their conclusions.

---

[6] In April 2000, the UK government estimated that the total cost of the BSE crisis to the public sector would be £3.7 billion by the end of the 2001–2002 fiscal year. *The Inquiry into BSE and variant CJD in the United Kingdom* (hereafter cited as *The Phillips Inquiry*) (2000).

The constitution of expert bodies reveals important aspects of what counts as legitimate expertise in German policy. The exceptionally inclusive character of expert advisory bodies, with memberships often specified in painstaking detail by law and with a frequent requirement that a substitute be provided for each member, underscores a commitment to creating a composite rationality that takes all relevant views into account – although, with rare exceptions, the criteria of inclusion remain mostly tacit. The quality of expert reasons and explanations derives from the strength of the collective. An expert within a committee functions essentially as an ambassador for a recognised institutional viewpoint. What emerges from the whole is a *view from everywhere*, because no relevant voice has been knowingly left out and none can adopt a credible oppositional stance towards the group's conclusions. A paradoxical consequence is that expert bodies, once formed, leave little room for ad hoc intervention by outsiders. Committees function as tightly enclosed systems out of which a collective will emerges, with no need for accountability to a wider, potentially disenchanted, and potentially irrational public. As in Britain, public scientific controversies are uncommon in German policymaking. On the rare occasions when sharp disagreements surface, as for example when the Greens in a parliamentary Enquete Kommission wrote a long, breakaway minority vote on the proposed Genetic Engineering Law of 1990 (Jasanoff 2005b), there is a strong impression of disorder, indicating that important rules of the deliberative game have been violated.

We see, then, that national attempts to improve the quality of policy-relevant science have addressed questions of goodness at multiple levels, using different mechanisms to integrate normative and cognitive concerns for each body: the science, the expert and the committee. Thus, the American system highlights the values of transparency and explicit public criticism while seeking to attain a 'view from nowhere' in relation to scientific knowledge. British political culture is less concerned with specialised knowledge and more with the character of the experts who serve the public. British policy stresses experts' personal commitment to the public good and seeks to ensure that experts will bring appropriate forms of experience to the issues before them. The German approach also implicitly embraces the idea of experts as society's delegates, but it does so by mapping the macrocosm of society onto the microcosm of committee structures. German expert bodies function not only as forums for knowledge-making and evaluation, but also as magnets for relevant, strongly institutionalised social interests. In effect, each of these national strategies acknowledges that fact and value are not separable in producing knowledge for policy, but rather that some essential values

Table 2.2 *Virtuous reason: the normative structures of expertise*

	Nature of objectivity	Normative commitments	Administrative practices
Bodies of knowledge (US)	View from nowhere (transcendental)	• Open access to information • Transparency • Public comment and criticism	• Freedom of information • Public comment • Legal challenge and review
Embodied experts (UK)	View from everywhere (empirical, observational)	• Issue-specific experience • Dedication to the public good • Balanced judgement	• Nominations from the public • Principles of public life • Conflict of interest rules
Advisory bodies (Germany)	View from everywhere (reasoned)	• Inclusion of all relevant voices • Willingness to accommodate reasons of others	• Representation of relevant institutional voices • Appointment of substitute members

(or virtues) must be cultivated in order to make judgements and offer reasons that reliably serve the public interest. Table 2.2 summarises these insights and briefly indicates how they have been translated into administrative procedures and practices.

Conclusion

Quality control in policy-relevant science, I have argued, needs to be fundamentally reconceived in the light of accumulating scholarship on science and technology as social and cultural institutions and of changing practices in the sciences themselves. Two moves are essential to this process of rethinking. The first is to recognise and factor into policy the social embeddedness of science, and hence the interpenetration of knowledge-making with norms and values. The second is to see that it is expertise, not science, that translates knowledge (or non-knowledge) into decisions, and expert legitimation is a different undertaking from securing the integrity of scientific studies and experiments. Once these insights are taken on board, it is no longer possible to hold on to the simplistic assumptions of the linearity-autonomy model of scientific quality control. More appropriate and empirically sustainable is the model of virtuous reason which moves quality out of the thin framework of truth and objectivity to the more complex framework of reason and legitimacy. This model takes better account of the social nature of science, the limitations of policy-relevant knowledge, and the importance of process values such as transparency and public engagement.

Unlike the linearity-autonomy model, that of virtuous reason makes no claim to universality. Virtue in politics is, after all, culturally situated, and democratic societies vary in their conceptions of public reason. Persistent national differences in the articulation of even the most widely shared quality control principles (see Tables 2.1 and 2.2) indicate that political culture matters profoundly in determining what societies are prepared to accept as reliable knowledge. By looking at each other's practices, nation states may be able to develop greater reflexivity in deciding how to legitimate expertise in their own policy systems. Abstract principles, of course, require concrete implementation, and other contributors to this volume offer examples of specific measures that may enhance the legitimacy of expertise in one or another policy context. My hope has been to show that, regardless of these specifics, the quest for good science in public decision-making cannot be divorced from deeper reflection on the ways in which democracies should reason.

REFERENCES

Angell, Marcia 1996. *Science on Trial: The Clash of Medical Evidence and the Law in the Breast Implant Case*, New York: Norton.

Beck, Ulrich 1992. *Risk Society: Towards a New Modernity*, London: Sage Publications.

Daubert v. Merrell Dow Pharmaceuticals, Inc., 509 U.S. 579 (1993).

Desrosières, Alain 1991. 'How to make things which hold together: Social science, statistics and the state', in Peter Wagner, Bjorn Wittrock and Richard Whitley (eds.), *Discourses on Society: The Shaping of the Social Science Disciplines*, Dordrecht: Kluwer, pp. 195–218.

Foucault, Michel 1979. *Discipline and Punish*, New York: Vintage.

Fox Keller, Evelyn 2000. *The Century of the Gene*, Cambridge, MA: Harvard University Press.

Gee, David and Stirling, Andy, 2003. 'Late lessons from early warnings: Improving science and governance under uncertainty and ignorance', in Joel Tickner (ed.), *Precaution, Environmental Science, and Preventive Public Policy*, Washington, DC: Island Press, pp. 195–213.

Gibbons, Michael, Limoges, Camille, Nowotny, Helga, Schwartzman, Simon, Scott, Peter and Trow, Martin 1994. *The New Production of Knowledge*, London: Sage Publication.

Gore, Al 2007. *The Assault on Reason*, New York: Penguin Books.

Halberstam, David 1972. *The Best and the Brightest*, New York: Random House.

Holmes, Oliver Wendell Jr. 1881. *The Common Law*, Boston.

Huber, Peter 1991. *Galileo's Revenge: Junk Science in the Courtroom*, New York: Basic Books.

Jasanoff, Sheila 1987. 'Contested boundaries in policy-relevant science', *Social Studies of Science* 17/2: 195–230.

Jasanoff, Sheila 1990. *The Fifth Branch: Science Advisers as Policymakers*, Cambridge, MA: Harvard University Press.

Jasanoff, Sheila 1992. 'Science, politics, and the renegotiation of expertise at EPA', *Osiris* 7/1: 195–217.

Jasanoff, Sheila (ed.) 2004. *States of Knowledge: The Co-Production of Science and Social Order*, London: Routledge.

Jasanoff, Sheila 2005a. 'Restoring reason: Causal narratives and political culture', in Bridget Hutter and Michael Power (eds.), *Organizational Encounters with Risk*, Cambridge, MA: Cambridge University Press, pp. 209–32.

Jasanoff, Sheila 2005b. *Designs on Nature: Science and Democracy in Europe and the United States*, Princeton, NJ: Princeton University Press.

Jasanoff, Sheila 2010. 'A New Climate for Society', *Theory, Culture and Society* 27/2–3: 233–53.

Jasanoff, Sheila, Markle, Gerald, Petersen, James and Pinch, Trevor (eds.) 1995. *Handbook of Science and Technology Studies*, Thousand Oaks, CA: Sage Publications.

Kuhn, Thomas 1962. *The Structure of Scientific Revolutions*, Chicago University Press.

Laski, Harold 1930. 'The limitations of the expert', *Harper's Monthly Magazine*, December 1930: 101.

Mooney, Chris 2005. *The Republican War on Science*, New York: Basic Books.

National Commission on Terrorist Attacks Upon the United States (9/11 Commission), *9–11 Commission Report*, available at: www.9–11commission.gov/report/index.htm (last accessed 25 March 2010).

Porter, Theodore M. 1995. *Trust in Numbers*, Princeton University Press.

Sanders, Joseph 1998. *Bendectin on Trial: A Study of Mass Tort Litigation*, Ann Arbor, MI: University of Michigan Press.

Summary of the Nolan Committee's First Report on Standards in Public Life, 1 October 2001, available at: www.archive.official–documents.co.uk/document/parlment/nolan/nolan.htm (last accessed July 2007).

The Phillips Inquiry 2000. *Volume 10, Economic Impact and International Trade*, available at: http://webarchive.nationalarchives.gov.uk/20090505194948/http://www.bseinquiry.gov.uk/report/volume10/toc.htm (last accessed 25 March 2010).

United States Office of Management and Budget, Proposed Bulletin on Peer Review and Information Quality, Summary, 68 Federal Register 54023, 15 September 2003.

Weinberg, Alvin 1972. 'Science and trans-science', *Minerva* 10/2: 209–22.

3   Reconciling representation with reality: unitisation as an example for science and public policy

Naomi Oreskes

Introduction: why 'getting the science right' is wrong

We live in a world where science is routinely called upon to provide information to policymakers under the presumption that science can identify and guide sensible decisions. But the presumption of clear guidance is undermined by the complexity of the natural world and the various uncertainties that surround scientific knowledge of it. Nowhere is this more so than in the arena of environmental policy, where we deal with complex natural systems with multiple relevant causal factors, and empirical parameters that may be difficult (or even impossible) to measure. There are always things we do not know; we never have *complete* information. So how do we know when we have *enough* scientific information to properly inform a decision?

In recent years, delay in the face of uncertainty has been developed as a political strategy. Given incomplete information, it can be comfortable and convenient for politicians to suggest that in the face of uncertainty it is prudent to do more research. It can also be expedient for those who have a vested interest in the status quo to insist that the available scientific information is insufficient to warrant change.

Scientists may inadvertently or implicitly bolster such strategies, because it is in the nature of scientific inquiry to focus on the unknown. Uncertainty defines the research frontier, so the habit of most scientists is to emphasise the unresolved aspects of problems rather than the settled ones. Science *is* always uncertain – there are always more questions to be asked, more details to be worked out, more causal factors to examine – and scientists rarely object to increased support for their endeavours. But when they focus on uncertainty and ask for more money for research, scientists may unwittingly give the impression that the scientific knowledge base is more insecure than it really is, contributing to strategies of delay (Weart 2003).[1]

---

[1] Weart emphasises that 'more money for research' became a mantra of US climate scientists in the 1980s and 1990s.

Many scientists also implicitly subscribe to the view that correct science leads to correct policy, and that their job is to 'get the science right' (Sarewitz 1996, 2004). Accurate, reproducible data and robust, well-tested theories are the proper goal of scientific research, and scientists are right to resist pressure to articulate results prematurely. Further research is clearly warranted if scientists have no consensus on the matters at hand. But if scientists have reached general consensus – despite perhaps a dissenter or two – then more research may not be warranted.[2] It may be a waste of time and resources better spent in other ways, and it can be damaging if it leads to delay in preventing harms (EEA 2001).

The tendency of scientists to want to *get the science right* is particularly evident when computer models are built in support of public policy. In areas as diverse as radioactive waste disposal, global climate change, forest ecology, protection of endangered species and economic forecasting, models have become a dominant tool of scientific investigation, and a primary tool of public policy and regulatory decision-making. In some cases, models are the only practical tool for investigating complex relationships and forecasting future outcomes, because when a system is too large in time or space to access directly, or an experiment would be unethical, both scientists and policymakers have to rely on models (Whipple *et al.* 2007).

Because models are so important, a great deal of effort over the past several decades has gone into making *better* models, and scientists often act in a manner that suggests that they are trying to *get the model right*. Most modellers seek to represent nature as fully as possible, and this typically leads them to add more and more parameters to their model. As Paul Gilman, former science adviser to the US Environmental Protection Agency, has put it, there is a tendency for models to become more

---

[2] Consensus in science is never absolute; there are always the occasional outliers who, for whatever reasons, continue to resist the general view. Albert Einstein never accepted acausality in quantum mechanics; Sir Harold Jeffreys never accepted plate tectonics. For an outstanding account of a scientific community coming to consensus through the process of empirical research and social interactions, see Rudwick 1985. In this case, where consensus was finally achieved after a decade-long debate, there were still a handful of dissenters in the end, but science proceeded despite their dissent, which, after a time, was finally forgotten. The same was true in the case of the long debate over continental drift and plate tectonics. In general, we can say that if, after some time, a minority position produces no new arguments or evidence, it typically gets ignored by the scientific community (see Oreskes 2001). If it has no policy implications, then it gets ignored by the general public as well (Oreskes 2004). In recent years, however, we have seen dissent on health and environmental issues, and its amplification beyond its proportions in the scientific community, exploited as a political tool (Boykoff and Boykoff 2004; Michaels 2005; 2008; Oreskes and Conway 2010).

and more elaborate (Gilman 2005; see also Whipple *et al.* 2007). That is to say, model elaboration leads to an elaborate model.

But is an elaborate model a better one? The presumption behind model elaboration is that the more complex a model, the better, more realistic representation of the natural world it is. Because nature is complex, complex models tend to look and feel more like the real thing.

However, there are real costs associated with model elaboration. An obvious cost is the time and money and human resources required. A second is the price of delay: if a policy decision awaits *completion* of an elaborate model, damage may meanwhile spread or become harder to reverse. A third cost lies in model transparency and public trust: complex models are typically harder to evaluate and understand than simple ones. This can increase public discomfort as affected parties feel excluded from the decision-making process because they cannot understand the model on which the decision was based.

Many modellers presume that these costs are compensated by greater model accuracy – that a more detailed model is a more faithful representation of nature, which will produce more reliable results. This presumption may not be correct.

I   Why the costs of complex models may not be not paid back

There are several reasons why model complexity is not necessarily paid back in better model results. The first is rather simple: it is the problem of being deceived by appearances. Complex, elaborate models often look more realistic than simple ones, and people therefore interpret them as good representations of reality. They confuse the model's sophisticated appearance with its accuracy, leading to over-confidence in the ability of the model to predict the behaviour of the natural world. In contrast, if a model is obviously highly simplified – when it is clear that it is a caricature, not a portrait – then there is less danger of confusing the representation with reality. Users understand that the model is an extraction of certain features of interest, and not a literal truth. But when a model looks highly realistic, there is a greater tendency to confuse the simulation with the reality and assume that the model forecasts will be correct.

The second reason that model elaboration does not necessarily yield a more reliable result is more subtle and has to do with model conceptualisation. Model elaboration usually involves fussing with model details – adding and refining parameters to achieve a better fit with available empirical data. It rarely involves changes to the basic model conceptualisation. Yet, experience shows that when models fail to predict the behaviour of the natural world, it is rarely because the modeller got the details wrong, and more often because the fundamental conceptualisation is incorrect – it describes the physical situation in a way that is inconsistent with what actually occurs in nature (Holling 1978; Bredehoeft 2000; Oreskes and Belitz 2001).[3]

Hydrologist John Bredehoeft has articulated the problem this way. Every model has a conceptual foundation: a basic idea or picture of how the natural system operates. The model-builder chooses a conceptual foundation based on prior experience, intuition or conventional wisdom, but it is not an empirical fact, and it cannot be independently tested. It is a choice, a form of expert judgement.

When models are put into use, nature often surprises us. The systems being modelled often do not behave in the way in which the model predicted. Why? There are relatively few studies that evaluate model performance retrospectively, but based on four decades of experience in groundwater investigations, Bredehoeft (2000) suggests that the most common reason is that the conceptualisation was wrong.[4] The model was not just wrong in the details, it was wrong in the way that the system was *pictured*.

Even if we recognise the possibility of conceptual error, it remains extremely difficult to detect in advance, because the available data are frequently compatible with more than one conceptual model and the

---

[3] Some readers might object that all model conceptualisations are *wrong* because they are idealisations, or, as Holling puts it, *caricatures*. But Bredehoeft is focusing on something far cruder: that the underlying assumptions were flatly incorrect. For example, a system is modelled as a homogeneous porous medium, when in fact its permeability is controlled by fractures. Or consider the classic picture of the hydrological cycle, with moisture controlled primarily by evaporation, precipitation, and infiltration and run-off. This picture appears in virtually every hydrology textbook in America, including those used in California, yet in reality the hydrological systems in many Californian cities are highly engineered, with rainfall captured before it has the chance to infiltrate or run-off, and recharge controlled by human artificial recharge systems. Where is the conceptual model that describes a system like that? If these analyses are correct, and models frequently fail because of underlying conceptual problems, then further model elaboration will not solve the problem. On the contrary, it may exacerbate it, by leading to a false sense of security and over-confidence in an inaccurate picture of the world.

[4] Bredehoeft offers several specific examples from his own experience. One is the Waste Isolation Pilot Plant, developed by the US government for military nuclear waste. Because the repository rests in salt formations, and because salt is highly soluble, it was presumed that the repository had to be dry, or else the salt would long ago have dissolved away, and that therefore the repository design did not have to account for moisture. When the salt formation was mined, considerable brine was discovered in the salt crystal interstices, brine that migrated into the openings where waste was to be stored. The basic picture was wrong; the repository design had to be modified. See Metlay (2000) for a discussion of changing conceptual models for Yucca Mountain.

various statistical techniques available to quantify error cannot reveal this. You cannot measure errors that you do not know you have made. The problem is revealed only when the model is put to use – and fails.

In short, the whole idea of *getting the science right* may be wrong.

My colleague, Kenneth Belitz, and I have reviewed the existing literature on model performance, and our results support Bredehoeft's conclusion. We found that models commonly failed to predict the future successfully because of changes in the forcing functions of the systems that modellers either failed to anticipate, or did anticipate, but did not incorporate into the model. Often these changes involved human action, such as groundwater pumping and land use (Oreskes and Belitz 2001).

Why do modellers fail to incorporate factors that they recognise as relevant to the system? In many cases the problem is how to handle human impacts. Human behaviour is notoriously hard to predict, and even harder to quantify, and therefore it is extremely hard to parameterise into a model variable. Moreover, most physical scientists have little training and experience in dealing with the human role in *natural* systems – the climate, predator-prey relations, the hydrological cycle, etc. Physical scientists in agencies like the US Department of Energy or the US Environmental Protection Agency are not trained to think about human behaviour. Being unsure how to incorporate dynamic human activities in a rigorous way, scientists may treat them in a static – and therefore highly unrealistic – way. Or, they may simply leave them out. Experience shows that scientists may omit factors and variables that they do not understand, or do not know how to quantify reliably, because to assign them an arbitrary value seems, well, arbitrary. But to leave them out is, in effect, to assign them the value of zero.

II   Uncertainty is inevitable, recrimination is not

Models are representations of the natural world, and we cannot say in advance how good a representation any particular model (or even any ensemble of models) will turn out to be. Nature is full of surprises.

Some scientists and philosophers have of course recognised this for some time. John Herschel in the nineteenth century, John Dewey, Alfred North Whitehead, and Werner Heisenberg in the twentieth century, and Silvio Functowicz and Jerome Ravetz more recently have all emphasised that uncertainty is intrinsic (see also Chapter 14). There are always unknowns. There are things we cannot measure, things we do not know how to measure, and things we do not even know to measure.

However, even if numerous details of a system under consideration are incompletely understood, the scientific parameters needed to inform policy may still be at hand. The history of science suggests that the success of science is not based on the achievement of certainty, but rather the reverse: on the willingness and ability of scientists to learn from experience. Therefore, we need mechanisms that do not deny the uncertainties, but enable us to live and work with them (Funtowicz and Ravetz 1985).[5]

How do we do that?

One place to look is the business community. Business models are often overlooked by scientists and academics who fancy themselves living the life of the mind, and they are often over-emphasised by American politicians who think that all problems can be solved by free markets. But business men and women constantly make decisions based on information at hand, in settings where delay can mean missed opportunities and lost market share. So it makes sense to think that business models could provide insight and guidance.

An immediate objection might be that business decisions are typically short-range choices rather than long-term policies, and are made in markets and manufacturing systems that are not comparable to complex natural systems. Perhaps. But there is at least one business community that frequently makes weighty, long-range decisions about complex natural systems, and based on incomplete information. That is the petroleum industry. The experience of evaluating oil fields demonstrates that while uncertainty is inevitable, recrimination is not.

III   Living with uncertainty: the unitisation model

Originating in finance, the term *unitisation* refers to the amalgamation of several small units into one larger one, as in the myriad cartons loaded into a single shipping container, or the numerous cargo cars that comprise a freight train. More recently, the term has been used to describe the joint development of an oil field that straddles leases held by different corporations.

Here is the basic idea. Oil fields, like most natural phenomena, have messy boundaries. They do not form neat circles, squares or rectangles. Yet the boundaries of oil leases do, so fields do not fit cleanly into the legal and social structures that humans have created to develop them. Moreover, the boundaries of a field, particularly a large one in a region

---

[5] This is the basic insight of pragmatist philosophy, as articulated by William James, John Dewey, and others. See, for example, Dewey 1929.

with many players, such as the North Sea, are unlikely to coincide with the boundaries of a single company's leases. This leads to questions about who owns how much of any particular field.

In other words, an oil field might look like Figure 3.1A:

In contrast, the leases look like Figure 3.1B:

Put them together and you get Figure 3.1C:

The problem is evident. If the field is owned by various parties, then they have to figure out a way to divide the proceeds, based on what part of the field rightly belongs to whom. However, sharing the proceeds implies that you know what it is that you are sharing, but it is very difficult – indeed, impossible – to determine, before a field is developed, exactly how large it is and how much oil it will yield. One never knows *exactly* how much a field will produce until the end of the day, when production ceases and the field is finally abandoned. This is so for two reasons, one having to do with nature, and the other with society.

From the perspective of the natural world, there are a large number of variables that determine the size and productivity of any oil field. These include the extent and thickness of the reservoir horizons, their porosity and permeability, the proportions of oil, gas, and water they hold, and the frequency of faults, fractures, pinch-outs and other geological

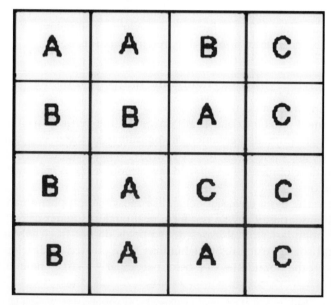

Figure 3.1A Distribution of leases over a potential oil field, 1

Figure 3.1B The actual shape of an oil field, straddling leases A, B, C shown in Figure 3.1A, 2

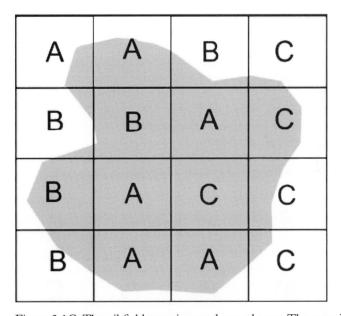

Figure 3.1C The oil field superimposed upon leases. The question is: How much of the oil, contained in the field, rightly belongs to companies A, B and C? 3

features. These variables affect oil quantity, quality, and flow, and are themselves variable. There is not *one* value for reservoir permeability, there is a range of values, spatially distributed and continuously varying across the field. Any estimate of reservoir permeability is exactly that: an estimate. Oil companies have developed sophisticated geophysical techniques to estimate the properties of a field, but none of the relevant variables can be fully and precisely determined up front, so the total amount of oil in the field cannot be fully predicted, either. It is only after a field has been exhausted that its operators know how much oil it contained, and even then, the operators will still not know the exact combinations of permeability, porosity, reservoir thickness and the like that produced the yield they actually got.

Moreover, the whole concept of an *oil field* is a human construct, because an *oil field* is not given in nature. Nature gives us rocks, with oil trapped in spaces between mineral grains. What makes those rocks into a *field* is that the oil can be extracted at a profit, which entails numerous human considerations, such as the price of oil, the cost of labour, the efficacy of available technologies, the will of the company, the stability of the political environment, and much more.

Even once a field is defined, its size remains somewhat indeterminate, because of fluctuations in the price of oil: if the price goes up, one can make a profit in a lower yielding field. One can also justify putting more resources into secondary and tertiary recovery. So a company can end up with a *larger* field than it would have had at a lower oil price. For similar reasons the *boundaries* or limits of a large oil field are not entirely fixed by nature. In an abstract sense it is never possible to say *exactly* how large a field is.

But if you do not know how big the field is, then how can you divide it? And if you do not know where the boundaries are, then how can you say how much belongs to whom?

In the early days of US Gulf Coast oil drilling, it was common for operators to sink wells near lease boundaries, deliberately removing as much oil as fast as possible, including oil pumped from adjacent leases. Operators followed the *law of capture* – whoever captured the oil, owned it. The obvious problems with this approach led many US states to impose production quotas and/or legal restrictions on well spacing (Ross 2003). But spacing restrictions are inefficient, and production quotas can create incentives for fraud. Moreover, the law of capture is unacceptable when leases cross international borders, because no country wants to see its resources siphoned off by another. The law of capture also fails in offshore situations, where the enormous technical difficulty and expense of constructing drilling platforms makes closely spaced wells highly impractical.

It would be better if adjacent leaseholders could figure out a way to cooperate.

The solution used by oil companies is unitisation: to treat the various leases as a single entity and find a way to divide the proceeds. Several leases or portions of leases are consolidated into a single *unit agreement*, which determines the terms by which both the costs and proceeds will be divided.[6]

How are the unit agreements forged? Typically, each party has its own set of experts, who perform extensive scientific studies before an agreement is forged. The experts make a set of predictions about the field performance, which provides the basis for the agreement.

But as the field is developed – as more wells are drilled and the performance of the reservoir is observed in practice – inevitably one discovers that the predictions on which the agreement was forged were not entirely correct. What happens then?

There are two possibilities. In some areas of the world, the answer is 'that's life'. The agreement is the agreement and that is that. You live with the result, and if you fare poorly, you try to do better next time. Perhaps your company hires different experts or tries to improve its in-house geological evaluation capabilities. Perhaps you get tougher lawyers the next time you have to negotiate.

But in many areas, unitisation agreements are subject to *re-determination*. After a predetermined time, perhaps five years, the parties reassess. They compare the predictions with the actual outcomes, and if they diverge (which invariably they do), they re-determine the features of the field and modify the agreement accordingly. The parties learn from experience and use this to adjust the agreement. Like NASA sending astronauts to the moon, they make a mid-course correction (Holling 1978).[7]

The crucial insight of re-determination is the recognition that one *cannot know in advance exactly how the natural system will perform when put into production*. To wait for perfect knowledge would be to wait forever; to wait even for nearly perfect knowledge would involve

[6] In some areas of the North Sea, for example the Norwegian sector, unitisation agreements are legally required. In the USA offshore environment, the Minerals Management Service reserves the right to impose unitisation if it determines that is desirable in order to prevent waste, conserve resources, and/or protect other rights, including the Federal Government's royalty interests. See Ross 2004; and Federal Code of Regulations, Mineral Management Services 30CFR250.1304 (2009).

[7] It is interesting that NASA engineers recognised the need for mid-course corrections in the early Apollo missions, without which the engineers would miss the moon! Engineers, being used to systems with both feedbacks and near-term consequences, are perhaps more pragmatic about dealing with uncertainty than scientists, with their ideals of truth-seeking, have traditionally been. It is therefore perhaps not surprising that early works on adaptive environmental management took inspiration from control systems engineering.

undesirable delays in recouping one's investment. Once a field is reasonably certain of producing oil at a profit, there is a strong incentive to move forward. Unitisation agreements are thus forged based on what is 'reasonably proven' by drilling and other geological and geophysical studies; re-determination allows the partners to modify the agreement in light of new information. In essence, it structures an opportunity to learn from experience, formally allowing one to live and work within a framework of acknowledged uncertainty.[8]

In an article recounting the history of unitisation agreements involving the Frigg Field, straddling Norwegian-UK waters in the North Sea, petroleum consultant James Ross explained:

One of the original problems with [the Frigg field] was that everyone thought they had to get all the details right first time. [Subsequently] parties decided right up front that they would decide on an approximate apportionment and sort out the details later through re-determinations as the field matured. This pragmatic approach ... allowed the project to go ahead unhindered by years of protracted negotiations ... [What one learned] was that while it was impossible to get all the details down pat at the start, it was more important for the projects to proceed with provisions in place for subsequent reviews and re-determinations (J. Ross 2003; J.G. Ross 2004).

Rather than spend time and money attempting to do the impossible – to make a perfect prediction of field performance – the companies involved use the agreement to move forward despite uncertainty.[9]

---

[8] For an example of an agreement that uses the language of *reasonably proven*, see US Mineral Management Service, www.gomr.mms.gov/homepg/pd/Model_agreement_Exp_Dev_Prod_Units.rtf. In practice, the details of agreements are far more complicated than the outline given here, and they may differ when more than one nation is involved. In the UK sector of the North Sea, the British government plays a large role in overseeing the agreements to ensure maximum recovery of the economic hydrocarbons (which may not be the same as maximum profit to the corporations involved), and there are annual consents for numerous aspects of production, such as annual volumes produced, flare volumes permitted, etc. In multinational situations, individual government oversight may play less of a role, and more rests on the unit agreement between the parties. For a sample Joint Operating Agreement in a multinational setting, see www.ukooa.co.uk/issues/stdagreements/worddocs/joint%20operating%20agreement.pdf.

[9] This should not be taken to minimise the difficulties involved. The knowledge available is understood to be highly imperfect and often involving considerable subjective judgement. Wiggins and Libecap (1985) suggest that the failure of many US firms in Oklahoma and Texas to enter into successful unitisation agreements results directly from lack of confidence in the available information, despite large net gains that could be achieved by such agreements. 'Because of the subjective nature and wide variation in estimates of subsurface parameters, negotiating parties rely on a small set of objectively measurable variables, but they are likely to be poor indicators of lease value' (379). Yet, despite these problems, many (most?) North Sea Operators do now enter into such agreements. Whether there is a larger pattern that European operators are better at cooperation than US ones is an interesting question, and worthy of study in its own right.

IV   You do not have to 'get all the details right the first time'

Agencies like the US Environmental Protection Agency (EPA) have a legal mandate to protect the environment, and if they discover that a regulation has failed to do that, they cannot simply say, 'Oh, well'. So unitisation without re-determination would be an unsatisfactory model for regulatory decisions. However, a regulatory model based on the concept of unitisation with re-determination addresses many of the problems that the EPA and similar agencies face, and has numerous advantages over the strategy of trying to get all the details right the first time.

Unitisation recognises the reality that all regulation is a form of dispute management. A regulation exists because of conflict: one party is regulated to protect the interests of another. An industry wants to make its products as best it sees fit, the residents in the area around it want to be protected from noxious emissions. A new drug is proposed for market, but patients and doctors are concerned about safety and efficacy. Mr Jones thinks he is perfectly entitled to dump his engine oil in his own backyard, but it could seep into the ground and affect Mr Smith's neighbouring water well. All regulation seeks to resolve or prevent potential disputes, to protect the interests of one individual or group against the actions of others.[10] Unitisation is a model that has been shown to work for dispute management.

Unitisation has been tested in the real world and it works. Life is not perfect, and no solution to complex environmental and regulatory problems will be either. In hindsight, one could surely find various unitisation agreements that were unfair or inequitable in an absolute sense. Nevertheless, *very few re-determinations have been subject to subsequent challenges by litigation.* In the United States, where legal challenges to regulation are rampant, any process that avoids prolonged, costly, and wasteful challenges would clearly be a step in the right direction. The track record of unitisation suggests that while uncertainty is inevitable, litigation is not.

Unitisation builds in flexibility. Dietrich Dörner (1996) has shown that systems often break down because their managers have a rigid idea of what needs to be done and fail to respond to new information. Systems that work tend to be flexible, and systems that are flexible are more likely

---

[10] This is not necessarily restricted to disputes between two parties. Regulation can also protect companies that have implemented pollution control and want others to do the same to maintain a level playing field, or new entries into marketplaces who want assurance what the rules will be. But no matter how many parties are involved, regulation always involves competing interests.

to work. Unitisation with re-determination formalises that concept, preparing for new information and structuring the opportunity for its incorporation. In this sense, it is a form of adaptive management, increasingly advocated in recent years in many spheres (Holling 1978; Walters 1986). A pioneering work on adaptive management summed up the issue perfectly decades ago: 'Attempts to eliminate uncertainty are delusory and often counterproductive. The appropriate concept for both assessment and policy design is recognition of the inevitability of uncertainty and the consequent selective risk-taking' (Holling 1978: 5).[11]

Unitisation does not rely on trust or confidence. Regulatory agencies often speak of building trust, and scientists often claim that their physical experiments or model evaluation exercises will 'build confidence'. But if there is no way to know in advance whether our confidence is justified, then the claim that certain scientific work builds confidence reduces to an appeal to authority; in effect, the claim that because *we* have confidence in our results, *you* should, too. In a regulatory environment, however, decisions often involve adversarial parties who do not trust one another, sometimes with good reason. Building trust between such adversaries may not be a realistic goal.

Confidence may also be misplaced. Experience and psychology experiments show that both experts and lay people are often *over*-confident in their knowledge (Kahneman, Slovic and Tversky 1982; Dörner 1996). Trust can get you into trouble. The unitisation model demands neither trust nor confidence – neither in experts, nor in science itself. It simply requires an agreed-upon process for re-determination. Moreover, if the process is decided up front – before either party knows whether they will be on the advantaged or disadvantaged side – the chances for agreement are improved.[12] Indeed, there is a striking difference between discussions of unitisation and those found in regulatory contexts. The former emphasise the goal of arriving at equitable, fair and workable solutions; the notion of trust or confidence simply does not come into play.

Unitisation provides a mechanism to avoid getting bogged down in details. The natural world *is* very complex, and many current environmental issues have got bogged down in details – what some call the 'fifth

[11] This point merits elaboration: regulators often view risk as something to be eliminated or at least minimised. Businesses, in contrast, view risk as essential to taking advantage of opportunities. Getting regulators to view risk in positive terms might be impossible, but what a change would ensue if they could!

[12] Somewhat like the Rawl's model for justice, the parties involved do not know who will benefit, and therefore can be expected to make fair choices, or at least untainted by informed self-interest.

decimal point'.[13] But often the direction of action needed to address an environmental issue is the same regardless of the fifth decimal place, or even the fourth, third or second. The unitisation model emphasises the *direction* of action – in this case, to get the field into production – with opportunity for adjustment of the magnitude when more details become known.

Unitisation avoids delay premised on uncertainty. In the United States, it has become a common and effective tactic to delay political action on the grounds of scientific uncertainty, on issues as diverse as tobacco control and greenhouse gas emissions (Oreskes and Conway 2010). The argument that in the face of uncertainty more information is needed seems logical enough on its face, and, as noted above, scientists rarely object to additional funding for their research. But to delay *is* to act – to act in favour of the status quo, which typically favours the wealthy and powerful. In regulatory matters, the results of the strategy of delay can be profoundly undemocratic. The unitisation model addresses this, acknowledging that while uncertainty is a fact of life, it is not grounds for presumptive preservation of the status quo.

Finally, the unitisation model acknowledges the reality of surprise. For nearly four centuries, Western scientists clung to the dream of knowing nature fully, completely, positively. In the past century, both scientists and philosophers have come to understand that this ideal is unobtainable: we can never know nature fully. All natural systems are complex, tricky, and subject to change over time. As philosopher of science Nancy Cartwright has stressed, the laws of physics do, indeed, lie – or at least mislead us (Cartwright 1983). They lead us to believe that nature is neat, when in reality it is messy, and that it is highly predictable when in reality it can be quite unpredictable.

V   Objections?

Some may object that environmental problems are sometimes so acute that we do not have the luxury of re-determination; we need to act now and cannot afford to wait five, seven or ten years to find out how we are doing. Such an objection would be misplaced, for in many cases we have already waited that long, if not longer.

Consider global warming. Scientists developed a consensus in the late 1970s that greenhouse gas emissions would likely lead to global climate

---

[13] Holling 1978, Ch. 1, esp. p. 4, offers a discussion of unnecessary detail, and the faulty assumption made by many scientists that more detail will improve overall understanding and predictive capacity.

change, and by 1995 they concluded that such change was indeed happening (Oreskes 2007; Oreskes and Conway 2010). If the model proposed here had been put in place to address global warming in 1995, when the Intergovernmental Panel on Climate Change first declared that the human effect on climate was discernible, the world might be a great deal better off than it is today (Houghton *et al.* 1996). Indeed, thinking about global warming leads us to note a paradox. Some fossil fuel companies have insisted that because global warming was not definitively proven, it was premature to act to control greenhouse gas emissions, but this was a standard that they did not apply in their own business decisions![14]

The past cannot be changed, and the challenge at hand is to move forward. The proposed model suggests a way to do so. The appropriate time frame for re-determination will vary with the problem and the capacity of available monitoring systems, but given how much time, effort and money has been spent in the United States on legal challenges to regulatory actions, it is hard to see how the delays involved in the model proposed here could be worse.

The objection might also be raised that regulated parties hate change: if a regulation is emplaced, they want assurance that any actions they take to comply will not be changed too abruptly or too soon. In effect, they want to know that the rules will not be changed in the middle of the game. Legal standards in the United States require that any changes that are made be consistent, and neither *arbitrary* nor *capricious*. Again, the model proposed here addresses these concerns, insofar as the time frame for re-negotiation can be chosen so as to be consonant with the temporal capacity of the regulated parties to adapt, and all parties will know in advance when that re-negotiation is scheduled to take place. In this sense, it may well be less capricious than agency reviews motivated by changes in the occupants of the American White House.

Conclusion

The history of science demonstrates that science is fallible. A robust approach to knowledge must acknowledge this and respond to it.

---

[14] On the other hand, there appears to be some evidence that US firms have not been as successful as North Sea operators in forging unitisations agreements, so perhaps there is a pattern here. See Wiggins and Libecap 1985: There is 'widespread failure of private crude oil producing firms to unitize US oil fields to reduce rent dissipation ... despite the fact that Unitization is the obvious private contraction solution to rent dissipation' (368).

When we apply scientific knowledge to environmental problems, our task should be to find a mechanism to recognise the reality of fallibility and allow us to learn from experience. One way or another we *will* learn from experience, the question is whether we will do it the hard way or the easy way. Pretending that we can *get it right* up front is the hard way; it sets up resistance and increases the difficulty of modifying our actions later. Later adjustment looks like failure, leading to embarrassment, recrimination and litigation.

The alternative proposed here is to acknowledge that we cannot get *it* right up front, no matter what the *it* is. If we can do this, then we can set up mechanisms to learn from experience and incorporate new information and insights. Adjustment in this case is not failure, it is simply part of the plan.

Acknowledgements

I am grateful to Charles Smith and Leonard Smith for comments on an earlier draft of this paper; to Lewis Gross for background on adaptive management; to Richard Wilson for patiently explaining how unitisation works in the North Sea; and to my research assistant, Krystal Tribbett. I thank Nancy Cartwright, Mary Morgan, Erik Conway, and Chris Whipple for numerous valuable discussions.

REFERENCES

Boykoff, Maxwell T. and Boykoff, Jules M. 2004. 'Balance as bias: Global warming and the US prestige press', *Global Environmental Change* 14: 125–36.
Bredehoeft, John D. 2000. 'The conceptualization problem – Surprise', *Hydrogeology Journal* 13/1: 37–46.
Cartwright, Nancy 1983. *How the Laws of Physics Lie*, New York: Oxford University Press.
Dewey, John 1929. *The Quest for Certainty: A Study of the Relation of Knowledge and Action*, New York: Minton, Balch & Co.
Dörner, Dietrich 1996. *The Logic of Failure*, New York: Metropolitan Books.
EEA 2001. 'Late lessons from early warnings: The precautionary principle 1896–2000'. *Environmental Issues Report No. 22*, Copenhagen. (Edited by: Poul Harremoës (chairman), Malcolm MacGarvin (executive editor), Andy Stirling, Brian Wynne and Jane Keys (editors), David Gee and Sofia Guedes Vaz (EEA editors).)
Federal Code of Regulations 2009. US Mineral Management Services 30CFR250.1304.
Funtowicz, Silvio O. and Ravetz, Jerome R. 1985. 'Three types of risk assessment: A methodological analysis', in Whipple and Covello (eds.), *Risk Analysis in the Private Sector*, New York: Plenum, pp. 217–32.

Gilman, Paul 2005. Testimony to Committee on Models in the Regulatory Decision Process, Board on Environmental Studies and Toxicology, Division on Earth and Life Studies, National Research Council, 2 December 2005.

Holling, C.S. (ed.) 1978. *Adaptive Environmental Assessment and Management*, New York: John Wiley & Sons.

Houghton, J.T., Meira Filho, L.G., Callender, B.A., Harris, N., Kattenberg, A. and Maskell, K. (eds.) 1996. *Climate Change 1995: The Science of Climate Change: Contribution of Working Group I to the Second Assessment Report of the Intergovernmental Panel on Climate Change*, Cambridge University Press, see esp. pp. 1–9.

Joint Operating Agreement for UKCS License 2007, available at www.ukooa.co. uk/issues/stdagreements/worddocs/joint%20operating% 20agreement.pdf (last accessed 14 October 2007).

Kahneman, D., Slovic, P. and Tversky, A. (eds.) 1982. *Judgment under Uncertainty: Heuristics and Biases*, New York: Cambridge University Press.

Metlay, Daniel 2000. 'From tin roof to torn wet blanket: Predicting and observing groundwater movement at a proposed nuclear waste site', in Sarewitz, Pielke and Byerly (eds.), *Prediction: Science, Decision Making, and the Future of Nature*, Washington DC and Covelo, CA: Island Press, pp. 199–230.

Michaels, David 2005. 'Doubt is their product', *Scientific American* 292: 96–101.

Michaels, David 2008. *Doubt is their Product*, New York: Oxford University Press.

Oreskes, Naomi (ed. with Homer Le Grand) 2001. *Plate Tectonics: An Insider's History of the Modern Theory of the Earth*. Boulder: Westview Press.

Oreskes, Naomi 2004. 'Science and public policy: What's proof got to do with it?', *Environmental Science & Policy* 7: 369–83.

Oreskes, Naomi 2007. 'The long consensus on climate change', *Washington Post*, 1 February 2007, p. A15.

Oreskes, Naomi and Belitz, Kenneth 2001. 'Philosophical issues in model evaluation', in M.G. Anderson and P.D. Bates (eds.), *Model Validation: Perspectives in Hydrological Science*. London: John Wiley and Sons, pp. 23–41.

Oreskes, Naomi and Conway, Erik M. 2010. *Merchants of Doubt: How a Handful of Scientists obscured the truth on Issues from Tobacco Smoke to Global Warming*. New York: Bloomsbury Press.

Ross, James G. 2004. 'Industry practice in equity redeterminations', *Transnational Dispute Management* 1/2, available at: www.transnational-dispute-management.com/samples/freearticles/tv1-2-article15a.htm (last accessed 8 March 2010).

Ross, Jim 2003. 'Unitization lessons learned from the North Sea', SPETT News, 1 September 2003, pp. 4–9.

Rudwick, Martin J.S. 1985. *The Great Devonian Controversy: The Shaping of Scientific Knowledge among Gentlemanly Specialists*. Chicago University Press.

Sarewitz, Daniel 1996. *Frontiers of Illusion: Science, Technology, and the Politics of Progress*. Philadelphia: Temple University Press.

Sarewitz, Daniel 2004. 'How science makes environmental problems controversies worse', *Environmental Science and Policy* 7: 385–403.

US Mineral Management Service 2010, available at: www.gomr.mms.gov/ homepg/pd/ Model_agreement_Dev_Prod_Units.rtf.(last accessed 14 March 2010).

Walters, Carl J. 1986. *Adaptive Management of Renewable Resources*, New York: Macmillan Publishers.

Weart, Spencer 2003. *The Discovery of Global Warming*, Cambridge, MA: Harvard University Press.

Whipple, Chris G. *et al.* (15 authors) 2007. 'Models in environmental regulatory decision making', Committee on Models in the Regulatory Decision Process, Board on Environmental Studies and Toxicology, Division on Earth and Life Studies, National Research Council, Washington DC: The National Academies Press.

Wiggins, Steven N. and Libecap, Gary D. 1985. 'Oil field unitization: Contractual failure in the presence of imperfect information', *The American Economic Review* 75/3: 368–85.

4 Looking for quality in all the wrong places, or: the technological origins of quality in scientific policy advice

Daniel Sarewitz

Quality control in scientific policy advice is a vexing problem because it seems to encompass two conflicting conditions. First, people believe that improved knowledge about the world, communicated by experts to politicians and policymakers, can improve our capacity to deal with many challenges to our well-being, from terrorism to climate change to pandemic influenza. Science advice must aim at providing the best picture of what we know, as a basis for making better decisions than those based on a less-good picture. Second, because the world is complex, complete scientific understanding of the problems that decision-makers seek to address can never be attained. Choices must always be made about how to frame a problem, what type of research should be pursued to characterise the problem, whose research results are reliable and relevant and whose are not, and so on. Science, that is, has an inherently social and political element, all the more when it is carried out and applied in contested political settings (see Jasanoff, Chapter 2, and Oreskes, Chapter 3).

Almost three centuries into *the Enlightenment* – in this case, meaning the broad social consensus to use reason, and especially scientific reason, as a guide to human understanding and action – and sixty years into an era of modernity where scientists are recognised as crucial contributors to policy processes at national and international levels, it is perhaps an embarrassment, yet nonetheless no surprise, that we are still trying to figure out how to ensure *quality*, and even what *quality* actually means, at the intersection of science and policy advice. Given the incommensurable conditions that seem to underlie the quest for quality, is there any reason to believe that the troubled state of scientific policy advice can become any less troubled; that notions of quality, or processes that yield quality, can be more broadly agreed upon and that science can therefore be more successfully employed to improve the capacity of decision-makers to deal with complex problems? Indeed, the past several decades have led to a general disintegration of anything surrounding a social consensus on what counts as *quality* in science advice, and who counts as a legitimate expert. Moreover, many academicians who work on these sorts of issues would likely view this disintegration as a positive development because it is accompanied by an increased transparency about the relations of power to expertise and legitimacy, and a heightened appreciation of the limits of science in providing authoritative understanding of problems that implicate both complex natural-human systems, and contested politics.

I will here stake out an unfashionable and I suspect unpopular position. For complex, contested challenges to human well-being, the identification and employment of effective technological interventions to facilitate the achievement of desired goals is a much more promising avenue of progress than the generation and deployment of scientific knowledge, of whatever quality, and via whatever mechanisms, aimed at improving decision-making and public policies.

I use the words *effective* and *progress* self-consciously and carefully. Much of this chapter will be devoted to what I mean by *effectiveness* in technology, which may perhaps be seen as roughly equivalent to *quality* in scientific policy advice. As for *progress* and technology, we have, of course, long ago lost our innocence. I do not mean just 'The Bomb' and 'Agent Orange' and big dams, but the idea of technology itself – the idea of a particular artefact or machine that just does its job. We have learned that technologies emerge from social systems that they – like science – reflect and internalise power relations and cultural assumptions. We recognise that social systems are actually techno-social systems; that these systems impose certain orders of behaviour on our lives about which we have little choice (who among us is not enslaved by email?); that these systems lock in paths of dependency that make a mockery of human agency (just try decarbonising the global energy system!); that they enable hierarchies of expertise, influence, and exploitation (who, anymore, can argue with their auto mechanic?). We know that socio-technological systems are now as complex and pervasive and incomprehensible as natural systems; in fact we know that the distinction between technological and natural systems is no longer very meaningful. We know that the dependence of modern market economies on continual growth means that we have to keep inventing and consuming new technologies, whether we really need them or not, and that this process of continual innovation and productivity enhancement leads to apparently unavoidable spasms of severe unemployment and socio-economic disruption and transformation, along with the wealth creation that is an underpinning for political stability in market democracies.

Technology seems to render more concrete and perplexing the conceptual ambiguity of the idea of progress. Writing in 1928, Lewis

Mumford (1963: 283; originally published in 1928) called this the *ambivalence* of the machine, which, he observed, 'is both an instrument of liberation and one of repression. It has economized human energy and it has misdirected it. It has created a wide framework of order and it has produced muddle and chaos. It has nobly served human purposes and it has distorted and denied them.'

Yet, while acknowledging all of this complexity and ambiguity, I want as well to posit the existence of something that no one of any intellectual sophistication could possibly believe in anymore: technology itself. For example, I want to claim that the watch I am wearing embodies a technological function that I find useful – letting me know what time it is. And in acknowledging this function I am not at all suggesting that, say, the development of the chronometer in the nineteenth century did not advance the pace of colonialism by allowing more precise marine navigation, or that my father was not manipulated into buying my particular watch by clever advertising, or even that my need to know the time is not a cultural expectation that assaults my individual autonomy. It is all probably true, and even so my watch helps me navigate my days because it reliably does what I want it to do.

With this in mind, let me start on what I hope is firm ground: Making and using and improving on technologies, like eating, sleeping, lying, procreating, imagining, is something that people do, is part of being a person. Mumford (1963: 60) wrote: 'The age of invention is only another name for the age of man.' And part of this innateness means that, at any given moment, humans are utterly, irrevocably, dependent on some set of technologies and technological functions for their survival. Of course, the nature of that dependency changes over time, sometimes in radical fits and starts, but it remains, nonetheless, a condition of our condition. And what this means is that assessments of future technologies are relative to the current technological state, not relative to some pre- or non-technological state. Technology is always part of the context.

Second, I want to reinforce this point about functionality. Technologies are meant to do things, to accomplish particular goals or tasks. Technologies are, in effect, cause-and-effect machines, linking a human intent to a particular consequence via the embedded function of the technology, and often doing so with very high reliability, often – but not always (Edgerton 2006) – more than could be achieved using an older technology aimed at the same function, or without the technology at all. And the fact that a technology emerges from a cultural and political choice process, or that a lot of technologies seem to serve no useful purpose other than to advance the profits of the producer, or are designed to do things like kill people, or end up doing things that they were not designed to do, is not problematic for my assertion of functionality.

Now I want to do something else academically incorrect and connect technology to a very modest notion of rationality. This modest notion is that when people make a decision, usually their intent is to achieve the objective at which their decision is aimed. I want to suggest that, at the level of individual use, technologies are volition enhancers: they often give us a better chance of accomplishing what it is we want to do than would otherwise be the case. I need, for example, to complete this chapter in fairly short order to meet a publication deadline, and my computer with its word processing software gives me a much better chance of meeting my obligation than if I were using pen and paper.

But this raises a third point, that technologies are, on the one hand, reliable cause-and-effect machines for our use, but they are also components of complex systems whose connections to the functionality of the individual technology is not necessarily very obvious or even salutary. Thus, for example, the very fact that I must complete this chapter in a rather short period of time is related to the compression of deadlines made possible by information and communication technologies and networks. If I did not have email, word processing and the World Wide Web, the editors of this volume could not possibly have expected me to complete this chapter in the time they have allotted me.

Technologies, that is, inhabit two rather independent realities. One reality is of the immediate effectiveness of the technology itself as it is used by those trying to accomplish something – for example, the jet airplane that carries me with incredible reliability from Washington DC to Phoenix, Arizona, and then back again, once or twice each month. The other reality is of systemic complexity – the air transportation system that seems in many ways to be the absolute embodiment of irrationality and dysfunction, whether it is the incomprehensible pricing system, the absurd inefficiency of boarding and security processes, the significant inequities in access, the constant delays, the inability to spend one's frequent flier miles, not to mention the almost continual financial insolvency of most airlines.

This system complexity that accompanies technologies raises another problem that provokes justifiable suspicions among technological scep- tics: the likelihood of unintended consequences. Technologies do not act in isolation, they are connected to other technologies, activities and phenomena that may interact in ways that no one is able to predict or control. So the functionality embodied in the airplane that reliably carries me from Washington to Phoenix is also implicated, for example, in the rapid spread of exotic infectious diseases such as AIDS and SARS, and of course in terrorist attacks that marked a major inflection point in recent US history. Technologies often surprise us because they introduce into society novel capabilities and functionalities whose diverse uses are constantly being expanded and discovered – that is just what we do, remember – and which interact with other technologies, and with natural and social phenomena, in ways that cannot be known in advance.

So here's a sharp contrast I want to bring out, where we as humans by definition live in a world of technology, in cultures of technological innovation, upon which we depend for our survival, and which condition our behaviour. And this dependency on one level reflects our efforts to exercise our intent across an increasing breadth of human domains to accomplish certain tasks with incredible reliability, even as it enmeshes us in complex socio-technical systems of Kafka-esque incomprehensibility and capriciousness, systems that themselves demand continual technological updating as part of the process of adjusting to their own unfolding and unpredictable complexities.

Let me focus in on the airplane. I experience it in two ways: as an extraordinarily reliable piece of technology, and as a component in an extraordinarily irritating transportation system. I remember when I first grew comfortable with the fact of airplane reliability – when I stopped gripping my arm rests during take-offs, landings and turbulence. It was 1975; I had dropped out of college and was working on a cod-fishing boat based in Boston Harbor. The boat was small and we fished within sight of the shore. The cod fishery was already in decline, and we had to switch from using gill nets to tub-trawls – long lines with hundreds of baited hooks on them – in order to get a decent catch. The costs of the bait and fuel were barely covered by the catch, and I was paid in sandwiches and all the cod I could eat. So we were using these rather elemental technologies, and meanwhile, we were usually within sight of Logan Airport, and planes were continually landing and taking off, every minute or so, with a reliability and precision that made our own elemental struggles to bring in a few fish seem out of a different world.

Our ability to succeed as fishermen depended, of course, on some technologies – the boat, the nets, and when they failed, the tub-trawls, but the most important parts of the system – the fish, and the ecosystem that sustained them – were outside of our control. The jets were part of a technological system that internalised almost everything that was necessary for their functioning. The design of the wings was such that the planes had no choice but to take off when a certain velocity was attained and the flaps were adjusted to a certain angle; the design of the jet engines was of an elegance and simplicity to provide tens of thousands of hours of reliable operation. Not only that, but the design of the planes was subject to continual, incremental improvement through, for example, the development of lighter, stronger alloys, more precisely machined parts, and more aerodynamic designs. But there was, in contrast, no engineering ourselves out of the absence of fish, in fact better engineering made the problem worse.

Of course, this is not the whole story. It is not just that the planes are reliable – it is that the reliability is completely obvious – and that unreliability is completely unacceptable. People agree on what constitutes the essence of a reliable airplane – one that gets you to your destination without crashing. This is a value that is widely shared. And pretty much everyone agrees that, if you want to travel many miles in the shortest possible time, airplanes are the best option. So there is a transparency to the effectiveness of airplanes that transcends ideological or religious or philosophical differences. Not only that, because the viability of the air transport system – for all its dysfunction and irrationality – depends utterly on the reliability of the airplane itself, the system has to figure out how to maintain that reliability at all levels of operation, from designing, building and maintaining aircraft, to managing air traffic, to detecting wind shear. The feedbacks from failure, and the incentives to learn and behave appropriately, are very clear and strong. According to the US National Transportation Safety Board (2009), there were 22 million scheduled US commercial air flights in 2007 and 2008, flying a total of about 16 billion miles – and zero fatal crashes, an incredible record that reflects continual learning and improvement as the size and complexity of the system grow. And yet I recently arrived at an airport only to find that my e-ticket seemed not to exist. Obnoxious persistence on my part led to the discovery that the ticket, which I thought I had purchased while on the phone with an airline employee who, it turns out, worked in Bangalore, had somehow not been entered into the system. So the airlines cannot even manage to reliably sell tickets to the customers who keep them in business. The feedback from my rage provided little opportunity for learning by the airline company. Yet not only do airlines manage to keep their planes in the sky – more and more of them, in fact – they keep developing improved planes – faster, more energy efficient, more reliable.

So our own experience with flight is filled with contradiction: we are powerless consumers, buffeted by the turbulence of organisational incompetence that seems to grow more pathological and even malevolent with the years, even as we can justifiably maintain a high level of confidence in the operation of the core technology, which itself is subject to pretty continual improvement. Very strange.

Now what can this possibly have to do with quality control in scientific policy advice? What I particularly want to call attention to is this difference between a level of action where people's intent has a good chance of being translated into a desired outcome, and the larger complex, dysfunctional system where the consequences of action become pretty much impossible to map out, so that projecting intent becomes at best a matter of trial-and-error, and at worse close to futile. I want in particular to focus on the way that a technology can, if the problem is appropriately defined, reliably do what it is supposed to do regardless of the complexity of the broader context, and contrast that reliability with the intransigence of complex problems for which no simplifying technological effectiveness exists, so that we are forced to depend on expert advice to make progress.

It would perhaps be an understatement to suggest that what I'm saying goes against the grain of much thinking about technology and society for the past forty years or so. Classic works that helped to define this field, like Jacques Ellul's *The Technological Society* (1967), and Langdon Winner's *Autonomous Technology* (1978), looked at the ways that societies restructure themselves to accommodate evolving technological systems and saw, for the most part, a ceding of human agency and authenticity and democracy to the demands of the system. The functionality of the technologies themselves was a trick, a sleight of hand aimed at distracting us from what was going on at the higher level. And it is true, complex technological systems do make a mockery of the Enlightenment fantasies of rational control over our affairs and dominion over nature. The works of Ellul, Winner, Mumford and others are suffused with an appropriate sense of befuddlement and resignation about what we can actually do to bring the technological systems that we create under our more direct and effective and democratic control.

Yet when, for example, Winner (1978: 228) talks about 'reverse adaptation – the adjustment of human ends to match the character of [technological] means' to describe our subservience to technological systems, the 'compared to what?' question kicks in. When was that golden age of harmony and agency and freedom from adjusting our ends to the available means? This is not, I want to emphasise, my apology on behalf of complex technological systems, it is my suggestion that technologies do not exist solely as vast, hegemonic and unthinking systems but also as local, homely, quotidian tools that people use to accomplish things.

Consider vaccines as an illustration of many of the possibilities, conflicts and dilemmas raised by this contrast between larger system and local use. In many ways vaccines represent everything one could possibly want in a technological intervention. Extended, and in some cases even life-long, immunity to a variety of diseases can be delivered through a process that takes seconds to administer and which confers its benefits with remarkable consistency and reliability. The vaccine can be administered easily, by people with minimal training, in just about any setting. The effectiveness of most vaccines is quite apparent; most famously, smallpox has been eradicated from the globe, we have come close with polio, and vaccines have played an important role in the reduction of childhood disease and mortality in many parts of the world. While vaccines have often stimulated opposition on both moral grounds and because of concerns over risks, on the whole they are widely accepted and embraced. Perhaps most interestingly, vaccinating against infectious disease has an inherently democratising aspect to it. The more people who get vaccinated, the better off everyone is. The benefits of herd immunity are a strong stimulus for public policies that encourage widespread and equitable distribution of vaccines. As I write this chapter, policymakers and citizens alike are hoping that vaccines can prevent a catastrophic outbreak of H1N1 (swine) flu. Vaccines provide rare instance where individual benefit is strongly linked by a technology to a wider communitarian benefit.

The contrast between the effectiveness of vaccines and the chaos of the system within which they are administered is perhaps even more conspicuous than for air transport. The US health care system, for example, has become an emblem of dysfunction, of inequity, and of immunity to beneficial political reform, regardless of the quantity or quality of *scientific policy advice* available for decision-makers. Yet most people manage to get necessary vaccinations, and enjoy the protection that they confer. Even in nations with little public health infrastructure, vaccines have often proven to be a powerfully effective intervention for improving health. So vaccines strongly illustrate the dual realities of technological effectiveness and system complexity.

But what makes a vaccine effective relative to other approaches to reducing the toll of infectious diseases? Consider one of the more conspicuous failures of modern science and technology policy: the relative neglect of research and effective treatment on diseases such as malaria that especially afflict poor people living in poor nations. In the past decade or so, private philanthropy, sometimes in partnership with international organisations, national governments and the private sector, has stepped in to try to reduce this imbalance. For example, research on malaria and malaria vaccines, has increased significantly. The technical challenges to developing a malaria vaccine are daunting, however, and it is unclear how long it will take for research to yield useful vaccines, or even if they are possible. In the meantime, malaria is killing at least a million people a year, most of them children, most of them in Africa (for example, Moorthy, Good and Hill 2004).

In the absence of a vaccine, there are several major cooperative efforts underway to promote prevention strategies centred around the distribution of insecticide-impregnated bed-nets, limited indoor spraying of insecticides, and other measures. In many ways impregnated bed-nets are a very appealing technology. Low cost, low tech, simple to use. Small is beautiful. Where impregnated bed-nets are in wide use, the spread of malaria declines rapidly. Yet the first decade of concentrated effort to promote widespread net use in malarial Africa was generally deemed a failure, with incidence of childhood malaria actually increasing. There are many reasons alleged for this failure, ranging from policy disagreements over appropriate distribution methods to bureaucratic incompetence at organisations like the US Agency for International Development and the cooperative Roll Back Malaria campaign (2009), to simple lack of use by those who received nets (Kyama and McNeil, Jr. 2007). As of 2006, despite significant expenditures and effort, only about 3 per cent of African children in malarial regions were sleeping under impregnated bed-nets (Hill, Lines and Rowland 2006).

In response to these disappointments, a policy consensus now seems to be emerging around an approach called Integrated Vector Management (IVM). IVM combines bed-nets with other interventions in a way that 'means tailoring a variety of preventative interventions to local context' (Africa Fighting Malaria 2009). As described by the World Health Organisation (2009), the characteristic features of IVM include 'selection of methods based on knowledge of local vector biology . . . rational use of insecticides . . . and good management practices. The specific mix of these interventions depends on local factors, such as the type of mosquito and malaria parasite, climate, cost, and available resources.'

'An IVM approach is evidence-based and an essential feature is development of the capacity to generate local data on disease epidemiology and vector ecology. IVM integrates all available resources to achieve a maximum impact on vector-borne disease' (World Health Organization 2004: 11). The alleviation of human suffering entailed in a radical reduction of malaria would be a magnificent achievement – true progress that we should all hope for. And surely IVM represents 'scientific policy advice' of high quality. Yet it is hard to be optimistic. Imagine that, instead of applying IVM to the prevention of malaria, we had a reasonably effective vaccine. What would be different?

Well, certain things might be the same. There would no doubt be controversies over appropriate policies for vaccine delivery, and organisational dysfunction at various levels, and lack of required health care delivery infrastructure and other challenges that have bedevilled efforts to improve public health in parts of Africa. But the essence of IVM, the key to its success, is 'tailoring a variety of preventative interventions to local context'. Yet surely the less tailoring that is necessary to achieve a desired result, the more likely success will be. To the extent that IVM is dependent on responding to local context, it is also dependent on managing and implementing knowledge and action in ways that are particular to that context. In any particular setting, the appropriate mix of interventions – 'a combination of bed nets, medication, spraying, and environmental management' – must be determined, and the institutions and people responsible for delivering the interventions must act appropriately. IVM, that is, is a complex combination of activities that require organisations to behave in particular ways in particular settings, and, crucially, where no single activity embodies the essence of malaria prevention. In these sorts of complex organisational settings, learning is particularly difficult because it is often not obvious how the lessons from one context might apply to another, and disagreement over competing approaches is common because the links from cause to effect are difficult to fully specify – numerous interpretations of success or failure may be plausible.

The key selling-point of IVM – its sensitivity to context – is nevertheless also its weakness. It is not that current approaches to controlling malaria should not be tailored to context – surely they must be – but tailoring to context is hard to do. A really effective intervention is one that renders context irrelevant. If a reasonably reliable malaria vaccine were developed no doubt there would be challenges related to cost, manufacturing, distribution and social acceptance of the vaccine, but much more of the intervention – the action that leads to the desired outcome – would be embodied in the technology itself. What you have to do to succeed is clear and always the same: vaccinate people. If people get vaccinated, they will with high reliability be immune, regardless of where they live, how they live, what they believe. A person may or may not reliably use the bed-net they are given, but once they have been vaccinated the problem is solved – the locus of reliability shifts from the individual or the organisation to the technology. The process of delivering the vaccination is what we might call a *shop-floor* activity, where effectiveness depends little if at all on the larger organisational setting beyond the capacity to deliver the vaccine. As with airplanes in the dysfunctional transportation system, most of the cause-and-effect directly relevant to solving the problem is localised in one particular technology whose performance can be easily measured, where performance is largely insensitive to the surrounding institutional context, where pretty much everyone agrees on what counts as success. Thus, questions of accountability and performance are easily assessed, and the difference between success and failure is apparent to all.

Solving a problem is hard when you do not have a way to condense the key cause-effect elements of the solution into a particular technology or routine that can be administered at the shop floor. Perhaps there will never be effective malaria vaccines, in which case IVM may well be the best path to reducing malaria in poor countries, but it is likely to be a very indirect path, one that does not always reach its goal. An effective vaccine would do the job better.

Of course many important problems cannot be technologically embodied in this way. Reducing the burden of malaria is sometimes portrayed as important for improving the economic performance of many African countries (for example, Sachs and Malaney 2002). One should expect that healthier people are better able to contribute productively to an economy, but there are so many other confounding factors, from education levels to environmental conditions to the quality of governance to the global trade situation that any prediction based on links between changes in malaria incidence and changes in wealth creation is at best a vague and hopeful guess about complex system behaviour. This problem is nicely illustrated by the work of anthropologist Peter Brown (1987), who tested the hypothesis that malaria was blocking economic development on the island of Sardinia in the period after World War II. He concluded that the 'macroparasitism' of landowners drained 30 per cent of the production capacity from peasants in the form of rents, while the 'microparasitism' of malaria accounted for less than 10 per cent reduction in their gross production. And here we should not expect a vaccine to do any better than bed-nets or IVM; now the goal – creating wealth – cannot be captured and internalised by a particular technology. In fact, if creating wealth is your goal, there could be much better routes to progress, for example changing patterns of land tenure, or improving levels of education. But, of course, these goals are themselves very hard to make progress on, and very resistant to improvement through 'scientific policy advice'.

I am arguing that the core functionality of a technology can offer a particularly reliable fulcrum for leveraging *quality* in scientific policy advice because an effective technology is one that reduces contextual complexity, and therefore also acts to reduce potential uncertainty and disagreement about competing approaches to a particular policy goal (like reducing malaria incidence). Those who are sophisticated about the social embeddedness of technologies might object that, for a variety of reasons, people often disagree about means as well as ends, and there is no reason to believe that a proposed technological solution will be ethically, politically or economically preferable to an alternative approach, even if that approach is more uncertain. Let me explore this problem through brief discussion of a different type of medical technology.

Cochlear implants are electronic devices that provide deaf people with a sense of hearing by direct stimulation of auditory nerves. Unlike hearing aids, which just amplify sound, implants can give profoundly deaf and severely hearing-impaired people the ability to sense and interpret sound, including speech. First tested in the early 1960s, cochlear implants were approved for use in the US by the Food and Drug Administration in 1985. By 2009, in the order of 190,000 devices have been implanted worldwide (National Institutes of Health 2009).

Opposition to cochlear implants has been centred around the idea that deafness is a reflection of human diversity, not a deficiency to be corrected. From this perspective, deaf culture is as rich and worthy of protection as any other distinctive culture, and deaf people do not need to be fixed. Using sign language, deaf people communicate richly with each other and with hearing people who also sign. Obstacles to complete and equal participation of deaf people in a society dominated by hearing people is a reflection of the structure of society, of institutionalised injustice, not of the attributes of deaf people. The appropriate ethical goals, therefore, are to eliminate obstacles to full participation in society by deaf people, and to adopt a stance of complete acceptance of deaf culture. Cochlear implants represent a threat to these goals, and to the sustainability of deaf culture (Tucker 1998). They should therefore be resisted. In support of this position, at least one deaf couple has sought out a sperm donor with a long history of family deafness to ensure that their child was also deaf (Spriggs 2002).

The reasons why, in contrast, many people do choose cochlear implants are apparent. The main ethical subtlety lies in the fact that many devices are implanted in young children who cannot consent to the operation or to the enhancement – but this is hardly a unique situation – and that in such cases it is presumably hearing people for the most part, rather than deaf people, who are making the decision. My point here is not to disparage opposition to cochlear implants; in fact, such opposition is based on a generous vision of social justice and equity that I support. But justice and equity can be served in different ways. If the goal is to create a society where deaf people have all the opportunities and benefits of hearing people, and two paths are open – the struggle for the complete and equal rights and access of those without hearing, and the widespread adoption of cochlear implants – it is likely that one path will be much more difficult, uncertain, frustrating and protracted than the other. As in the case of malaria, one option pushes the complexity of the larger system to the background by embodying most of the relevant cause-and-effect of the immediate problem, and in so doing it radically reduces the political and organisational challenges involved in making progress to achieving the goal.

Apparently, though, the problem is not just one of means, but of ends. Is the goal to ensure that deaf people can participate as fully and equally as possible in society? Or is it to ensure that deaf culture is sustained and fully accepted and included in a vibrantly diverse society? It might well be true that a society that openly embraced deaf culture as an expression of human diversity would be a more just and equitable society than one which radically reduced deafness through the widespread use of cochlear implants. But because cochlear implants exist, modifying deaf individuals technologically so that they can participate in hearing culture is simply an easier task – a much easier task – than stimulating the political and behavioural change necessary to fully include, nurture and sustain deaf culture across an institutionally diverse society and in the process make implants irrelevant. The dilemma exemplifies Langdon Winner's complaint about adjusting our ends to match the character of our technological means. But this adjustment also allows us to act more effectively. I am not making an ethical argument for or against cochlear implants, I am making an observation about the likely success of different paths of social change, and a weak prediction about the choices that people on the whole – exercising my version of modest rationality – are therefore likely to make.

So this is a tough dilemma that pits the ease of a reliable technological intervention against the hard and unpredictable slog of political struggle. What gives the technological option the key political advantage is its functionality, its effectiveness – if it did not actually do what it claimed to do, its competitive advantage against the non-technological option would be harder to sustain. And so the effectiveness of the implant itself has a political meaning, a built in political impetus, and the implant becomes an attractor of various constituencies that want to get a certain thing done, because it does so more reliably than other avenues to a related end. The dilemma is particularly disturbing because it rubs our noses in the possibility that what seems like right action – the quest for a more tolerant and inclusive society – may in the end be a less beneficial path to follow than the use of the technological intervention – not because it would not be better to have a society that did not need the technological fix, but because the effectiveness of the fix is so much more reliable and predictable and rapid than the political path towards progress.

I want to pursue this tension between technological and political effectiveness one uncomfortable step further, using, again, an aspect of human health and medical technology as an illustration. One of the most conspicuous sites for technological intervention in human health is childbirth. The influence of technology on the birthing process has been pervasive and profound and will likely become more so. One may also feel it has been alienating and dehumanising. At the same time, the industrialisation of childbirth, through the application of technologies like labour-inducing drugs and heart monitors, and through standardised procedures like the Caesarean section and the Apgar score, has also transformed childbirth into an extraordinarily reliable and predictable process relative to what it once was, where, in rich countries, infant mortality at childbirth has declined from several hundred per thousand in the eighteenth century to ten or less per thousand today, and maternal mortality has declined from as high as one-in-ten as recently as the late nineteenth century to less than one in 10,000 today (for example, Porter 1997). When you combine these trends with the rise of assisted reproductive technologies like *in vitro* fertilisation, and the increasing ability to nurture radically premature babies to term, one can imagine that we may be on a course towards pregnancies that are completely technologically mediated, perhaps even outside the womb, to deliver, as it were, utter reliability in the outcomes of childbirth.

This is a trajectory whose wonderful benefits are undeniable even as the continual intrusion of technology on pregnancy and childbirth may reasonably offend our sense of what is appropriate. The offence may seem to be magnified when we think about a related problem: the entrenched inequities in birth outcomes in the United States. Infant mortality among African Americans, for example, is on the order of twice what it is among whites; and the overall rates of US infant mortality have long been unconscionably high relative to other rich countries, mirroring America's greater levels of socio-economic disparity. So we pursue all this technological change in our affluent society but meanwhile we cannot even do what is necessary to ensure that poor and minority babies have the same chance of surviving as white babies and babies born to families that are well-off.

But there are, it turns out, two twists to this tale. First, over the last few decades, infant mortality rates among poor and minority babies in the United States have actually declined pretty much at the same rate as declines among the babies of more well-to-do parents. While the disparities remain distressingly resistant to change, the absolute outcomes have improved for everyone. These declines are apparently explained almost entirely by technologies: shop-floor interventions, in the delivery room, that have provided tremendous benefits to poor and well-off alike.

The second twist is that there have been substantial efforts to address the inequity problem – supported by a continual effusion of *scientific policy advice* from diverse sources – and they have largely failed. More than forty years of policies aimed at increasing the quality of prenatal and maternal health care and nutrition among poor women in the United States through Medicaid and other programmes have had little or no positive effect on birth outcomes nationwide. These worthy efforts turn out not to have narrowed the mortality disparities (Lantz *et al.* forthcoming; Gortmaker and Wise 1997). The specific reasons for lack of progress are, of course, debated among the experts who provide scientific policy advice. The causes of high infant mortality rates among poor people are complex, and deeply embedded in broader problems of socio-economic inequity that continue to resist political solution and effective policy intervention.

Obviously I am not arguing against engaging in the hard political battle for greater socio-economic equity in our society; the growing concentration of wealth in this already wealthy nation and world is a continuing moral affront. Rather, my point again is that when the essence of a problem is amenable to capture by a technological intervention, real progress can sometimes be made very rapidly, whereas political paths to solving a bigger, underlying problem are likely to be much slower and less satisfactory, regardless of the quantity and probably even the quality of expert policy advice. This is what we are seeing in the infant mortality case.

The technological path may seem less ethically satisfactory than the political path because it fails to directly confront the underlying social failures that contribute to the inequity. Again, we adjust our ends to suit the available means, and this may create some reasonable sense that the technological path provides an excuse for not taking the political path – that the available means are distracting us from the more important end, from doing what is right, which is to solve the problem by making society better, by reducing inequality, rather than by isolating the problem from its social context through a technological fix.

But why would we think that in the absence of a technological fix we would do any better? No amount of *quality in scientific policy advice* will allow decision-makers to intervene in complex systems to reliably yield particular desired results over the long term. How did all of our advanced economic modelling and theoretical capacity help us to avoid the subprime mortgage meltdown?[1] Hundreds of thousands of academic

---

[1] Here perhaps it is worth emphasising the distinction between the use of technologies to embody key cause-effect relations of a problem – the subject of my chapter – and their use to aid in the scientific diagnosis and analysis of policy problems, for example with numerical models run on computers, as discussed by Oreskes (Chapter 3).

publications on subjects ranging from ecosystem restoration to weapons non-proliferation to organisational management to international governance to immigration policy to improving the conditions of our inner cities have certainly added in some sense to expert understanding, but without adding much to our capacity to act with consistent or increasing effectiveness. The remarkable absence of increasingly effective practice in these broad areas of human affairs, despite all the effort aimed at better understanding, is not a statement about the lack of *quality* in expert or scientific policy advice, but about the inherent limits on intelligibility relevant to potential action when the future is uncertain and values conflict.

Yet there is a scale of experience where one does not have to give up one's sophistication about the complexity of the world to accept the possibility of significant and relatively rapid progress in social affairs. This progress substantially derives from our innate capacity and apparent compulsion as a species to technologically innovate – to take certain types of problems and capture much of what is difficult about them in physical artefacts (or, less commonly, in rather prescriptive organisational procedures) that allow us to get around those difficulties.

In making this kind of progress, we are creating a domain of increasing control related to solving a particular problem, even as we are also feeding into the complexity of socio-technical systems whose comprehensibility continually slips from our grasp, and often presents us with new types of problems. This seems to me like a fundamental dilemma of the human condition, one that requires continual, balanced attentiveness. Technology is no more the cure for politics than politics is for technology; they need each other, can benefit from each other, evolve with each other, and we are forever stuck with both. Yet there is something different, and special, about technology that under certain circumstances allows humans to act in the world with much greater effectiveness than they could otherwise do. What if the greatest source of reliable action in human affairs is not our knowledge, our institutions, cultures, norms, or experts, but our inventions? In that uncomfortable case, we should expect that *quality* in scientific policy advice is most on display when technology can chart the path between intent and desired outcome, and thus make more transparent the difference between actions that reliably achieve a desired end, and those that do not.

REFERENCES

Africa Fighting Malaria 2009. 'Prevention', available at: www.fightingmalaria. org/issues.aspx?issue=4 (last accessed 25 October 2009).

Brown, P. 1987. 'Microparasites and macroparasites', *Cultural Anthropology* 2/1: 155–71.

Edgerton, D. 2006. *The Shock of the Old: Technology and Global History since 1900*, Oxford University Press.

Ellul, J. 1967. *The Technological Society*, New York: Vintage Press.

Gortmaker, S.P. and Wise, P.H. 1997. 'The first injustice: Socioeconomic disparities, health services technology, and infant mortality', *Annual Review of Sociology* 23: 147–70.

Hill, J., Lines, J. and Rowland, M. 2006. 'Insecticide-treated nets', *Advances in Parasitology* 61: 77–126.

Kyama, R. and McNeil, Jr., D. 2007. 'Distribution of nets splits malaria fighters', *New York Times*, 9 October 2007.

Lantz, P., Shultz, C., Sieffert, K., Lori, J. and Ransom S. (forthcoming). *The Impact of Expanded Models of Prenatal Care on Birth Outcomes: A Critical Review of the Literature.*

Moorthy V.S., Good, M.F. and Hill, A.V. 2004. 'Malaria vaccine developments', *Lancet* 363/9403: 150–6.

Mumford, L. 1963 [1928]. *Technics and Civilization*, New York: Harvest Books.

National Institutes of Health 2009. *Cochlear Implants*, available at: www.nidcd. nih.gov/health/hearing/coch.asp (last accessed 25 October 2009).

Porter, R. 1997. *The Greatest Benefit to Mankind: A Medical History of Humanity*, New York: W.W. Norton.

Roll Back Malaria 2009. *Economic Costs of Malaria*, available at: www. rollbackmalaria.org/cmc_upload/0/000/015/363/RBMInfosheet_10.htm (last accessed 25 October 2009).

Sachs, J. and Malaney, P. 2002. 'The economic and social burden of malaria', *Nature* 415: 680–5.

Spriggs, M. 2002. 'Lesbian couple create a child who is deaf like them', *Journal of Medical Ethics* 28: 283.

Tucker, B.P. 1998. 'Deaf culture, cochlear implants and elective disability', *The Hastings Center Report*, p. 28.

US National Transportation Safety Board 2009. *Table 6. Accidents, Fatalities, and Rates, 1989 through 2008, for U.S. Air Carriers Operating Under 14 CFR 121, Scheduled Service (Airlines)*, available at: www.ntsb.gov/aviation/Table6.htm (last accessed 25 October 2009).

Winner, L. 1978. *Autonomous Technology: Technics-Out-of-Control as a Theme in Political Thought*, Cambridge, MA: MIT Press.

World Health Organization 2004. *Global Strategic Framework for Integrated Vector Management*, Geneva: World Health Organization, p. 15, available at: http://apps.who.int/malaria/integratedvectormanagement.html (last accessed 25 October 2009).

World Health Organization 2009. *Integrated Vector Management*, available at: www.who.int/malaria/vector_control/ivm/en/index.html (last accessed 25 March 2010).

Part II

Collegial science advisory bodies

5   Knowledge, advice and influence: the role of the UK Royal Commission on Environmental Pollution, 1970–2009

Susan Owens

Introduction: in search of theory

We do not have a well-developed theory of policy advice, let alone of 'good advice', which is an altogether more demanding concept. In one sense this is surprising, given the growing propensity of governments to seek counsel from committees, commissions and think tanks of various kinds, as well as from individuals and institutions deemed to have relevant expertise. In another sense, the lack of a coherent theory should not surprise us, because policy advice is complex, both conceptually and in practice. Advice can take a myriad of different forms, depending on the credentials of the advisers, their relation to governmental institutions, the issues they address, and the time horizon over which their recommendations might be expected to take effect. Nor is it easy to determine what is 'good' in this context, though we might reasonably agree that it has something to do with both the intrinsic qualities and the consequences of the advice.

If we seek to understand the nature and practice of advice, and its role and influence in policy and political processes, then we need to do conceptual work on (at least) three levels. We have to think about the ways in which advice and advisers might themselves be characterised; we need to explore the processes through which policies are formulated, developed and modified; and if we are to make sense of outcomes, we must pay attention to the many ways in which power is exercised in modern democratic societies. Cutting across these levels of analysis is the interplay between cognitive factors, including knowledge, ideas and argument, and the more familiar categories of policy and political analysis such as networks, interests, bargaining and institutions. We need to know how knowledge travels, and under what circumstances it comes to have effect.

Theory building in this area demands insights from a range of different disciplines. However, the literatures with most to offer in the field of policy advice have often been curiously independent of one another, running in parallel tracks with little or no cross-fertilisation of ideas.

So, for example, scholars concerned with the uptake of natural or social scientific research in policy (for examples of each, see Weiss and Bucuvalas 1980; Collingridge and Reeve 1986) have engaged only to a limited extent with research in science and technology studies (STS), though the latter has offered important insights into the contingency of scientific knowledge and the social construction of boundaries separating 'science' from 'politics' (Gieryn 1983, 1995; Jasanoff 1990; Miller 2001; and see Chapter 2, Sheila Jasanoff's contribution). In yet another stream, political scientists focusing on the processes of policy formulation and change have traditionally paid little attention to research and advice, seeing knowledge as a relatively uninteresting variable in systems driven primarily by institutions, interests and power.

To the extent that there has been a convergence between these approaches, it lies in the growing recognition that knowledge and ideas can have an important, quasi-independent role in the policy process. Hugh Heclo (1974) was among the first to demonstrate that cognitive factors may be as important as power and interests in the political system: '[p]olicy-making', he argued, 'is a form of collective puzzlement on society's behalf; it entails both deciding and knowing' (305). A number of scholars have subsequently developed cognitive theories of the policy process, in which knowledge is in dynamic interaction with other variables, and 'policy learning' can help to bring about change (see, for example, Sabatier 1987, 1988, 1998; Majone 1989; Hall 1993; Jenkins-Smith and Sabatier 1994; Kingdon 2003, and for overviews, Bennett and Howlett 1992; Radaelli 1995). Among this group are some who place particular emphasis on what they see as the crucial, discursive dimensions of policymaking, bound up with the mutually constitutive roles of knowledge and power (Rein and Schön 1991; May 1992; Litfin 1994, Hajer 1995, Hajer and Wagenaar 2003a; Hajer and Versteeg 2005). It is this work, together with critiques of classical policy analysis (see, for example, Fischer 1990, Torgerson 1986) that has the closest affinity with approaches developed in STS.

The literature dealing specifically with policy advice is well established, but fragmented. It focuses variously on experts and expert advisory bodies, inquiries set up by governments, and external organisations such as think tanks. Within it one can find a range of classificatory, conceptual and evaluative frameworks (see, for example, Nichols 1972; Clark and Majone 1985; Boehmer-Christiansen 1995; Renn 1995) and case studies from a diversity of sectors and national contexts (Everest 1990; Jasanoff 1990; Barker and Peters 1993; Peters and Barker 1993a; *Science and Public Policy* 1995; Stone and Denham 2004). Government-appointed commissions and committees have been the subject of extensive commentary, with mainly descriptive and typological research (Wheare 1955; Chapman 1973; Cartwright 1975; Rhodes 1975; Bulmer 1980a; Everest 1990) gradually giving way to more critical and analytical accounts (for example, Bulmer 1983, Jasanoff 1990; Hawes 1993; Williams 1993; Owens and Rayner 1999; Bal, Bijker and Hendriks 2004; Hendriks, Bal and Bijker 2004[1]).

Relatively little has been said, beyond the familiar appeal to 'sound science', about the intrinsic qualities of good advice, though more effort has been devoted to identifying the conditions under which advice might be heeded. We can, however, glean certain characteristics from the literature. There is a general consensus that advice should be independent, at least in what Diane Stone (2004: 3) calls a 'scholarly' sense, and that it should be transparent, in as far as this is practicable, and defensible in the public domain. Outside the academic literature, we have seen the emergence of guidelines which, implicitly at least, associate good advice with adherence on the part of advisory bodies to certain principles and rules of conduct. The UK, for example, has a code of practice for scientific advisory committees (Government Office for Science 2007) and expects all members of advisory bodies to uphold the *seven principles of public life*.[2] In terms of effectiveness, there is a sense not only that advice should be heeded, but that it should be seen to influence public policy for the better, enabling governments to identify policy problems and pre-empt or address them through legislation and the creation of effective institutions.

The impact of individual advisory bodies over extended periods of time has not generally been the subject of in-depth analysis (Hendriks, Bal and Bijker 2004 and a number of the contributions to this book provide interesting exceptions). However, the detailed, longitudinal study of a specific body is promising if we seek to understand the role of policy advice, particularly if we see cognitive factors as significant in policy evolution, in dynamic interplay with 'the balance of organized forces' (Kingdon 2003: 163; see also Gottweis 2003). Within such perspectives, expertise and advice are implicated in processes of policy-learning (see, for example, Haas 1992; Hall 1993; Jenkins-Smith and Sabatier 1994; Litfin 1994), and sometimes in learning of the *double-loop*

---

[1] Note that Hawes 1993 and Williams 1993 assess the work of parliamentary select committees in the UK, rather than external advisory bodies.

[2] The seven principles, first set down by the Nolan Committee (Committee on Standards in Public Life 1995), are: selflessness, integrity, objectivity, accountability, openness, honesty and leadership. Further details may be found at: www.public-standards.gov.uk/About/The_7_Principles.html (accessed 31 August 2009). In Chapter 7 Michael Rogers provides an example of guidelines in operation at European level.

variety, which challenges existing norms and can be a precursor to fundamental policy change (Argyris and Schön 1978; see also May 1992). Learning may be facilitated not only directly, through the processes of analysis and reporting, but through the embedding of advisory bodies, and their members and secretariats, in a variety of policy networks (for a more extended discussion of networks, see Marsh and Rhodes 1992; Hajer and Wagenaar 2003a and 2003b).

With these processes in mind, this chapter draws on a detailed study of one of the longest-standing advisory bodies in the field of environmental policy – the UK Royal Commission on Environmental Pollution. The study combines extensive archival research, interviews with many of those involved in, or interacting with, the Commission, and the author's own participation, as a member, between 1998 and 2008.[3] It covers a period of unprecedented development in environmental policy, spanning four decades, in which the Commission has been both a subject and an agent of policy change. The chapter considers how the role of such a body might be conceptualised, and then identifies a number of different ways in which the Commission could be said to have exerted influence. It suggests that certain key characteristics of the Commission have been crucial to the quality of its advice, and concludes by identifying some of the challenges it faces in the new political conditions of the twenty-first century. First, however, it is necessary to provide a brief outline of the Commission's origins and working practices, in order to locate its activities in a wider historical and political context.

The Royal Commission on Environmental Pollution

The Royal Commission on Environmental Pollution was created in 1970, at a time of considerable turmoil in environmental politics. Its establishment can be seen as part of a more generalised institutional response to mounting public and political concern about these issues: broadly similar moves were made in countries on both sides of

[3] The original project (1995–97) was supported by grants from the Leverhulme Trust and the Royal Commission on Environmental Pollution. The author would like to acknowledge this support and the contribution of Tim Rayner as Research Assistant. Approximately 100 in-depth interviews were conducted, in addition to extensive analysis of published material and unpublished documentary evidence from the Royal Commission and government archives. The author was appointed to the Commission in 1998, so that insights from the earlier work have been enriched by participant observation (as well as further documentary analysis). This is not the place to discuss the benefits and pitfalls of 'insider' accounts, though both are acknowledged to be considerable.

the Atlantic at around this time.[4] Some four decades later, the Commission's terms of reference (set out in its Royal Warrant[5]) remain unchanged. They are:

... to advise on matters, both national and international, concerning the pollution of the environment; on the adequacy of research in this field; and the future possibilities of danger to the environment.

By 2010 the Commission had produced thirty-two reports (see Appendix 1), ranging from overviews of pollution and regulatory arrangements, through detailed investigation of contentious issues (such as lead in the environment, waste incineration and the release of genetically modified organisms) to scrutiny of the environmental impacts of policy sectors including agriculture, transport, energy, aviation and fisheries. Some of the most important contributions have been concerned with the underlying frameworks – institutional and philosophical – for regulating pollution and setting environmental standards. Significantly, in all but three cases, the Commission has chosen its own topics for investigation, sometimes to the discomfiture of governments or particular ministries. Reports are submitted to the Queen and laid before Parliament, and there is an expectation of a formal governmental response.[6] The publication of a report constitutes a 'concentrated moment of influence',[7] the more so if the topic is one that attracts media attention. As we shall see, however, the Commission's impacts have not always been apparent in the immediate aftermath of a study.

Many interviewees, unprompted, described the Commission as *a committee of experts* rather than an expert committee. Interestingly, it is often characterised as a scientific body, perhaps because its establishment in the late 1960s was bound up with a quest to base environmental

---

[4] For example, the German Advisory Council on the Environment (Sachverständigenrat für Umweltfragen), the Council for Environmental Quality in the United States and the Swedish Environment Council (Miljövårdsberedningen) were also part of this wave of institutional change.

[5] The full text can be viewed on the Commission's website. See www.rcep.org.uk/about/index.htm (accessed 2 September 2009).

[6] The Commission is a UK-wide body. Its remit extends to the devolved administrations in Northern Ireland, Scotland and Wales, which (in addition to the UK government) receive, and sometimes respond separately to, its reports.

[7] Interview, former Deputy Secretary, environment ministry. Unless otherwise specified, quotations in the text are from interviews conducted during the study described in footnote 3 above. The ministry responsible for environmental affairs in the UK has had several different names (and different overall remits) during the period of the Commission's existence. For simplicity, it is referred to throughout as *the environment ministry*. At the time of writing, it is the Department for Environment, Food and Rural Affairs – Defra.

policy on *sound science*. In fact its members, predominantly academic and usually numbering around fourteen, have always been drawn from a range of disciplinary backgrounds, including anthropology, economics, engineering, geography, law and philosophy, as well as the physical and biological sciences. However, all eight of the Commission's chairs (in the period 1970–2009) have been distinguished natural scientists and Fellows of the Royal Society, the UK's prestigious academy of sciences. Members serve in an individual capacity, for periods normally limited to around six years.[8] Indeed, it is an important characteristic of the Commission that, while some individuals bring experience from sectors such as industry and agriculture, it is not (and has never been) a stakeholder body of the kind that governments have tended to favour in recent years. In this respect, it differs from bodies like the Dutch Advisory Council for Research on Spatial Planning, Nature and the Environment (RMNO), discussed by Bert de Wit in Chapter 8, but bears some resemblance to the European Group on Ethics in Science and New Technologies (EGE), considered by Michael Rogers in Chapter 7.

The Commission is served by a small, permanent secretariat, based in London. Its investigations typically involve in-depth and comprehensive analysis of the selected topic, with shorter, more specifically focused, studies sometimes being undertaken in parallel. Some studies have taken several years to complete, though over its lifetime the average time taken to produce a report has been about sixteen months. Meetings take place each month, over two days, most frequently in London but also regularly in Scotland, Wales and Northern Ireland, and sometimes elsewhere. Outside the formal meetings, members and the secretariat are involved in visits, discussions with interested parties, and dissemination of the Commission's work (and it is here that professional and policy networks become particularly important in the transmission of arguments and ideas).

Once a topic is chosen, information is gathered from a range of sources, including the published literature, written and oral evidence, visits and, occasionally, public meetings. Drafts of reports, usually with input from both the secretariat and the members, are discussed in successive meetings until a final version is agreed. Interestingly, this drawn out and often frustrating process (described by one former member as 'a nightmare') has almost always secured consensus, and has produced reports that are widely regarded as authoritative. The

---

[8] Some members (including the author) have served for much longer, but norms governing public appointments introduced in the 1990s have made extended terms of service more unusual than they were in the past.

Commission meets in private, and has resisted pressure to do otherwise, but in latter years its minutes and (normally) the transcripts of written and oral evidence have been made publicly available on the internet.

We have, then, a body that has provided advice in the field of environmental policy for around four decades, both in the tangible form of reports and recommendations and, less visibly, through networks in which its members and secretariat have been active. Scrutiny of the Royal Commission's work over this period ought, therefore, to offer important insights about the functions and effectiveness of expert advice and, indeed, about change and stability in key domains of environmental policy.

Conceptualising the role of advisory bodies

Advisers and advisory committees come in many forms (as this book amply demonstrates), and standing royal commissions are unusual, so we need to be wary of generalisations. Nevertheless, royal commissions exemplify a form of advice in which public bodies established by government 'consider specific policy problems, ... gather evidence about them, and ... report and make recommendations for action' (Bulmer 1980b: 1). From the literature we can distil three broad conceptualisations of the function of such bodies: as rational analysts, providing information upon which governments and others can act; as symbols and legitimisers, enabling the powerful to pursue their favoured objectives; and as cognitive or discursive agents, 'creating the intellectual conditions for problem solving' (Bulmer 1983: 664), by developing new ideas and frames.[9] These are not, of course, mutually exclusive models, but they tell different stories about the interplay of rationality, interests and power; and they are both challenged and intersected by insights from sociological studies of science.

Commissions[10] have frequently been represented as analysts and synthesisers of information, excavating 'the facts' (Wheare 1955: 89) or 'filtering and making usable expert knowledge' (Bulmer 1993: 48). In what amounts (at least implicitly) to a linear-rational model of policy advice, it is assumed that facts exist independently of values, and can be

---

[9] Frames are used in this chapter to mean discursive strategies through which certain considerations are included in, or excluded from, the policy process; in this sense, framing is a means of selecting and organising information to make sense of complex realities (Rein and Schön 1991).

[10] A few authors have looked particularly at royal commissions, others at a wider range of commissions, advisory committees and committees of inquiry. To avoid repetition, the term 'commission' is used in a generic sense in the remainder of this chapter.

tracked down, distilled and conveyed to decision-makers in order to inform their policies. Commissions might act, in the process, as conduits for the views of other agents, but the rational model sees the advisers themselves as disinterested and objective in their approach. This conception of the knowledge-policy interface has been roundly criticised by scholars from a variety of different traditions. We can accept its limitations, however, without precluding the possibility that governments do sometimes seek advice 'because they want to make the right decisions' (Peters and Barker 1993b: 2). The origins of the Royal Commission on Environmental Pollution seem to be attributable, at least in part, to such a motive.[11]

There is a different perspective, in which the setting up of advisory bodies serves a more overtly political purpose. It is widely recognised, for example, that commissions can function as 'symbolic responses' (Bulmer 1983: 661), removing contentious issues from the political arena and buying time for governments who are unable or unwilling to act (see also Wheare 1955; Rhodes 1975; Jasanoff 1990). They can also be used, in strategic or opportunistic ways, to provide authority for favoured policies or to allow governments 'to change their minds without losing face or having to admit error' (Boehmer-Christiansen 1995: 97; see also Wheare 1955, Rhodes 1975; Baker 1988). And of course in pluralist polities, the findings of authoritative bodies can be used as ammunition by many groups, especially when *the facts* are in dispute; in extreme cases, as recognised elsewhere in this book (see Jasanoff, Chapter 2; Kurth and Glasmacher, Chapter 15), advisers might even be captured or co-opted. A standing body like the Royal Commission on Environmental Pollution, which can choose its own topics, may be less easily manipulated (by governments or other political actors) than one that is established and populated for a specific purpose. Even so, there have been some occasions (discussed later) on which governments have sought to depoliticise issues by referring them to the Commission, and many instances of its findings being deployed by various parties as legitimising discourse.

A thread running through these predominantly instrumental characterisations of advisory bodies is the tendency on behalf of

---

[11] As *the environment* emerged as a distinctive category for political action during the 1960s, the need was felt within government for scientific and expert advice on the relevant issues (see, for first hand accounts, Kennet 1972; Zuckerman 1988; Holdgate 2003). At the end of 1969, the Prime Minister, Harold Wilson, told the House of Commons that there would be a standing Royal Commission on Environmental Pollution, to act as an independent watchdog, and a new Central Scientific Unit on Pollution within the Cabinet Office.

governments to appeal to objectivity and *sound science* as a basis for policies and decisions. When issues are complex, their referral to specialist advisers implies, if not a wholesale transfer of power from elected politicians to experts, then at least a danger that political choices will be made under the guise of scientific or technical neutrality – an insidious form of legitimation. We might debate at length the extent to which modern democracies have actually drifted towards technocracy, but the growing dependence on expert advice must at least raise questions about the 'interface' between science and politics, and the mutual influence, interpenetration or even co-production of these spheres in contested regulatory domains (Funtowicz and Ravetz 1993; Weingart 1999; Jasanoff 2004a and 2004b, and Chapter 2 in this book; Irwin 2007). This shifts our conceptualisation of advisory bodies laterally, as it were, from simple rational-analytic or strategic-symbolic models. Such bodies are implicated, for example, in *boundary work* – in constructing, negotiating and defending the borders that demarcate science from politics (Jasanoff 1990).[12] Yet at the same time they can become bound up in a process of hybridisation, through which the production of knowledge and the production of policy become inextricably intertwined. In the case of the Royal Commission, its own conception of where the boundaries lie has evolved in interesting ways over time – a point that will be considered in further detail below.

Returning, for the moment, to more traditional representations, we find that whilst the symbolic and strategic potential of policy advice is widely recognised, many observers have emphasised the positive contribution of commissions rather than, or in spite of, their 'manipulative potential' (Bulmer 1983: 662; see also Wheare 1955; Rhodes 1975; Jasanoff 1990; Owens and Rayner 1999). Significantly – and this is the third broad conceptualisation – if we look beyond the immediate function of providing advice (whether to inform or legitimise), we can postulate a more autonomous role, involving innovation and education in the longer term. Thus, for Cartwright (1975: 217), commissions could 'go where ministers and their officials might hesitate to tread', and Wheare (1955: 89) observed that even when a government had little

---

[12] Boundary work is used here as an analytic category rather than an actor category (a distinction made by Sheila Jasanoff during the Workshop from which this book originated). The concept is used in the latter sense by Sven Dammann and David Gee (see Chapter 13) in their discussion of the European Environment Agency as a 'boundary organisation', one that does boundary work in that it 'communicates, translates and sometimes mediates between the arenas of science and policy'. Boundary work in both senses can be seen as skilled and productive.

intention of acting on its advice, a committee's work could perform 'an educative function' which might ultimately result in change. Such diffuse, long-term effects, sometimes referred to as 'atmospheric influence' (James 2000: 163) or 'enlightenment' (Weiss 1977), resonate well with the equally subtle processes of policy-learning. They imply that in assessing the value of policy advice, we have to look well beyond the immediate effects of a commission's reports and recommendations.

The circumstances of influence

Influence, like advice, is a complex concept. In the present context, it can most usefully be conceived of in terms of a continuum, with direct, rapid responses to recommendations at one extreme and atmospheric influence or enlightenment at the other. In trying to capture this range of effects, there is a risk, on the one hand, of false positives – crediting advisers with changes that might well have happened anyway – and, on the other, of overlooking significant impacts because the line of influence has been indirect or obscure. With such caution in mind, we can now attempt to delineate the diverse ways along the continuum in which the Royal Commission has exerted influence.

Visible, short-term responses

We can begin with what seem at first sight to be the most straightforward cases – when governments accept recommendations and act upon them immediately, or at least without undue delay. Instances of such effects span all four decades of the Commission's existence. The influence of specific reports (RCEP 1972, 1983, 1989 and 2000, respectively) can be seen, for example, in the 1974 Control of Pollution Act (UK Government 1974); in a dramatic policy reversal on lead in petrol in 1983 (Department of the Environment 1993); in the precautionary approach to the release of genetically modified organisms (GMOs) adopted in the Environmental Protection Act of 1990 (UK Government 1990); and in the reframing of UK energy policy in 2003 around a long-term target for reducing CO_2 emissions (DTI 2003). There are numerous other examples, including the quiet acceptance of many lower-profile proposals and changes to institutional arrangements, in addition to visible impacts on legislation. If we looked only for the sequence of *recommendation-acceptance-action*, therefore, we could agree with a former Chair of the Royal Commission that its influence has been 'moderately satisfactory' (Southwood 1985: 347; see also Owens and Rayner 1999).

Even in such *obvious* cases, however, the Commission has rarely been the *only* influence at work. Rather, it has added an authoritative voice to the debate at particular moments, and has sometimes been able to frame or re-frame difficult issues in ways that have made them amenable to political action. But what is most distinctive about the 'direct hits', including those outlined above, is that they occur when recommendations resonate with the political temper of the times. The Commission's earliest work, particularly its third report (RCEP 1972), presented clear guidelines at a time of mounting pressure for government to 'do something' about gross pollution; in a policy vacuum, the Commission fulfilled something close to its rational analytical role, and was helped in this endeavour by its casting as a scientific body. It filled a vacuum again in relation to the emergent issue of GMOs in 1990. In the case of lead in petrol, the key recommendation of the Commission's ninth report (that lead additives should be phased out as soon as possible) was seized upon by a government 'wriggling on a hook' in the run-up to a general election.[13] The Energy Report of 2000 came at a time of heightened awareness of climate change, when there was a willingness on the part of government to add a long-term emissions reduction target to its more immediate actions and strategies, and for a number of other reasons it was timely for the state to re-engage with the energy sector. Thus the first comprehensive policy statement on energy for several decades accepted that the UK should 'put itself on a path' towards a 60 per cent reduction in CO_2 emissions by 2050 (DTI 2003: para 1.10).[14]

---

[13] The phrase was used by a former senior civil servant in the environment ministry. Government policy at the time was to reduce rather than to eliminate the lead content of petrol. However, a vigorous campaign for total elimination, focusing on children's health, was mounted by the Campaign for Lead Free Air (CLEAR), and lead-free petrol became an election issue (see Wilson 1983 for further detail). Rather nimbly, and demonstrating its propensity for re-framing, the Commission side-stepped the intractable controversy over the impacts of airborne lead on children's health. Acknowledging that lead was a poison, already widely distributed in the environment by human action, it asked whether lead additives in petrol were really needed, and demonstrated that eliminating lead would incur only modest costs (or 'benefits foregone'). On the grounds of precaution, the Commission then advocated such a policy. There were fascinating discussions about the role of *the science* during preparation of the report, but the framing of the issue around need and precaution kept both the scientists and the non-scientists in the Commission on board. Ministers accepted the recommendation within an hour.

[14] It is interesting to see how such policies can solidify. In 2008, a Climate Change Act (UK Government 2008) enshrined an even more stringent, 80 per cent reduction, target in law and established an independent Climate Change Commission to set interim quinquennial carbon budgets for the UK.

Dormant seeds

In less propitious political circumstances, recommendations that challenge the *status quo* are unlikely to have effect, particularly when they run counter to 'deep core' and 'policy core' beliefs and values (Jenkins-Smith and Sabatier 1994: 180). So, for example, the Commission's proposals to bring together spatial and environmental planning regimes within *Integrated Spatial Strategies* (RCEP 2002) held little appeal for a government bent on 'modernising' the land use planning system and delivering more land for development. Key recommendations of the twenty-second report have therefore, to date, been ignored. Even when proposals seem at first to have had an impact, inertia and the power of a dominant discourse can conspire to stifle change. In the 1990s, two reports on transport (RCEP 1994, 1998) added considerable weight to an emergent discourse coalition that wanted to see travel demand managed with respect to environmental constraints. For a brief period around the turn of the century, these ideas were in the ascendancy, and were reflected in a key policy document in 1998 (DETR 1998) and, to a lesser extent, in the Transport Act of 2000 (UK Government 2000). But causal beliefs linking transport to economic growth and competitiveness proved extremely resistant to change, and older priorities have subsequently been reasserted (compare DETR 1998 with Eddington 2006; see also Owens and Cowell 2002).

Over time, however, even the deepest policy cores can be challenged. Certain proposals have acted like dormant seeds, generating little activity in the first instance but coming to fruition much later. The best documented example is that of integrated pollution control (IPC), first advocated by the Commission in its fifth report in the mid-1970s (RCEP 1976), but not taking full effect in legislation and practice until the 1990s (for more detailed discussion, see Owens 1990; Weale, O'Riordan and Kramme 1991; Smith 1997). The Commission's inquiry into air pollution control had, unusually, been requested by the Secretary of State for the Environment, attempting on this occasion to use his advisers in a strategic, depoliticising capacity. But the Commission, which has never much enjoyed being directed, went 'way off remit'.[15] It pressed for the introduction of a cross-media approach to pollution and a new integrated national inspectorate, all to be subject to the guiding principle of 'best practicable environmental option' (BPEO), which it had formulated in the course of its deliberations. These unexpected and deeply unwelcome

---

[15] Interview, former Secretary of the Royal Commission.

proposals had little immediate effect. Ten years later, however, the political climate had changed, allowing cross-media pollution to be acknowledged as a problem and *integration* attached to it as a solution. An integrated inspectorate was duly created, essentially as envisaged by the Commission.[16] The new system was given a statutory basis in the Environmental Protection Act 1990 (UK Government 1990), and influenced the European Integrated Pollution Prevention and Control Directive,[17] adopted in 1996. It is interesting, given that the trend towards integration was observable across the Western world, that integrated pollution control in the UK has remained closely identified with the work of the Royal Commission. What is clear, though, is that the idea as presented in the 1976 report was not enough. Borrowing Kingdon's (2003) terminology, we might say that the shift to integration was not feasible until external events allowed problem, policy and political streams to merge, but that the Commission itself, as an advocate and policy entrepreneur, had something to do with this convergence.[18]

In a similar way, but over a less extended period of time, the important *duty of care* concept in waste management, developed and promoted in the Commission's eleventh report (RCEP 1985), was incorporated into the Environmental Protection Act 1990 some five years later. In other cases, the Commission's influence in the waste sector has verged on the *atmospheric*. A controversial report on incineration (RCEP 1993), for example, had limited short-term impacts but, according to an environment ministry official, it gave 'a spur to [the ministry's] efforts to come up with [a more] strategic approach'. A waste strategy for England and Wales was finally published in 2000 (DETR 2000a), with a revised version[19] appearing in 2007 (Defra 2007a). Reflecting generally on the Royal Commission's role, a former environment ministry official (later head of the European Environment Directorate General) said that it had done 'good work on waste', and had made a major contribution to the development of better institutions for pollution control in the

---

[16] Plans to set up her Majesty's Inspectorate of Pollution (HMIP) were announced in 1986, and the Inspectorate began operating in April 1987. There was further consolidation to create an Environment Agency under the *Environment Act* 1995 (UK Government 1995).

[17] Council Directive 96/61/EC of 24 September 1996 concerning integrated pollution prevention and control.

[18] The Commission continued to press for integrated pollution control and the principle of BPEO in further reports (for example, RCEP 1984) and in other ways. One former chair likened it to a fire that was nearly going out, 'but ... there are some glowing embers there, and you've got a chance to keep it alive'.

[19] For England.

UK: 'we are now better set up than we were ... although it took a long time, a very long time ...'

Another interesting case of influence without a clear, direct lineage, is that of agriculture, on which the Commission produced a dedicated report in its first decade (RCEP 1979). Many of its recommendations, and indeed the decision to examine agriculture and pollution at all, encountered stiff resistance from the then Ministry of Agriculture, Fisheries and Foods (MAFF).[20] But as the post-war productivist philosophy in the agricultural sector gradually weakened, change became feasible. Thus, according to a former Chair of the Commission:

> the response [to the seventh report] was largely in the hands of the Minister of Agriculture, not the Minister of the Environment. [MAFF] pretty well rubbished almost every part of the report, and then if you follow agricultural policy over the next five or six years, they've adopted almost everything ...

A senior civil servant from the environment ministry encapsulated the way in which ideas can slowly percolate into a policy sub-system, coming to fruition when external circumstances change:

> even the things ... [that] aren't worth pushing, because there is simply too much opposition, they're still there, on the table, they haven't gone away. And over time some of those also get picked up ... [The agriculture report] in particular was interesting because when it came to the legislation, it was written very much along the lines that I think the Royal Commission would have approved of ... it was MAFF who wrote the legislation ... *it got into their consciousness* that some of the things they'd been doing ... now was the time to change them. (Emphasis added)

Changing frames

As we have seen, delayed effects merge along the continuum into atmospheric influence or enlightenment, in which the work of an advisory body helps to condition the intellectual environment within which policymaking takes place. So, for example, we see the Commission from the outset espousing important, emergent principles of environmental governance, refining them in the context of particular studies and promoting them in successive reports (a persistence made possible by its survival as a standing body). It has championed the cause of public access to environmental information, for example, and has been impatient with counter-arguments about commercial confidentiality,

---

[20] Several interviewees claimed that MAFF cooperated in the study only on condition that agricultural policy and cropping strategy would not be questioned by the Commission.

potential misuse or public alarm (RCEP 1972, 1976, 1984, 1998, 2004). Here, as in the case of precaution discussed below, it added its authoritative voice to more general pressures for reform. As one civil servant described it, the changing ethos of government (particularly in the 1980s) 'was a slow process, but there were milestones along the way and certainly the Royal Commission's interest in the subject was one of the things that kept the impetus going'. In similar vein, a prominent freedom of information campaigner nicely encapsulated the concept of enlightenment:

The Royal Commission [reports] were helpful, but they didn't succeed in changing things immediately; they were of assistance to people who were trying to change things and *they did condition attitudes*. But there was obviously considerable resistance to doing what the Royal Commission was calling for. (Emphasis added)

The Commission has also developed and promoted a broadly precautionary approach to pollution and environmental harm (Owens 2006). Although in earlier reports it stoutly defended the British 'science-based policy approach' (Hajer 1995: 141), it was inclined even then to place less emphasis on the assimilative capacities of the environment and more on eliminating dangerous pollutants at source, a position which it refined over time (see, for example, RCEP 1976, 1984, 1992). It is in this context that the *boundary work* performed by the Commission has developed in some extremely interesting ways. From the outset it recognised that environmental regulation must be a matter of political judgement as well as science (for example, RCEP 1971, 1972, 1976), though its reports in the 1970s and 1980s tended to reinforce the notion of a clear separation between the two. In later studies, however, it moved towards a view that boundaries between science and politics cannot be unambiguously drawn (RCEP 1998, 2003). Space does not permit full discussion of these developments here, but it is worth noting that they did not proceed in a smooth trajectory. The nuclear and lead reports (RCEP 1976, 1983), for example, could be said to have blurred the boundary, while the GMO and incineration reports (RCEP 1989, 1993) seemed to construct a firmer division. In *Setting Environmental Standards* (RCEP 1998), one can read a tension between the desire to separate facts and values and the recognition that they are inevitably intertwined; intriguingly, when the report was being drafted, one of the issues discussed by members was whether it 'shed light on where science stops and policy begins'.[21] Later reports, for example those on chemicals in

---

[21] Minute 8, eighth meeting, 1997.

products, pesticide spray drift and nanotechnologies (RCEP 2003, 2005, 2008), are more robust in their acknowledgement of what Jasanoff (see Chapter 2) calls the 'hybrid cognitive-normative character of regulatory science' – so here we have a body whose own (*scientific*) authority owes much to a form of boundary work critically reflecting on the processes of demarcation involved. When the Commission clashed publicly with the government's Advisory Committee on Pesticides (ACP) in 2005–06, the disagreement was essentially a boundary dispute, focusing on the role of science, the ethics of risk governance and the appropriate degree of precaution in the face of deep uncertainties and ignorance.[22]

Invisible influence

The discussion above has already touched upon one of the less visible ways in which a body like the Royal Commission can have influence – through the personal, professional and policy networks in which its members and secretariat have been involved. Within these networks they have been able to disseminate, test and promote concepts being developed within the Commission: one member described, for example, how they would 'talk up' the subject that was currently under scrutiny as they went about their regular affairs. Undoubtedly also, members have

---

[22] The controversy concerned a Royal Commission report on bystander exposure to pesticides (RCEP 2005). In 2004, the government had declined to introduce buffer zones between residential properties and arable land that was regularly sprayed with pesticides. Nevertheless, a group of *bystanders* (as neighbouring residents were called) remained convinced that their health was suffering as a result of exposure to spray drift. The responsible Minister asked the Commission to examine the science on which the risk assessment, and claims about the safety of the public, had been based (so this was another instance of a study being requested, here in the hope that it might help to resolve a controversy). The Commission agreed but decided in addition to address issues of risk governance. In its report, it said that firm conclusions about causality could not be drawn, but argued that the regulatory science provided insufficient grounds for the degree of confidence in the ACP's advice to ministers and the level of assurance given to the public. It recommended (inter alia) the introduction of five-metre buffer zones as a precautionary measure, pending further research. Unusually, the ACP issued a critical commentary on the report, emphasising what it saw as scientific shortcomings in the argument (ACP 2005). It was 'unconvinced by the scientific case' for five-metre buffer zones, which it saw as a 'disproportionate response to uncertainties' (paras. 3.27 and 3.44), and claimed that its own view was 'shared by most other scientists' in the field of pesticide risk assessment (para. 3.45). This is classic boundary work. The Commission subsequently responded, robustly defending its original views (RCEP 2006). It suggested that its main difference with the ACP 'relates to what action it is appropriate to take in the absence of scientific certainty, where human health may be at stake' (para. 4) and emphasised its view that '[p]olicy must be informed by scientific evidence, but in complex situations such evidence may well not be conclusive' (para 24). The government agreed to further research but did not accept the Commission's recommendation concerning buffer zones.

absorbed ideas in currency within a particular community, and brought them to the Commission to be further developed and transmitted: the *duty of care*, a concept borrowed from the field of health and safety and advocated within the Commission by one of its then industrial members – is an interesting case in point. In such ways, networks within which knowledge and ideas circulate become a mechanism for policy-learning, and for fostering the conditions that can ultimately bring about change (Heclo 1974, Sabatier 1987; May 1992; Hall 1993, Hajer 1995; Hajer and Wagenaar 2003b).

To the above we might add a wider and more diffuse network – that of the educational community. As noted, the majority of members have been academics and over the years they (and many others) have drawn upon Royal Commission inquiries and reports in their graduate and under-graduate classes. The effect, as one member put it, was that these students 'were in part educated by the Royal Commission'. What is significant here is that concepts and analysis emanating from the Commission have influ-enced many cohorts of graduates going into government, industry, the media, academia and environmental professions. This is another poten-tially powerful mechanism for the transmission of new ideas.

Doing good by stealth

It is worth commenting on one further process through which influence has been exercised in a relatively invisible way. The very fact that a study is being undertaken by the Commission can itself raise the profile of an issue, and even stimulate action, not least when government depart-ments and other organisations are called upon to present evidence and 'establish their line'.[23] One senior civil servant said:

we do a lot of our best thinking on a subject not in response to a Royal Commission *report* but in response to their request for evidence, and it can easily happen that, in a sense, that's the really influential thing ... (Emphasis added)

If we include other forms of engagement and discussion, and gentle threats and pressures behind the scenes, we have an important (though not always transparent) mechanism for influence, even before the publi-cation of a report. A former member described how civil servants would 'get wind' of recommendations and pre-empt them – 'inevitably they change tack before your report comes out, and so it appears to be giving retrospective advice', and another claimed that to concentrate on the post-publication response would reveal only 'about a third of what

---

[23] Former Deputy Secretary, environment ministry.

[the Commission's] influence really is'. Developments during the incineration study (RCEP 1993) provide a good example, as noted by one academic observer: the environment ministry had already 'done its bit' before publication of the report, so it was able to claim that an integrated waste strategy was in preparation. Similarly, in the author's own experience, the study of urban environments (RCEP 2006) had an impact on the environment ministry's engagement with this issue in advance of publication. Cognitive factors are clearly in evidence in such cases: the policy context, if not policy itself, is being influenced, much as Majone (1989) envisages, by evidence, argument and persuasion.

Giving good advice?

The question to which we must now turn is whether, and in what sense, the Royal Commission on Environmental Pollution has given good advice over the four decades of its existence. Ultimately, of course, we should ask whether the Commission's work has contributed in a positive way to the protection and enhancement of the environment, but this question would be extremely difficult to answer directly, because of the many other factors at play. We must look, instead, at the nature of the Commission's advice and its consequences for environmental policy.

Our study suggests that the Commission has, for the most part, offered good advice in terms of its intrinsic qualities, and that its recommendations have often, though not always, been influential. The two dimensions are connected, in the sense that certain features of the Commission and its working practices, discussed below, have been crucial to its effectiveness, even when the impacts of its studies have not immediately been apparent. We can say with some confidence that over its lifetime the Commission has influenced policy in numerous ways, sometimes quickly, sometimes after a considerable lapse of time, sometimes through mechanisms that are diffuse and indirect. As well as initiating or advancing many specific legislative or institutional developments, the Commission has helped to shift modes of thinking in ways that have shaped the policy environment. It is itself a product of, and has been carried along in, a broader stream of cognitive and policy development, in which public and political attitudes to the environment have changed beyond recognition. But within this stream, and within and sometimes beyond the UK, it has at least been a significant influence on the flow and diffusion of ideas.

In many ways, the Royal Commission presents a paradox. It is, after all, a relatively small, unrepresentative, predominantly academic group, which nevertheless deliberates and pronounces on important matters of public policy. It explores issues in depth, will not be hurried, and for the most part conducts its business in private (and sometimes behind the scenes). Though its reports (and latterly its minutes and other papers) are in the public domain, it is not particularly transparent in its operation. It has no 'lay members' as such, is seen by some critics as elitist (Defra 2007b), and is not at all in line with the pragmatic, participatory and interactive approaches to complex problems that many analysts and policymakers now favour (Nowotny, Scott and Gibbons 2001; Hajer and Wagenaar 2003b). The paradox is that the Commission has enjoyed an unusual degree of legitimacy and trust (Williams and Weale 1996; Owens and Rayner 1999; DETR 2000b), and has been admired as a body willing to challenge, rather than defend, the status quo. We might usefully reflect on the characteristics that have contributed to this standing, and consider how these relate to the properties of good advice. Since one of the Commission's roles has been that of 'enlightenment', we might ask, in addition, what it is that gives certain proposals an enduring quality, enabling them to survive and ultimately to disrupt a hostile policy environment.

A crucial factor has been the ability of the Commission to step outside the dominant discourse, problematising taken-for-granted assumptions in particular policy domains. Such a role has been greatly facilitated by its constitution as a 'committee of experts', which means that its approach to any given subject involves a highly effective combination of specialist expertise, alternative disciplinary lenses and what amounts in every study to an intelligent lay perspective.[24] The body as a whole *deliberates*, subjecting cherished assumptions to scrutiny: it is this that members referred to when they spoke of 'being educated by each other', and the 'evolutionary process' of producing reports. The constant testing of ideas has contributed substantially to the robustness, and defensibility, of the Commission's analyses. Perhaps more importantly, it has fostered individual learning which, in turn, has enhanced the Commission's ability to challenge conventional wisdoms, adopt new frames and stimulate learning in wider policy communities. This would seem to be good advice, even if it is sometimes unwelcome.

Just as important to the Commission's effectiveness has been what one civil servant called 'the independence thing'. External observers, as well as insiders, almost always perceived the Commission to be independent, and regarded its autonomy as crucial. We might ask why this view is so widely held, given that the Commission's funding is actually channelled

---

[24] Several former members, from different disciplinary backgrounds, described themselves as 'lay members' in relation to topics on which they possessed no specialist expertise.

through the environment ministry,[25] and ministers and civil servants have invariably been involved in the appointment of members and chairs.[26] Furthermore, while ministers have only infrequently exercised their powers to request studies, it has been customary to consult the environment ministry and other government departments on the choice of topics for investigation. Since the late 1990s, the Commission has also been subject to quinquennial, independent reviews, so that it has become publicly accountable for its procedures, outputs and impacts.[27] Ultimately, it could, of course, be abolished, or absorbed into another institution – the fate of several standing royal commissions in recent years.

The Royal Commission is not, then, independent in a financial sense, nor is it free of all opportunities for political interference. And yet it has retained a 'scholarly independence' (Stone 2004: 3), largely choosing its own topics, investigating them in its own way, and producing (for the most part) challenging and critical reports. Cooperation with the environment ministry has been 'on the understanding that [the Commission] makes its own mind up and it may in the end say things which are inconvenient to the government'.[28] Both its choice of topics and its recommendations have certainly been inconvenient on numerous occasions, and if bureaucratic manipulation has been attempted, it has not been notably successful. Nor has the Commission obviously been captured by particular interests, a feature that is probably related to the breadth of its membership. It is in these important senses that the Commission has been independent. But autonomy of this kind should not be confused with disinterestedness, or with the notions of objective

---

[25] This has been the case since the early 1990s. Previously, funding came through the Cabinet Office.

[26] The formal position is that appointments are made by the Queen, on the advice of the Prime Minister who is, in turn, advised by the Secretary of State for the Environment. The appointments process, which used to be an opaque one relying on internal agreement and nomination, has been opened up since the late 1990s to involve public advertisement of vacancies and interviews of shortlisted candidates (by a panel including the Chair of the Commission as well as representatives from the environment ministry and the devolved administrations). Members, as noted earlier, are appointed to serve in an individual capacity but, as a British parliamentary committee has observed, '[t]here will always be questions about the independence of experts chosen by government' (House of Commons Public Administration Select Committee 2007: 28).

[27] The Labour administration elected in 1997 introduced regular *Financial and Management Performance Reviews* for non-departmental public bodies and statutory agencies. Although the Royal Commission falls into neither of these categories, it agreed to be subject to such reviews. The first was completed in 2000 (DETR 2000b) and the second (conducted by management consultants PricewaterhouseCoopers) in 2007 (Defra 2007b).

[28] Interview, former Secretary of the Royal Commission.

purity implied in some characterisations of good advice. For one thing, members are clearly not disinterested. They come with their own values and preconceptions ('hobbyhorses', according to one member of the secretariat), even if they have to rationalise them in the process of deliberation, and they have intellectual interests, as defined by Geoffrey Podger in Chapter 12. More importantly, perhaps, the Commission has not remained aloof from policy, but has often engaged in advocacy and persuasion. It has also, at different times, constructed, defended, softened and reconstructed the boundaries around 'science' and 'policy' with which its work has invariably been concerned. It has, in significant ways, been an agent through which these entities are co-produced.

What can this experience tell us about policymaking more generally, and about the role of advisory bodies in this process? Looked at in the round, the reception and impact of the Commission's advice are consistent with perspectives on the policy process that see it as an inherently messy, non-linear affair in which 'powering' and 'puzzling' (Heclo 1974: 305) are intertwined. In the majority of its studies, the Commission can be seen to have performed a role as 'knowledge broker' (Litfin 1994: 4), whether by sifting and synthesising a complex mass of information, or by subtly reframing problems and potential policy responses.[29] But depending on the wider context, its advice has at different times been accepted gratefully, used strategically, sidelined or even ignored. It is tempting to conclude that the degree to which knowledge matters must depend, at any particular point in time, on the 'balance of organised forces' (Kingdon 2003: 163), and on their ability (including their discursive power) to determine which facts and rationalities are admissible. But our analysis confirms the view that ideas themselves can have power. They can challenge the dominant discourse and, if initially unsuccessful, can reassert themselves as the balance of organised forces shifts. Because this can take years, or even decades, the continuity of the Royal Commission, and its long institutional memory, have been powerful assets in its ability to promote a progressive environmental policy.

A few, final comments should be made about the Royal Commission's continuing existence, in a public policy climate very different from the one in which it was established. It is noteworthy that the review of the Commission conducted by management consultants in 2006–07 suggested that while it had 'historically exhibited independence, scientific rigour and depth of study in its advice', and its important functions were unlikely to be performed by any other body, it was 'in need of

---

[29] Bert de Wit (see Chapter 8) identifies a similar function for the Dutch RMNO.

modernisation' (Defra 2007b: 3). Among the proposals for reform were that the Commission should take less time to produce its reports, and that its membership should be re-balanced to include fewer academics and a higher proportion of individuals with experience of business, regulatory and policy sectors. The government accepted these recommendations in a qualified way, while reaffirming its support for the Commission: 'The great value of RCEP to Government ... has rested on its combination of independence and scientific authority. We value its reports which are often highly influential and deliver policy benefits ...' (Defra 2008: 3).[30] It is too early to tell how much change there might eventually be as a result of the review. It is to be hoped, however, that any reforms will protect those characteristics of the Commission that have enabled it, over time, to offer challenging and effective advice, including its capacities for frame reflection and sustained deliberation.

Ultimately, the project of *good advice* involves a contradiction. Advisory bodies, at least when they are funded from the public purse, must conform with modern notions of accountability, and must be scrutinised periodically to judge whether they remain efficient, effective and useful. But they must also retain a capacity to be disruptive, since it is clear that the best advice may be the least welcome, particularly in the short term. Their survival may depend, then, on whether occasional disruption is regarded by those in power as useful. On the whole, when we look at the Royal Commission, this seems to have been the case. Looking to the future, however, a number of developments may make this delicate balance increasingly difficult to maintain.

One such development, already noted, is the new form of accountability, which exposes the Commission more directly to both its friends and its critics, including those who have been discomfited by its

---

[30] The government agreed in principle that there should be greater diversity and undertook to work with the Commission to address this issue and in particular to 'seek applicants with experience in business, policymaking and regulation' (Defra 2008: 4). At the same time, however, it recognised 'that the RCEP is a committee of experts and not an expert committee which will lead it to consist mainly of academic members' (2008: 4). It welcomed the recommendation that reports should be produced more quickly, with fewer iterations of drafts, but again with a slight softening: 'The RCEP is already exploring new ways of working in its current study to increase the speed at which drafts are prepared without compromising the quality of outputs' (2008: 8). Other recommendations concerned management practices within the Commission and its communication with policy communities and the public. One significant outcome of the review was that, in order to make budgetary savings to finance some of the recommended reforms, the Commission agreed to move from its independent premises into government offices – a move that it had always resisted, in part for symbolic reasons, in the past.

procedures or its reports.[31] More generally, the Commission's determined adherence to an environmental remit, and its concern that environmental considerations are being marginalised within the broader, tripartite structure of sustainable development (see, for example, RCEP 2002), have not endeared it to governments for whom the latter concept quite often provides rationalisation for business-as-usual (House of Commons Environmental Audit Committee 2004). Finally, we might observe that while the Commission's early reports dealt primarily with the gross externalities of production, much of its later work, including reports on transport, energy, chemicals, aviation, and the urban environment, has dealt with intractable issues of much greater complexity, and forced it to grapple with the more difficult politics of consumption. Arguably, the problems that the Commission confronts in the twenty-first century are less amenable to ecologically modern solutions, and it may find deep policy cores increasingly difficult to penetrate.

Soon after the May 2010 General Election in the UK, the new Conservative/Liberal Democrat Coalition Government decided to abolish a large number of advisory bodies, including the Royal Commission on Environmental Pollution. In a written ministerial statement, Caroline Spelman, Secretary of State for Environment, Food and Rural Affairs, offered the following rationale:

When the RCEP was set up in 1970, there was very little awareness of environmental issues, with few organisations capable of offering relevant advice. The situation now is very different, and the Government have many such sources of expert, independent advice and challenge. Protecting the environment remains a key Government aim, and DEFRA intends to draw on the full range of expertise available . . . I pay tribute to the work of the Royal Commission and its current chair, Sir John Lawton. Over the last 40 years the commissioners have made a significant contribution to raising the profile of environmental issues in the UK.[32]

The Commission will complete its final report, on demographic change and the environment, and will cease to exist from March 2011.

---

[31] The 2006–07 review, for example, depended heavily on a consultation exercise with a range of governmental and non-governmental actors who had been involved in some capacity with the Commission's studies since 1999 (Defra 2007b). Twenty-seven people were consulted individually and forty-seven responses to an on-line survey were received.

[32] Written Ministerial Statement, 22 July 2010, full details at http://ww2.defra.gov.uk/news/2010/07/22/arms-length-bodies-statement/ (accessed 13 January 2011).

Appendix 1 *Reports of the UK Royal Commission on Environmental Pollution (published up to September 2010)*

1st	February 1971	First report, Cm 4585
2nd	March 1972	Three Issues in Industrial Pollution, Cm 4894
3rd	September 1972	Pollution in Some British Estuaries and Coastal Waters, Cm 5054
4th	December 1974	Pollution Control: Progress and Problems, Cm 5780
5th	January 1976	Air Pollution Control: an Integrated Approach, Cm 6371
6th	September 1976	Nuclear Power and the Environment, Cm 66
7th	September 1979	Agriculture and Pollution, Cm 7644
8th	October 1981	Oil Pollution of the Sea, Cm 8358
9th	April 1983	Lead in the Environment, Cm 8852
10th	February 1984	Tackling Pollution – Experience and Prospects, Cm 9149
11th	December 1985	Managing Waste: The Duty of Care, Cm 9675
12th	February 1988	Best Practicable Environmental Option, Cm 310
13th	July 1989	The Release of Genetically Engineered Organisms to the Environment, Cm 720
14th	June 1991	GENHAZ: A System for the Critical Appraisal of Proposals to Release Genetically Modified Organisms into the Environment, Cm 1557
15th	September 1991	Emissions from Heavy Duty Diesel Vehicles, Cm 1631
16th	June 1992	Freshwater Quality, Cm 1966
17th	May 1993	Incineration of Waste, Cm 2181
18th	October 1994	Transport and the Environment, Cm 2674
19th	February 1996	Sustainable Use of Soil, Cm 3165
20th	September 1997	Transport and the Environment, Cm 3762
21st	October 1998	Setting Environmental Standards, Cm 4053
22nd	June 2000	Energy – the Changing Climate, Cm 4749, 292pp
23rd	March 2001	Environmental Planning, Cm 5459
Special	November 2002	The Environmental Effects of Civil Aircraft in Flight
24th	June 2003	Chemicals in Products – Safeguarding the Environment and Human Health, Cm 5827
Special	May 2004	Biomass as a Renewable Energy Source
25th	December 2004	Turning the Tide – Addressing the Impact of Fisheries on the Marine Environment, Cm 6392
Special	September 2005	Crop Spraying and the Health of Residents and Bystanders
26th	March 2007	The Urban Environment, Cm 7009
27th	November 2008	New Materials in the Environment: the Case of Nanotechnology, Cm 7468
Special	November 2009	Artificial Light in the Environment
28th	March 2010	Adapting Institutions to Climate Change, Cm 7843

All reports have been published by Her Majesty's Stationery Office (HMSO), latterly The Stationery Office (TSO).

REFERENCES

Note: Reports of the Royal Commission on Environmental Pollution are listed separately in Appendix 1.

Advisory Committee on Pesticides (ACP) 2005. *Crop Spraying and the Health of Residents and Bystanders: A Commentary on the Report published by the Royal Commission on Environmental Pollution in September 2005*, London: ACP, December, available at: www.pesticides.gov.uk/uploadedfiles/Web_Assets/ ACP/RCEP_Response_vfinal.pdf (last accessed 1 September 2009).

Argyris, C. and Schön, D. 1978. *Organizational Learning: A Theory of Action Perspective*, Reading, MA: Addison Wesley.

Baker, R. 1988. 'Assessing complex technical issues: Public inquiries or commissions?', *Political Quarterly*, April–June: 178–89.

Bal, R., Bijker, W. and Hendriks, R. 2004. 'Democratisation of scientific advice', *British Medical Journal* 329: 1339–41.

Barker, A. and Peters, B. Guy (eds.) 1993. *The Politics of Expert Advice*, Edinburgh University Press.

Bennett, C.J. and Howlett, M. 1992. 'The lessons of learning: Reconciling theories of policy learning and policy change', *Policy Sciences* 25: 275–94.

Boehmer-Christiansen, S. 1995. 'Reflections on scientific advice and EC transboundary pollution policy', *Science and Public Policy* 22/3: 195–203.

Bulmer, M. (ed.) 1980a. *Social Research and Royal Commissions*, London: George Allen and Unwin.

Bulmer, M. 1980b. 'Introduction', in M. Bulmer (ed.) 1980a.

Bulmer, M. 1983. 'Does social science contribute effectively to the work of governmental commissions?', *American Behavioural Scientist* 26/5: 643–68.

Bulmer, M. 1993. 'The Royal Commission and Departmental Committee in the British Policy-making process', in B. Guy Peters and A. Barker (eds.), *Advising West European Governments: Inquiries, Expertise and Public Policy*, Edinburgh University Press, pp. 37–49.

Cartwright, T.J. 1975. *Royal Commissions and Departmental Committees in Britain: A Case-Study in Institutional Adaptiveness and Public Participation in Government*, London: Hodder and Stoughton.

Chapman, R.A. (ed.) 1973. *The Role of Commissions in Policy-making*, London: George Allen and Unwin Ltd.

Clark, W.C. and Majone, G. 1985. 'The critical appraisal of scientific inquiries with policy implications', *Science, Technology and Human Values* 10/3: 6–19.

Collingridge, D. and Reeve, C. 1986. *Science Speaks to Power: The Role of Experts in Policy Making*, New York: St Martin's Press.

Committee on Standards in Public Life 1995. *First Report*, Cm 2850, London: HMSO.

Department for Environment, Food and Rural Affairs (Defra) 2007a. *Waste Strategy for England*, Cm 7086, London: The Stationery Office.

Department for Environment, Food and Rural Affairs (Defra) 2007b. *Review of the Royal Commission on Environmental Pollution: Final Report, prepared for Defra by PricewaterhouseCoopers*, London: Defra, May.

Department for Environment, Food and Rural Affairs (Defra) 2008. *Government Response to the Review of the Royal Commission on Environmental Pollution*, London: Defra, June.

Department of Environment, Transport and the Regions (DETR) 1998. *A New Deal for Transport: Better for Everyone*, Cm 3950, London: HMSO.

Department of Environment, Transport and the Regions (DETR) 2000a. *Waste Strategy 2000*, London: The Stationery Office.

Department of Environment, Transport and the Regions (DETR) 2000b. *Financial Management Policy Review of the Royal Commission on Environmental Pollution*, London: Defra.

Department of the Environment (DoE) 1993. *The Government Response to the Ninth Report of the Royal Commission on Environmental Pollution*, Pollution Paper No. 19, London: DoE.

Department of Trade and Industry (DTI) 2003. *Our Energy Future: Creating a Low Carbon Economy*, London: The Stationery Office.

Eddington, R. 2006. *The Eddington Transport Report. The Case for Action: Sir Rod Eddington's Advice to Government*, London: The Stationery Office (with agreement of HM Treasury).

Everest, D.A. 1990. 'The provision of expert advice to government on environmental matters: The role of advisory committees', *Science and Public Affairs* 4: 17–40.

Fischer, F. 1990. *Technocracy and the Politics of Expertise*, Newbury Park, CA: Sage.

Funtowicz, S. and Ravetz, J. 1993. 'Science for the post-normal age', *Futures* 25/7: 739–55.

Gieryn, T. 1983. 'Boundary work and the demarcation of science from non-science: Strains and interests in professional ideologies of scientists', *American Sociological Review* 48: 781–95.

Gieryn, T. 1995. 'Boundaries of science', in S. Jasanoff, G.E. Markle, J.C. Petersen and T. Pinch (eds.), *Handbook of Science and Technology Studies*, Thousand Oaks, London and New Delhi: Sage, pp. 393–443.

Gottweis, H. 2003. 'Theoretical strategies of poststructuralist policy analysis: Towards an analytics of government', in M. Hajer and H. Wagenaar (eds.), *Deliberative Policy Analysis: Understanding Governance in the Network Society*, Cambridge University Press, pp. 247–65.

Government Office for Science (UK) 2007. *Code of Practice for Scientific Advisory Committees*, London: Department of Innovation, Universities and Skills, November.

Haas, P.M. 1992. 'Introduction: Epistemic communities and international policy co-ordination', *International Organisation* 46/1: 1–35.

Hajer, M. 1995. *The Politics of Environmental Discourse: Ecological Modernisation and the Policy Process*, Oxford University Press.

Hajer, M. and Versteeg, W. 2005. 'A decade of discourse analysis of environmental politics: Achievements, challenges, perspectives', *Journal of Environmental Policy and Planning* 7/3: 175–84.

Hajer, M. and Wagenaar, H. (eds.) 2003a. *Deliberative Policy Analysis: Understanding Governance in the Network Society*, Cambridge University Press.

Hajer, M. and Wagenaar, H. 2003b. 'Introduction', in M. Hajer and
    H. Wagenaar (eds.) 2003a, pp. 1–32.
Hall, P.A. 1993. 'Policy paradigms, social learning, and the state: The case of
    economic policymaking in Britain', *Comparative Politics* 25/3: 275–96.
Hawes, D. 1993. *Power on the Backbenches?*, Bristol: School for Advanced Urban
    Studies.
Heclo, H. 1974. *Modern Social Politics in Britain and Sweden*, New Haven, CT:
    Yale University Press.
Hendriks, R., Bal, R. and Bijker, E. 2004. 'Beyond the species barrier: The
    Health Council of The Netherlands, legitimacy and the making of
    objectivity', *Social Epistemology* 18/2–3: 271–99.
Holdgate, M. 2003. *Penguins and Mandarins*, Spennymoor, County Durham:
    The Memoir Club.
House of Commons Environmental Audit Committee 2004. *The Sustainable
    Development Strategy: Illusion or Reality?* Thirteenth Report Session
    2003–04, HC 624, London: The Stationery Office.
House of Commons Public Administration Select Committee 2007. *Governing
    the Future*, Third Report Session 2006–07, HC 123, London: The
    Stationery Office.
Irwin, A. 2007. 'STS perspectives on scientific governance', in E.J. Hackett,
    O. Amsterdamska, M. Lynch and J. Wajcman (eds.), *The Handbook of Science
    and Technology Studies*, 3rd edn., Cambridge, MA: MIT Press, pp. 583–607.
James, S. 2000. 'Influencing government policymaking', in D. Stone (ed.),
    Banking on Knowledge: The Genesis of the Global Development Network,
    London: Routledge, pp. 162–79.
Jasanoff, S. 1990. *The Fifth Branch: Science Advisers as Policy Makers*, Cambridge,
    MA: Harvard University Press.
Jasanoff, S. 2004a. 'The idiom of co-production', in S. Jasanoff (ed.), *States of
    Knowledge: The Co-Production of Science and the Social Order*, London:
    Routledge, pp. 1–12.
Jasanoff, S. 2004b. 'Ordering knowledge, ordering society', in S. Jasanoff (ed.),
    States of Knowledge: The Co-Production of Science and the Social Order,
    London: Routledge, pp. 13–45.
Jenkins-Smith, H. and Sabatier, P.A. 1994. 'Evaluating the advocacy coalition
    framework', *Journal of Public Policy* 14/2: 175–203.
Kennet, W. 1972. *Preservation*, London: Temple Smith.
Kingdon, J. 2003. *Agendas, Alternatives and Public Policy*, 2nd edn., New York:
    Longman.
Litfin, K. 1994. *Ozone Discourses*, New York: Columbia University Press.
Majone, G. 1989. *Evidence, Argument and Persuasion in the Policy Process*, New
    Haven, CT, and London: Yale University Press.
Marsh, D. and Rhodes, R.A. 1992. *Policy Networks in British Government*,
    Oxford: Clarendon Press.
May, P. 1992. 'Policy learning and failure', *Journal of Public Policy* 12/4: 331–54.
Miller, C. 2001. 'Hybrid management: Boundary organizations, science policy,
    and environmental governance in climate change', *Science, Technology, and
    Human Values* 26/4: 478–500.

Nichols, R.W. 1972. 'Some practical problems of scientist-advisers', *Minerva* X/4: 603–13.

Nowotny, H., Scott, P. and Gibbons, M. 2001. *Re-thinking Science: Knowledge and the Public in an Age of Uncertainty*, Cambridge: Polity Press.

Owens, S. 1990. 'The unified pollution inspectorate and best practicable environmental option in the UK', in N. Haigh and F. Irwin (eds.), *Integrated Pollution Control in Europe and North America*, Washington DC and IEEP, London: The Conservation Foundation, pp. 169–208.

Owens, S. 2006. 'Risk and precaution: Changing perspectives from the Royal Commission on Environmental Pollution', *Science in Parliament* 63/1: 16–17.

Owens, S. and Cowell, R. 2002. *Land and Limits: Interpreting Sustainability in the Planning Process*, London: Routledge.

Owens, S. and Rayner, T. 1999. ' "When knowledge matters": The role and influence of the Royal Commission on Environmental Pollution', *Journal of Environmental Policy and Planning* 1/1: 7–24.

Peters, B. Guy and Barker, A. (eds.) 1993a. *Advising West European Governments: Inquiries, Expertise and Public Policy*, Edinburgh University Press.

Peters, B. Guy and Barker, A. 1993b. 'Introduction: Governments, information, advice and policy-making', in Peters and Barker (eds.) 1993a, pp. 1–19.

Radaelli, C.M. 1995. 'The role of knowledge in the policy process', *Journal of European Public Policy* 2/2: 159–83.

Rein, M. and Schön, D. 1991. 'Frame-reflective policy discourse', in P. Wagner, C. Weiss, B. Wittrock and H. Wolman (eds.), *Social Sciences and Modern States*, Cambridge University Press, pp. 262–89.

Renn, O. 1995. 'Styles of using scientific expertise: A comparative framework', *Science and Public Policy* 22/3: 147–56.

Rhodes, G. 1975. *Committees of Inquiry*, London: Allen and Unwin for Royal Institute of Public Administration.

Royal Commission on Environmental Pollution (RCEP) 2006. *Response to Commentary of the Advisory Committee on Pesticides on the RCEP's Report on Crop Spraying and the Health of Residents and Bystanders*, London: RCEP, July 2006, available at: www.rcep.org.uk/reports/sr-2006-cropspraying/sr-cropspraying.htm (last accessed 25 March 2010).

Sabatier, P.A. 1987. 'Knowledge, policy-oriented learning and policy change: An advocacy coalition framework', *Knowledge: Creation, Diffusion, Utilisation*, 8/4: 649–92.

Sabatier, P.A. 1988. 'An advocacy coalition framework of policy change and the role of policy-oriented learning therein', *Policy Sciences* 21/2–4: 129–68.

Sabatier, P.A. 1998. 'The advocacy coalition framework: Revisions and relevance for Europe', *Journal of European Public Policy* 5/1: 98–130.

Science and Public Policy 1995. Special issue on scientific expertise in Europe, 22/3.

Smith, A. 1997. *Integrated Pollution Control: Change and Continuity in the UK Industrial Pollution Policy Network*, Aldershot: Ashgate.

Southwood, T.R.E. 1985. 'The roles of proof and concern in the Royal
Commission on Environmental Pollution', *Marine Pollution Bulletin* 16/9:
346–50.
Stone, D.A. 2004. 'Introduction: Think tanks, policy advice and governments',
in D. Stone and A. Denham (eds.) 2004, pp. 1–16.
Stone, D.A. and Denham, A. 2004. *Think Tank Traditions: Policy Research and the
Politics of Ideas*, Manchester and New York: Manchester University Press.
Torgerson, D. 1986. 'Between knowledge and politics: The three faces of policy
analysis', *Policy Sciences* 19: 33–59.
UK Government 1974. Control of Pollution Act 1974, Chapter 40, London:
HMSO.
UK Government 1990. Environmental Protection Act 1990, Chapter 43,
London: HMSO.
UK Government 1995. Environment Act 1995, Chapter 35, London: TSO.
UK Government 2000. Transport Change Act 2000, Chapter 38, London: TSO.
UK Government 2008. Climate Change Act 2008, Chapter 27, London: TSO.
Weale, A., O'Riordan, T. and Kramme, L. 1991. *Controlling Pollution in the
Round*, London: Anglo German Foundation.
Weingart, P. 1999. 'Scientific expertise and political accountability: Paradoxes of
science in politics', *Science and Public Policy* 26/3: 151–61.
Weiss, C.H. 1977. 'Research for policy's sake: The enlightenment function of
social research', *Policy Analysis* 3/4: 531–45.
Weiss, C.H. and M.J. Bucuvalas 1980. *Social Science Research and Decision-
Making*, New York: Columbia University Press.
Wheare, K.C. 1955. *Government by Committee: An Essay on the British
Constitution*, Oxford: Clarendon Press.
Williams, A. and Weale, A. 1996. 'The UK's Royal Commission on
Environmental Pollution after 25 years', *Environmental Management and
Health* 7/2: 35–9.
Williams, R. 1993. 'The House of Lords Select Committee on Science and
Technology within British science policy and the nature of science policy
advice', in Peters and Barker (eds.) 1993a, pp. 137–50.
Wilson, D. 1983. *The Lead Scandal*, London: Heinemann Educational.
Zuckerman, S. 1988. *Monkeys, Men and Missiles: An Autobiography 1946–1988*,
London: Collins.

6 International Commission on Radiological Protection: policy and worldwide standards

Christian Streffer

1 Introduction

The International Commission on Radiological Protection (ICRP) was established in 1928 as a Commission linked to the International Congresses of Radiology with the name *International X-Ray and Radium Protection Committee*. The original aim of the Commission was to develop principles and standards in order to protect medical staff and patients against possible health damage after the exposure to ionising radiation. In 1950, the Commission was restructured and given its present name. Formally, its parent organisation is still the International Society of Radiology, but its field of work has widened from protection in medical radiology to all aspects of protection against ionising radiation in medicine, research and technologies. The Commission has always been an advisory body (ICRP 1999). The Commission is supported by a number of international organisations and by many governments. It issues recommendations on the principles of radiological protection. Its recommendations form the basis for more detailed codes and regulations in radiological protection issued by other international organisations and by regional (for example EU) and national authorities.

The main objective of the Commission is to provide recommendations on an appropriate standard of protection for humans without unduly limiting the beneficial practices giving rise to radiation exposure. It has been the position of the Commission that under conditions where mammals including humans are protected, the environment is also protected (ICRP 1991). This conviction developed from the fact that mammals (including humans) are the most radiosensitive organisms. In recent years, the state of the discussion on this matter has changed somewhat. There may be certain situations where it is necessary to pay more attention to environmental aspects. This is especially the case in regions where a release of radionuclides and uptake of these radionuclides into non-human organisms takes place and no humans are present, for example, dumping of radioactive waste into the depths of the ocean, or the release of sunken nuclear submarines in the deep sea (ICRP 2003).

In order to set standards of radiological protection, solid scientific knowledge about the possible health effects after exposure to ionising radiation is essential. The quality of scientific policy advice depends very much on sound scientific data and on the plausibility of the used concepts. However, the aim of providing an appropriate, optimal standard of protection, rather than achieving the lowest possible standard regardless of costs and benefits, cannot be achieved on the basis of scientific concepts alone. Members of the Commission and its committees have the responsibility to supplement their scientific knowledge by value judgements about the relative importance of different kinds of risk and about the balancing of risks and benefits. All those concerned in the preparation of documents should be aware of the Commission's publications and of the policy decisions already made by the Commission. The use of value judgements by scientists and engineers working in the practical application of their expertise is very common and is not confined to safety and environmental issues. The Commission believes that the scientific basis for such judgements should be made clear and transparent, so that readers are able to understand how the decisions have been reached.

2   Structure, operation and members of ICRP

ICRP is composed of the Main Commission and five standing committees. The Main Commission consists of twelve members and a chairman (ICRP 1999). The members are elected for a term of four years by the Commission itself, under its rules, which are approved by the International Society of Radiology. At least three and not more than five members must change at each election. The Commission's secretariat is managed by a *Scientific Secretary* with a minimum of bureaucracy and administrative help. A broad range of scientific disciplines is necessary for the work of ICRP. Therefore, the members come from various fields of biology, epidemiology, medicine and physics. While for the selection of the members of the committees the essential criterion is primarily their expertise, the members of the Commission are also elected on the basis of their expertise but the geographical/national distribution has some significance as well. The present members of the Commission come from the following countries: Argentina, China, France, Germany/Switzerland, Japan, Russia, South Korea, Spain, Sweden, the UK and the US.

The committee members are appointed by the Commission for the same term. Re-appointments are possible. Each committee is chaired by a member of the Commission. The committees cover certain important fields of radiological protection: Committee 1 on Radiation Effects (Biology and Medicine), Committee 2 on Physics and Dosimetry, Committee 3 on Protection in Medicine, Committee 4 on Application of the Commission's Recommendations (Regulatory processes) and Committee 5 on Environmental Issues. ICRP uses task groups and working parties which are usually appointed for shorter time periods in order to work on specific topics. These task groups prepare reports which are discussed in one or two committees responsible for the corresponding field of radiological protection. After approval of the reports by the committee, the document is discussed in the Main Commission and is finally adopted by the Commission.

Nowadays the internet is used to present the drafted reports in advance of publication to the scientific community for three to four months in order to receive comments. This can happen during the discussion period in the committees or after approval by the committee. The received comments are taken up and discussed in the committee or Commission which can then lead to changes in the document before the final publication. Depending on the importance of the document and on the extent of changes, such a presentation of the drafted report on the internet may be repeated. Further scientific congresses and meetings of regulatory bodies especially on an international level (for example IRPA, IAEA, EU) are used for the presentation of a drafted report which is discussed with the scientific and also the administrative community in order to achieve transparency and receive necessary feedback during the process. It is essential to include the most recent scientific data and experience from the practice of radiological protection. Through these mechanisms the development of a document can take several years.

3   Scientific basis for radiological protection

In order to assess the health risks of ionising radiation, it is primarily necessary to measure or estimate the radiation doses from external radiation exposures and internal exposures after incorporation of radioactive substances as well as to study the possible health effects after these exposures in dependence on radiation dose. When matter is exposed to ionising radiation, the radiation energy is absorbed which leads to physico-chemical processes, molecular changes (for example ionisations occur), cellular changes with genetic mutations and cell death (UNSCEAR 2000; Streffer *et al.* 2004). The radiation dose is a measure for the radiation energy which is absorbed in the matter/tissue (absorbed energy dose). It is given in Gray (Gy).

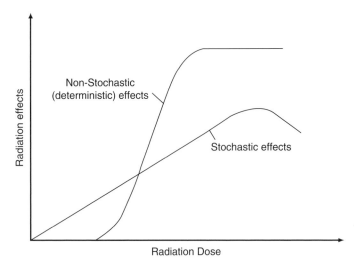

Figure 6.1 Schematic presentation of the two categories for Dose Response Curves occurring in Toxicology in general and in Radiotoxicology in particular (from Streffer *et al.* 2004)

With external radiation exposures the radiation fields can be measured by physical techniques and the radiation doses in the tissues can be estimated. With internal exposures after the incorporation of radio-nuclides such a direct measurement is not possible. The kind and amount of incorporated radioactivity has to be estimated, for example by whole body counters, by measuring radioactivity in urine and the radiation dose is then assessed through biokinetic models. Biological studies and clinical experiences have shown that the amount or extent of radiation effects is not only dependent on the absorbed dose, but also on the kind of radiation (for example Alpha-, Beta- or Gamma-radiation) and on the radiation energy. Therefore, radiation weighting factors have been introduced through which the equivalent dose is calculated by multiplication with the absorbed energy dose. This dose is given in Sievert (Sv) (ICRP 1991). For risk evaluation the dose response is of decisive significance.

There are two types of harmful radiation effects with respect to the dose response which are important for radiological protection. Higher doses (in the range of >1 Gy) will cause inevitable harm, the determin-istic effects, which do not appear if the dose does not exceed a threshold value (see Figure 6.1). Direct evidence on deterministic effects in humans is obtained from observations on individuals who have been exposed to high doses through accidents or intentionally in radiotherapy where unwanted side effects have been observed. The primary protection policy with respect to deterministic effects is therefore to prevent doses which are higher than these threshold doses. Both low and high doses may cause stochastic, i.e. randomly occurring, effects (cancer and hereditary disorders). Hereditary effects have been reported from a number of animal experiments especially with mice. The dose response can be best described with a linear dose response without a threshold. No such genetic data are available after radiation exposures of humans. However, it is not doubted that such effects also occur in humans.

The induction of cancer in humans has been measured by epidemiological studies after whole body radiation doses in the range of 100 mSv and higher. For stochastic effects, no direct cause-effect relation can be observed and assessments of risks to humans must be based on epidemiological studies with statistical methods. Because these effects are not different from cancers caused by other agents or by endogenous processes, statistical limitations prevent significant observations at low doses. In such situations the radiation effects are smaller than the *noise* of the spontaneous cancer rates. The epidemiological information therefore has to be supplemented by inference from radiobiological research on mechanisms for stochastic effects. At low doses, of the order of those caused by natural sources of radiation (usually 1 to 10 mSv), these effects have not been observed. However, for radiological protection it is assumed that these effects will occur with a small degree of probability, which is judged by the Commission to be in proportion to the dose (see Figure 6.1) (ICRP 1991). This proportionality (the linear, no-threshold dose-response relationship, LNT) has characteristics that facilitate the administration of radiological protection. For example, it makes it possible to consider each source and exposure separately from other sources and exposures; the probability of harm per unit dose will always be the same. The probabilistic nature of the stochastic effects makes it impossible to make a clear distinction between *safe* and *dangerous*, a fact that causes problems in explaining the control of radiation risks.

The LNT model has not scientifically been proven for cancer; it is a matter of debate. Cancer develops through a number of biological steps which are based on mutations and changes in cell proliferation (UNSCEAR 2000). These steps can be modified through a number of biological processes (for example, DNA repair, adaptive response, genomic instability) of which the impact on the dose response in the low dose range is unclear. Therefore deviations from the LNT model may occur as demonstrated in Figure 6.2 (UNSCEAR 2000; Streffer *et al.* 2004; BEIR VII 2005; ICRP 2006). Some experimental data (for example, DNA damage, chromosomal aberrations after irradiation) indicate that

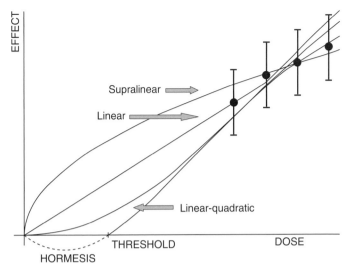

Figure 6.2 Discussed possibilities of the extrapolation of data from high and medium dose range to the low dose range (from Streffer *et al.* 2004)

biological effects of ionising radiation can be observed below 100 mSv down to 1 mSv) (Streffer 2009). For these and precautionary reasons, ICRP has come to the conclusion that it is reasonable to stay with the LNT model for the assessment of stochastic risk for radiological protection (ICRP 2007).

All living organisms are exposed to ionising radiations from a number of natural as well as man-made sources. There are workplaces with increased radiation exposures and there are exposures to patients in diagnostics and therapy (see Table 6.1). Besides radiation therapy where high radiation doses have to be applied in order to eradicate malignant tumours, in the other fields the radiation doses are usually below 100 mSv. However, the main radiation exposure to the population in industrialised countries comes from radiation diagnostics and this is growing.

As these radiation exposures show, the standards of radiological protection have to be set in the low dose region in order to guarantee safe workplaces and a reliable protection of the public. For risk assessments in the low dose range, a high degree of uncertainty exists for various reasons (these are mainly biodiversities with respect to individual radiosensitivity, to physiological, to anatomical data, etc., as well as uncertainties in dose estimation). As already stated, uncertainties are connected with dose estimates which are larger for internal than for external

Table 6.1 *Radiation exposures to humans in medical practices, at workplaces and in the environment*

1. Medical practices (dose per treatment)	
Therapy, usually local doses	several 10.000 mGy(mSv)
Diagnostics, local, regional (X-rays; radionucl.)	1–50 mSv
2. Workplaces (effective dose per year)	
Staff in control areas (Nuclear Techn.; Medic.)	average 4–5 mSv
Flying staff (exclusively North Atlantic route)	6–8 mSv
Welders (electrodes with Th)	6–20 mSv
Workplaces with high Rn–concentrations e.g., water industry, Fichtel-, Erzgebirge, Germany	6–20 mSv
3. Environment (effective dose per year)	
Average of natural exposure in Germany	2.4 mSv
High regional natural exposures in Germany	8–10 mSv
High regional natural exposures in India (Kerala)	20–100 mSv
Nuclear facilities Germany in 2003 (BMU 2005)	<0.01 mSv
Chernobyl in Germany in 2003 (BMU 2005)	<0.015 mSv

radiation exposures. In the low dose range, the uncertainties increase further due to the heterogeneity of microdosimetric distribution of energy deposition events in tissues. Furthermore, the radiation risk in the low dose range can only be assessed by extrapolation from the high and medium dose ranges to the low dose range. This procedure again implies uncertainties.

4   Principles of radiological protection

Three fundamental principles are important for radiological protection (ICRP 2007):

1. *Justification of radiation exposure*: Each new radiation exposure or changes of radiation exposures have to be justified by a benefit to the exposed individual (for example, patient or indirectly to a worker or to the society); there has to be a net benefit. Any decision which alters the radiation dose has to be justified by the fact that it does more good than harm.

2. *Optimisation of procedures and protection*: The likelihood of incurring exposures, the number of people exposed and the magnitude of their individual doses should all be kept as low as reasonably achievable, taking into account economic and societal factors. An optimised margin of benefit should be reached over possible harm. In order to avoid inequitable outcomes of the optimisation procedures, there should be restrictions on the radiation doses to individuals from

a particular source. These are called dose constraints. Appropriate constraints or reference levels should be agreed on between the regulator and the operator of a radiation source. Optimisation is an iterative process. It can only be reasonably performed for single sources. The smallest dose is not always the most appropriate dose. Thus, for an X-ray study in medical diagnostics, a certain dose is needed in order to get an appropriate image.

3. *Dose limits for workers and public*: The total dose for any individual from all planned exposure situations should not exceed the appropriate dose limits recommended by the Commission. Dose limits are decided by the national regulatory authorities on the basis of international (ICRP) recommendation. There are different dose limits for workers and for members of the public in planned exposure situations (twenty times higher for workers than for members of the public). Dose limits for male and female workers are the same although female workers show a higher radiosensitivity for stochastic effects than males. Special dose limits are recommended for pregnant female workers. Dose limits do not apply to medical exposures to patients.

Because of the complexity of radiological protection and of the need to achieve consistency across a wide range of applications in medicine, research and technologies, the Commission has established a formal system of protection. The main aim of this system is to encourage a structured approach to protection. The Commission distinguishes between three types of exposure situations: planned exposures, emergency exposures and existing exposures (ICRP 2007). It also lists three categories of exposures: occupational, public and medical. The total system of radiological protection is described using these types and categories of exposure. The principal subdivisions in the system are summarised as follows:

- Practices that increase the exposure of people or the number of persons exposed have to be considered and certain regulations are recommended dependent on radiation dose.
- Interventions that decrease the exposure from existing sources and in emergency situations. There are reference levels recommended for occupational and public exposures. Effective doses higher than 100 mSv are only allowed in cases of life-saving actions and also in prevention of a serious disaster.
- Source-related and individual-related assessments of radiation doses and their possible risks should be carried out not only in the case of emergency but also in existing situations. In such situations, it may be useful to estimate the collective dose by multiplying the average individual dose by the number of exposed individuals.

- Justification of a practice, optimisation of protection, and dose limits have been developed.
- Justification of intervention and optimisation of the type and scale of intervention has to be performed.
- Potential exposures and accident prevention have to be considered.
- Emergency planning has to be carried out.
- Implementation of the recommendations by operating managements and regulators is necessary. Good cooperation between these parties is essential for an efficient radiological protection.

The Commission's recommendations are widely used by international and regional agencies, by national regulatory agencies, and by operating managements and their protection advisers. The timescale on which these bodies can respond to a change in recommendations varies widely, but none of them welcomes frequent changes. The Commission recognises this and avoids making frequent changes in its principal recommendations. Intervals of not less than ten to fifteen years seem to be appropriate. There is also an expectation that the recommendations be internally consistent. This is fairly straightforward in the principal recommendations but more difficult in the recommendations for special fields when detailed guidance is issued on specialised topics.

5   Aspects of decision processes

Solid scientific data about the effects of ionising radiation with special emphasis on health effects in humans and the mechanisms involved are essential requirements for consistent radiological protection. A better knowledge of the mechanisms as to how radiation effects develop is important for the extrapolation of dose response relations from measured data in the high and medium dose range to the low dose ranges which are most significant for standard setting and dose limits in radiological protection. These procedures and facts have been described in principle above.

Under the assumption of the LNT model, even the smallest radiation dose is connected with a radiation effect although in the low dose range it is small, not measurable and has a high uncertainty. There is no *safe* dose and therefore the setting of a dose limit for stochastic effects is not a sole scientific decision. The question arises which dose limit at a workplace is tolerable. Furthermore, it has been reported that females are significantly more radiosensitive than males. Therefore, it has been frequently discussed whether separate dose limits are necessary for males and females. Such a decision could lead to a discrimination of the two sexes at certain workplaces, for example, in nuclear medicine. ICRP has therefore decided to recommend dose limits for workers at such a level that good protection is also achieved for women but to recommend only one dose limit for both sexes. These circumstances and other situations show that ethical and societal questions are included in the decision process.

The following aspects and points are considered and included in this connection:

- aspects of acceptability;
- aspects of just distribution;
- transparency during the procedures;
- communication of risk and benefit;
- participation of external scientists as well as concerned groups in the process of making decisions;
- decisions with respect to the *critical group*, for example, children, pregnant women, future generations.

In the task groups which establish the fundamental drafts for a new scientific report, usually experts for the corresponding scientific fields who are not members of ICRP are invited to participate as full members. This means that the scientific field is covered in a broader way and it reduces or even prohibits *inbreeding* of ICRP thinking. It is a further instrument for communication within the scientific community. Such a procedure also makes it possible to include views from countries which are not represented by members in the ICRP commission or committees (ICRP *family*).

The ICRP is therefore convinced that transparent risk-benefit-communication is absolutely necessary. Such procedures have to be involved in the process of decision-making. During the period of working out the general recommendations for regulations in radiological protection, the ICRP communicates drafts of the documents in a broad sense to the scientific community at congresses all over the world, to regulatory bodies and concerned groups. The ICRP uses the possibilities of the internet for such communication. Feedback from various organisations improves the documents with respect to comprehensibility and appreciation of practicability. The acceptability of the recommendations is thus enhanced, and this has certainly contributed to the fact that principles and standards for regulations in radiological protection are comparatively identical worldwide.

For the protection of the public, it is necessary to consider the differences in individual radiosensitivity. The differences of radiosensitivity between males and females have already been discussed. A further point is the increased radiosensitivity of children and juveniles in comparison to adults. For the dose limits, the effective dose (E) is the fundamental quantity and this quantity is calculated through the following equation:

$$E = \sum_T w_T \sum_R w_R D_{T,R}$$
$$= \sum_T w_T H_T$$

The absorbed dose, $D_{T,R}$, in a tissue or organ is multiplied with the radiation weighting factor, w_R, which takes into account the different biological efficiency of various radiation qualities (alpha-, beta-, gamma-radiation and neutrons) and then yields the equivalent dose, H_T, in a tissue or organ T. The equivalent dose is then multiplied with the tissue weighting factor, w_T, which takes into account the differences of various tissues and organs with respect to their radiosensitivity for causing stochastic radiation effects. These tissue weighting factors are averaged over sex and age and are therefore the same for all members of the population. Effective dose is calculated for a reference person with anatomical and physiological parameters which have been published (ICRP 2002). The reference person and the connected effective dose should mainly be used for prospective radiological protection and for compliance with dose limits. In the case that an individual person has been exposed to radiation doses above the dose limits and the risk of that individual must be assessed, individual parameters (for example, sex, age) then have to be considered.

From clinical experiences it is well known that a small number of humans have higher radiosensitivity due to genetic predispositions. However, the number of these individuals is small. Therefore, no special care has been considered for such a group. However, their higher radiosensitivity must be considered in medical treatment. Radiotherapy is obsolete for such patients if they suffer from cancer. The problems for future generations have to be considered in the case of radioactive contaminations of wide regions as was the case after the reactor accident in Chernobyl as well as for waste management of long-living radioactive material. For the regulations in radiological protection, legal and constitutional aspects are certainly important. However, although the ICRP has no special expertise in this field and the worldwide range of typical constitutional situations and laws in this area are very large, such considerations nevertheless play a role in the discussion of the Main Commission.

6   Summary

- The International Commission on Radiological Protection recommends principles and standards including dose limits for the regulation in radiological protection. The advice is given to international organisations and national authorities. The ICRP recommendations have been transferred into national laws and regulations.
- The ICRP consists of a Main Commission with a chairman and twelve members and additional five committees with around fifteen members each. The various disciplines of radiological protection are represented. The members come from all continents worldwide. However, expertise in science and radiological protection practice is most important. The scientific policy advice is based on an interdisciplinary approach.
- Solid scientific data in physical radiation dosimetry as well as in biological and health effects provide the fundamental basis for working out sound recommendations. Experimental and epidemiological data and clinical experiences after radiation exposures provide the necessary basis for these recommendations.
- Transparent communication of the data and their consequences within the scientific community with regulatory organisations and with representatives of the public is extremely important. Feedback between the ICRP and these groups is desired and it is attempted to achieve this through discussions during scientific meetings as well as with the aid of the internet. For general recommendations this is an iterative process which often takes several years.
- Ethical and societal aspects, for example, acceptability, just distribution of risk-benefit and other risk-benefit considerations have to be discussed.
- Legal and constitutional aspects are important and must be kept in mind although this is very difficult for worldwide consideration.

All these mechanisms have contributed so that principles, standards and dose limits are comparatively uniform for radiological protection all over the world.

REFERENCES

BEIR VII (National Research Council of the National Academies of USA) 2005. *Health Risk From Exposure to Low Levels of Ionizing Radiation*, Pre-publication version, July 2005.
BMU 2005. *Umweltpolitik. Umweltradioaktivität und Strahlenbelastung, Jahresbericht 2003*, Bonn: Bundesministerium für Umwelt, Naturschutz und Reaktorsicherheit.

ICRP 1991. 'Recommendations of the International Commission on Radiological Protection' (ICRP Publication 60), *Ann. ICRP* 21(1–3): 1–201.

ICRP 1999. *International Commission on Radiological Protection: History, Policies, Procedures.*

ICRP 2002. 'Basic anatomical and physiological data for use in radiological protection' (ICRP Publication 89), *Ann. ICRP* 32(3/4): 1–277.

ICRP 2003. 'A framework for assessing the impact of ionising radiation on non-human species' (ICRP Publication 91), *Ann. ICRP* 33(3): 201–70.

ICRP 2006. 'Low-dose extrapolation of radiation-related cancer risk' (ICRP Publication 99), *Ann. ICRP* 35(4): 1–142.

ICRP 2007. 'The 2007 Recommendations of the International Commission on Radiological Protection' (ICRP Publications 103), *Ann. ICRP* 37(2/4): 1–332.

Streffer, C. 2009. *Radiological Protection: Challenges and Fascination of Biological Research. StrahlenschutzPRAXIS* 2/2009, 35–45.

Streffer, C., Bolt, H., Follesdal, D. *et al.* 2004. *Low Dose Exposures in the Environment: Dose-Effect Relations and Risk Evaluation*, Berlin, Heidelberg, New York: Springer.

UNSCEAR 2000. *Sources and Effects of Ionizing Radiation*, New York: United Nations.

7 The European Commission and the collection and use of science and technology advice

Michael D. Rogers

1 Introduction: scientists advise – policymakers decide

Winston Churchill said: 'Scientists should be on tap not on top.' The quotation is taken from an interview with his son (Churchill 1965: 127).

Randolph Churchill:

Experts must always be firmly controlled by men with rather perhaps less nimble and exact minds but men with broader minds and well-established characters.

Irving:

Your father had a lot of people round him in the war who today would be called managers, who were at the time some of them unorthodox.

R. Churchill:

Well, once he said *scientists should be on tap, but not on top* – a little-known remark of his.

Irving:

You think he had his scientists under control? What about Lindemann[1] – don't you think he got a bit too much influence?

R. Churchill:

He was never allowed to interfere in politics; I often heard my father say to him 'Now, now, Prof, that's politics. You mustn't interfere in that.' He did have a lot of influence because he was able to translate complicated scientific facts and theories in a way my father could understand.

One of these British wartime scientists, J.D. Bernal, put it more succinctly:

But certain arbitrariness must and will remain; there often comes a point when it has to be recognised that we lack the knowledge to make an important decision and that someone will have to make the decision before we can possibly hope to

---

[1] Frederick Lindemann was Professor of Experimental Philosophy at Oxford University and Director of the Clarendon Laboratory. He was a close friend of Winston Churchill and became the British government's leading scientific adviser during World War II.

get that knowledge. The function of a scientist as a scientist does not extend into this field. Responsibility for making decisions which are basically indeterminate and must take unassessable factors of human attitudes into account is the proper field of executive authority. The scientist is, however, responsible for seeing that executive authority is fully aware of the assessable factors and of the consequences of different decisions, insofar as they can be known, and it is his duty, not only to make this information available at request, but to force this into those in control by all the means of his power. There was a saying in the services that the scientist must be on 'tap' but not on 'top'! Now this, although apparently plausible, contains a very dangerous implication. The scientist does not claim or want to be on top, but it is not nearly enough to have him merely on tap. In most cases the executive authority will not be able to see for himself when the scientist should be called in or what questions he should be asked. (Bernal 1944)

Note the reference to lack of knowledge in this quotation and the need for dialogue between the policymaker (posing the question) and the expert (providing *an* answer), a point that was emphasised in the dialogue between Irving and Randolph Churchill above. Lindemann was valued by Winston Churchill because he could 'translate complicated scientific facts and theories in a way [that Churchill] could understand'. Furthermore, this dialogue between Irving and Randolph Churchill coupled with the views of Bernal lead directly to the problem of executive action based on limited information and uncertain knowledge and thence the question of precaution in risk management (see Section 4).

So we draw a clear distinction between *advice* and *action*, if you like between risk assessment and risk management. However, in life, the boundary between advice and action is rarely this *black and white*.

There is also an obvious tension between those who *know* (or claim to know) and those who *act*. Those who *act*, the policymakers or regulators, have to balance sometimes conflicting interests – interests primarily related to three dimensions, namely equity, economy and the environment, the *three Es*: whereas, the experts (those who *know*) are concerned only with the state of knowledge and the uncertainties in this knowledge in their fields. However, policy actions can affect the state of knowledge, for example when legislation mandates the monitoring of technological impacts as with planting permits for GMO crops in the EU,[2] so that in practice there is no

---

[2] Directive 2001/18/EC introduced *mandatory monitoring* for *direct and indirect* effects on human health and the environment after the placing on the market of GMOs, or derived products, linked to an authorisation granted for a fixed time period. See Art 4.3, etc. Directive 2001/18/EC of the European Parliament and of the Council of 12 March 2001 on the deliberate release into the environment of genetically modified organisms and repealing Council Directive 90/220/EEC, *Official Journal of the European Communities* No L 106, 17 April 2001, pp. 1–38. Available at: http://eur-lex.europa.eu/LexUriServ/LexUriServ.do?uri=CELEX:32001L0018:EN:HTML (last accessed 29 January 2007).

convenient strict demarcation between knowledge and action (any more than there is between risk assessment and risk management) (Rogers 2004). (The boundary between advice and action is also discussed elsewhere in this book; see in particular the first part of Chapter 2 by Sheila Jasanoff. However, the distinction between advice and action is being blurred by, for example, the European Environment Agency, as the Conclusions of Chapter 13 by Sven Dammann and David Gee make clear.)

2 Governance: science advice in the European Commission

An improvement in the way Europe is governed was one of the priorities of the Prodi Commission.[3] President Prodi,[4] in his first address to the European Parliament, informed the parliamentarians that the objective of this policy was to develop proposals for a 'new more democratic partnership between the different levels of governance in Europe' (Prodi 2000). Under the umbrella of the Commission's subsequent governance exercise, which culminated in a Governance White Paper (European Commission 2001a), the Commission established a working group to look at the specific issue of scientific advice (see Section 2.2 and 2.3 below) of which I was a member.

The introduction to this chapter suggests that we are dealing with a relatively simple scientific advice governance model, namely experts are consulted by policymakers in order to obtain a basis for effective policy action. The fact that (current) EU practice does not fit with such a simple model is, for example, reflected in the organisation of food safety advice (which was also set up under the Prodi Commission). Under the General Food Law Regulation (Regulation (EC) No 178/2002) the European Food Safety Authority (EFSA) is asked for advice by the European Commission, which then takes action on the basis of this advice. However, it was recognised at an early stage that such a strict separation of responsibilities could lead to less optimal decisions and it was decided to establish a unit that would oversee the interface between the two bodies (to ensure that there is an effective 'dialogue between the policymaker that asks the question and the expert that

---

[3] Communication from the Commission to the European Parliament, the Council, the Economic and Social Committee, and the Committee of the Regions, *Strategic Objectives 2000–2005*, Commission of the European Communities, Brussels 9 February 2000, COM(2000) 154 final. See website at: http://eur-lex.europa.eu/LexUriServ/LexUriServ.do?uri=COM:2000:0154:FIN:EN:PDF (last accessed 11 November 2010).

[4] Romano Prodi, President of the European Commission 2000–2005.

provides the answer') (Regulation (EC) No 178/2002: Article 8). (The need for a dialogue between those asking the questions and those providing the answers is also discussed by Geoffrey Podger in Chapter 12 of this volume: See in particular his section 'On the perils of risk assessment'.) A similar system is intended for the European Chemicals Agency (ECHA) that will provide the advice concerning the regulation of chemical safety under the new REACH legislation (see, for example, Rogers 2003). The growth in expert committees (such as the European Commission's Scientific Committee on Health and Environmental Risks[5] (SCHER)) and expert agencies (such as EFSA) gives experts considerable influence in setting the policy agenda. However, expert influence is challenged by stakeholder dissent and this has inevitably resulted in a greater focus on the governance of such scientific advice.

2.1   *Dissent*

Randolph Churchill's comment above that '[e]xperts must always be firmly controlled' brings out rather sharply the view that experts advise whereas policymakers decide. The expert must be unfettered in his advisory function but the resultant advice remains just that – advice. A clear example is provided by Opinion Number 5 of the Group of Advisers on the Ethical Implications of Biotechnology to the European Commission (GAEIB, which was the predecessor of the European Group on the Ethics of Science and New Technologies – see Section 3 below). Opinion Number 5 (dated 5 May 1995) concerned the Ethical Aspects of the Labelling of Foods Derived from Modern Biotechnology. GAEIB recommended that where the use of modern biotechnology resulted in a substantial change in the food then labelling was appropriate. However, where it does not, it is not appropriate.[6] This was a clearly expressed expert view but there remains considerable public dissent concerning this issue and the policymakers decided to set this particular recommendation aside and to require the labelling of all foods derived from GMOs (Directive 2001/18). Here, the division of responsibility is made manifest – advisers advise, policymakers decide! However, how the policymakers respond to *dissent* is, as Churchill said, *politics* and as such is unlikely to be consistent. Churchill clearly agreed with Aristotle

---

[5] See website: http://ec.europa.eu/health/ph_risk/committees/04_scher/04_scher_en.htm (last accessed 29 January 2007).

[6] Paragraph 2.4 of Opinion No 5 of the Group of Advisers on the Ethical Implications of Biotechnology to the European Commission (GAEIB) on the Ethical Aspects of the Labelling of Foods Derived from Modern Biotechnology. See website: http://ec.europa. eu/european_group_ethics/docs/opinion5_en.pdf (last accessed 25 March 2010).

who taught that politics arbitrates between all the activities which take place in communities. Of course, the process can be hijacked by vested interests (Whiteside 2006) which remains an obvious danger in the advisory system.

A particular problem arises when the policymaker finds it convenient to encourage advice that makes his role easier. According to the *Science* journal, this has been the case with some advisory committees in the US (Michaels *et al.* 2002). As the journal article emphasises, '[s]cientific advisory committees do not exist to tell the [policymaker] what he wants to hear' but to help the policymaker address complex issues. This temptation does not only exist on the other side of the Atlantic. Some members of the European Parliament have objected to the advice that the Commission receives from the European Group on the Ethics of Science and New Technologies (the EGE, see Section 3 below). Following the appointment of new EGE members in 2005, MEPs Peter Liese and Miroslav Mikolášik issued the following press statement:[7] 'Up to now, the EGE has been composed in a very unbalanced way. Most of the members supported a relatively unlimited freedom of research. This was particularly obvious in its statement on the patenting of human embryonic stem cells.' The MEPs welcomed the composition of the new EGE and went on to state that: 'One can therefore expect more balance in the newly composed group.' Clearly, they hoped for future advice to be closer to their own views rather than to provide independent opinions on complex issues.

Dissent has been a feature of a number of important science and technology issues in the EU over the last few years, from BSE (mad cow disease) to GMOs (genetically modified organisms) to stem cell research. Perhaps the most promising approach to dissent is to involve the public in the research policy process – upstream of decisions. The DEMOS think tank has one such project, which they call 'See-through Science' (Wilsdon and Willis 2004). DEMOS argues that '[s]cientists need to find ways of listening to and valuing more diverse forms of public knowledge and social intelligence' and that the public 'want answers to the more fundamental questions at stake in any new technology: Who owns it? Who benefits from it? To what purposes will it be directed?' This was precisely the line taken by the participants in the citizens' consultation project run by the King Baudouin Foundation on brain science – the Meeting of Minds project.[8] One of the citizens'

---

[7] Link to press statement: www.peter-liese.de/cms/front_content.php?idcat=120&idart=300 (last accessed 29 Januray 2007).

[8] Meeting of Minds project website: www.meetingmindseurope.org/europe_default_site.aspx?SGREF=14 (last accessed 30 January 2007).

recommendations was to promote 'citizens' participation in the definition and monitoring of the research quality'. Through such initiatives, policymakers can more effectively respond to public concerns – not by manipulating the advisory process!

2.2   Democratising expertise

There can be no doubt that the general public has lost trust in the risk regulation process, not least because of BSE (mad cow disease) in Europe and its consequences both for agriculture and for human health. If we are to move forward, then trust in the process will have to be rebuilt and this will only be possible if the public becomes directly involved in transparent, risk management decisions. *Educating the public*, so that they will accept regulatory decisions which are informed by expert judgement behind closed doors, is no longer sufficient. Certainly, the current process of *competing megaphones*, such as occurred during the Brent Spar dispute[9] between Shell and Greenpeace, will not result in optimum risk decisions. These competing megaphones often make excellent media headlines, *Golden Rice* against *Frankenfoods*, but otherwise only help to continue a sterile debate.

Consequently, as part of the Governance White Paper preparation (referred to earlier) a number of working groups were created. Working Group Ib (Democratising Expertise and Establishing European Scientific References) was given the following mandate:

To formulate proposals to improve the contribution of expertise to European governance, taking into account its increasing involvement in risk management and its linkages with all levels (sub-national, national, international). This involves a better understanding of the sources and functioning of expertise itself, and of its use for public policy and societal debate in areas involving uncertainty and risk.[10]

The Group's Report[11] makes a number of valuable recommendations concerning scientific advice. They were concerned about the sources and breadth of expertise used by the Commission and called for a *mapping* of expertise. The Group recommended that expertise should

---

[9] Much has been written about the Brent Spar dispute (concerning the disposal of an offshore oil platform owned by Shell). A short summary is available at: www.angelfire.com/falcon/sociology/brentspar.pdf (last accessed 29 September 2009).

[10] Democratising Expertise, see website: http://ec.europa.eu/governance/areas/group2/index_en.htm (last accessed 17 November 2007).

[11] Report of the Working Group *Democratising Expertise and Establishing Scientific Reference Systems* available at: http://ec.europa.eu/governance/areas/group2/report_en.pdf (last accessed 29 September 2009).

be more accessible making the advisory process more transparent (for example through open meetings). They considered that the interfaces between the various components of risk analysis (assessment, management, communication, etc.) should be improved particularly between risk assessment and risk management where the assessment (advisory) function has been devolved by the Commission to an agency (as with the European Food Safety Authority). Here, we see again a recognition that the *Churchillian* strict separation between advice and action may result in less optimal risk management decisions, and that a dialogue between those who ask the questions and those that provide the answers (on which action will be based) is necessary.

The recommendations of Working Group Ib have had considerable influence on the scientific advisory process in the Commission. One of its consequences was a European Commission Communication on the *Collection and Use of Expertise by the Commission: Principles and Guidelines*.[12] This Communication stresses that the core principles for selecting expertise are:

- *Quality*: The Commission should seek advice of an appropriately high quality.
- *Openness*: The Commission should be open in seeking and acting on advice from experts.
- *Effectiveness*: The Commission should ensure that its methods for collecting and using expert advice are effective (and proportionate).

The appointment and mandate of the current members of the European Group on Ethics in Science and New Technologies followed these core principles (see Section 3 below). (These three principles have been criticised in the report of an expert group set up under the Commission's Sixth Framework Programme – Wynne *et al.* 2007. Their report considers that the three principles are too narrow and that in particular the potential contribution of citizens to such advice is overlooked. However, the White Paper Working Group's report makes clear that advice 'needs to be "socially robust"' which requires expertise beyond the 'traditional and professional "peer" community to include those with practical or other knowledge about the issue at hand' (European Commission 2001c)).

---

[12] European Commission Communication, 'The Collection and Use of Expertise by the Commission: Principles and Guidelines – Improving the Knowledge Base for Better Policies', available at: http://eur-lex.europa.eu/LexUriServ/LexUriServ.do?uri=CELEX:52002DC0713:EN:HTML (last accessed 29 September 2009) (COM (2002) 713 final).

2.3   *The Bureau of European Policy Advisers (BEPA)*

The Commission's central think tank

The Forward Studies Unit (more commonly known by its French name, the Cellule de Prospective) was set up in 1989 by European Commission President Jacques Delors as a small think tank reporting directly to himself. This was a time of great change in the European Community coming between the signature of the Single European Act in 1986, the completion of the Internal Market programme in 1992 and the signature of the Maastricht Treaty in 1992. Consequently, it was essential that the Commission received advice that focused on the progression of European integration and its longer-term prospects. Hence the Commission's decision on setting up the Unit set out three main tasks:

- to monitor and evaluate European integration;
- to establish permanent relations with bodies involved in forecasting; and
- to work on specific tasks.

This mixture of prospective and responsive tasks rapidly resulted in a wide range of publications (see, for example, Jacquemin and Wright 1993) and underpinned critical policy papers (see, for example, European Commission 1994), and this output has continued as the think tank has evolved to meet the needs of subsequent Commission Presidents and changed its name to the Group of Policy Advisers (under President Prodi) and to the Bureau of European Policy Advisers (under President Barroso).

The policy needs have changed over time, ranging from competitiveness to environment to food, but the essential need of the Commission to receive balanced and impartial advice remains the same. To widen the basis for such advice the Forward Studies Unit established the Carrefours series of European Seminars on Science and Culture in 1992. These were seminars which brought together eminent intellectuals to debate a specific topic usually in the presence of the President of the Commission. In 1993, the Carrefour seminar was 'Science, Conscience and Society'. This was held in Oxford and brought together a remarkable constellation of scientists and philosophers that included three Nobel laureates (Rogers 1993). More recently, BEPA has created three *permanent* external high level advisory groups to fulfil this need (and replacing the previous ad hoc Carrefours series), namely the Group of Political Analysis, the Group of Economic Policy Analysis and the Group of Societal Policy Analysis. It also provides the Secretariat for the European Group on Ethics in Science and New Technologies.

In 1988, the Commission also established the Institute for Prospective Technological Studies (IPTS) as part of the reform of the Joint Research Centre.[13] This was initially formed in Ispra (Italy) and then moved to its current location in Seville (Spain) in 1994.[14] In 1990, one of the IPTS scientists was seconded to the Forward Studies Unit to ensure coordination between the two think tanks and, in 1992, this transfer was made permanent providing a scientific advisory function within the Forward Studies Unit. As a result of this link, the IPTS provided research support for the Forward Studies Unit in several areas of the Unit's work.

Science was an essential component of advice on a number of important policy issues affecting the Delors Commission (notably environmental issues and employment), the Prodi Commission (notably food safety and the creation of the European Food Safety Authority) and the Barroso Commission (notably the new chemicals legislation and stem cell research). The growing importance of science advice to the President of the European Commission was analysed by the European Policy Centre (EPC) in their working paper *Enhancing the Role of Science in the Decision-Making of the European Union* (Ballentine 2005). The EPC made a number of interesting recommendations one of which was to establish an independent Chief Scientific Adviser to the President of the European Commission (Recommendation E).

3   Ethics: the European Group on Ethics in Science and New Technologies

In 1991 (19 April 1991), the European Commission issued a Communication to the European Parliament and Council entitled 'Promoting the Competitive Environment for the Industrial Activities Based on Biotechnology within the Community'.[15] This Communication stated: 'It is desirable that the Community have an advisory structure on ethics and biotechnology which is capable of dealing with ethical issues where they arise in the course of Community activities.' It went on to provide the essential *raison d'être* for setting up such an advisory group: 'The Commission considers that through addressing explicitly the ethical challenges, it is helping to improve the climate of public understanding

---

[13] Interestingly, the European Parliament established its own technology assessment think tank at about the same time. The Scientific and Technological Options Assessment (STOA) unit was established in March 1987.

[14] See the IPTS website at www.jrc.es/ (last accessed 17 November 2007).

[15] SEC(91) 629 final, PDF version available at website: http://aei.pitt.edu/5970/01/ 003168_1.pdf (last accessed 30 January 2007).

and opinion concerning the responsible development of biotechnology; hence facilitating the acceptance of its benefits, and ensuring a single market for its products.' Consequently, the European Commission, under President Jacques Delors, decided (Decision of 20 November 1991) to set up a Group of Advisers on the Ethical Implications of Biotechnology (GAEIB). The Group was established early in 1992 and issued its first Opinion in 1993 (on performance enhancers in agriculture and fisheries). In 1997, under President Jacques Santer, the Commission decided (Decision of 16 December 1997) to rename the Group and to broaden its mandate, thus creating the European Group on Ethics in Science and New Technologies (EGE). The Opinions (advice) of the two Groups are numbered sequentially in a single series, indicating the essential continuity in the ethics advice to the European Commission.

3.1   The role of the EGE

The GAEIB had three main tasks:

- to clarify the underlying issues in the ethical debate in order to provide ethical guidance to Community Institutions on developments in biotechnology and thus contribute to regulatory evolution in this field;
- to initiate an open dialogue on ethical problems that the member states or other concerned parties consider need resolution; and
- to provide an ethical input to the Community's legislative process.

Although the field has been broadened from the GAEIB's focus on biotechnology, the EGE's tasks remain essentially the same. The current EGE mandate states that the 'task of the EGE shall be to advise the Commission on ethical questions relating to sciences and new technologies, either at the request of the Commission or on its own initiative'. Thus, the EGE is primarily an advisory committee to the European Commission. However, the EGE mandate states that the European Parliament and the Council may draw the Commission's attention to questions they consider of major ethical importance and which might be taken up by the EGE.[16] Therefore, the EGE has also in a small way an inter-institutional character.

---

[16] For background on the EGE, its mandate and its activities (past and present), see the website at: http://ec.europa.eu/european_group_ethics/index_en.htm (last accessed 30 January 2007).

3.2   Governance and the EGE

The EGE is an independent, pluralist and multi-disciplinary body. The members come from different EU member states but do not represent their member states. They are appointed for their high level expertise and personal qualities by the European Commission following an open call for applications. There is a broad balance between male and female members, between members coming from large member states and coming from small member states, and between science, philosophy (including theology) and law. The emphasis is on a transparent recruitment process that results in a balanced, high level committee of experts. This is all in strict accord with the Commission's Communication on the use of expertise (European Commission 2002).

The EGE deliberations contribute to the preparation and implementation of Community legislation or policies. This contribution is increasingly recognised in legislative acts. For example, Article 7 of Directive 98/44 on the legal protection of biotechnology inventions states 'the Commission's European Group on Ethics in Science and New Technologies evaluates all ethical aspects of biotechnology'. A second example is provided by Directive 2001/18 on the deliberate release of genetically modified organisms. Recital 57 of the Preamble states that: 'The Commission's European Group on Ethics in Science and New Technologies should be consulted with a view to obtaining advice on ethical issues of a general nature regarding the deliberate release or placing on the market of GMOs.' In the body of this Directive, Article 29.1 states:

Without prejudice to the competence of Member States as regards ethical issues, the Commission shall, on its own initiative or at the request of the European Parliament or the Council, consult any committee it has created with a view to obtaining its advice on the ethical implications of biotechnology, such as the European Group on Ethics in Science and New Technologies, on ethical issues of a general nature.

Since its inception (as the GAEIB and then the EGE) it has issued twenty-four formal Opinions and a number of other reports. Its influence has become considerable and thus the governance question is very important.

The EGE meetings are private. (However, their meeting agendas are published in advance on the Group's website.) For each Opinion, the EGE Chairman appoints one or more rapporteurs from amongst the members of the EGE. Before finalising their Opinions the

Group always receives input from external experts and always holds a public roundtable meeting with as wide a participation as possible. Once in every six months they hold their meeting in the member state holding the EU Presidency, further broadening the range of inputs to the EGE Opinions. The eventual Opinions are adopted by consensus. When there is dissension, the Opinion includes any dissenting point of view. Once the Opinion has been adopted by the Group it is presented to the Commission President and then immediately published and distributed widely. All the information is also available on the EGE website (see footnote 16).

Opinion No 20 on the ethical aspects of information and communication technology (ICT) implants in the human body is an example of the EGE providing advice on its own initiative (rather than at the specific request of the Commission). This right of initiative helps to ensure that the advice provided by the EGE remains neutral and independent. The Opinion covered current and potential future applications ranging from the correction of health problems, to enhancing human capabilities, to surveillance applications. It included both passive and active implants. This forward-looking Opinion is likely to have a significant impact on future legislation – particularly in the human rights area. Nevertheless, the boundaries of responsibility remain clear. The EGE advises in total transparency. What the Commission decides to do with this advice is the Commission's business. This right of initiative also ensures that the EGE is able to undertake a more prospective or forward-looking role and not just respond to requests concerning current problems.

As indicated earlier, the EGE's recommendations are often incorporated into EU legislation but this is not always the case. As discussed in Section 2.1, Opinion No 5 (GAEIB), entitled *Labelling of Foods Derived from Modern Biotechnology*, provides a clear example of the distinction between advice and action (Churchill's 'on tap not on top'). The advisers recommended one course of action (not to label when there was no substantial change in the food) but the policy-makers, taking the wider perspective, decided to act differently (requiring labelling for *all* foods derived from genetically modified organisms, whether there was a substantial change or not). This policy dilemma crops up under many guises and remains very topical. In a recent debate on the labelling of food additives in the UK's House of Lords, Lord Krebs (former Head of the UK's Food Standards Agency) said 'that it would be disproportionate in this circumstance to demand labelling of substances that have not been shown to be harmful'.[17]

4 Technology: advice and the regulation of risks arising from the application of new technologies in the EU

The prospect of shaping the future is fundamental to human behaviour. Obviously, the future is not *written* and in principle cannot be forecast. However, the very process of thinking about the future, exploring the implications of alternative futures, and providing advice derived from this process can have a profound impact on policy formation. In this sense the future can be *influenced* and this possibility lies at the root of all prospective studies. In an uncertain world, good foresight improves societies' chances of avoiding potential unpleasant consequences of technological progress. In fact, the neglect of prospective studies in the 1970s and 1980s might have contributed to the lack of anticipation of many significant difficulties during this period. Whether this speculation is correct or not, the European Institutions certainly established a number of prospective studies units in the late 1980s and early 1990s (which was a time of considerable societal and technological difficulties and of increasingly rapid change). The European Parliament's Scientific and Technological Options Assessment (STOA) unit was set up in 1987. The European Commission's Institute for Prospective Technological Studies was set up in 1988; the Forward Studies Unit in 1989; and the Group of Advisers on the Ethical Implications of Biotechnology in 1992. There are two obvious reactions to difficulties, to accept them in a stoical manner or to try to do something about them. Creating these advisory bodies was clearly a positive and prospective reaction to the difficulties of the time. The ways in which science and technology advice from the various bodies affected policy in three fields (food safety, GMOs, and chemical safety) are discussed in the following sections.

The critical difficulty in all of these areas is the extrapolation from past knowledge to future action in fields where there exists significant scientific uncertainty. Here, we are concerned with *epistemic* uncertainty, i.e. the uncertainty linking a particular hazard (for example, planting a specified GMO crop) and a particular harm (for example, postulated negative impacts on specified beneficial insects). Above a certain level of uncertainty a full risk assessment on which risk management actions can

---

[17] House of Lords Debate, 11 October 2007, minutes available at: www.publications. parliament.uk/pa/ld200607/ldhansrd/text/71011-0001.htm (last accessed 11 November 2010).

be based becomes problematic. In such circumstances the Precautionary Principle (PP) is applicable within the EU.[18] The PP is both retrospective and prospective in nature. It is *retrospective* in that its use is dependent on looking back at the existing evidence for a postulated causal relationship and deciding whether this is sufficient to justify precautionary action (see, for example, Rogers 2003). It is *prospective* in the sense that past knowledge is used to predict possible future effects and hence decide on appropriate risk management decisions. It is this Janus-like character of the PP that makes the interface between advice and action so important and endorses Bernal's qualification of Churchill's dictum 'on tap, not on top' (see introduction to this chapter).

4.1   Food safety

The decision in the early days of the Prodi Commission to make food safety a priority was not just a reaction to the BSE crisis (for a discussion, see, for example, Wiener and Rogers 2002): The focus on food safety was more general in nature and reflected concern at the highest level that the loss of public confidence (resulting from the way in which various food safety issues had been dealt with), and the resultant growth in dissent (discussed earlier) necessitated structural changes to the way in which the EU handled food safety in order to restore consumer trust in food safety. If consumer confidence could not be restored then this threatened the cornerstone of the European Union, namely the operation of the Single Market. The Commission strategy for improving the governance of food safety and thus restoring public confidence was set out in the White Paper on Food Safety (EC White Paper 2000) in 1999. The White Paper introduced the objective of establishing a European Food Safety Authority (EFSA), which would become 'the scientific point of reference for the whole Union' and would 'contribute to a high level of consumer health protection', and hence 'help to restore and maintain consumer confidence'. Hence, this strategy involved delegating the responsibility for advice concerning risk assessments relating to food to an independent, *neutral* agency. This arm's length approach to sensitive issues is increasingly used by the European Commission. (However,

---

[18] The Precautionary Principle was first formally introduced in the Maastricht Treaty in 1992. See: European Union 1999; Office for Official Publications of the European Communities, Luxembourg. Subsequently, the European Commission described its approach to the use of the Precautionary Principle in its *Communication from the Commission on the Precautionary Principle*, COM(2000) 1 final, Brussels, 2 February 2000 (available on the Europa website at: http://eur-lex.europa.eu/LexUriServ/LexUriServ.do? uri=COM:2000:0001:FIN:EN:PDF (last accessed 11 November 2010)).

it should be stressed that this is a delegation of executive power, to carry out risk assessments, but not a delegation of responsibility.)

A rigid separation of risk assessment from risk management can result in poorer decision-making. Hence, in order to improve regulatory decisions, it is essential that the risk assessment process, with all its uncertainties, is fully appreciated by the regulator. As the US National Research Council has noted, the '[s]eparation of the risk assessment function from an agency's regulatory activities is likely to inhibit the interaction between assessors and regulators that is necessary for the proper interpretation of risk estimates and the evaluation of risk management options. Separation can lead to disjunction between assessment and regulatory agendas and cause delays in regulatory proceedings' (US National Research Council 1996). It is, of course, essential that the preparation of the initial risk assessment (the scientific advice) is not influenced by the range of regulatory actions that are possible or desired, but this functional separation is a normal administrative requirement. In fact, the linkage between risk assessment under uncertainty and risk management via the PP makes the risk assessment–risk management interface of critical importance. In recognition of this the EU General Food Law (European Council 2002) includes an important clause in the Preamble, namely:

(35) The Authority should be an independent scientific source of advice, information and risk communication in order to improve consumer confidence; nevertheless, in order to promote coherence between the risk assessment, risk management and risk communication functions, the link between risk assessors and risk managers should be strengthened.

Consequently, the European Commission established a unit to manage the interface between the Commission's risk management function (seeking advice from EFSA) and EFSA (responding to the requests for advice). This new model is much closer to Bernal's view of the proper relationship between advice and action than Churchill's.

EFSA was established in January 2002, and in November 2007, the fifth anniversary was celebrated with a *food safety summit* meeting in Brussels.[19] This meeting emphasised the range of issues on which EFSA now provides scientific advice, from food to feed and from biotechnology to nanotechnology. It covers existing and emerging risks and is networked with similar food safety agencies in the EU member states and around the world. Within Europe it is accepted that food safety agencies

---

[19] See website: www.efsa.europa.eu/EFSA/efsa_locale-1178620753812_1178621168192. htm (last accessed 1 December 2007).

should be independent of regulatory bodies. In terms of the Commission Communication on the use of expertise[20] it clearly meets the criteria of *quality, openness and effectiveness* (see Section 2.2). It is perhaps too soon to know whether this formal separation of risk assessment and risk management (advice and action) has resulted in improved food safety in the EU.

4.2   GMOs

The first field trial of a genetically modified organism, or GMO, crop was authorised in the US in 1987. GMO crops were heralded as possessing considerable potential benefits such as increased food supplies, improved health, reduced inputs (pesticides and fertilisers), reduced land use and protection of biodiversity, and reduction in pollution. However, they were also considered by some scientists to be potentially hazardous to human health and the environment. In the face of these conflicting views the European Council adopted Directive 90/220 on the 'deliberate release into the environment of genetically modified organisms'.[21] Two key reasons for the new regulation are presented in the preamble to Directive 90/220. First, that preventative (i.e. precautionary) action should be taken with regard to the environment. Second, that the protection of human health and the environment requires that any risks from the release of GMOs to the environment should be controlled. However, a growing body of scientific evidence that some of the earlier fears were not substantiated, coupled with criticism from industry concerning the regulatory burden being placed on the application of this new technology, persuaded the Commission to accept in 1994 that 'the Community should be open to review its regulatory framework' with respect to GMOs. This response was contained in the White Paper on Growth, Competitiveness and Employment.[22] The review took longer than expected, and the revised Directive (2001/18) (European Council 2001) finally entered into effect on 17 October 2002, replacing Directive 90/220 which was repealed on the same date. However, whatever the

---

[20] See website: www.efsa.europa.eu/EFSA/efsa_locale-1178620753812_1178621168192. htm (last accessed 1 Decemebr 2007).

[21] Directive 90/220/EEC of 23 April 1990 on the deliberate release into the environment of genetically modified organisms, *Official Journal of the European Communities*, No L 117/15–27.

[22] European Commission *Growth, Competitiveness, Employment – The Challenges and Ways Forward Into the 21st Century*, White Paper, Luxembourg, Office for Official Publications of the European Communities, 1994.

original thoughts behind the above decision might have been, public opinion broadly dissenting from expert advice (in the wake of the BSE crisis) had swung strongly against GMO releases to the environment and GM foods in particular, and this had a major impact on the revision process. The decision to revise the Directive responded to advice that increasing knowledge and experience indicated that the regulation was too precautionary. However, the revised Directive 2001/18[23] is in many ways more precautionary. The regulators clearly decided that restrictive regulations concerning the safety of GMOs, and their robust enforcement, were a *sine qua non* for obtaining public trust and hence effective progress in this field. Yet again, we see that science advice was not *on top*.

The new *deliberate release* Directive was followed in 2003 by a new Regulation on GM food and feed.[24] Under this Regulation, EFSA was made responsible for advice (risk assessments) on GM food and feed and 'genetically modified food and feed should only be authorised for placing on the Community market after a scientific evaluation of the highest possible standard, to be undertaken under the responsibility of the European Food Safety Authority, of any risks which they present for human and animal health and, as the case may be, for the environment' (Preamble Paragraph 9). All opinions of EFSA are open to the public (except where commercial confidentiality is involved) and numerous GMOs have been authorised following EFSA advice. Under the earlier system, the Commission relied on its internal advisory system and then had to take a decision when there were objections raised by some member states to a positive recommendation concerning a GMO made by the sponsoring member state. Now it is required to refer such cases to EFSA. Thus EFSA recently gave a positive Opinion on herbicide tolerant GM maize (see EFSA-Q-2003–003, Opinion adopted 25 November 2003[25]). With such contentious issues it is obviously politically easier where the advice (on which action should be based) is provided by an independent body. (In brief, the EFSA Opinion in this case was that the GM maize under consideration was as safe as conventional maize.)

[23] European Council Directive 2001/18/EC of the European Parliament and of the Council of 12 March 2001 on the deliberate release into the environment of genetically modified organisms and repealing Council Directive 90/220/EEC, *Official Journal of the European Communities* No L 106, 17 April 2001, pp. 1–38.

[24] Regulation (EC) No 1829/2003 of the European Parliament and of the Council of 22 September 2003 on genetically modified food and feed.

[25] See website: www.efsa.europa.eu/EFSA/Scientific_Opinion/opinion_gmo_03_summary_final_en1,0.pdf (last accessed 1 December 2007).

4.3   Chemical safety

About four years after the enactment of the General Food Law in 2002, the regulator's approach to advice on chemical safety (risk assessments) followed the same path.[26] However, the driving forces were different. Certainly, there was no equivalent to the BSE crisis. However, there was general concern that the then existing chemical regulatory framework had two major flaws. First, there were large numbers of chemical substances on the EU market, often in high volumes, of which little was known about the risks they might represent. Second, the regulatory framework was complex. There were separate regulatory systems for *existing* chemicals (about 100,000 chemicals that were on the market before 18 September 1981) and *new* chemicals (about 2,700 substances introduced to the EU market after 18 September 1981). Advice on the safety of individual chemicals under this system was taking too long to obtain and a simpler, more efficient system was clearly necessary. Furthermore, during the 1970s and 1980s, there had been widespread stories in the media about *cancer-causing chemicals* and a concern about the degree of ignorance of the possible adverse effects of chemicals on human health and the environment. Consequently, in the White Paper (European Commission 2001b) that preceded the legislation, the European Commission stated:

Currently there is wide-spread public concern about the effects of chemicals on human health and the environment as well as fear about new potential threats as in the case of endocrine disrupters. This concern is exacerbated by the so-called 'burden of the past'. Since the notification procedure has only been in place since 1981, all chemicals marketed prior to that date have never been scrutinised according to this procedure. Thus, for the majority of these chemicals few data are available. The immediate concern is therefore that man and the environment are potentially exposed to a large number of chemical substances for which the hazardous properties have not been identified and/or the risks have not been assessed.[27]

The new EU law on chemical safety came into force on 1 June 2007. On the same day the new European Chemicals Agency (ECHA) started operations in Helsinki (mirroring EFSA in Parma, Italy). However, there is a key difference from EFSA concerning the advice source. Under the previous chemicals regulatory system, data concerning primary and

---

[26] Regulation (EC) No 1907/2006 of the European Parliament and of the Council of 18 December 2006 concerning the Registration, Evaluation, Authorisation and Restriction of Chemicals (REACH) and establishing a European Chemicals Agency, etc. See website: http://eur-lex.europa.eu/LexUriServ/site/en/oj/2006/l_396/l_39620061230en00010849. pdf (last accessed 2 December 2007).

[27] For a general review of the rationale and risk assessment aspects of the new chemicals regulatory strategy, see Rogers 2003.

secondary uses of the substances under consideration and hence information on exposure proved difficult to obtain. The new Regulation breaks through this impasse and expedites the advisory procedure by reversing the burden of proof, requiring industry to carry out the initial risk assessments. ECHA oversees this process and will play a direct role with its own committees where the risk is considered to be serious or where there are conflicts concerning the data. Underpinning the legislation, as with food, is the precautionary principle. Thus, where the process is delayed excessively, or where there is an early indication of unacceptable risk, the PP will be invoked in deciding on risk management actions. Again, the European Commission expects that this arm's length approach to scientific advice in this major area of EU economic activity will help to restore trust in the operation of the chemicals safety system.

5   Concluding comments

Major changes in the European Commission system for receiving scientific advice have taken place at the beginning of the twenty-first century. These changes could be characterised as *Churchillian* because they involved a clear administrative separation of the advisory function from the policy function. Here, science advice is demonstrably 'on tap but not on top'. The two chief exemplars of this new approach, which involves setting up advisory agencies, are the European Food Safety Authority and the European Chemicals Agency. At the same time, the European Commission has retained some internal advisory bodies such as the European Group on the Ethics of Science and New Technologies, which could be characterised as *Bernalian*; since the bodies remain neutral and independent but, because they are internal, the dialogue that Bernal considered essential is facilitated. ('The scientist does not claim or want to be on top, but it is not nearly enough to have him merely on tap. In most cases the executive authority will not be able to see for himself when the scientist should be called in or what questions he should be asked.') Of course, the new agencies (such as EFSA and ECHA) can ensure that this dialogue takes place (and in the case of EFSA a formal interface unit exists). However, their geographical location (Palma and Helsinki) makes this difficult. By contrast, the US Food and Drugs Administration (FDA) has both risk assessors (advisory function) and risk managers (policy function) in the same body while preserving their functional separation. Clearly, this follows the Bernal approach to the provision of advice and could be replicated in the EU by ensuring a regular exchange of staff between the European Commission and the agencies concerned with the provision of this safety critical advice.

Certainly, the regulator does not possess the resources or expertise to undertake all aspects of risk regulation – from assessment to communication. Furthermore, it is not efficient to try to replicate expertise that exists elsewhere, for example in industry. However, this recognition of practicalities does not abrogate the regulator's responsibility. This may not even be possible. The European Court of Justice (ECJ) has concluded that delegation of powers to a Community agency is permissible, but only when 'it involves clearly defined executive powers the exercise of which can, therefore, be subject to strict review in the light of objective criteria determined by the delegating authority' (*Meroni v High Authority*).[28] Additionally, the ECJ proceeded to state that a delegation of authority 'implying a wide margin of discretion which may, according to the use which is made of it, make possible the execution of actual economic policy' is unconstitutional as 'it replaces the choices of the delegator by the choices of the delegatee, bringing about an actual transfer of responsibility'.

Ensuring that the European Commission retains the competence to exercise its responsibilities in these areas would be facilitated by the exchange of staff referred to above. It is beyond question that two of the three criteria that the Commission established for the use of expertise (quality and openness) have been demonstrated in the new advisory systems. The third (effectiveness) may be dependent on adopting Bernal's recommendation concerning dialogue between those that ask the question and those that provide the answer. This requires a mechanism for breaking down the geographic separation that the new system has put in place. Another way towards the same end might be to take up the EPC recommendation (see Section 2.3) and appoint a Chief Scientific Adviser to the European Commission. Such an appointment would inevitably involve coordinating the various sources of scientific advice to the Commission. However, as Bernal clearly recognised, scientific advice is not and should not be purely a passive process. A recent article in *The Times of London* emphasises this point (Linklater 2007). According to the article, the new UK Chief Scientist will be required to place 'science at the heart of government while at the same time telling government things that it will simply not want to hear'. In the European Commission, where much of the scientific advice has been delegated to agencies, there is perhaps a greater need for such a chief scientific adviser at the heart of the Commission.

---

[28] ECJ Case 9/56, *Meroni & Co, Industrie Metallurgische SpA v High Authority of the European Coal and Steel Community* [1958] ECR 133.

REFERENCES

Ballentine, Bruce 2005. *Enhancing the Role of Science in the Decision-Making of the European Union*, EPC Working Paper No. 17, March 2005.

Bernal, J.D. 1944. 'Lessons of the war for science', *Reports on Progress in Physics* 10: 418–36.

Churchill, Randolph S. 1965. *Twenty-One Years, Epilogue*, London: Wiedenfield and Nicolson.

European Commission 1994. *Growth, Competitiveness, Employment – The Challenges and Ways Forward into the 21st Century*, White Paper, Luxembourg: Office for Official Publications of the European Communities.

European Commission 2000. *White Paper on Food Safety*, COM(1999) 719 final, 12 January 2000.

European Commission 2001a. *European Governance – A White Paper*, COM (2001) 428 final, 25 July 2001, available at: http://eur-lex.europa.eu/ LexUriServ/site/en/com/2001/com2001_0428en01.pdf (last accessed 28 January 2007).

European Commission 2001b. *White Paper – Strategy for a Future Chemicals Policy*, COM(2001) 88 final, available at: http://eur-lex.europa.eu/ LexUriServ/LexUriServ.do?uri=CELEX:52001DC0088:EN:HTML (last accessed 2 December 2007).

European Commission 2001c. *Report of the Working Group Democratising Expertise and Establishing Scientific Reference Systems*, Brussels, available at: http://ec.europa.eu/governance/areas/group2/report_en.pdf (last accessed 11 April 2010).

European Commission 2002. 'Improving the Knowledge Base for Better Policies', Communication on the Collection and Use of Expertise, COM (2002) 713 final.

European Council 1991, *Promoting the Competitive Environment for the Industrial Activities Based on Biotechnology within the Community*, SEC(91) 629 final, Brussels.

European Council 2002. Regulation (EC) No 178/2002 of the European Parliament and of the Council of 28 January 2002 laying down the general principles and requirements of food law, establishing the European Food Safety Authority and laying down procedures in matters of food safety, available at: http://eur-lex.europa.eu/pri/en/oj/dat/2002/l_031/ l_03120020201en00010024.pdf (last accessed 1 April 2010).

European Court of Justice 1959. Case 9/56 *Meroni & Co, Industrie Metallurgiche SpA v. High Authority* [1959] ECR 133.

European Union 1999. Treaty Establishing the European Community. Article 174 (ex 130r) in Selected Instruments Taken from the Treaties, Vol. I, pp. 253–4.

Jacquemin, Alexis and Wright, David (eds.) 1993. *The European Challenges Post-1992*, Aldershot: Edward Elgar.

Linklater, Magnus 2007. 'Go on, upset your masters. The new Chief Scientist must not shy away from speaking unwelcome truths', *The Times of London*, 12 December 2007.

Michaels, David, Bingham, Eula, Boden, Les, Clapp, Richard, Goldman, Lynn R., Hoppin, Polly, Krimsky, Sheldon, Monforton, Celeste, Ozonoff, David and Robbins, Anthony 2002. 'Advice without dissent', *Science* 298: 703, 25 October 2002.

Prodi, Romano 2000. 'Shaping the New Europe', *European Parliament Strasbourg*, 15 February 2000, available at: http://europa.eu/rapid/pressReleasesAction.do?reference=SPEECH/00/41&format=HTML&aged=1&language=EN&guiLanguage=en (last accessed 28 January 2007).

Rogers, M.D. 1993. *Carrefours Européene des Sciences et de la Culture, No. 2*, July 1993, Forward Studies Unit.

Rogers, M.D. 2003. 'Risk Analysis under uncertainty, the precautionary principle, and the new EU chemicals strategy', *Regulatory Toxicology and Pharmacology* 37: 370–81.

Rogers, M.D. 2004. 'Genetically modified plants and the precautionary principle', *Journal of Risk Research* 7: 675–88.

US National Research Council 1996. *Understanding Risk – Informing Decisions in a Democratic Society.*

Whiteside, K.H. 2006. *Precautionary Politics: Principle and Practice in Confronting Environmental Risk*, Cambridge, MA: MIT Press.

Wiener, J.B. and Rogers, M.D. 2002. 'Comparing precaution in the United States and Europe', *Journal of Risk Research* 5/4: 317–49.

Wilsdon, J. and Willis, R. 2004. *See Through Science – Why Public Engagement Needs to Move Upstream*, London: Demos, available at: http://www.demos.co.uk/publications/paddlingupstream#media#media (last accessed 29 September 2009).

Wynne, Brian, Felt, Ulrike, Eduarda Gonçalves, Maria, Jasanoff, Sheila, Jepsen, Maria, Joly, Pierre-Benoît, Konopasek, Zdenek, May, Stefan, Neubauer, Claudia, Rip, Arie, Siune, Karen, Stirling, Andy and Tallacchini, Mariachiara 2007. *Taking European Knowledge Society Seriously*, Report of the Expert Group on Science and Governance to the Science, Economy and Society Directorate, Directorate-General for Research, European Commission; EUR 22700, available at: http://ec.europa.eu/research/science-society/document_library/pdf_06/european-knowledge-society_en.pdf (last accessed 12 October 2009).

Part III

Collegial science policy advisory bodies

RMNO and quality control of scientific advice to policy[1]

Bert de Wit

1 RMNO, the Advisory Council for Research on Spatial Planning, Nature and the Environment in the Netherlands

RMNO, the Advisory Council for Research on Spatial Planning, Nature and the Environment, is a knowledge broker, focusing on the knowledge for the mid- to long-term that is needed in order to solve or mitigate societal problems. This knowledge is thought to be relevant for societal groups, policymakers and politicians. Policymakers can use this knowledge to underpin their strategic policies.

RMNO's main clients are five ministries, but RMNO nowadays also works for provinces and other decentralised authorities.

RMNO deals with the articulation of strategic knowledge needs, the assessment of available knowledge, the formulation of research questions, the evaluation of research programmes and the utilisation of knowledge in policymaking. Advice about knowledge infrastructure and networks is also one of the products of RMNO.

RMNO is an independent advisory council, financed by the five ministries mentioned above. The leading ministry is the Ministry of Housing, Spatial Planning and the Environment which also appoints RMNO's members. They fall into three categories: policymakers (directors of departments, research coordinators), scientists who are interested in societal problems and people from business and societal groups.

Advice and studies provided by the Council have either been requested by one or more ministries or have been produced on the Council's own initiative. RMNO does not allocate research money or

---

[1] RMNO ceased to exist in 2010. The Dutch government decided to put an end to the advisory council expecting the so-called knowledge chambers within ministries to take over the advisory role on strategic research. The Council's activities in the field of methodology of boundary work have been taken over by the PBL Netherlands Environmental Assessment Agency in The Hague. The email address of Bert de Wit is bert.dewit@pbl.nl.

research grants. That is the task of universities and the NWO, the Dutch Foundation for Scientific Research.

2   What does the RMNO do?

To provide an idea of the activities of the RMNO, the following figure can be used. It shows interactions that take place at the interface of science and policy, based on the idea that there are two definite and separate arenas (*worlds*) of science and policy. The interface with society is left out for reasons of simplicity. Of course, similar interactions can be seen at this interface as well as specific problems, such as the representativeness of stakeholders and questions concerning participation.

The figure shows two arenas, a policy arena and a knowledge arena. Why do we talk about a knowledge arena and not a scientific arena? The reason is because sometimes informal knowledge is also used and can be very important in elucidating policy decisions.

Several mismatches may occur in this scheme. These are indicated by slashes. For example, a well-known problem is the articulation of the strategic knowledge needs of policymakers. Recently, a survey was carried out for the Council to see what the people involved thought the main problems are (for example, pressure from short-term policy, disinterest at the highest political level, etc.). There are several reasons why policymakers cannot easily say what knowledge they need to underpin strategic policy. Work on everyday policy is very predominant and time for reflection about possible future developments is scarce. There is often no reward for those policymakers who really bother about future problems they will have to deal with. Moreover, money for strategic research has become increasingly scarce in recent years. Of course, some intermediary organisations can offer help in this case to shape the strategic research policy.

Other mismatches may occur at the level of the utilisation of research products. One of the most obvious reasons for ignoring research results is that they do not fit with the policymaker's or the minister's policy theory. Another reason why knowledge does not fit might be that it is too abstract, needing some kind of contextualisation before it can be of use. The knowledge produced might also be mono-disciplinary, whereas the real life problem cannot be split up according to disciplinary boundaries. Other, more common reasons why knowledge is not utilised are that the knowledge is produced too slowly (the life cycles of research and policymaking are quite different) or that some policy questions are not researchable.

As a matter of fact, the whole figure of interactions between the policy arena and the knowledge arena can be understood as a portrayal of the core business of the RMNO. But the focus of the RMNO on strategic

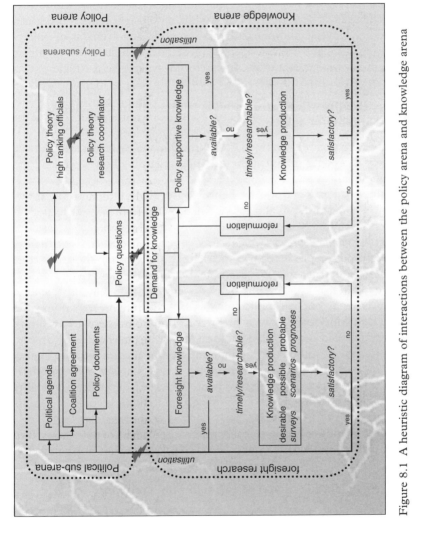

Figure 8.1 A heuristic diagram of interactions between the policy arena and knowledge arena

knowledge brings about a special interest in demand articulation for the mid- to long-term future as well as foresight exercises and future scanning as these can point towards possible new developments in society and policy. Of course, the implementation of foresight knowledge in policymaking is a problem in itself, as the position of strategic policy is often crowded out by short-term concerns. A study in the field of environmental policy and spatial planning in the late 1990s shows that very little use has been made of the results of foresight reports produced by various agencies and departmental sections. Involvement of policymakers in foresight exercises seems to be advisable in order to utilise foresight knowledge in a more satisfactory way (In't Veld 2001).

3   Quality of scientific advice is more than the scientific quality of advice

The question regarding how to guarantee the quality of scientific advice to policy is broader than just the question regarding how to control the scientific quality of advice.

As one may gather from the figure above, RMNO is not only interested in the scientific quality of knowledge that is presented to policymakers. We think in terms of *optimising the interactions between policymakers and researchers (and societal groups, business)*. If a high quality research product, produced by top scientists, does not fit the knowledge needs of policymakers, for example because the knowledge is too abstract and too little contextualised, one can say that its scientific quality is high, but its applicability is low. Therefore, expanding the notion of quality control to a broader notion about knowledge fitting the original need is quite obvious for a knowledge broker.

It goes almost without saying that one cannot speak about the quality of a product of a professional group in terms that are only based on internal procedures, ignoring the client. That kind of quality is a quality of days gone by when the professional group thought it could dictate its ideas to the rest of society.

Therefore, not only the scientific procedures will have to be taken into consideration, but also the interactions of scientists with policymakers.

4   The classic model of rational policymaking

Most people who are involved in giving policy advice have only implicit ideas about how the relations between politics, policymakers and scientists should ideally be characterised. If you ask them, all kinds of implicit ideas about responsibilities, relations, power and trust will surface.

These implicit assumptions might be summarised in a kind of model of rational policymaking. First, there is the politician with his or her political rationality, asking the policymaker who has to provide the answers for questions that arise from a particular political problem. A solution for policy problems that is linked to their policy theory is often already in their minds, but they need to legitimise this solution. Further supporting evidence is needed. The policymaker formulates the policy question. A translation into questions about available knowledge and knowledge gaps follows. Often, after that, research questions are formulated by special research coordinators.

In the next step, research is carried out by a scientist who has his or her own scientific rationality and bears the responsibility to come up with an answer to the research question. The scientist considers him or herself strictly independent. The results of research are finally translated into information and knowledge that can be used – or ignored – in policymaking. This is more or less the implicit model that a great number of scientists and policymakers have in mind. See Figure 8.2.

Of course, this implicit idea about who is predominant and what the respective responsibilities are is time-dependent and depends on the institutional context.

5   The rational model and reality

Four cases of knowledge use in complex policy problems have been analysed in the late 1990s and are described in *Willingly and Knowingly. The Role of Knowledge About Nature and The Environment in Policy Processes* (In't Veld 2000).

The Betuwe Cargo Railway from Rotterdam to Germany, costing about €5 billion, is one case. In the 1990s, hundreds of reports were written by consultants, university professors, departmental sections and state planning agencies. Most of these reports taking different starting points were not very compatible, and quite a few did not take a comprehensive view of the problem. It took four years after the original policy decision was made until a commission was asked to make a survey of the usefulness and necessity of the whole project (whereas nowadays this is compulsory for megaprojects). Some reports, for example a rather favourable report of RIVM (State Institute for Health and the Environment) about the environmental benefits of this new cargo railway track, in later years proved to be based on incorrect figures provided by the Ministry of Transport and Water Management.

A parliamentary inquiry into this case showed several shortcomings in the way Parliament was informed. The Duijvestein commission

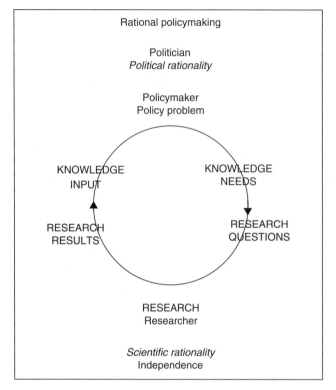

Figure 8.2 The classic model of rational policymaking

(Parliamentary Commission Duijvestein, Tweede Kamer 2004/2005) concluded that Parliament was systematically misinformed or incompletely informed by ministers and that critical reports had been smuggled away on purpose. Parliament should get its own investigation office to monitor progress of megaprojects. It should be able to check scientific reports to Parliament.

One can doubt whether this solution will be adequate. It will certainly not be if the knowledge that is produced conflicts with the policy theories of the Members of Parliament ...

The analysed cases in *Willingly and Knowingly* show that knowledge is often strategically used in complex policy problems. It is a kind of two-level game between the knowledge arena and the political arena. The inevitable conclusion is that the classic model of rational policymaking is not adequate for describing and explaining the observed phenomena.

One should be aware of the fact that different actors may have very different problem definitions when dealing with complex policy problems. A policymaker may describe the problem as 'how to construct a new railway from Rotterdam to Germany at the lowest cost for the economy and the environment'. That is a purely technical question. A local inhabitant is worried about the noise that will be produced and mistrusts reassurances that there will be no problem. Taxpayers and the General Auditor are interested in the question what the costs and benefits of the proposed railway are. Environmentalists want to include a comparison to other types of transport in the calculations.

The error many policymakers commit, is that they think a problem is structured, when in fact it is not. Thus, a *paper war* may explode, one party ordering research that shows favourable results and the other party showing research results that lead to the opposite conclusion. Strategic use of knowledge is the consequence of the battle in the political arena being fought out in the knowledge arena.

The question arises as to how one should deal with knowledge utilisation and production in complex policy problems.

6   The nature of the policy problem should be the point of departure for scientists

A *structured problem* is characterised by consensus about relevant values and knowledge. A simple principal-agent relationship between policymaker and scientist seems adequate. That is, the scientist delivers the knowledge the policymaker wants and assures its quality by mono-disciplinary peer review procedures. In this case, the former model of rational policymaking applies.

Unstructured problems are problems that are characterised by lack of consensus on relevant knowledge and relevant values. For unstructured problems, the rational model is not appropriate. These should be dealt with in a different way than structured problems (Hisschemöller 1998). The role of scientists, policymakers and stakeholders should also be different. Scientists and policymakers should engage in a dialogue with stakeholders. Research should become a co-production of knowledge (Jasanoff 2004).

This means that several problem definitions have to be taken into consideration. Different problem definitions are linked to social and cognitive configurations (groups of persons who more or less share the same view on the problem). Social and cognitive interventions should aim at including variation and enhancing dynamics to bring about new meanings and new solutions (innovation). Interaction should produce new shared problem definitions and provide an opportunity for learning.

Wherever knowledge is conflicting, procedures will have to be devised to get things sorted out. One example where this has been done can be found in the mediation procedure regarding the extension of the Frankfurt Airport. A group of local citizens and business stakeholders were involved in a process identifying conflicting knowledge. Expert hearings were organised and expert reports on specific subjects were ordered.

Mono-disciplinary scientific advice from one specialist is not adequate for an unstructured problem, because not only is knowledge from several disciplines usually needed but also informal knowledge from stakeholders.

If for example, in the case of biodiversity loss, only scientific advice based on taxonomic data and research is provided, the problem will be how to interpret the expected loss of species, their significance for ecosystem functioning, their cultural and recreational value for the local society and the rest of the world, the economics of species richness, etc.

Furthermore, the uncertainties related to future projections should be explicitly stated. Uncertainties are often used in political debates to undermine the position of the other party.

When the policy problem is *badly structured*, the problem is mainly about conflicting values – stem cell research for example – and a means of reconciliation has to be found. Science plays only a subordinate role. However, new scientific information might be of use in order to refine definitions (for example, what is death? Or at what point in time does an embryo have functions that can be considered as belonging to a human being?) or to devise instruments for reconciling the conflict.

In Figure 8.3, the typology of problems is linked to the recommended approach to the problems by scientists and policymakers.

Our conclusion is that the role of scientists (and policymakers alike) should vary according to the nature of the problem: from speaking the truth to power in case of research into a structured problem to taking part in a dialogue between researchers, policymakers and stakeholders in transdisciplinary research. If a scientist thinks he or she can simply go on doing what he or she has always done without taking the context into account, the quality of scientific advice might be very good according to the peer group, but very bad in all other aspects. This is not to say that good quality research should provide knowledge that fits with the policy theory of the policymaker. We simply want to underline that the nature of the problem should define the way scientific expertise is put to work. It should also be the starting point for considering the need for a mono-, inter- or transdisciplinary approach in research.

7   Assessment of societal quality of scientific advice: a possible instrument?

There have been interesting efforts to try to define the societal quality of research and advice and to develop an instrument for

Consensus on existing values		
Consensus about relevant knowledge	**Yes**	**No**
Yes	**Structured problem** Approach: match the need for and supply of knowledge; contextualisation of knowledge	**Poorly structured problem** Approach: make value orientations more explicit and look for possibilities for reconciliation
No	**Slightly structured problem** Approach: expert hearings joint factfinding	**Unstructured problem** Approach: (learning) dialogue or argumentation. Joint fact finding, etc.

Figure 8.3 A typology of problems

assessment of societal quality. Quality of research up until now is often only measured in terms of peer reviewed articles and visitations by foreign researcher- colleagues. But a widely accepted instrument to measure the *societal quality of research* is not yet available. If it were available, it might also be of use to assess the quality of scientific advice to policy.

Of course, a simple survey of the client's satisfaction may suffice. However, a more elaborate framework has been worked out by Spaapen *et al.* (2004).

Steps in constructing an operational framework include:

- defining the relevant characteristics of the communication structure in a particular field;
- deciding what the relevant issues are between science, technology and society; and
- integrating different elements into a single procedure.

From the main elements of the interaction structure between researcher, client and surroundings, one can conclude which indicators of communication, research output and societal demand are relevant. Graphs can be constructed using eight indicators of relevant types of input, output and media, thus producing a kind of amoeba-figure. The indicators are sector bound. Graphs of different research groups may show differences in orientations as a consequence of different organisational missions and goals. A stakeholder analysis is part of the procedure (Spaapen, Dijstelbloem and Wamelink 2004).

Assessing the societal quality of research by the method of Spaapen *et al.* is quite laborious. That means that it will not often be applied if there is not some kind of reward system connected to it that is comparable to that for scientific quality.

8   Evaluation of scientific advice in the Netherlands

In the Netherlands, several institutionalised procedures and routines for the quality control of scientific advice exist. Most of these procedures and routines are internal (criticism and support from colleagues, codes of conduct) and external as far as peer groups are concerned. The Royal Academy of Sciences (KNAW 2005) recently underlined the importance of independence of researchers giving advice for policymakers.

Peer review is a very common method of quality control, not only with regard to university research. Visitation committees are also familiar instruments for quality control in research institutes and planning agencies that produce advice for policymakers. Examples are visitation reports of the RIVM (State Institute for Public Health and the Environment) and the Alterra (the research institute linked to and part of Wageningen University that carries out much policy-relevant research in the field of agriculture, nature and food quality).

Nowadays, the evaluation procedure for university research in the Netherlands is a self-evaluation procedure.

Some ministries try to measure the utilisation of scientific advice in policymaking. The Ministry of Agriculture, Nature and Food Quality wishes to know whether effective use has been made of scientific reports that have been ordered by the Ministry.

When assessing the quality of foresight knowledge, one should bear in mind that probability is often not the key variable, but rather plausibility and feasibility (In't Veld 2001). Evaluation reports on the utilisation of foresight knowledge clearly indicate that these are the crucial factors, and of course the process is important in this respect, too. Policy preferences and institutional and organisational aspects should be taken into consideration when putting foresight knowledge to work.

Quality control of research is best developed for mono-disciplinary research. The reward system of universities and the career-making possibilities are determined by the quest for excellence in disciplinary research. In general, quality assessment of inter- and transdisciplinary research is problematic if it follows the standard procedures for disciplinary research. There are no evaluations of transdisciplinary research available in the Netherlands. Evalunet, the international network for evaluation of transdisciplinary research, has produced guidelines for this purpose, based on very detailed criteria of quality and methods used, also taking into account the aspect of learning (Bergmann *et al.* 2005).

As we have argued before, research into policy problems, especially the unstructured problems, necessitates an inter- or transdisciplinary approach. For these approaches in research, only recently have some guidelines become available (see the Evalunet criteria), but the procedures are not mandatory. For transdisciplinary research, quality control is not reserved to peers only. In this case, other persons are involved too, making the review an extended peer review. In the Netherlands, up until now, there have been no examples of an institutionalised extended peer review.

To sum up, in the Netherlands:

- for disciplinary research, a well-developed system of quality control and a corresponding reward system exist;
- for research institutes, an internal quality assessment and control exists; external quality assessment and control is by means of peer review and visitation committees;
- for assessing and controlling the societal quality of research, no institutionalised system exists;
- for inter- and transdisciplinary research, no institutionalised system of quality control exists.

9   Institutionalised patterns of advising in the Netherlands

In general, one can say that what is considered to be *sound advice* to policy depends also on the policy field and the way the relations between policymakers and scientists and scientific institutions are institutionalised.

Willem Halffman (Halffman and Hoppe 2005) points out that practices of science-based expert advice to government are not deployed in an institutional void. Several institutionalised patterns of advice can be seen. The institutions concerned develop a body of knowledge, formal and informal rules about how they should operate, they have a more or less guaranteed budget, and a conception of what is their business and what not.

One way to look at policy expertise is to study what institutions have formed over time and how they frame boundary work. The premise of international comparison is often that there is something in the socio-political constitution of a society that forces expertise into specific patterns.

Halffman describes three key trends in Dutch science-policy with respect to expert policy advice: a neoliberal, a corporatist, and a network pattern of institutionalisation of science-policy interfaces.

(1) Halffman considers CPB, the Central Agency for Economic Advice, an example of the *corporatist* pattern. Drawing the lines of negotiations in Dutch policy, CPB has the role of a referee defining the playing field for corporatist negotiations. There is a gradual accumulation of knowledge in the planning bureaus (CPB, RIVM, SCP, RPB). Disadvantages are the monopolistic position, a possible systematic bias through the dominance of certain professions or modelling practices and the potential exclusion of policy alternatives.

(2) The *neoliberal* pattern expresses itself in an increasing contractuali-sation of expertise, i.e. the commodification of expertise. Expertise for policymaking should be located in agencies or companies. Policymakers in this view should be able to tap into a wider range of expert organisations, reach beyond the accepted wisdom of one policy belief system and its concomitant expert professional para-digm. While the proponents of this model stress that government can reduce the cost of expertise through the competition of experts on the market, there are also considerable disadvantages linked to this model. Knowledge accumulation is accidental at best. Know-ledge is stored in the worst possible location: reports. Only the bigger consultancies are able to cope with this problem. They can deliver tailor-made advice. It is more difficult for them to develop and refine models, to foster extended learning processes between policymakers and experts and to sustain groups of experts. Know-ledge providers cannot afford to be too critical or to object to excessive instrumental use of expertise by policymakers.

(3) The *distributed expertise* (network) pattern: here, expert knowledge is not commodified, but a public good that is produced, evaluated and integrated in a wide variety of places. This pattern can be found in several Dutch knowledge centres, in the increased use of expertise by NGOs and citizens, and the increasing higher education levels as well as the expanding role of the media in reporting on science and expertise. The pattern breaks through the limitations of access to expertise, and through professional barriers, and follows more easily new policy issues as they appear in the risk society. Weaknesses include the problematic nature of quality standards or a possible tendency to

package complex knowledge issues into sound bites and overly simpli-fied one-liners (Halffman 2008). More than 100 knowledge centres have been founded in the Netherlands. The RMNO as a tripartite advisory council fits well in this distributed expertise pattern.

Of course, there are also examples of institutionalised expertise that can be compared to expert committees in other countries.

The Health Council is an example of an expert council. Its committees consist of professionals, specialists who give advice to gov-ernment about, for example, the scientific basis of medical treatments, the risks of substances and how to deal with them (safety limits for standards). They also propose standards for reducing environmental pollution.

A similar expert model is at the basis of the Committee for Environ-mental Impact Assessment. Ad hoc committees of experts give their judgement about the scope and planning of environmental impact assessments and also give their opinion about the quality of EIA reports. The EIA committees are not quite comparable to committees of the Health Council, as the former only have a control function and do give their advice to other actors (companies, provinces, etc.) than just minis-tries. It is, by the way, problematic that the legally obliged *ex post* evaluation of EIA's is often missing, making it difficult to learn from past advice.

Some spokesmen in the Dutch government seem to prefer the expert model, imitating the Anglo-Saxon model of specific expert committees, whereas ironically, in the UK, after the BSE crisis, a more deliberative approach for complex policy issues is now recommended (see Hajer and Wagenaar 2003).

These institutionalised patterns of expertise reflect various discourses about the relations between science and policy (see Hoppe and Huijs 2003).

10   Discourses on the interface of science and policy

Institutionalised patterns of expertise can be seen as the crystallisation of discourses about the way scientists and policymakers see their roles. The discourses people adhere to can very strongly influence the inter-actions between policymakers and scientists (Hoppe and Huijs 2003). Some scientists think their role is primarily speaking truth to power. They will not take part in a dialogue with policymakers and stakeholders (example of the enlightenment discourse or the technocratic discourse). Other scientists see themselves as being part of the bureaucratic

Table 8.1 *Discourses of boundary work between science and politics*

Operational code	Primacy of Science	No primacy: Dialogue	Primacy of Politics
Divergent functions	(1) *Enlightenment* discourse (science as supplier of ideas)	(2) *Advocate's* discourse (science as supplier of arguments)	(3) *Bureaucracy* discourse (science as data-supplier)
Convergent functions	(4) *Technocracy* discourse (science as [virtual] power)	(5) *Learning* discourse (community of researchers as political role model)	(6) *Engineer's* discourse (science as market for [social] technologies)

(*Source: Hoppe and Huijs 2003*)

organisation which does not allow them to enter an open dialogue with stakeholders (bureaucratic discourse). For the sake of the optimisation of utilisation of knowledge in policymaking, such role reversals are, however, sometimes necessary when the unstructured nature of the problem requires a dialogue.

Sometimes several discourses at the same time can be traced from policy documents and from interviews of research coordinators of institutes and ministries. The Ministry of Agriculture, Nature and Food Quality, for example, has long been an example of the bureaucratic discourse. It finances its own agricultural university (Wageningen University), its own system of agricultural schools, and these were closely linked to state-financed information services to farmers and to the agricultural industry. The system was very successful from the 1870s until the 1970s. The great disadvantage of this kind of system is groupthink. Environmental problems caused by external effects – such as overproduction of manure from intensive pig breeding – are at first not recognised and not acknowledged. Later on, technological solutions were thought to be adequate, the policy option of reduction of livestock was not considered until the beginning of the 1990s.

In the meantime, the dominant position of bureaucratic discourse in the knowledge system of this ministry has come to an end. Other discourses like the engineer's discourse, technocratic discourse and learning discourse are now of more importance. The enlightenment discourse always has been part of the thinking as Wageningen University is a university and should not only produce knowledge that is directly applicable in agricultural practice, although application of knowledge was and is still a very important basis for its work.

11   Lessons learned

From the above examples, one can gather that for an advisory council like RMNO, quality of scientific advice to policy depends on several factors.

In 2001, RMNO organised an annual conference about disasters, failures and successes in the field of scientific advice to policymakers (RMNO 2001). The idea was to find out what are considered to be good and bad practices of boundary work. The conclusion RMNO drew from this conference is that what is considered to be an example of good or bad practice depends on the following factors:

- the nature of the problem and the way scientists, policymakers and stakeholders see their roles with regard to knowledge production; and
- the existing evaluation routines and institutions.

These factors have been dealt with in the previous sections. But an important factor has not yet been mentioned: 'the paradigmatic view of science-policy interactions: a positivist view or a social constructivist view of knowledge' (see Hajer and Wagenaar 2003).

Quality of scientific advice is according to Spaapen *et al.* (2004) a *relative concept, relative to an environment and to particular actors*. Let me finish by some provoking thoughts about how quality control could be conceived from a constructivist point of view and what difference it makes to the common positivist point of view.

12   A knowledge auditor

My personal opinion is that the quality of scientific advice might be further improved by introducing an accountability mechanism for research institutes that regularly produce advice to the government. An audit might be carried out by an independent *knowledge auditor* whose chief responsibility is quality assurance of knowledge produced for policymaking. Audits of research institutes are already quite familiar, and they have to satisfy certain quality criteria which are often defined by peers. However, quality of scientific advice should be more broadly defined as described above, pertaining to the interactions between relevant actors, and not narrowly conceived as quality in a disciplinary sense or as quality defined only by (scientific) peers. Clearly, quality assessment in a broad sense should be done from a constructivist point of view.

When an audit is carried out from a strict positivistic point of view, the focus is on performance management and measuring using standard criteria. Some people call this type of quality control (in case of policy evaluation) 'McDonaldization' (Leeuw 2001), measuring the effectiveness of scientific work by well-chosen citation and publication indices.

One could argue that the idea underlying the institution of a *chief scientist* in Great Britain is positivist. The Chief Scientist reviews the quality of the knowledge that has been used for policymaking every three years. Experts from outside the ministry analyse how scientific knowledge is utilised inside the ministerial system. Every year the department produces a Science and Innovation Agenda. The idea is that one person (with the help of experts) has the responsibility for saying whether a particular kind of knowledge has been utilised for policymaking.

Complementary to this quality control mechanism is the idea of an ethical code of conduct for researchers. This kind of solution for problems on the interface of science and policy by making an appeal to the ethical principles of the researcher is also known to exist in other countries. It fits well with the positivist way of thinking.

The intriguing question is of course: how does a Chief Scientist deal with complex policy problems like genetic modification? It proves that for these cases a different approach is chosen. An open forum called *Science Wise*, an ambulant platform, gives the citizens an opportunity to communicate their opinions on these matters and to present their questions to a panel of experts. The citizens can even make their own suggestions for solutions. The whole idea is, in my opinion, not that of science speaking truth to power but it is more like a dialogue (see Weingart and Lentsch 2006). From a positivist point of view, the procedure for this type of complex policy problems is a step too far, but from a constructivist point of view, it is a logical step and the beginning of adequate interaction.

In conclusion, I would like to emphasise that quality assessment from a broader social constructivist point of view is necessary when evaluating the interactions between science and policy. A strict positivist view excludes a social constructivist point of view, but a constructivist view does not exclude a positivistic point of view.

One can draw a parallel to ideas about policy evaluation. Policy evaluation according to some authors should also be broadened to become a so-called inclusive policy evaluation (Abma 2001). Inclusive policy evaluation is adequate for complex policy problems, when the persons involved have different problem perceptions. The active participation of interest groups is not seen as an obstacle, but as a possibility to make use of the informal knowledge of stakeholders.

Needless to say, a knowledge auditor, in my opinion, should have a broad, constructivist view on the interactions between science and policy. Important elements are a critical examination of the organisation of the research process, how different problem perceptions are dealt with, the methodological choices with regard to the nature of the policy problem at hand, etc.

Elements of the evaluation method for societal quality of research devised by Spaapen *et al.* (2004) could be of use to a knowledge auditor. Such an auditing mechanism can also help in propagating good practices of research outside the strict disciplinary domain. A probable effect is that learning in the field of inter- and transdisciplinary research is boosted and the position of this kind of research is made more secure.

REFERENCES

Abma, T. 2001. 'Variatie in beleidsevaluaties/Variations in policy evaluation', in T. Abma and R. In't Veld (eds.), *Handboek beleidswetenschap (Handbook of Policy Sciences)*, Meppel: Uitgeverij Boom.

Bergmann, Matthias, Brohmann, Bettina, Hofmann, Esther, Loibl, M. Céline, Rehaag, Regine, Schramm, Engelbert and Voß, Jan-Peter 2005. *Qualitätskriterien transdisziplinärer Forschung. Ein Leitfaden für die formative Evaluation von Forschungsprojekten. – Quality Criteria for Transdisciplinary Research. A Guide for the Formative Evaluation of Research Project*, ISOE-Studientexte Nr. 13, *Frankfurt am Main*.

Hajer, M.A. and Wagenaar, H. (eds.) 2003. *Deliberative Policy Analysis: Understanding Governance in the Network Society*, Cambridge University Press.

Halffman, W. and Hoppe, R. 2005. 'Science policy boundaries: A changing division of labour in Dutch expert policy advice', in Sabine Maasen and Peter Weingart (eds.), *Democratization of Expertise? Exploring Novel Forms of Scientific Advice in Political Decision-Making*, Dordrecht: Kluwer, pp. 135–52.

Halffman, W. 2008. *States of Nature: Nature and fish stock reports for policy*, Report for the Netherlands Consultative Committee of Sector Councils for research and development, RMNO preliminary study V.13, The Hague.

Hisschemöller, M. 1998. *Kennisbenutting en politieke keuze: Een dilemma voor het milieubeleid? (Knowledge Utilisation and Political Choice: A Dilemma for Environmental Policy?)*, Werkdocument no. 65, Den Haag, Rathenau-Instituut.

Hoppe, R. and Huijs, S. 2003. *Werk op de grenzen van wetenschap en beleid. Paradoxen en dilemma's (Work on the Boundaries of Science and Policy)*, Paradoxes and Dilemmas. RMNO nr. 157, Den Haag.

In't Veld, R.J. 2000. *Willingly and Knowingly. The Role of Knowledge About Nature and The Environment in Policy Processes RMNO*, Utrecht, The Netherlands: Lemma.

In't Veld, R.J. 2001. *Eerherstel voor Cassandra/Rehabilitation for Cassandra* (available in English) WRR, RMNO, Den Haag.

Jasanoff, S. 2004. 'The idiom of co-production', in Sheila Jasanoff (ed.), *States of Knowledge: The Co-Production of Science and Social Order*, London: Routledge, pp. 1–12.

Leeuw, F. 2001. 'Evaluatieonderzoek, auditing en controle in Nederland anno 2000/Evaluation Research, auditing and control in the Netherlands in 2000', in T. Abma and R. In't Veld (eds.), *Handboek beleidswetenschap*, Meppel: Uitgeverij Boom.

KNAW 2005. *Verklaring van Wetenschappelijke Onafhankelijkheid/Declaration of Scientific Independence*, Amsterdam: KNAW.

RMNO 2001. *Disaster, Failure Or Success? Towards a Better Interaction Between Scientists, Policymakers and Societal Groups*, RMNO nr. 152, Den Haag.

Spaapen, J., Dijstelbloem, H. and Wamelink, F. 2004. *A Model for the Evaluation of Research in the Context of Application. Self-Evaluation of Two Pharmaceutical Faculties in a New National System of Evaluation*, Den Haag: COS.

Tweede Kamer (Dutch Parliament) 2004/2005. *Grote Projecten uitvergroot. Een infrastructuur voor besluitvorming/Mega Projects Magnified. An Infrastructure for Decision-Making, TK vergaderjaar* 2004/2005, nr. 29283, nr 6.

Weingart, Peter and Lentsch, Justus 2006. *Standards and Best Practices of Scientific Policy Advice*. Round Table Discussion with Sir David King, Chief Scientific Adviser to the British Government, Berlin: Berlin-Brandenburgische Akademie der Wissenschaften.

9   Quality assurance through procedures –
policy advice by the German Science Council

Andreas Stucke

1   The Science Council as an arena for science policy

Science policy is a relatively new field, not only in Germany, being developed systematically with the appropriate consulting structures only in the second half of the twentieth century. There may have been attempts at the level of university policy in Germany or, more precisely, in Prussia as early as in the nineteenth century (System Althoff[1]), in the form of long-term planning of professorial appointments. But that kind of policy was fundamentally different from science policy as it took shape in Germany in the second half of the twentieth century, leading to the establishment of the first systematic funding procedures for scientific research and the foundation of new scientific organisations (for an overview, see Stichweh 1994). From 1945, almost all developed industrial nations started long-term scientific research programmes, significantly increased their investment in research and development, created new, centralised agencies of national science policy (ministries, coordination and funding bodies), and established forms of finance allocation for scientific research. In this context, there also emerged institutions to provide science policy advice, such as the President's Science Advisory Committee (PSAC, US), the Council for Science and Technology (CST, UK) or the Wissenschaftsrat (Science Council, Germany).

The Science Council (founded in 1957) is one of the first science policy advisory bodies in Europe. For Germany it is – even after the significant and noticeable broadening of the science policy advisory scene over the last decade – the central consulting institution for a national science policy for the federal government and the federal states (Länder). Founded in the context of post-war reconstruction, its original mission was to 'develop a comprehensive plan to promote the sciences' and to 'provide recommendations for the use of funds as available in

---

[1] Named after Friedrich Althoff (1839–1908), the Prussian senior civil servant, who represented by his activities a long-term national appointment policy at universities.

federal and *Länder* budgets for the promotion of science'. Since then, this spectrum of tasks has changed and was extended considerably. Today, the predominant tasks of the Science Council are (Bartz 2007; Stucke 2002):

- to provide recommendations for the institutional development of universities and non-university research institutions and to propose or evaluate the related structural reforms in research and education;
- to contribute to quality control and quality assurance in the German science system by evaluating individual research institutions as well as disciplines or fields of scientific research and by accrediting private universities;
- to provide recommendations for the development of university infra-structure (buildings, large-scale facilities) with regard to specific research programmes.

Apart from that, the Science Council also fulfils funding responsibilities by organising the competition between universities outstanding in research within the Excellence Initiative in Germany since 2006.

With all its activities and decisions, the Science Council constitutes an *intermediary organisation* of science policy. As such, its function is to mediate between the diverse interests of science and politics, as well as between the federal government and the Länder, and to coordinate the activities of these actor-groups (Braun 1997).

The basic organisational characteristics of the Science Council have remained virtually unchanged over the past decades. Some of these characteristics clearly distinguish the Science Council from most other scientific advisory bodies and are, as we will see, of immediate consequence for the quality of the policy advice. These peculiarities are found in the composition and mode of operation of the Science Council but also, and more importantly, in the interesting fact that although it is scientists who act as advisers, their advice can not be regarded as *scientific* policy advice.

The first peculiarity of the Science Council is that the predominant addressees of its advice, i.e. the science policymakers on the federal and Länder levels, are themselves full members of the Science Council, contributing to the development of recommendations and statements at all levels of the consultation process. In contrast to many areas of scientific policy advice, where individual scientists or panels of scientists develop assessments and then deliver them to politicians, the Science Council is essentially a hybrid organisation. The Council intentionally applies an integrative model of policy advice. This becomes evident from the organisational structure of the Science Council (see Figure 9.1), which is made up of a Science Commission (with twenty-four scientists

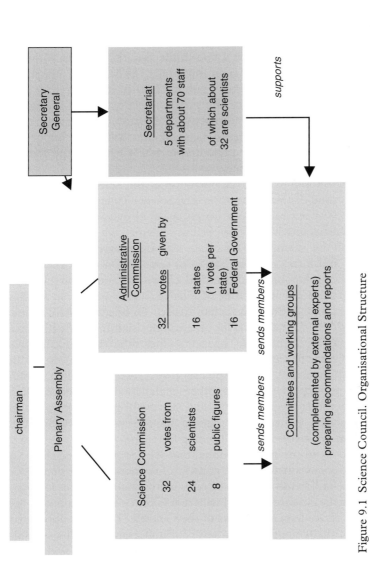

Figure 9.1 Science Council. Organisational Structure

appointed *ad personam* by the President of the Republic and eight other public figures) and an Administrative Commission (consisting of thirty-two members from federal and Länder governments). Both commissions meet separately, one after the other, and then together in the Plenary Assembly. Since all recommendations and statements of the Science Council have to be ratified by a two-thirds majority of the plenum, there is pressure to consent. Also of importance: each commission has to agree to a recommendation by a two-thirds majority starting with the Scientific Commission. Under such conditions, the Science Council can neither be an agent of science nor of politics. Rather, it is an arena where the relevant actors from science and politics meet to achieve a consensual understanding about the perspective and institutional structures of science in Germany. The Science Council thus fulfils the important function of 'interest pooling' (Thompson 1967) between the federal government, Länder and science.

The organisation and mode of operation of the Science Council are linked to a second distinctive feature: The Science Council is not a body for *scientific policy advice*, but one for *policy advice by scientists*.

The main areas of advice by the Science Council are the institutional structures of the science system, i.e. funding programmes, funding instruments and forms of organisation of science. On these areas now exist a significant amount of theoretical knowledge and empirical findings by the sociology and history of science, higher education studies and, not least, management research focused on scientific institutions. All of these can be instrumental for practical decision-making within the science system. If, for instance, science studies show that the cognitive structures of some disciplines, for example, computer science, do not fit a certain funding model, for example, *big-science* research funding (Hohn 1998), this provides not only another explanation why the funding record of computer science is less than successful in Germany; it also presents practical evidence that should be considered by politicians when making organisational and funding decisions.

Compared to this, it has to be noted that science policy decisions – in contrast to decisions made in the context of economic, environment or social policy – are hardly ever based on scientific findings. This is definitely true for the Science Council, where it is particularly evident in the recruitment of academic members of the Council. These are appointed explicitly as outstanding representatives of important disciplines (medical sciences, physical and life sciences, technology, arts and social sciences), but not as *scientific* experts for the concerns of *science as an institution*. This fact requires explanation as it is relevant for the type of quality of the advice, too.

In the understanding of the agents involved, this peculiarity is explained by the special function of the Science Council. Accordingly, the expectations the Science Council is confronted with clearly transcend the expectations faced by a purely scientific expert commission, for example, for pensions, for climate change or foreign policy. While scientific expertise is expected only from the latter – even if they also consider the confinements of political implementation – the Science Council is in fact *expected* to take part in bargaining about possible solutions. This is especially true for questions such as the foundation of a new university, the establishment of new types of university degrees, or the polytechnics' right to award doctoral degrees. Consequently, issues of practical implementation become highly significant. According to current opinion, though, scientific knowledge as such cannot contribute much to the consensual settlement of these issues between scientists and politicians. More likely, it may be seen as an obstacle against achieving any consensus. The hidden assumption seems to be that it is, mainly, broad *institutional experience* of scientists and politicians that enables the Council to arrive at consensual recommendations. The physicist, chemist, or professor of philosophy in the Science Council may not have a special scientific expertise regarding the structure of the science system. However, often as long-standing members of a university or research institution, mostly in leading roles with abundant international experience, they can rely on exclusive practical experience and contacts. In the end, this also creates a symmetric relationship between scientists and politicians in the council, relying equally on their institutional experience as a basis for policy advice. Therefore, there is a cognitive basis to the 'equal footing' of scientists and politicians within the Science Council.

From the point of view of a sociologist of science, it is an interesting question whether this recourse to knowledge accumulated through practical institutional experience results in a functional equivalent to or even functional advantage over the use of scientific knowledge in the consultation process. I cannot treat this question in general. What I will do is to describe, in more detail, what constitutes the quality of this type of integrative policy advice drawing less on scientific expertise but mainly on broad institutional experience, and how the Science Council generates and assures this quality.

2   What is good science policy advice?

There is a number of criteria aimed at consultation procedures and processes that are frequently cited as standards for *good scientific policy advice*. These include, for instance, independence, transparency, participation, and disclosure of uncertainties as attributes of the consultation process (Berlin-Brandenburgische Akademie der Wissenschaften 2006). The Science Council itself recommended these criteria as standards for good scientific policy advice on several occasions in the past.[2] But where the quality of an advice of the Science Council itself is at stake, it would be justified only to a very limited extent to expect that the results of the consultations reflect up-to-date scientific knowledge. Its specific concentration on *institutional* questions of the science system and the *hybrid structure* of its consultations lead, as mentioned above, to a marginalisation of scientific knowledge as a basis for its work. Scientific expertise may be called upon in a targeted way, for instance when the Science Council employs working groups and recruits external experts to evaluate the research performance of an institute or to assess innovations in certain fields of research. These types of judgements can be provided reliably only by scientific experts. But the core product, i.e. the *science policy recommendations*, remains untouched by this part of the process and is still based, primarily, on the Council members' practical experience. Consequently, the quality of the recommendations depends predominantly on the question whether the ways in which the Science Council organises the exchange of practical experience and knowledge generates a sufficient volume of new ideas for initiatives that are desirable and, at the same time, realistic. This requirement to come up with new ideas promising implementation in the medium term brings me to the point where I differentiate between three main quality indicators for the consultation products of the Science Council: intersubjective plausibility, political connectivity and practicability.

Intersubjective plausibility

Intersubjective plausibility means that the proposals seriously discussed in the Science Council should be relatively new but, at the same time, *pre-discussed* within the science system to the extent that the actors in science and politics can see some plausibility in these proposals. *Revolutionary* suggestions by individuals, such as cutting by half the resources of the Deutsche Forschungsgemeinschaft, the major funding organisation for universities in Germany, and to use the money *gained* by this measure to establish junior professorships at some universities (see Münch 2007: 403, who in this way intends to break up *monopoly-style structures* in the

---

[2] For example, when the Science Council gave recommendations on economic research at universities and the role of scientific policy advice in this field. See Wissenschaftsrat 2002.

German science system), have little chance to be even discussed in the Science Council. Even the fact that the Science Council could recently recommend the 'Teaching Professorship' as an independent career path at German universities (Wissenschaftsrat 2007a) is essentially connected to the fact that the importance and quality of teaching at universities has been massively pushed on the general agenda in recent years. Thus, in a sense, the ground was already prepared for this recommendation, which would not have had a chance to be adopted by the Science Council only ten years ago. The recommendation could only be released because various scientists within the Science Council can now envisage an improvement of the situation through introducing teaching professorships, based on their specific knowledge about the institutions. In any case, this plausibility test is more decisive than any possible congruency of the recommendations with the latest empirical studies on higher education policy.

Political connectivity

The particular construction of the Science Council as an advisory body integrating science and politics leads to another indicator of quality: The recommendations must offer a high degree of *political connectivity*. In this sense, the good quality of recommendations from the perspective of the scientific members of the council may be necessary as a condition, but not sufficient. The recommendations must also be built on the existing science policy agenda, providing a possible solution from the perspective of politics, and, most importantly, taking into account the present room for manoeuvre available to politicians. Only then will the politicians be prepared to vote for these recommendations in the Plenary Assembly. The introduction of tuition fees, for example, was considered a bridge too far by most politicians even in the early 1990s, with the result that a recommendation prepared by several scientific members of the Science Council did not materialise in the end. Since then, however, the political climate has changed significantly, so that the Science Council does not have to take a position on this question anymore.

Practicability

Finally, the third quality criterion is the *practicability* of the recommendations, which is, to an extent, already determined by their intersubjective plausibility and political connectivity. Practicability means that the recommendations of the Science Council have to work, in principle, in a real world with all its political, legal or financial possibilities and constraints. In contrast to many other advisory bodies, scientists and politicians are both users of the recommendations of the Science Council. Therefore, both sides are driven by a strong interest to not oblige themselves to implement unrealistic proposals. This is an essential aspect at all stages of the consultation process.

Procedures play a prominent role when it comes to the question how the Science Council can assure a high degree of intersubjective plausibility, political connectivity and practicability and thus maintain the fundamentals of the quality of their work. Procedures are regulated and, to a certain degree, standardised social processes. They open up certain roles and options for action to the individuals involved and, usually, lead to a decision. In this function they set and bind the expectations of the participants and generate, post festum, a high degree of legitimacy of the result (Luhmann [1969] 1983). This will be illustrated by the following example of an increasingly important task of the Science Council: institutional evaluation.

3   Quality assurance through procedures – the example of institutional evaluation

Institutional evaluations have developed an increasing importance for science policy over the past twenty years. They have also become one of the core tasks of the Science Council. At many occasions the Science Council was asked by the federal government and Länder governments to evaluate individual research facilities or entire fields of research organisations. The so-called 'system evaluation' of the Leibniz-Gemeinschaft, including all of their eighty individual institutes (1995–2000) (Wissenschaftsrat 2001a), and the system evaluation of the Helmholtz-Gemeinschaft Deutscher Forschungszentren (2001) (Wissenschaftsrat 2001b) are prominent examples of such statements. Still, how does the Science Council assure the quality of its own evaluations and science policy statements? The answer is: by rules and procedures that are binding for all who are actively involved. The following procedural elements have emerged as particularly important: (a) evaluation criteria; (b) selection of experts; (c) participation of involved parties; and (d) multi-level procedure and monitoring of the implementation of recommendations.

Evaluation criteria

The evaluation criteria applied by the Science Council are essentially guided by the criteria commonly used for science evaluations, such as the originality of the research programme, publications (preferably in peer-reviewed journals), patents, number of doctorates, etc. Beyond that, the Science Council adjusts its evaluation criteria according to the specific evaluation subject or evaluation assignment. For the evaluation of government research labs, for example, a catalogue of criteria was developed that takes into account not only the usual criteria of science evaluations, but also, prominently, criteria of knowledge transfer (Wissenschaftsrat 2007b). This is intended to do justice to the complex mission of such research establishments.

Recruitment of experts

Naturally, the recruitment of the experts is of great importance in science evaluation procedures. In its recruitment of experts, the Science Council ensures that candidates are proven experts in their respective field, independent and unbiased, and that the panel as a whole reflects the spectrum of the tasks undertaken by the establishment being evaluated. Both in its committees, which control the evaluation procedures, and in the individual evaluation groups installed by them, it is ensured that the members represent a broad spectrum of backgrounds, meaning: not only university scientists, but also scientists from non-university research facilities, research intensive industries, and representatives of relevant professional organisations, associations, etc. are selected. In addition, wherever this is possible and appropriate, scientists from abroad or representatives from corresponding reference institutions in other countries should take part in the evaluations. Furthermore, the selection of experts by the Science Committee is subject to strict rules concerning conflicts of interest. Candidates who have, or had in the last five years, close connections to the institution to be evaluated, for example, as a member of its scientific advisory council, as an important partner in a scientific collaboration, as a project contractor or applicant for a leading position, are not considered for selection as referees. In almost every evaluation, especially if there is only a small circle of prospective specialist referees available, questions of referees' conflicts of interest are decided strictly according to an unassailable procedure.

Participation of involved parties

In the case of evaluations of national research establishments, there are mainly two groups involved: the institutions themselves and the governmental departments that finance them. The procedural rules of the Science Council provide for participation of the involved parties at all stages of the process:

- In the selection of experts, the institutions and departments can comment on the list of experts and point to missing or unsuitable competence profiles of referees, as well as to potential conflicts of interest. These notes are always followed up in consultation with the chair of the evaluation panel. As a result, professional re-appointments among the referee groups are the rule rather than the exception.
- For visits of the evaluation groups to the respective institute (*inspections*), the procedure expressly demands that the leadership of the institute, the relevant department and the staff of the visited institution are heard. The departments responsible are also given guest status in the evaluation group, which allows them to participate at all stages of the evaluation – except for internal closed sessions of the referees.
- Once the evaluation report has been set up, the departments, which are asked to consult appropriately with the research establishments involved, are given the opportunity to comment on the evaluation report. These comments are heard by the relevant committee of the Science Council, which discusses the comments and considers them for their further deliberations.
- For the adoption of the statement in the Science Council, the interests of the relevant departments are represented by the Ministry for Education and Research acting as their advocate and representing the federal government in the Council.

Multi-level procedure

Another central element of quality assurance in evaluations is the multi-level procedure practised by the Science Council (see Figure 9.2). At its core, multi-level procedure means that there is, on the one hand, a clear procedural separation between expert scientific judgements about research establishments and the resulting science policy recommendations on the other. This separation is based on the awareness that the assessment of science and research must be a matter for independent peers alone and must not be subject to political negotiation processes. Consequently, an evaluation report drawn up and passed by peers remains unchangeable throughout the subsequent levels of the procedure, up to the discussion in the plenary assembly of the Science Council. This also provides protection for the expert referees, so that they can be confident that their expert advice, even if it is seen as politically inconvenient, will not be watered down or distorted. On the other hand, the multi-level procedure takes account of the fact that a specific, expert

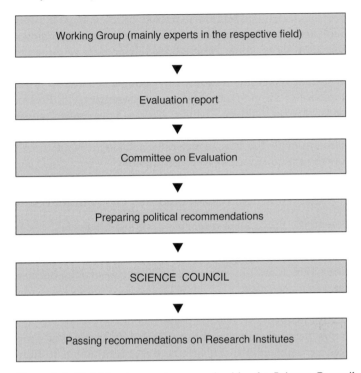

Figure 9.2 Multi-level procedure practiced by the Science Council

scientific evaluation does not automatically suggest certain conclusions. The finding, for example, that the staff members of a scientific establishment have not published sufficient papers in recognised journals, does not lead directly to certain science policy conclusions. Depending on other conditions, the conclusion may be a recommendation to close the research establishment because of its lack of performance. There could also be a recommendation to have the establishment carry on if, for instance, its scientific potential is manifest, the field of research involved is of high national importance, and the low output of publications is mainly the result of understaffing. Such conclusions are always drawn on comparable cases, too. As described at the beginning, the science-policy recommendations on individual research establishments or research organisations have to be passed by a two-thirds majority in the plenary assembly of the Science Council. Here, my initial observation applies: that this decision on a science-policy level is mainly based on the institutional experience of the Science Council members and not on scientific expertise.

Once the statement has been passed by the plenary assembly, the Science Council monitors the implementation of its recommendations. Usually after three years, research establishments or departments are asked whether and how the recommendations were implemented. For major system recommendations, for example, on the 'role and future development of the governmental research agencies with R&D activities' (Wissenschaftsrat 2007c), which address the entire governmental research programme, it holds information events for agencies and departments with the aim to promote a dialogue with the addressees on how to implement the recommendations.

4   Uncertainties, typical conflicts and conflict resolution

Despite all the procedures of quality assurance, especially the participation of the addressees (mainly federal government and the Länder government) in the development of statements, the recommendations of the Science Council are not only discussed controversially but are actually attacked in some cases.

However, as far as the purely scientific expertise in the evaluation process (judgement on research performance) is concerned, such attacks are rather rare. The conceivable grievances in such cases – that certain referees were unsuitable; the specific mission of the institution in question was not taken into account sufficiently; or the procedure had not allowed the institution to present its strengths – are largely anticipated by the procedure described above.

The situation is more difficult with the actual science-policy conclusions and recommendations, especially if a statement impacts on an area that is politically charged at the time. If, for example, the Science Council concludes that an establishment does not operate according to the state of the art in safety-relevant areas, as it did in 2006, and, at the same time, the issue attracts considerable political importance, there are always efforts to discredit the Council and its advice. In the case I refer to, for instance, it came to press briefings by the department and the publication of a counter report. Events of this kind are simply unavoidable and form part of a pluralistic structure of the advisory process.

In other cases, where dissent arises with addressees or clients of evaluations, the conflict is resolved within the Science Council, again through procedures, for example, by setting up a new working group with a modified or extended remit. This opens up a meta-level with the purpose to create a new, consensual frame of interpretation for a controversial statement. One such example was the evaluation by the Science

Council of the large economic research institutes in Germany between 1995 and 2000.[3] The expert commission of the Science Council came to the conclusion that the scientific foundation of some of those institutes was not satisfactory to provide good science policy advice. In one case, the Science Council even argued for discontinuing joint federal and Länder financing of the institute as a deserving research establishment. This was met with fierce resistance from the responsible government body, the Federal Ministry of Economics and Technology, which criticised the strong reference to scientific foundations (in contrast to the application-oriented mission of the institute) in the Science Council's evaluation. In the same context, the department also criticised that the overall situation of the economic sciences in Germany were not sufficiently taken into account. The politicians expressed their concern about the strong theoretical bias of the economic sciences at the universities and called for a stronger empirical basis and a stronger orientation to praxis. The negotiations in the Science Council between the Science Commission and the Administrative Commission (in the latter especially with the representatives of the Ministry of Economics and Technology) resulted in a *General Aspects* section drawn up in cooperation with the Ministry, preceding the individual statements in the report (Wissenschaftsrat 1998: 29–5I). That preamble emphasised, among other points, the need for a broad study, including international comparisons, on the state of empirical economic research at German universities, so that the critique of the economic research institutes could be seen from a new perspective and was somehow weakened.

These examples show that the Science Council, as a consensual body between politics and science, is in a way constitutionally equipped to resolve conflicts. Since politics and science act together at all stages of the consultation process within the Science Council, any possible conflicts can either only be resolved internally and cooperatively, or not at all. Therefore, the Science Council must decide even before accepting a subject whether it is appropriate for a consensual consultation process. Highly controversal issues such as the question of the future use of nuclear energy in Germany are not suitable for deliberation by the Science Council.

Lessons learned

The Science Council represents a special case: as a policy advisory body in which scientists participate, it nevertheless differs from a body

---

[3] For the 'whole story' including recent developments, see Gert G. Wagner, Chapter 11.

of *scientific* policy advice like many other expert bodies or advisory councils associated with the executive branch of government. In contrast to those well-known scientific advisory bodies serving the politicians, the *core product* of the Science Council is not scientific knowledge. For its advice the Science Council does not rely on scientific knowledge, neither of the hard kind nor of the soft variety. Its advice is also not based on expertise in the sense that it would derive its recommendations from somehow processed scientific knowledge (Weingart 2006: 7). Rather, the Science Council brings together the *institutional experience* of scientists and politicians, contributing to proposals as realistic and viable as possible for the further development of the institutional structures of the science system. This knowledge accumulated through experience is socially robust in the sense that it creates an entanglement between the diverse experiences, interests and expectations of scientists and politicians and, from that, develops shared perspectives on the promotion and organisation of the sciences. The legitimacy for the Science Council recommendations can not be found in scientific knowledge as such,[4] but in the social reputation of the individuals assembled in the Council. As far as the scientists are concerned, this reputation is, of course, crucially related to the scientific achievements of the individual Council members. Still, these scientific achievements do not predestine any privileged access to issues of science policy. To make it quite clear: with all his or her proven scientific excellence, a Nobel Prize-winning physicist does not have any automatic advantage when it comes to questions on how to improve the teaching at universities.

Now, what are the conclusions for the field of (scientific) policy advice?

1. One has to be very careful to not overlook any manifest or hidden functions of the advisory body in question, apart from its task to provide (scientific) policy advice. In the case of the Science Council, it is its function to *mediate* between the political actors from the federal government and the Länder and, most importantly, between politics and science, what primarily determines the expectations and quality standards. In this way we can also understand why knowledge gained from institutional experience and institutional contacts can be an essential resource for an advisory body. Scientific knowledge, on the

---

[4] This even applies to evaluations in which the expert assessment of the performance of an institution is based on sound, scientific findings, whereas the science policy recommendations can in no way be scientifically derived from these findings.

other hand, as provided, for example, by sociology of science, could be a considerable irritation in the mediation process and makes it more difficult to achieve the desired consensus between politics and science.

2. The problems with and the qualities of this kind of negotiated advice are fundamentally different from those encountered in scientific policy advice. The predominant quality criterion for this negotiated advice is that its recommendations actually work (or can work). I suspect that almost all of the policy advice bodies whose recommendations are not science-based achieve the quality of their advice in two ways: First, by internal consultation procedures, which generate a maximum of rationality and legitimacy through consensual determination of the aims and criteria of the advice process, inclusion of experts, participation of the parties involved, and through multi-level (iterative) consultation processes; and second, by successful practical implementation. In their application, the recommendations of the Science Council are nothing more than social techniques of the science system. What counts is that they actually work. The quality of the Science Council's recommendations lies in the fact that it can be documented that they work (or, for new recommendations, that it is conceivable that they will work).

3. Apart from that, there remains the unexplained fact that science policy has not experienced the radical process of scientification (Weingart 2001: 127–70) seen in other fields of policy. The advisory institutions of science policy, in particular, hardly ever explicitly recur to the scientific knowledge about science. If the causes for this situation cannot be found primarily on the supply side (scarcity of applicable knowledge), one has to look for other reasons for the lack of reception. In any case, scientifically interesting is that science as a social system did avoid the scientification of its decisions. It is unclear whether a determined and successful effort of social closure (Bourdieu) of the actors in the science system is behind this, or rather some deeply engrained scepticism of the scientists with regard to the possibility that science as a social system could be controlled and organised on a scientific basis. However, there remains the irritating observation that successful advice for an important subsystem of modern societies is perfectly possible without any recourse to scientific knowledge.

Acknowledgements

I would like to thank Uta Bielfeldt, Wedig von Heyden, Magnus Rüde and Uwe Schimank for helpful comments.

REFERENCES

Bartz, Olaf 2007. *Der Wissenschaftsrat, Entwicklungslinien der Wissenschaftspolitik in der Bundesrepublik Deutschland 1957–2007*, Stuttgart: Franz Steiner Verlag.

Berlin-Brandenburgische Akademie der Wissenschaften 2006. *Standards and 'Best Practice' of Scientific Policy Advice (Akademie-Debatten)*, Berlin.

Braun, Dietmar 1997. *Die politische Steuerung der Wissenschaft. Ein Beitrag zum 'kooperativen Staat', Schriften aus dem MPI für Gesellschaftsforschung Bd. 28*, Frankfurt am Main, New York: Campus.

Hohn, Hans-Willy 1998. *Kognitive Strukturen und Steuerungsprobleme der Forschung. Kernphysik und Informatik im Vergleich*, Frankfurt am Main, New York: Campus.

Luhmann, Niklas [1969] 1983. *Legitimation durch Verfahren*, Darmstadt/ Neuwied: Luchterhand.

Münch, Richard 2007. *Die akademische Elite. Zur Sozialen Konstruktion wissenschaftlicher Exzellenz*, Frankfurt am Main: Suhrkamp.

Stichweh, Rudolf 1994. 'Differenzierung von Wissenschaft und Politik: Wissenschaftspolitik im 19. und 20. Jahrhundert', in Rudolf Stichweh (ed.), *Wissenschaft, Universität, Professionen*, Frankfurt am Main: Suhrkamp, pp. 156–74.

Stucke, Andreas 2002. 'The role of "councils" in research and technology policy: The case of the German Wissenschaftsrat', *Plattform Forschungs- und Technologieevaluierung* 16: 2–5.

Thompson, James D. 1967. *Organisations in Action*, New York: MacGraw-Hill.

Weingart, Peter 2001. *Die Stunde der Wahrheit? Zum Verhältnis der Wissenschaft zu Politik, Wirtschaft und Medien in der Wissensgesellschaft*, Weilerswist: Velbrück.

Weingart, Peter 2006. 'Erst denken, dann handeln? Politikberatung aus der Perspektive der Wissens(chafts)soziologie', Svenja Falk *et al.* (eds.), *Handbuch Politikberatung*, Wiesbaden: Verlag für Sozialwissenschaften, pp. 35–44.

Wissenschaftsrat 1998. *Stellungnahme zu den Instituten der Blauen Liste. Wirtschaftsforschungsinstitute in den alten Ländern, Band III (see Report on the West German Economic Research Institutes on the Blue List – General Aspects*, pp. 29–51), Cologne.

Wissenschaftsrat 2001a. *Systemevaluation der Blauen Liste – Stellungnahme des Wissenschaftsrates zum Abschluß der Bewertung der Einrichtungen der Blauen Liste*, Band XII, Cologne.

Wissenschaftsrat 2001b. *Statement of the German Science Council on the Hermann von Helmholtz Association of German Research Centres* (Executive summary), Cologne.

Wissenschaftsrat 2002. *Empfehlungen zur Stärkung wirtschaftswissenschaftlicher Forschung an den Hochschulen* (Drs. 5455–02), Saarbrücken.

Wissenschaftsrat 2007a. *Empfehlungen zu einer lehrorientierten Reform der Personalstruktur an Hochschulen*, Cologne.

Wissenschaftsrat 2007b. *Kriterien des Ausschusses Ressortforschung für die Begutachtung von Bundeseinrichtungen mit FuE-Aufgaben* (Drs. 7693–07), Cologne.

Wissenschaftsrat 2007c. *Empfehlungen zur Rolle und künftigen Entwicklung der Bundeseinrichtungen mit FuE-Aufgaben* (Executive Summary in English see pp. 6–15), Cologne.

Part IV

Research-based advisory organisations

10   The industrial organisation of economic policy preparation in the Netherlands

Frank A. G. den Butter

1   Introduction

The ultimate aim of (economic) policy is to enhance social welfare. In an ideal world with perfect competition, no externalities and transaction costs, and with a perfect distribution of property rights, the optimal path of social welfare is reached automatically when all individuals maximise their own welfare. There is no need for coordination by the government since the market mechanism will do the job. However, the real world is not ideal. Various externalities, the provision of public goods and problems of distribution require government intervention. The discipline of public economics provides the theoretical foundation and practical solutions as to how to deal with problems of market failure and redistribution of income and wealth. Policy prescriptions on the most efficient ways for governments to intervene and solve the coordination problem at the macro level are widely discussed in the literature. Moreover, the problems of government failure, and of politicians and civil servants seeking to serve their own interests instead of the public interest of enhancing social welfare, are also subject of much academic debate.

However, the (economic) literature has paid far less attention to the way the process of policy preparation is organised. In democratic societies, the final step for policy measures to be implemented is that they are legitimised according to the existent democratic rules. However, before policy measures obtain parliamentary approval, a long and often winding road has to be followed to move from the first ideas about the policy measures to their final formulation. To some extent, this organisation of the process of policy preparation is institutionalised in various procedures and implicit or explicit rules. There is an analogy here with the organisation of production processes and coordination procedures in industry, which is described by the economic discipline of industrial organisation. Therefore, when considering the institutional setup of the design and shaping of policy measures, we may speak of *the industrial*

177

organisation of policy preparation. Apart from getting parliamentary approval for policy measures, it is essential that these measures obtain public support. Although parliamentary consent and public support are required in all democratic societies, there appear to be remarkable differences in the institutional setup of the policy preparation in these countries. Obviously there is no one best *model* to arrive at policy measures which enhance welfare.

This chapter considers the organisation of economic policy preparation in the Netherlands. Here, the model is often referred to as the *polder model* because the social dialogue plays a prominent role in obtaining public support for the policy measures. A background to this way of organising public consent may be that in the Dutch polders all inhabitants had to agree about the water management and division of costs. That is because they were all involved in the implementation of the measures.

The focus of this chapter is on the role of scientific knowledge and of quality control in the process of policy preparation. Formally there is a one-way direction in the use of scientific knowledge by policymakers, but in practice much interaction takes place (see, for example, Den Butter and Morgan 2000). In the Netherlands, part of this interaction is formalised in the institutional setup of policy preparation, which may contribute to the quality of the policy measures, but, as we will see, may also lead to a deadlock of ideas about beneficial policies. In such cases, there should be enough room for outsiders to start a dispute on these leading opinions of academics and policymakers. Thus, the main question for the industrial organisation of economic policy preparation is to find a good balance between, on the one hand, fixed procedures which guarantee a fruitful exchange of ideas between scientists, policymakers and representatives of interest groups, and, on the other hand, a great degree of flexibility in order to avoid deadlocks and the premature exclusion of opinions coming from outside the mainstream.

The contents of the remainder of the chapter are as follows. The next section gives an overview of the history of economic policy preparation in the Netherlands with special attention to the important role of data collection at the level of the state. Section 3 discusses the present institutional setup of policy preparation in the Dutch polder model, which has been greatly inspired by the practical elaboration of Tinbergen's theory on economic policy. The working of the interaction between empirical analysis and policymaking is illustrated in Section 4 by the unique procedure in the Netherlands in which the CPB Netherlands Bureau for Economic Policy Analysis estimates the effects of the election programmes of the major political parties (see Graafland and Ros 2003).

Section 5 assesses the standards and mechanisms of quality control in this institutional setup of policy preparation in the Netherlands. It considers criteria for quality and provides examples of the debate and controversy with respect to policy measures. In order to illustrate how the industrial organisation of policy preparation can differ between countries, the organisation in France is compared with that in the Netherlands in Section 6. Section 7 is the conclusion.

2   Early history of economic policy preparation in the Netherlands

Today empirical analysis and measurement play an essential role in the debate on policy measures in the Netherlands. It is especially this part of economic science which dominates the policy discussions. However, in the nineteenth century, Dutch science had not yet developed a strong academic orientation towards actual measurement and experience. This had to do with the Protestant background of the Dutch government where measurement and divine authority had a complicated relationship. Thus, natural philosophy and empiricism had to become acceptable within the framework of essentially religious means and goals. First and foremost, measurement was intended to develop knowledge about the greatness of God. This orientation did not provide a very fertile ground for the development of an experimental, empirical and quantitative approach. This disinterest in actual measurement disappeared only slowly and partially between 1750 and 1850 (see Klep and Stamhuis 2002; Den Butter 2004).

It was mainly through the private initiatives of individual scientists and practitioners, and not so much of the government, that this change in attitude was brought about.

Kluit and Vissering

An early protagonist of actual measurement in the Netherlands was Adriaan Kluit (1735–1807). He was the first Dutch professor to teach statistics under that name. One of the reasons that Kluit began to deliver lectures in statistics was his winning a prize contest by the de Hollandsche Maatschappij der Wetenschappen (Dutch Society of Sciences) at Haarlem, a learned society founded in 1752, which, in those days, tried to promote scientific research by posing practical questions. This learned society still exists and was granted the label *Royal* by the Queen when it celebrated its 250th anniversary in 2002. The question to which Kluit reacted was 'What is the overall situation, both in general and especially with respect to the economy in our fatherland, and what are the reasons why our country lags so far behind as compared to our neighbours?' So it was in fact a quest for economic data which inspired Kluit to get involved in statistics. Kluit did not distinguish between political economy and statistics, and in his specification the state was the centre of attention. So in his work we observe the beginning of the connection between the workings of political economy (in Dutch: staatkunde or staathuishoudkunde) and statistics. In this respect it is noteworthy that in Germany political economy or economic political science was called statistica or statistik. This connection can also be traced back to the Italian word statista or statesman, which has given the discipline of statistics its name.

Although he was a lawyer by education, Simon Vissering (1818–88) can be regarded as one of the main protagonists of statistical quantification of the state of the economy at the macro level in the Netherlands. He was one of the leaders of the Statistical Movement, a group of lawyers who dedicated themselves to the advancement of statistics, especially during the period in which the government did not take its statistical task very seriously. Although Vissering was more quantitatively oriented than his predecessors in political economy, his ideas about the kind of data needed for the description of the national economy are still rather naive as compared to the data nowadays used to analyse the economy. In the course of the nineteenth century, quantification came to play a more important role, but it was nevertheless Vissering's opinion that qualitative information was needed to make the statistical description of a state complete (see Klep and Stamhuis 2002).

Descriptive versus mathematical statistics

It is interesting to note that in the development of measuring the state of the economy (and society) in the nineteenth century, not much reference seems to be made to the work of early *quantitative* economists such as Petty and King in the UK, or Keuchenius and Metelerkamp in the Netherlands, who are nowadays considered pioneers in national accounting (see Den Bakker 1993; Bos 2003). Moreover, there was still a large gap between descriptive and mathematical statistics. In the latter discipline the Belgian statistician Lambert Adolphe Jaques Quetelet (1796–1874) was one of the protoganists. In 1834, Quetelet was one of the founders of the London Statistical Society, nowadays the Royal Statistical Society. Morgan (1990) describes how, in the history of statistics, Quetelet's statistical characterisation of human behaviour proved to be of great importance. He noted that individuals behave in an unpredictable way, but that taken together these apparently disorganised individuals obey the law of errors in deviating from the ideal *average man*. Obviously, this is one of the basic notions in econometric methodology, used in the evaluation of economic policy measures. So Quetelet can be seen as an initial bridge-builder between the mathematically oriented statistical approach and the descriptive and qualitative-quantitative approach.

However, Quetelet's ideas did not reach Vissering and his colleagues. It was only after the 1930s that, with Tinbergen as the great inspirer and teacher, a full integration of both lines of thought in statistics took place in the Netherlands. It is remarkable that, whereas these two lines in statistics had been separated for such a long time, from then on the Netherlands assumed the strong position in econometrics and applied economics that it holds until today, and that is at the heart of the institutional setup of the polder model.

Statistics as a public good

Vissering and his colleagues have played a major role in promoting the idea that the government should regard statistical data collection as a public good and therefore should assume responsibility for the collection of these data. However, in the second half of the nineteenth century, the government was very reluctant to take up this responsibility. Therefore, Vissering took the initiative in compiling and publishing general statistics for the Netherlands in 1866. However, this large project was never finished (see Stamhuis 1989, 2002). In 1884, when the Dutch government was still not willing to collect statistical data in the public domain, a Statistical Institute was established by these private persons. At last, in 1892, after inquiries in the Second Chamber of the Parliament by, amongst others, the socialist member of parliament, F.J. Domela Nieuwenhuis, the Centrale Commissie voor de Statistiek (Central Committee for Statistics) was established. Finally, in 1899, the Central Bureau of Statistics (CBS) was founded, which from then on has collected independent and undisputed data for public use in the Netherlands. The Central Committee for Statistics still exists and has a role as supervisory board for the Central Bureau of Statistics. Its responsibilities were even extended by decision of the Parliament in 2003. In fact, the lobby to have the government collect statistical data at the level of the state through the Society of Statistics, which was founded in 1849, can be regarded mainly as an association of economists (see Mooij 1994). After 1892, when the lobby of the society for data collection by the government had finally been successful, the main focus of the society turned to economics. Therefore, in 1892, its name was changed to the Society for Political Economy and Statistics. Yet, it was more than half a century later, namely in 1950, that the focus of the society became clearly reflected in its name which now was called the Netherlands Economic Association. Finally, in 1987, the Queen honoured the society by granting it the label *Royal*. So since 1987 we have the Royal Netherlands Economic Association, which is probably the oldest association of political economists in the world.

Micro- versus macrodata

National measurement of data and the way indicators from these measurements are used in policy practice relate to the debate in the field of statistics, whether to collect data at the micro- or macro-level, and consequently to the problem of aggregating individual data when these data are used to analyse the state of the nation as a whole. It seems that these problems only began to be systematically dealt with in the construction of modern national data measurement by Stone and Meade as protagonists in the late 1930s. In this respect Van den Bogaard (1999: Ch. 5) gives an interesting description of the long discussions between Tinbergen and the CBS on transforming individual data from budget surveys to national data on consumer behaviour which could be used in consumption functions of the Keynesian macro models of those days. These consumption functions describe how aggregate consumption is explained by various macro-economic variables. Nowadays the construction and definition of data on aggregate consumption are well established and undisputed within the context of National Accounts. However, in the 1930s, consumption was still something related to individual income, social class and social role in society. It was indeed only in the early 1950s that data collection and statistical methodology for analysing data at the macro-level were really integrated. This is closely related to the development of National Accounting (see, for example, Den Butter 2007).

3   The polder model and the Tinbergen legacy

The present institutional setup of policy preparation in the Netherlands can, in a way, be seen as an off-shoot of Tinbergen's theory of economic policy, where scientific insights on how instruments may effect policy goals are separated from political preferences on trade-off between these policy goals (see Tinbergen 1952, 1956).

These ideas were, of course, very much inspired by the political and societal landscape in the Netherlands in the period between World Wars I and II (see also Van Zanden, 2002, for a broad historic perspective). In the years just after World War II, when Tinbergen designed his theory of economic policy and was active in the institutional setup of policy preparation in the Netherlands, the Dutch society was still very much *pillarised*. The four main pillars were the liberals, the Catholics, the Protestants and the socialists. Each of them were represented by one or more political parties with implicit preferences on policy goals in their own, so to say, social welfare function. As they all are minority parties, there has always been a need for the formation of a coalition government. The chairmen of the political parties or pillars did realise that it is impossible to meet all of their own party's policy goals in such a coalition government. Although the pillarised society has changed very much since then and there has been a steady *depillarisation*, all parties are still minority parties, even more so than before, so that the need for a compromise agreement for the coalition government has remained.

As will be elaborated below, the analysis of the Dutch Central Planning Bureau has from its founding played an important role in the design of policy preparation in the Netherlands. Nowadays the bureau calls itself CPB Netherlands Bureau for Economic Policy Analysis, because there is no true *planning* involved in the activities of the bureau. More specifically, the analysis is an important input for the negotiations and social dialogue on policy issues in what has become known as the Dutch polder model.

In its first few years, there was a fierce internal discussion in the CPB about the way the bureau should give shape to its advice and perform its task in policy preparation (see Van den Bogaard 1999). On the one side was Van Cleeff, who had the view that the CPB should follow a normative approach, while, on the other side, Tinbergen supported the idea of disentangling the positive and normative elements of the analyses. Crucial in this controversy was in which way economic policy advice would be the most successful in the pillarised economy. Van Cleeff tried to develop an all-embracing normative theory which would integrate the ideas of the different pillars. As in industry, that would lead to a formal policy *plan* which could be implemented by the government in a coordinated effort of all citizens. On the other hand, Tinbergen wanted to develop a method that would provide the most objective description of reality. The differences between the pillars would then be minimised to their different normative proportions. In other words, he wanted to make a clear distinction between the workings of the economy (model) and the policy goals (welfare functions), and then 'try to agree on the first and compromise on the second issue'. Tinbergen won this battle. Since then, economic policy preparation in the Netherlands is organised in three autonomous parts: (i) data, (ii) model and (iii) norms. As discussed in the previous section, the data and statistics are collected by the Central Bureau of Statistics (CBS) in an independent and (hopefully) undisputed manner. The CPB tries to reach, from a scientific perspective, *consensus* about the workings of the economy as described by its empirical models. The balancing of different points of view is done by the government in dialogue with unions, employer organisations and other associations of organised interest. This method of splitting data, analysis and politics has up to now always been a prominent feature in creating agreement on, and support for policy measures in the Dutch society where all belong to a cultural minority or minority party. Yet, as political preferences of all of these parties are different, such agreement will always have the character of a *compromise*.

Many organisations and stakeholders are involved in this institutional setup of the social dialogue in the Netherlands. Below we discuss the influence and working of two institutions more thoroughly. First, the role and position of the CPB is elaborated on how it tries to come to a consensus view on economic developments and the effects of policy measures. The second institution is the Social Economic Council (SER) that plays (together with the Foundation of Labour) the central role in negotiations between the various stakeholders in coming to compromise agreement on matters of economic and social policy (see for a more elaborate survey: Den Butter and Mosch 2003). This is the arena where interaction between scientific knowledge and the policy dispute takes place. Finally, some other institutions are discussed that play an even broader role in policymaking in the Netherlands.

Netherlands Bureau for Economic Policy Analysis (CPB)

The Central Planning Bureau (CPB) started in 1945 but obtained a formal status by law only in 1947. In spite of the fact that the CPB is formally part of the Ministry of Economic Affairs, it fulfils its advisory task independently from government interference. This status of independence is recognised by all parties and stakeholders in the policymaking process, which provides the analyses of the CPB with high reputation and esteem. The two major periodic publications of the CPB are the Central Economic Plan (CEP) and the Macroeconomic Outlook (MEV). The CEP is published each year in springtime and contains a survey and analysis of economic developments in the Netherlands and abroad. It contains economic forecasts for the current and for the following year. The MEV is published together with the government budget in September each year. The forecasts of the economy in the next year are formal in the sense that the government budget has to be based on these data. Moreover, the MEV also gives revised projections for the current year. In fact, nowadays the CPB has two major tasks. The first is the task of national auditor: this implies economic forecasting and assessment of the effects of policy measures for the government and for other groups involved in the policymaking process, such as the social partners. The second task consists of the CPB conducting, in a more general sense, applied economic research (see Don 1996). Nowadays the following have gained in importance: extensive scenario analyses and cost benefit analyses are conducted with respect to various aspects of the Dutch economy. There is also a shift towards micro-economic research and evaluation studies. Typical for the institutional setup of Dutch policymaking are the numerous formal and informal contacts between the staff of the CPB and the economists in ministries, researchers in academia and the staff of the social partners. On the one hand, they provide relevant information to the CPB, but, on the other hand, they will, if needed, be critical of the work of the CPB.

Since Tinbergen (1936) built the first econometric policy model, it is understandable that model-based policy analysis has, from the beginning, constituted an important part of the work of the CPB. The CPB's *model* early on acquired high status in academic circles and has come to be regarded in Dutch society as an objective piece of economic science (Den Butter and Morgan 1998). The analyses of the CPB are widely used as input for social economic policy discussions, for example, in the Social Economic Council (see below). The next section elaborates a typical example of the role of the CPB in using their model-based analysis for policy purposes, namely the calculation of the effects of the policy proposals in the election programmes of the political parties on economic growth, employment, income distribution and so on.

Seemingly, it is almost a realisation of Tinbergen's dream to separate the knowledge on the working of the economy, which is contained in the models used by the CPB, and the normative preferences on trade-offs between policy goals, which will differ for each political party.

Foundation of Labour and Social Economic Council

It is typical for the institutional setup of the social dialogue in the Netherlands (i.e. the polder model) that the social partners are at the heart of the consultation structure for economic and social policy. The Foundation of Labour (STAR) is the formal platform where employees and employers meet each other on a structural basis. It was founded in 1945 as a private organisation and acts as a bilateral discussion forum in the field of labour standards for unions and employer associations. The seats are equally divided between the two, and each side delivers one of the two chairmen. The results of the discussions are stated in so-called *central agreements*. This occurs about once in two or three years.

Yet, the major forum for political discussions is the Social Economic Council (SER). The SER is the main policy advisory board for the government regarding social economic issues. Its constellation is tripartite. Labour unions, employer associations and *independent members* each possess one-third of the seats. The independent members consist of professors in economics or law, politicians, the president of the Dutch Central Bank and the director of the CPB. They are appointed by the Crown. It is through these independent members that the policy discussions within the SER benefit from the insights of scientific research. In this way, also the members from the trade unions and from the employers' organisations are bound to be professionals who are knowledgeable of the scientific framework of the discussions, and speak the same language as the independent members. The analyses of the CPB and also of the Dutch Central Bank carry a great deal of weight in these discussions. Policy advice by the SER is prepared in committees, in which representatives of the three categories discuss and amend texts drafted by the SER. Representatives of various ministries attend these committee meetings, but formally they are observers. They do not take part in discussions unless they are asked to provide relevant information. So, unlike in other countries, where the third party in tripartite council discussions is the government, in the Netherlands independent experts as third party in the discussion see to it that the social partners do not come to agreements which are harmful to society as a whole. This would be the case when the costs of the policy measures agreed upon are shifted to the society as a whole. A major reason that the government is not an official partner in the discussions in the SER is that the SER gives formal advice to the government. It is clear that the government should not have a say in the preparation of such advice.

Obviously, it is important for the impact of the SER recommendations that they are supported unanimously. It is quite uncustomary that the government would disregard a SER unanimous policy recommendation. The independent members can be helpful in reaching a consensus recommendation in informal discussions. Obviously, the SER chairman has, as independent member, a crucial position in this institutionalised social dialogue. It is true that the independent members are selected and appointed in such a way that their political backgrounds more or less reflect the political landscape in the Netherlands. This may somewhat obscure the division between statements based on scientific insights and political preferences in the discussion. Recently the political background of the independent members of the SER has become more important and former politicians with little experience in academic research have been appointed as independent members. So there is a risk that scientific insights will play a less substantial role in the discussions, and that the discussions will focus on bridging political differences. On the other hand, at least in the past, on some occasions the political background of the independent members has been quite instrumental in reaching an agreement. It happened that an academic member associated with the socialist left wing party would interfere in the discussions and tell the trade unions that their demands were unfair, or that an academic member associated with the liberal, right wing party would tell the members of the employers' organisations that their demands were too high.

Other institutes

As in most other countries, the Central Bank – The Netherlands Bank (DNB) – plays a major role in economic policymaking. Nowadays, the major task of the DNB is to enhance and guarantee the stability of the payment system, whereas its former main task, namely to conduct monetary policy in order to combat inflation, has been delegated to the European Central Bank. Yet, the role of DNB in the policy discussions in the Netherlands is not restricted to banking supervision or (advice on) monetary policy. Officers of the Bank take part in the prominent forums for policy discussions in the Dutch polder model. As mentioned before, the president of the DNB is a member of the Social Economic Council and DNB officers participate in various meetings where SER advice is formulated. Moreover, there is ample informal coordination with fiscal policy: The president of the DNB has regular lunches with the Minister of Finance and the Treasurer General (a high-ranking civil servant in the Ministry). DNB officers are members of various ad hoc and regular committees in The Hague which are an important part of the policymaking process.

Sometimes, when no consensus can be reached about difficult policy problems within the formal institutional framework of the polder model, special committees are established for policy advice on these problems. An example was the new design for the social security arrangement for disabled workers. At the end of the twentieth century there was a long period of disagreement about how to solve this problem. Finally, in 2001, the government established a committee which consisted of members representing various political backgrounds and which was chaired by Piet Hein Donner (a prominent member of the Christian Democratic Party, former chairman of the Scientific Council for Government Policy, Minister of Legal Affairs in the Balkenende II cabinet, and Minister of Social Affairs and Employment in the Balkenende IV cabinet). This committee reached an agreement about a new arrangement for disabled workers which was thereafter – with some minor changes – approved by the Social Economic Council. However, the advice was not unanimous because three independent members did not consider the new arrangement an improvement.

Apart from the CPB, at the end of the twentieth century three other so-called *planning bureaus* were established in the Netherlands. In 1972, the Social and Cultural Planning Bureau (SCP) was founded. As in the CPB, the task of this bureau is not so much formal planning but rather monitoring and indicating future developments with respect to the social and cultural level of welfare of the Netherlands' population. In the late 1990s, an Environmental and Nature Planning Bureau was established within the existing large Institutes for Public Health and the Environment (RIVM). In 2006, this Environmental Planning Bureau became fully independent from the RIVM (see also Sluijs *et al.*, Chapter 14).

A Spatial Planning Bureau was founded in January 2002. However, in May 2008, this Spatial Planning Bureau merged with the Environmental and Nature Planning Bureau to form a new 'planning bureau' for the strategic analysis and policy research in the field of environment, nature and spatial planning. In English, the bureau calls itself the Netherlands Environmental Assessment Agency (in Dutch: Planbureau voor de Leefomgeving, PBL). The division of tasks between these three planning bureaus, CPB, SCP and PBL, is described in a protocol.

All directors of the three planning bureaus and the general director of the CBS are external members of the Scientific Council for Government Policy (WRR) which was founded in 1972 to provide advice to the government about long-term policies. The WRR is a multi-disciplinary council with about eight members and a small staff of about twenty persons. Most members have an academic background and have, in one way or another, already been involved in the policy consultation process in the Netherlands. The council is part of the Prime Minister's office, but it is completely independent in its long-term policy advice. The major part of the subjects of advice on which the WRR writes its reports to the government is initiated by the members of the council themselves. The advice of the WRR is required to be unanimous, although the possibility exists for individual members to write a minority recommendation. One of the functions of the WRR has grown to be ringing the alarm bell when the closeness of the consultation structure in the Netherlands leads to inertia and even to deadlocks in the process of policymaking, so that radical changes were not able to be initiated. Some reports of the WRR have been very influential in this respect.

There are many more institutions and committees which act, in a more broader sense, in the interface between science and policy in the setup of the polder model. An example is the RMNO (see De Wit, Chapter 8).

In 2005, a Council of Economic Advisors, consisting of five leading Dutch economists, was established in order to strengthen the role of the Parliament in discussions on economic policy. The council's role was to function for the Parliament as a counteracting power and to produce second opinions regarding the economic outlooks and the advice of the CPB, of the OECD and of the IMF. However, as members of the Parliament were not keen in using the critical reports of the council, it was dissolved in 2008. Apparently such an advisory body, where experts suggest, from a science-based perspective, policy changes directly to the members of Parliament, does not fit into Tinbergen's setup of the division of responsibilities in the policymaking process.

4   An example: economic effects of election programmes

The fact that the major political parties ask the CPB to calculate the economic effects of their election programmes is to conform with the institutional setup of policymaking in the Netherlands where knowledge on the working of the economy is, according to the theory of economic policy, separated from the normative preferences on trade-offs between policy goals. These policy preferences will differ for each political party (or pillar). Therefore, it is not remarkable that the CPB conducts these assessments; it may be even more remarkable that it only started to do so in 1986. In that year the three major parties, the Christian Democrats, the Liberals and the Socialists, asked the CPB to look at the effects of their economic policy proposals. In 1989, the Liberal Socialists of D66 also participated in the exercise and, in 1994, the Green-Left party, after some fierce internal discussions, became the fifth party to participate. In 1998, the assessment also included the policy programmes of these five political parties whereas the exercise was extended to eight political parties in 2002. It should again be emphasised that the CPB conducts the assessment at the *request* of the political parties and does not, apart from the timing of the exercise, take any initiative on its own. So it is the free choice of each of the political parties whether or not they want their programme to be examined by the CPB. In this way, they aim to obtain the stamp of approval of the CPB. Although there may be some herding involved in the decision of the political parties to participate (it may be regarded as a negative signal when parties do not participate) and although the smaller political parties complain that the exercise is relatively costly and time consuming for them, the impression is that the major political parties consider the assessment as useful as it brings discipline and budgetary consistency when it comes to drafting the programme.

Thus, it actively contributes to quality improvement in the political process. Moreover, in the larger political parties, with many hobby horses and shades of opinions between the active members, the assessment makes life easier for the person who has the responsibility for budgetary consistency of the programme. So, in the exercise in 2002, the financial spokesman of the Socialist party, Ferd Crone, discussed his input into the assessment of the CPB with two persons only, namely the political leader (Melkert) and the chairman of the party (Koole).

Of course, there is a major dilemma that the CPB faces in the assessment. On the one hand, there is much value in obtaining quantitative information on effects of various policy proposals in the election programmes. However, a completely objective and politically unbiased judgement on these policy proposals can never be given. Although a good quantitative economist will conduct his or her analysis as objectively as possible, a complete separation, as especially political scientists would emphasise, can never be made between analysis and normative preferences. It must be said that the CPB has put much effort into the design of the assessment procedure to guarantee the unbiasedness of the outcomes, but the selection of the models and the input of much tacit human knowledge into the assessment (see Don 2003 for a description of the procedure) will not completely prevent value judgements from creeping into the procedure. Therefore, apart from the value-creating elements in the assessment, some objections have also been raised against this procedure (see, for example, Review Committee of the CPB 1997).

In the following, a number of pros and a number of cons of the assessment are discussed.

Pros

There are a number of reasons why the assessment exercise can be regarded as a contribution to the qualified use of scientific knowledge in policy preparation. Some of these reasons have already been alluded to above. The first source of value of the exercise is that all policy proposals in the election programmes are calculated using a consistent model-based framework. It implies that the calculated effects on the policy goals are comparable for all political parties. In this way, the assessment gives the impression of the implicit social welfare function of the various political parties. Thus, the voters may decide which of the parties has a welfare function that agrees most with their own preferences.

In fact, the assessment procedure consists of three steps. The first step is that the political parties are confronted with a basic scenario which is somewhat cautious about future developments and which is *policy poor*. It means that trends in government expenditures in the main fields of policy concern (health care and insurance, education, social security) have been extrapolated on the assumption of no additional policy efforts. So the policy proposals of the political parties are defined as changes with respect to trend growths implicit in this basic scenario. It implies that when the political parties propose a cut in spending in one policy field in order to be able to intensify expenditure in another policy field, it does not mean that there is an absolute decrease in spending in that first policy field, but only a relative decrease as compared to the basic scenario. Of course, this makes a careful wording of the assessment in the public debate necessary. A second step in the assessment procedure is budgetary accounting. A definition equation describes in what way the political parties are planning to use the so-called *budgetary space* according to the basic projection plus cuts in spending which they propose. This can be used in three ways: namely, for additional spending, for reduction of the tax and premium burden and for reduction of the government debt. Obviously this accounting rule is not based on model assumptions and on economic behaviour, and contains no value judgement in that respect. It is noticeable that the rules and procedures for this budgetary accounting, including the norm for the budget surplus, are extensively discussed in policy advice of the Social Economic Council (SER) and in the so-called Studiegroep Begrotingsruimte, which is a committee of high-ranking civil servants of Ministries and of experts of the Central Bank on budgetary policy.

This is another example of the interaction between scientists and various stakeholders in the policy discussions in the polder model.

The working of the models and the assumptions on the economic behaviour implicit in these models do play a major role in the third step of the assessment procedure. Here, the effects of the policy proposals on the labour market, on product markets and on income distribution are calculated. There is, moreover, some feedback to the second step of the procedure as the model-based exercise may yield negative or positive second order effects for the government budget. However, in the most recent assessments of the CPB, the second order effects are relatively small as compared to second order effects found in previous assessment exercises (on which there has been much debate).

Therefore, a second major advantage of the assessment procedure is that the political parties are forced to think about this budgetary consistency. It means that the political parties have to be very strict on their proposals and cannot promise mountains of gold at no cost. More generally, this discipline in making consistent policy plans can be regarded as a major value added in the use of models for economic policy analysis. It does not only bring discipline into the policy plans, but there is also ample interaction between the policymakers and the modelling experts on what kind of policy instruments are most effective in achieving the warranted policy goals. This interaction also occurs in the discussions of the CPB experts and makers of the election programmes of the political parties. Yet, the CPB's procedure is strict in the sense that the final outcome cannot be influenced by the political parties any longer. Moreover, during the procedure there is no information and discussion between the political parties on how they proceed in the assessment procedure and on the CPB's implementation of their policy proposals. A proof of the fact that the assessment procedure brings consistency is that during the elections of 2003, when no assessment could be made due to a short election period, there were many complaints in the media about financial inconsistencies in the political programmes.

A third source of value of the assessment procedure is that the policy discussion takes place in line with the CPB's belief in the working of an economy which is based on sound economic theory, on empirical research and on a deep knowledge of economic institutions in the Netherlands. The policy analysis of the CPB provides a kind of common language as framework for the policy discussions. This common language lowers the transaction costs in, for example, the negotiations between the social partners. It is even remarkable how much, to give an example, the advice of the SER on medium-term policy for the period 2002–06 has heavily relied on studies conducted by the CPB (see SER 2002). Thus, the economic framework used in the assessment of the programmes of the political parties is familiar to all professional participants in the policy discussions in the Netherlands. They all use the terminology of the CPB and accept and interpret the outcomes of the analyses of the CPB accordingly. Moreover, the CPB has, in these circles, a high reputation for the quality of its analysis. It would take a long time for other institutes to build up a similar reputation. Because of the large investment costs in specific knowledge on this type of calculations, proliferation of such policy assessments of the election programmes would bring about huge costs given the size of the Dutch economy. In this respect the Dutch economy cannot be compared with the German economy, which has six major institutes for economic policy analysis.

A final and most prominent source of value of the assessment is that the calculations contribute considerably to lowering the negotiation costs when after the elections a coalition government has to be formed. Due to the assessment, the negotiators in the formation process are aware of the effects which the proposals of the various election programmes have, according to the calculations of the CPB, on the policy goals. This has proven to be useful information in order to come to a compromise and reach a government agreement which consists of a combination of the most effective policy proposals from the programmes. So, in an informal way, the assessment contributes to establishing an overall social welfare function that combines the individual preferences of the political parties which constitute the government.

Cons

Most arguments in favour of the assessment of the programmes of the previous section also contain a seed from which doubt may grow on the value of this task of the CPB. It is already mentioned that it is impossible to calculate the effects of policy proposals in a completely objective way. There will always be normative aspects and some subjective interpretations in the implementation of the policy proposals in the modelling. On previous occasions, as part of the learning process, there have been ample discussions between the makers of the programmes and the staff of the CPB on this implementation. In the recent exercise, the length of time for these discussions has been restricted by keeping a tight time schedule. As yet, all three steps in the calculation procedure discussed in the previous section contain elements of judgement by the CPB officers. In that sense the assessment is not fully codified. The basic scenario and the resulting calculation of the budgetary space are based on sound projections of structural growth, but, since, in the calculations discussed here, a cautious trend projection underlies the scenario, the probability of higher structural growth is greater than the probability of lower structural growth. This makes the basic scenario somewhat difficult to interpret.

There is no room for differences in interpretation in the second step: here, the budget constraint says that by definition the budgetary allowance plus cuts in spending should be equal to additional government expenditure plus tax reductions plus additional reduction of the government debt. However, the third step, where a mix of the models of the CPB is used for calculating the effects and propagation dynamics of the various policy proposals, is bound to many underlying assumptions. It may occur that the makers of the policy programmes disagree with the major mechanisms of the models used for the calculations. A first and not very complicated disagreement would be about calibrated or estimated values of the parameters of the models. Graafland (2003) shows that such differences in parameter values may already give rise to huge differences in the calculated effects of the policy proposals. A second and more fundamental disagreement would be about the dynamics of the model, namely the lag structure and the propagation speed of the policy proposals. This has been a cause of disagreement between the Christian Democratic Party and the CPB in the previous assessment of the election programmes in 1998 (see Verbon 1998; and Don 1998).

The most serious objection of the makers of the policy programmes would be when they disagree with the working and specification of the model and its theoretical underpinnings. In that case, their request would be for the use of different model specifications. All in all, the political parties may ask for a sensitivity analysis with respect to these kinds of specification changes. However, that would be very time consuming and would also involve the danger that the political parties go shopping for more positive results.

Although ideally the assessment is supposed to reveal the social welfare function of each political party, in reality the assessment does not provide a clear-cut insight into the trade-offs between policy goals and into the preferences of the political parties. The outcomes are rather complicated in their mix of policy goals, input of various instruments and propagation dynamics. Thus, some parties will have favourable effects in the short run, whereas their long-term economic performance may be lower than that of other parties. This rich diversity of outcomes makes it difficult to select the political party with preferences that come closest to one's own individual welfare concept. That is why the assessment, apart from its technical character, is not very helpful to laymen voters trying to decide about their favourite party. The CPB tries hard to present the outcomes in a clear and understandable way, and all political parties will stress that their outcomes are the best given their own criteria of judgements for them. On the other hand, the policy debate may be very selective with respect to the outcomes.

Politicians can be, in their election campaigns, rather eager to exaggerate specific policy consequences, mainly with respect to the effects on employment, and give them much more weight than the uncertainties which the calculations allow. For instance in 1998, a leader of the Liberals argued that the Christian Democrats were not ready for government because the calculations of the CPB showed that their programme did not enhance employment. In the assessment of 2002, there were some misunderstandings in the press about the effect on purchasing power of lower and higher incomes, due to the CPB's definition of lower and higher incomes in which the class of higher incomes also comprised (lower) middle incomes.

Another problem with the assessments, unavoidable though, is that the calculations of the CPB are highly technical so that they are very difficult for laymen and relative outsiders to judge. It is really an insider's exercise, the scope of which can only be fully understood by experts. Only a few professionals are fluent in the language of the CPB and really know how to interpret the working of the models. Moreover, it is questionable whether the results can be reproduced completely by outsiders (see also Graafland 2003). In fact, the calculations are made by different models which generally do not yield the same impulse response effects. So a great deal of not fully documented judgement is included in the assessment in combining the effects according to the various models.

A further source of concern regarding the assessments is that a number of aspects, which political parties (and the public) may consider as important, cannot be taken into account in the calculations. These may be either positive effects, such as policy measures to enhance the quality of education, or to make the health system more efficient without additional expenditures, or negative effects of high transaction and transition costs that policy measures may bring about. More in general, the assessment is confined to a quantification of the economic effects of the policy proposals. Although the assessment of 2002 extended the analysis to a quality assessment with respect to the environment, the public health sector and disability, the danger was that other important issues in the election campaign would remain underexposed such as values, norms and the preservation of social capital, safety and crime prevention and government failure. This problem could be solved if the other planning bureaus would also make an assessment, albeit qualitatively, in their field of competence. As a matter of fact, the Environmental Planning Bureau publishes its assessment in line with the assessment of the CPB.

A final and most interesting problem, or side effect of the assessment, is that the makers of the party programmes have become familiar with the properties of the models of the CPB and will, in the policy proposals, see to it that they are effective in terms of the CPB models. In fact, a bad performance in the CPB calculations, especially with respect to employment, has, on previous occasions, proved to lead to a loss of votes in the elections. The result is that this procedure generates those policy proposals of the political parties which are most beneficial according to the models of the CPB. This has led to a remarkable convergence of policy plans, especially between the established parties, which would help qualify them for participation in the government. For example, in the assessment of 2002, the policy proposals of the Green-Left party (Groen-Links) were so much in line with the proposals of the other parties that they were not excluded by other parties from taking part in the government beforehand. This convergence of plans may have contributed to the lack of interest of the Dutch population for general elections – apart from *depillarisation* which may be another course.

Moreover, there is a risk that the way the CPB models describe economic reality is not correct, so that all political parties are betting on the wrong horse in the design of their programmes. This would imply an extraordinary example of a political bind.

It is true that, as Don (2003) argues, it enhances welfare when the designers of the political programmes exploit the properties of the CPB models when these models provide an adequate description of reality. However, the dominant role of the models of the CPB and their implicit conceptual framework with which all economists in the country have been educated, may lead to path dependence in the analysis. A kind of discourse coalition will emanate, which may exclude new and relevant conceptual ideas (see Van den Bogaard 2002). That is why, in the institutional framework of the Dutch polder model, with its frequent interactions between professionals in the policymaking process who all speak the same scientific language, some counteracting power of outsiders should be organised and facilitated in order to prevent such conceptual binds.

5   Quality control of scientific advice

The description above of the institutional setup of the process of policy preparation in the Netherlands already implicitly deals with some questions regarding quality control and certainty in scientific advice to policy. This section contains a more explicit discussion of these questions. There are two basic questions. The first is how to guarantee that the scientific advice itself is of good quality, makes use of state-of-the-art scientific knowledge and is policy-relevant. This is a question of quality control and reputation formation within the scientific community itself. The second question regards the propagation of the scientific knowledge and advice to the policymakers.

Here, it is important how the propagation of scientific knowledge and the interaction between scientists and policymakers is organised.

What is quality?

From an operational point of view the quality of scientific advice for policymaking is very difficult to assess. Of course, from a highly theoretical perspective, that scientific advice to policy has the highest quality which contributes most to social welfare.

However, even with the benefit of hindsight, the contribution of scientific advice to welfare cannot be measured. First, that is because social welfare itself is difficult to measure. Social welfare functions are a theoretical construct, which are difficult to quantify. At most some information on (political) trade-offs between various policy goals (for example, income per head, equality, environmental quality, employment) can be obtained by surveys, or, *ex post*, by revealed preferences (see, for example, Merkies 1973, Van Eijk and Sandee 1959). Moreover, in modern economic thinking, the concept of a social welfare function representing political preferences no longer has its former prominent role in political economy. Instead, the actual implementation of policy plans is seen as the outcome of a process of negotiation between various stakeholders with different interests. In that theoretical model the outcome depends on the negotiation power of the stakeholders.

A second reason why the quality of the advice is difficult to assess is that at the macro-level there is no control experiment. It is only in a model-based calculation that the difference between the development without and with a policy measure can be computed. This is what an *impulse-response analysis* does. Such analysis (spoorboekjes – railroad timetables – as Tinbergen called it) is used by the CPB to estimate the effects of policy measures before they are implemented, for instance in the calculation of the effects of the election programmes. A suggestion in this respect for further quality control is to perform a similar calculation after the policy plan has been put into effect.

Which criteria for quality?

Because of these difficulties in assessing the quality of scientific policy advice, one should be pragmatic in setting criteria for the judgement of that quality. Criteria can be related to the two questions posed above. A first set of criteria should describe the quality of the advice insofar as it is based on state-of-the-art scientific knowledge and empirical observations. Here, the usual criteria used in the scientific community hold: the analysis should be peer reviewed, reproducible and based on public sources open to the scientific debate (see, for example, Jasanoff, Chapter 2) These criteria are discussed and used widely in science policy, so that they do not need further attention in this chapter. In fact, these criteria relate to the consensus part of the setup of the polder model. In order to comply with these criteria, the CPB organises discussions and collaboration with researchers at universities, invites international experts and supports publications of staff members in peer reviewed journals.

The second set of criteria has to do with the propagation of the scientific knowledge to the policymakers, and with the way interaction between scientific knowledge and policymakers (and/or stakeholders) is organised in order to gain public support for the policy measures. Here, the criteria are associated with the compromise part of the polder model. These criteria should enable a judgement on: (i) whether the scientific knowledge is implemented in a correct way in the policy plans, (ii) whether feedback from politicians and stakeholders have been sufficiently incorporated in the policy plans, (iii) whether the independence of the scientific advice has been preserved when incorporating this feedback and no political pressure has been exerted on the scientific advisers to adapt the results to predicted outcomes, (iv) whether an open debate on policy measures and their measured effects has been organised so that stalemates are avoided, (v) whether public support for the policy plans has been obtained in an open and honest way (no cheating or window dressing), (vi) whether the calculated effects of the policy plans sufficiently fulfil the preferences (or best interests) of stakeholders, and (vii) whether, in a follow-up analysis, the implementation costs of the policy measures turn out to be reasonably low.

Whereas the first set of criteria is directly related to the way the production of scientific knowledge is organised, a good performance on the second set of criteria depends on the institutional setup of the process of policy preparation. The quality control in scientific advice to policy depends a great deal on the way the propagation of scientific knowledge to policy practice is institutionalised in formal and informal procedures. That is why this chapter puts so much emphasis on the history and working of the polder model in the Netherlands.

Institutions and formalised procedures

As mentioned before, in the institutionalised procedures of the polder model to obtain public support for policy measures, discussions and compromise advice of the SER play a major role. Therefore, most of the above criteria of judgement on the quality of the scientific advice are applicable to the SER. It is the task of the independent members to see to it that advice is based on and is consistent with up-to-date scientific knowledge. These persons thus play an important role in the use of scientific knowledge for policy practice. It is through these independent members that the policy discussions within the SER benefit from the insights of scientific research.

The SER has an important function in promoting trust between the various policymakers by acting as a platform of discussion for social partners, government, central bank, CPB and scientists. The positive role of the SER has, however, not always been recognised by the government. The legal provision that the government was obliged to ask the SER for advice on all proposals for socio-economic legislation was abolished in 1995. The feeling had arisen at the government level that this procedure took too much time and caused too much *stickiness* in the policy preparation procedures.

However, instead of weakening the position of the SER in the process of policy preparation, this measure seems to have strengthened it. The measure worked, probably unintended by the government, as a trigger mechanism for the members of the SER to reach consensus in its policy recommendations. Recommendations that are signed unanimously by the three parties involved give a strong signal to the government of societal consensus on specific policy measures, and are therefore much more powerful than recommendations that reflect divided opinions. As mentioned above, the Dutch culture of consensus puts strong pressure on the government to follow unanimous recommendations. The government is, however, not bound to act in the way the SER recommends, although it is obliged to give a formal statement of reaction to every published recommendation.

In this institutional setup the SER thus fulfils two main purposes. First, it works as a device for the government to become informed about the points of view of trade unions and employer organisations about socio-economic questions. Especially the unanimous recommendations give the government clues about what policy measures will be supported by society. Second, the SER works as a platform that brings together trade unions and employer organisations to talk with each other about socio-economic matters. The presence of economic and legal scientists makes sure that the discussions are based on solid arguments. In this way, they learn about each other's motives and objectives for and against certain policy measures. This prevents misunderstandings and makes it possible to form a basis for developing mutual trust (see Den Butter and Mosch 2003; Mosch 2004). It also promotes that policy plans are based on consistent and good quality economic knowledge.

One of the major aspects in the negotiations in the SER, which is related to the idea of trust, is that the main negotiators meet each other regularly both in formal and in informal meetings. It is the repeated frequent interactions of the negotiators in meetings that contribute to trust formation which plays an important role here. An example of this attitude can be found in an interview by Klamer (1990) on the occasion of the fortieth anniversary of the SER. Klamer posed the following question to Jan Stekelenburg, at that time the chairman of FNV, the largest trade union:

My impression is that you and Van Lede – chairman of the largest employers' organisation – are very much on speaking terms and that you are more friendly to each other than the outside world believes you are.

Stekelenburg's answer is:

No, no, that is not true! It is certainly not true that we're constantly fighting with each other, but at the moment of conflict it is clear and apparent and we don't ease the problem when we are together.

Then Klamer asked:

Did it happen that you were really angry with Van Lede?

Stekelenburg replied:

Yes, when there is really a large conflict I may be angry. However, it will happen in a way which does not harm our future relationship, because we are committed to each other. We need each other in these negotiations on labour relations, so that we should be aware that after a big quarrel we will always be forced to come back to business in a next situation. So the real hard and definite battle will never be fought.

These examples illustrate that the Dutch institutional framework for socio-economic policy preparation has several characteristics that favour the formation of trust and cooperation.

To begin with, there is, as explained before, a cultural trait prevalent in the Netherlands that is favourable to cooperation and consensus. In other words, there seems to be a sort of *basic trust* upon which actual mutual trust can be developed. This can also be related to the idea of the path-dependency of trust (see, for example, Putnam 1993). Given the fact that most people in a society feel inclined to act in trustworthy ways, it is beneficial for all people to keep to this way of transacting, because it will reap extra benefits for the involved parties when it comes to solving coordination types of activities.

The Dutch institutional framework seems to fit almost completely with micro-findings on how to build trust-enhancing networks. The group of players in the Netherlands is relatively small. As we have seen from the interview by Klamer (1990), there is much repeated contact between the players. A substantial part of it is face-to-face and informal (see, for example, Ostrom and Walker (1997) for an analysis of public good games in which face-to-face communication leads to substantial increases in cooperation). Each player belongs to an organisation, so reputations can be smoothly inferred from one representative of the organisation to the other. In other words, a reputation of trustworthiness does not disappear (completely) when individual persons are replaced. Reputations are important, because policymaking is a dynamic process. Organisations meet each other over and over again, and know that this will not change in the coming years. Along with the fact of the small group, this leads to the fact that the possibilities for learning and control are substantial. It also has implications for the way unanimity is reached in the recommendations. Occasionally, when opinions of the social partners are too far apart, trying to reach unanimity is not desirable as it may prevent them from coming to a unanimous agreement in a repeated round of the discussions in the SER at a time when such unanimity may be even more urgent.

All in all, trust formation and the use of trust between the leaders of the various groups of stakeholders is one of the major mechanisms in the Netherlands for the quality control of scientific policy advice. In a broad respect Hoppe and Halffman (2004) distinguish three patterns of institutionalisation of scientific advising in policy preparation in the Netherlands. The first is the corporatist approach of organising scientific input in the policy debate and negotiations between the social partners. Advantages of this way of institutionalising have been discussed above: stable platforms of negotiation, consistent use of scientific knowledge and trust formation between various stakeholders. A disadvantage can be that outsiders and outsiders' knowledge are excluded from the discussions and that the discussion is locked within the dominant discourse coalition (see Van den Boogaart 2002).

According to Hoppe and Halffman, the second pattern is the neoliberal, decisionistic way of obtaining scientific advice for the design of policy measures. Here, policymakers *buy* advice from independent and often commercial centres of expertise.

This pattern is linked to the increased focus on efficiency through the working of markets in economic policy. A third pattern is a tendency towards a more interactive and deliberative way of organising the debate between stakeholders (see, e.g., Van de Kerkhof 2004). From the (Tinbergen) viewpoint of economic policy, such stakeholder participation can be useful in order to obtain more information on, and/or to shape and sharpen the preferences and interests of stakeholders, so that they become more explicit. More generally, it is important to be clear about the aim of stakeholder participation when it is to be organised and eventually institutionalised. The aim can be to: (i) obtain insight in stakeholder preferences; (ii) articulate stakeholder preferences; (iii) strive at convergence of preferences; (iv) obtain information on negotiating power of stakeholders. Each case requires a specific setup for stakeholders' participation.

Debate and controversy

The separation in the polder model between data collection, the working of the economy and policy goals derived from political preferences, should also apply to the public debate and controversy about policy plans. Data collection should be indisputable so that here the debate should be confined to internal discussions between the experts. CBS has been quite successful in this respect. The most disputed part of the institutional setup of the polder model is the separation of the debate and the controversy on scientific knowledge on the working of the economy and on policy preferences. Of course, in practice such clear separation of responsibilities is impossible so that often the public debate is obscured by mixing opinions on the working of the economy with opinions on policy goals and their contribution to welfare. In particular, this problem arises when expert economists become opinion leaders and disguise their political preferences in debates on economic effectiveness of policy measures. Indeed, the discussions in the SER will not always reflect the ideal setup of Tinbergen's polder model either and arguments on the working of the economy will be mixed with political preferences (see Woldendorp 2005).

The most relevant arena of debate from the perspective of this chapter is the scientific debate on the working of the economy and consequently the appropriateness of measures of economic policy. Here, the institutional setup of the polder model makes it possible to find a subtle balance between reaching agreement amongst experts and widening the scientific debate. Much and long lasting disagreement between experts would weaken the position of scientific knowledge and would make policy preparation less efficient.

On the other hand, early exclusion of outsider opinions would lead to deadlocks and to dominant discourse coalitions. In illustration of this aspect of the polder model, some examples of debate and controversy on the role and work of the CPB are given below.

Monopoly versus competition

The CPB's reputation of conducting independent analyses has been challenged from time to time both in academia and by the press, especially with respect to its task as formal auditor for the government. The position of the CPB is in fact that of a monopoly and it is true that the CPB has a special situation as it has access to confidential information on government policy. This position is needed in order for the CPB to be able to react promptly on policymakers' questions pertaining to technical and accounting aspects in policy discussions. Yet, in the institutional framework for policymaking in the Netherlands, a number of checks and balances have been installed in order to prevent the CPB from misusing its monopolistic position. For one, there is a regular evaluation of the work of the CPB by external expert commissions. Moreover, misuse of its monopolistic position would also immediately destroy much of the good reputation that the bureau has built up so carefully. Besides, as already mentioned, it is a question of efficiency to have, in a relatively small country like the Netherlands, only one institute which is responsible for this kind of macro-economic forecasting and policy evaluations. This task requires a lot of specific investments and hence the institute has to be quite sizeable. It is typical for the institutional setup of Dutch policymaking that there are numerous formal and informal contacts between the staff of the CPB and the economists at ministries, researchers in academia and the staff of the social partners. On the one hand, they provide relevant information to the CPB, but, on the other hand, they will, if needed, be critical of the work of the CPB.

The CPB does not hold a monopolistic position for its second task, namely that as an institute of applied economic research. Here, it competes both with other Dutch institutes and with institutes abroad. Nowadays the CPB is asked more frequently than earlier on to give a second opinion on research conducted by other institutes. Similarly, there is, for instance, no objection that political parties ask other researchers, including research institutes at universities for second opinions on the effectiveness of parts of their programmes. Yet, a full economic assessment of the programmes as conducted by the CPB, cannot be done by other institutes because of the costs involved in investments in specific knowledge and building up of reputation in the institutions of policy preparation in the Netherlands. In this respect the situation is different compared to, for example, Germany where six independent research institutes assess economic developments and the policy plans from various economic perspectives. This may result in diverse and sometimes competing views on the adequacy of plans (see Wagner, Chapter 11).

Wage moderation

The policy of wage moderation, which is, in retrospect, generally supposed to be very beneficial to the Netherlands, has been subject to much controversy and debate. In the 1950s and 1960s, years of prosperous economic growth and almost full employment, the Dutch government conducted an active counter-cyclical policy of demand management. This policy was supported by the first generation of models of the CPB, which were short-term Keynesian demand models. According to these models, a rise in government spending, but also wage increases, resulted in more demand and higher economic activity. When unemployment and inflation were rising in the 1970s – the phenomenon of stagflation – a new generation of policy models of the CPB challenged this policy prescription (see Den Butter 1991). The first turning point was around 1975 when the CPB started to use the Vintaf-model. The clay-clay vintage approach by Den Hartog and Tjan (1974, 1976) in this model showed that a rise in real wages exceeding the rate of technical progress caused increased scrapping of capital goods and hence increased unemployment. So, according to this model, the negative neoclassical effect on employment of a wage increase was larger than the positive Keynesian spending effect. In 1977, the Central Economic Commission, one of these important commissions of highly ranked government officers in the polder model, based its projections and policy advice for the medium term on the outcomes of the Vintaf-model. This evoked a vivid and unique debate among academics and government specialists on the merits and shortcomings of the model (see Driehuis and Van der Zwan 1978). Yet, finally some consensus emerged from this discussion that a policy of wage restraint was a suitable medicine against stagflation and would be helpful in enhancing employment. This consensus resulted in the famous Wassenaar agreement between the social partners in 1982. This agreement, which couples wage restraint with working time reduction, is seen as the starting point of the improvement of the Dutch economy, with increased labour participation and a reduction of unemployment. It has become known as the transition from the *Dutch disease* to the *Dutch miracle*.

Yet, occasionally the policy of wage restraint, and restraint in government spending, is challenged again. This is especially true during periods of cyclical recessions. One of the arguments, most prominently put forward by Kleinknecht (1994, 2003), is that wage restraints lead to fewer investments in labour-saving technical progress so that the growth rate of (labour) productivity decreases. The other side of the coin of this debate is that empirical evidence does not reveal a negative relationship between wage restraint and labour productivity growth, and that wage restraints lead to a higher rate of return on capital. These profits are partly used for investments in R&D which enhance total factor productivity and therefore (more than) compensate the adverse effect of wage restraints on labour productivity.

Equilibrium modelling

Another debate on modelling and the working of the economy was held around 1990. This time the debate was initiated outside the CPB, amongst others by experts at the Ministry of Economic Affairs (see Van Bergeijk and Van Sinderen 2000). Model outcomes of the CPB were becoming more and more *policy resistant*, i.e. the calculated effects of policy measures were small compared to the large effects needed for restructuring the economy. The plea was to put more emphasis on the supply side of the economy, such as competition policy and deregulation, and use applied general equilibrium models for long-term analysis of structural policy measures (see Don, Van de Klundert and Van Sinderen 1991). This debate urged the CPB to construct a new model, the MIMIC-model, which has since then been used intensively to calculate the general equilibrium effects of policy measures with respect to taxation and social security reform. Moreover, it initiated a shift in the research of the CPB towards cost benefit analysis and studies of the effects of institutional change.

All in all, these examples show that scientific debate has indeed influenced the ideas and more or less the consensus about the working of the economy in the institutional setup of policy preparation in the Netherlands. However, there is always the danger of, on the one hand, too much debate so that policymakers and politicians are tempted to cherry-pick – i.e. selecting those opinions which are in conformity with their a priori assumptions – and, on the other hand, too much path dependence in the scientific research programmes, with the result that paradigm changes are hindered.

6   A comparison with France

In order to illustrate that there are large differences between countries in the industrial organisation of economic policy preparation, this section compares labour market institutions and the organisation of policy preparation in France and the Netherlands.

The Dutch polder model can be classified – if any classification is possible: see Esping-Andersen (1990) and the critics of this classification – as a mixture between the liberal Anglo-Saxon model and the Social-Christian

Rhineland model. The French model can be regarded as an example of the *Latin rim* or Mediterranean model, although a large number of the actual social security regulations in France mimic the Rhineland model. The reason for this focus on the differences between France and the Netherlands is that, as far as we know, not much literature on comparing these two countries exists. Blanchard and Tirole (2004) discuss some institutional differences between these two countries with respect to employment protection. However, much more economic literature is available on the institutional differences between Germany and the Netherlands (see, for example, CPB Netherlands Bureau for Economic Policy Analysis 1997; Blien and Den Butter 2003, Eichhorst and Wintermann, 2005). With respect to institutional differences (and similarities) between the UK and the Netherlands, Nickell and Van Ours (2000) show how partly overlapping and partly different supply-oriented policies resulted in a substantial reduction of unemployment rates in both of these countries.

Policy institutions in France

In order to compare with the Netherlands, we must first have a closer look at institutions which play a role in the social dialogue and policy preparation in France. The French institutional organisations which are regarded as the most influential on policy preparation are the Institut National de la Statistique et des Etudes Economiques (INSEE), the Direction de Prévision (DP), the Commissariat Général du Plan and the Conseil Economique et Social (CES).

INSEE, DP and CGP

The Institut National de la Statistique et des Etudes Economiques (INSEE) and the Direction de Prévision (DP) conduct quantitative analyses of economic developments in France, which are used in the CES recommendations. Both institutes are closely related and in a department of the Ministry of Finance. The INSEE has the combined role of a bureau of statistics and of an institute of applied economic research. Besides data collection and analysis, the INSEE is actively involved in economic research and education. In addition to applied research focused on policymaking, the INSEE also conducts high quality fundamental research.

Although both institutes are involved in economic forecasting, each institute has its own specific responsibilities. The DP focuses primarily on short-term forecasting for economic policymaking concerning public finance, foreign relations and the financial sector. The INSEE specialises in extremely short-term forecasting and also on long-term forecasting. In order to secure data collection independent of policy analysis, forecasting and analysis of policy proposals which are relevant for actual policymaking are prepared by the DP, and not by the INSEE. A second institution which separated data collection and its analysis from policy preparation was the Commissariat Général du Plan (CGP). The CGP was a platform where current policy problems were discussed. The predictions and policy analyses of the DP and the INSEE served as input for these discussions. During its existence, the CGP status was subordinate to that of the Ministry of Finance and depended heavily on the prestige of its members. Today the CGP no longer exists. An important feature of the French system are the close interrelations between the Ministry of Finance, the country's most powerful economic body, and the INSEE, the DP and the CGP. Staff members are often employed by one of these institutions using short-term contracts, which results in frequent mutual rotations and increased interaction possibilities. In his study on the French financial elite, Kadushin (1995) demonstrates that board membership is heavily determined by social circle membership. Concentration of social economic power in France resides largely with the elite.

Conseil Economique et Social

In France, the Conseil Economique et Social (CES) advises the Parliament or the government on legislation with a social and economic character. In the CES, a great variety of social organisations are represented, with the restriction that only organisations seen as the most representative are eligible to be members in the CES. CES members include delegates from employee organisations, employer organisations, free professions, French citizens who live abroad and agricultural organisations. The CES functions as a discussion forum for the various organisations represented in it. In the CES, information exchange takes place and assessments are made with respect to future policy. Every policy plan or project concerning socio-economic legislation is liable to compulsory assessment by the CES. The French government may consult the CES on other policy matters as well if such advice seems appropriate. However, the government is not compelled to comply with CES advice and the influence of these recommendations seems to be rather limited. 163 of the 231 CES members are appointed directly by the social member organisations, the government selects the remaining sixty-eight members. Initially the purpose of this appointment procedure was to combine independence and representation with a converging force to serve the national interest (Frayssinet 1986). Furthermore, the government adds seventy-two specialised section members to the 231 CES members. Although section members do not enjoy the full CES membership, they contribute to discussions in their discipline.

Comparison of institutions in France and the Netherlands

One of the most striking differences between the two countries is that France lacks an equivalent organisation for the Dutch Foundation of Labour (STAR). Unlike the Netherlands, the French employers' organisations and trade unions are not involved in negotiating collective labour agreements at a central level. This implies that no national coordination of wage bargaining exists in France. Central coordination in the Netherlands provoked effective cooperation and prevented important rivalry between the various unions, although they might have been founded around different ideological principles. The French situation without central coordination and the competitive system of CES representation encourages competition between the various union organisations.

Although the Dutch SER and the French CES appear to have about the same role in the social dialogue in both countries, considerable differences surface. Within the CES, many more stakeholder organisations and lobby groups have claimed representation than in the SER, where the social partners play a major role. Implicitly this results in a weaker voice for the French social partners in the CES and therefore less influence on government policy. The second related dissimilarity is that in the Netherlands, the SER is institutionalised to be much more independent of government intervention than the CES in France. The Dutch government has no say in the appointment of SER members, whereas in France about one-third of the CES members and all of the section members are appointed by the government. The Dutch SER and the French CES differ also in the way they draft their policy recommendations. Whereas CES recommendations usually comprise a number of different views on policy issues and a count of the number of votes showing how many members share each of these views, the SER tries hard to reach agreement on policy issues and come to unanimous recommendations. When unanimous agreement is not reached, disagreement is minimised and the text of the recommendations indicates by name which members have different opinions about specific aspects of the policy proposals.

In principle, the CPB in the Netherlands, and the INSEE, the DP and the CGP in France have about the same role in policy preparation. Within the INSEE, data collection is carried out independent from the data analysis, whereas in the Netherlands the Central Bureau of Statistics (CBS), which is nowadays placed at a distance from government control, conducts independent data collection. Yet, it seems that INSEE and DP analyses have far less influence on the French policy discussions than CPB analyses have on policy discussions in the Netherlands. A similarity in the institutional setup of labour relations in both countries is that most collective labour agreements between the social partners are made binding by the government for all workers – union members and non-union members – in the sector to which the agreement applies. This is remarkable as in both countries the rate of union membership has fallen and is nowadays rather low. France even has the lowest membership rate of the European Union (Besancenot and Vranceanu 1999).

Furthermore, the number of workers that is bound by collective agreements is very high in France, with coverage of about 90 per cent. In the Netherlands, 70 to 75 per cent of the workers are covered by collective agreements.

All in all, it can be concluded that the major differences between France and the Netherlands arise from the extent of governmental interference in labour relations. In the Netherlands, the government has refrained more and more from interfering in the social partners' negotiations on labour relations. Yet, the threat of possible interference has motivated the social partners to be cooperative and to avoid such interference. The need to cooperate enhances trust in the negotiation process (see the previous section).

In France, much direct government intervention in the negotiations between the social partners can traditionally be found. This large governmental influence on the outcome of the negotiations causes distrust and enhanced feelings of powerlessness between the social partners. Whereas in the Netherlands social partners try hard to reach a compromise agreement within the setup of the polder model, in France we see what we may call *the productive conflict model* at work. In this model social partners try to resolve disputes by confrontation. This has also to do with the republican tradition in France and the social-Colbertism with a dominant role for the centralised state, which tries to monopolise power to make decisions in order to reach certain political and social goals. In France, it is the political elite that decides about policy matters without much consultation. It will withdraw or adapt the policy measures when they evoke too much protest and lead to conflict. In the Netherlands, however, the institutional setup is much more directed to consultation. The advantage of the Dutch model is that less conflicts arise, so that the final implementation of policy measures is less costly.

However, the disadvantage as compared to the French conflict model is that coming to an agreement may be very time-consuming and that compromise policy measures may be inefficient (see, for example, the long-lasting efforts in the Netherlands to come to a reform of the costly disability provisions). Subsequently, in France, obstacles lie with the implementation of policy while in the Netherlands policy preparation is most time consuming.

7   Conclusion

The process of policy preparation is organised in the Netherlands in such a way that scientific knowledge plays an important role in the shaping of (economic) policy. Moreover, the formal and informal procedures of the institutional setup guarantee that there is ample interaction and quality control in the use of scientific knowledge in the policy proposals. This interaction is favoured by the fact that there is a relatively small number of key actors in the process of policy preparation and that they meet each other frequently in various committees, commissions and councils. It happens quite often, and probably more frequently than in other countries, that academic experts become high-ranking government officers and even Ministers. There is also much mobility of experts between academia, planning bureaus, advisory councils and think tanks at ministries.

The consultation structure of the Dutch polder model puts much emphasis on compromise in the social dialogue and on obtaining public support for policy measures. The advantage is that much social unrest is avoided and implementation costs of policy measures are relatively low. The disadvantage is that it may take a long time before agreement is reached on urgent policy measures and that policy arrangements, for instance the system of social security, become very complicated and inefficient as they are the result of extensively debated and amended compromise agreements.

The separation between undisputed data collection, consensus on the working of the economy and compromise about policy goals, as inspired by Tinbergen, still seems to be a workable institutional setup. A problem which becomes increasingly evident is that policy recommendations and the resulting policy debate increasingly have a very technocratic character so that they are difficult for the layman to understand. More in general, this is an important information problem in highly developed societies.

Apparently the trade-offs between risk insurance by the government and individual responsibilities of citizens, and between moral hazard and solidarity, are difficult to understand and communicate. It urges a rethinking of how more attention to communication on the dilemmas in policymaking because of these trade-offs can be included in the institutional setup of the polder model.

In the industrial organisation of economic policy preparation, there is no one model to be preferred. Different countries have different models which can partly be attributed to cultural differences. In the institutional setup of policy preparation after World War II, the concept of *planning* played a major role in most continental European countries. Yet, the decentralised discussion-based culture in the Netherlands and the centralised, power-based culture in France have given rise to a much different interpretation of *planning*, and of the way the policy preparation has been institutionalised. However, part of the differences can also be attributed to the way the protagonists and opinion leaders in economic policy have been involved in the institutional setup of policy preparation. The obvious examples here are Norway (see Bjerkholt 1998) and the Netherlands, where both Nobel Prize-winners in economics, Frisch and Tinbergen, were the forerunners in making economic policy preparation empirical. In Norway, policy plans were set up like production plans in industry, with much detail, whereas in the Netherlands policy analysis was much more macro-oriented, with the separation of responsibilities between data collection, knowledge on the working of the economy and political preferences described extensively in this chapter.

Acknowledgements

The author acknowledges useful comments by Henk Don, Johan Verbruggen, Jaap Woldendorp and the editors of this book.

REFERENCES

Bakker, G.P. den 1993. 'Origin and development of Dutch National accounts', in W.F.M. de Vries *et al.*(eds.), *The Value Added of National Accounting*, Voorburg/Heerlen: CBS, pp. 73–92.

Bergeijk, P.A.G. van and van Sinderen, J. 2000. 'Models and macroeconomic policy in the Netherlands', in Den Butter and Morgan (eds.), 2000, pp. 26–38.

Besancenot, D. and Vranceanu, R. 1999. 'A trade union model with endogenous militancy: Interpreting the French case', *Labour Economics* 6: 355–73.

Bjerkholt, O. 1998. 'Interaction between model builders and policy makers in the Norwegian tradition', *Economic Modelling* 15: 317–39.

Blanchard, O. and Tirole, J. 2004. 'Redesigning the employment protection system', *De Economist* 152: 1–20.

Blien, U. and Butter, F.A.G. den (eds.) 2003. *Labour Participation and Unemployment; A Comparison of Developments and Institutions in Germany and The Netherlands*, The Hague: WRR Working Documents W133.

Bogaard, A.A. van den 1999. *Configuring the Economy. The Emergence of a Modelling Practice in the Netherlands, 1920–1955*, Amsterdam: Rozenberg Publishers (Thela Thesis).

Bogaard, A.A. van den 2002. *De verwevenheid tussen toekomstverkenning en beleid; het ontstaan van vertoogcoalities*, The Hague: Working Document W127, Scientific Council for Government Policy (WRR).

Bos, F. 2003. *The National Accounts as a Tool for Analysis and Policy; Past, Present and Future*, University of Twente: Academic Thesis.

Butter, F.A.G. den 1991. 'Macroeconomic modelling and the policy of restraint in the Netherlands', *Economic Modelling* 8: 16–33.

Butter, F.A.G. den 2004. 'Statistics and the origin of the Royal Netherlands economic association', *De Economist* 152: 439–46.

Butter, F.A.G. den 2007. 'National accounts and indicators', in M. Boumans (ed.), *Measurement in Economics: a Handbook*, Amsterdam/Boston: Elsevier Inc., pp. 189–229.

Butter, F.A.G. den and Morgan, M.S. 1998. 'What makes the models-policy interaction successful?', *Economic Modelling* 15: 443–75.

Butter, F.A.G. den and Morgan, M.S. (eds.) 2000. *Empirical Models and Policy Making: Interactions and Institutions*, London: Routledge.

Butter, F.A.G. den and Mosch, R.H.J. 2003. 'The Dutch miracle, institutions, networks, and trust', *Journal of Institutional and Theoretical Economics* 159: 362–91.

CPB Netherlands Bureau for Economic Policy Analysis 1997. *Challenging Neighbours: Rethinking German and Dutch Economic Institutions*, Berlin, Heidelberg: Springer.

Don, F.H.J. 1996. 'De positie van het Centraal Planbureau' (The position of the central planning bureau), *Economische Statistische Berichten* 81: 208–12.

Don, F.J.H. 1998. 'Verbons verwijten aan CPB onterecht', *Christen Democratische Verkenningen* 9/10: 406–10.

Don, F.H.J. 2003. 'Economic analysis of election programmes: What, how and why?', in J.J. Graafland and A.P. Ros (eds.), *Economic Assessment of Election Programs: Does it Make Sense?* Dordrecht, Boston: Kluwer, pp. 21–30.

Don, F.H.J., van de Klundert, Th. and van Sinderen, J. (eds.) 1991. *Applied General Equilibrium Modelling*, Dordrecht, Boston, London: Kluwer Academic Publishers.

Driehuis, W. and Van der Zwan, A. (eds.) 1978. *De voorbereiding van het economisch beleid kritisch bezien*, Leiden: Stenfert Kroese.

Eichhorst, W. and Wintermann, O. 2005. *Generating Legitimacy for Labor Market and Welfare State Reforms: The Role of Policy Advice in Germany*, the Netherlands and Sweden, IZA Discussion Paper No. 1845.

Eijk, C.J. van and Sandee, J. 1959. 'Quantitative determination of optimum economic policy', *Econometrica* 27: 1–13.

Esping-Andersen, G. 1990. *The Three Worlds of Welfare Capitalism*, Cambridge: Polity Press and Princeton University Press.

Frayssinet, J. 1986. *'Le conseil economique et social'*, *Notes et Etudes Documentaires*, Paris: La Documentation Française.

Graafland. J.J. 2003. 'Balancing information and uncertainty', in J.J. Graafland, and A.P. Ros (eds.), pp. 61–79.

Graafland, J.J.and Ros, A.P. (eds.) 2003. *Economic Assessment of Election Programmes: Does it Make Sense?*, Dordrecht, Boston: Kluwer.

Hartog, H. den and Tjan, H.S. 1974. *Investeringen, lonen, prijzen en arbeidsplaatsen*, Occasional Paper no. 2, The Hague: Central Planning Bureau.

Hartog, H. den and Tjan, H.S. 1976. 'Investment, wages, prices and demand for labour (a clay-clay vintage model for the Netherlands)', *De Economist* 124: 32–55.

Hoppe, R. and Halffman, W. 2004. 'Wetenschappelijke beleidsadvisering in Nederland; trends en ontwikkelingen' (Scientific policy advice in the Netherlands, trends and developments), *Beleidswetenschap* 18/1: 31–61.

Kadushin, C. 1995. 'Friendship among the French financial elite', *American Sociological Review* 60: 202–21.

Kerkhof, M. van de 2004. *Debating Climate Change; A Study of Stakeholder Participation in Integrated Assessment of Long-Term Climate Policy in the Netherlands*, Utrecht: Lemma Publishers.

Klamer, A. 1990. *Verzuilde dromen: 40 jaar SER* (Pillarised dreams, 40 years SER), Amsterdam: Uitgeverij Balans.

Kleinknecht, A. 1994. 'Heeft Nederland een loongolf nodig? Een neo-Schumpeteriaans verhaal over bedrijfswinsten, werkgelegenheid en export', *Tijdschrift voor Politieke Ekonomie* 17: 5–24.

Kleinknecht, A. 2003. 'Causes of the Dutch job miracle: There is no free lunch', *De Economist* 151: 329–33.

Klep, P.M.M. and Stamhuis, I. (eds.) 2002. *The Statistical Mind in a Pre-statistical Era: The Netherlands 1750–1850*, Amsterdam: Aksant, NEHA Series III.

Merkies, A.H.Q.M. 1973. *Van Prognoses naar Programma's*, Inaugural lecture, Amsterdam: Vrije Universiteit, 13 April 1973.

Mooij, J. 1994. *Denken over Welvaart, Koninklijke Vereniging voor de Staathuishoudkunde, 1849–1994*, Utrecht: Lemma.

Morgan, M.S. 1990. *The History of Econometric Ideas*, Cambridge University Press.

Mosch, R.H.J. 2004. *The Economic Effects of Trust; Theory and Evidence*, Tinbergen Institute Research Series no. 340, Amsterdam: Thela thesis.

Nickell, S. and van Ours, J. 2000. 'The Netherlands and the United Kingdom: A European employment miracle?', *Economic Policy* 30 (April 2002): 137–80.

Ostrom, E. and Walker, J. 1997. 'Neither markets nor states: Linking transformation processes in collective action arenas', in D.C. Mueller (ed.), *Perspectives on Public Choice: A Handbook*, Cambridge University Press, pp. 35–72.

Putnam, R.D. 1993. *Making Democracy Work: Civic Traditions in Modern Italy*, Princeton University Press.

Review Committee CPB 1997. *Scanning CPB; A View from the Outside*, The Hague: Central Planning Bureau.

Social Economic Council (SER) 2002. *Advies sociaal economisch beleid 2002–2006*, The Hague: SER.

Stamhuis, I.H. 1989. Cijfers en Aequaties en Kennis der Staatskachten; *Statistiek in Nederland in de negentiende eeuw*, Amsterdam, Atlanta: Rodopi.

Stamhuis, I.H. 2002. 'Vereeniging voor de Statistiek (VVS); een gezelschap van juristen', *STAtOR* 3/2: 13–17.

Tinbergen, J. 1936. 'Kan hier te lande, al dan niet na overheidsingrijpen een verbetering van de binnenlandse conjunctuur intreden, ook zonder verbetering van onze exportpositie? Welke lering kan ten aanzien van dit vraagstuk worden getrokken uit de ervaringen van andere landen?', in *Praeadviezen voor de Vereeniging voor de Staathuishoudkunde en de Statistiek*, Den Haag: Nijhoff, pp. 62–108.

Tinbergen, J. 1952. *On the Theory of Economic Policy*, Amsterdam: North-Holland.

Tinbergen, J. 1956. *Economic Policy: Principles and Design*, Amsterdam: North-Holland.

Verbon, H.A.A. 1998. 'Vernieuwing van de partij – CPB modellen verwijtbaar ondeugdelijk', *Christen Democratische Verkenningen* 7–8: 345–9.

Woldendorp, J.J. 2005. *The Polder Model: From Disease to Miracle? Dutch Neocorporatism 1965–2000*, Thesis, Vrije Universiteit Amsterdam.

Zanden, J.L. van 2002. 'Driewerf hoera voor het poldermodel', *Economisch Statistische Berichten* 87: 344–7.

11 Quality control for the leading institutes of economic research in Germany: promoting quality within and competition between the institutes

Gert G. Wagner

Introduction

This paper deals with a special branch of the publicly financed system of research-based policy advice in Germany: the *leading institutes* for economic research. These institutes have the task of providing *non-partisan advice* to the public, the government, political parties, and NGOs of all kinds.

Following a short introductory discussion of concepts and problems of research-based policy advice and of some of the specific problems of economic and social policy advice that arise in this context, this chapter describes the idea and the system of quality control in the aforementioned institutes for economic research, whose shared aim is to provide non-partisan, *independent* advice. The system of quality control is (1) established within the individual institutes for economic research and (2) enhanced by competition between the institutes.

A major conclusion of this chapter deals with the common interest of governments, political parties and NGOs in obtaining partisan, and often confidential, advice – in other words, advice which is based on certain value judgements and political goals. The system of publicly funded non-partisan research institutes is not able to provide this kind of *internal* advice. One possible solution – that of founding private research institutes capable of providing such research- *and* value-based advice – is discussed in the outlook section below.

This chapter does *not* discuss the non-research-based policy advice that is becoming increasingly prevalent within the German government, especially in the fields of economic and social policy. Thus, we do not address the quality of consulting services provided, for example, by the Bertelsmann Foundation or consultants like McKinsey or Roland Berger. It is worth mentioning that this kind of consultancy, which is often confidential (*internal advice*), is not the solution to policymakers' desire for fast and tailored research-based advice. The reason is simple: consultants who are not researchers are not able to give research-based policy advice – neither public nor private.

1   General discussion

1.1   *Basic problems of research-based policy advice*

Research-based policy advice is difficult by its very nature, due to the inherently conflicting aims of politics and policymakers on the one hand, and science and researchers on the other: while politicians want to make *final* decisions, good researchers want to constantly raise new questions (see Kaube 2006). In other words, while good scholars will never stop asking questions, policymakers – and the general public – will always seek clear-cut answers. From the individual policymaker's point of view, in the best-case scenario, his answer will be clearly identifiable by the unambiguous scientific arguments on which it is founded. Unfortunately, this dream is far from the realities of politics and policymaking.

Most problems of politics and policy cannot be solved through scientific research because they are problems of political objectives. In other words, policy problems are inherent in the conflicting interests and priorities of the different groups in any given society. This raises the problem not just of finding the best instrument for achieving a particular goal effectively and efficiently, but also of determining which set of objectives can be realistically agreed upon by majority decision within a society and its parliament(s). As a result, political decisions must necessarily be based on the values and preferences of the citizens and voters. For example, there is no scientific answer about the *right* (or *just*) pension level or the *correct* level of government health care coverage. In other words, tax rates and the structure of the tax system, for example, depend on preferences (political aims), and they must be determined by truly political decisions. There is no best level of taxation based on purely scientific insights.

Science and research cannot legitimate policy goals, but this is clear only in theory.[1] In the real world, politicians – and even the general public – not only demand scientific results and research-based prognoses in order to achieve their aims effectively; they also want advice on the aims themselves. Furthermore, policymakers like to *upgrade* the rationale underlying their political aims by bringing in researchers – in their

---

[1] The author is grateful to Juergen E. Zoellner (Senator for Education and Research of Berlin) for a very valuable discussion of the problems discussed in this section and his hint on Sarewitz (2004).

capacity as researchers, not as citizens (Weingart 1999). And since many researchers – as citizens – have their own political goals that they would like to promote, many cannot resist the temptation when given the opportunity to provide policy advice.

Some researchers even decide to become *covert* politicians, campaigning for their political goals in a clandestine manner. In the natural sciences, this covert campaigning often has the simple aim of shaping the research agenda and perhaps raising money for own research. In the social sciences, i.e. in economics, sociology and political science, where research is not so expensive, it is more likely that researchers want to influence the economic and social agenda of the government and political parties. For example, it may be that so many economists want to reduce tax rates because, as high-income earners, they do not need public schools for their children or a national health care system (or at least: they *believe* that they do not need such systems).

Sarewitz (2004) stresses the delicate issue of scientists possibly having hidden value agendas. In this context, self-selection of young people into different scientific disciplines may be affected by their values and preferences. For example, it could be that teenagers with more egoistic values and materialistic financial ambitions will more often choose economics and business administration as their fields of study. If this is the case, economists may overrate the role of egoistic values and objectives in the general public and thus in political goals. And, in fact, we have empirical evidence that students of economics are more selfish than other students (see Frank, Gilovich and Regan 1993; Frey and Meier 2005).

When policy advice is given to the public, quality control is crucial. The public might be confused by poor advice, due either to poor scientific quality itself or to (hidden) values and political agendas. When policymakers turn to publicly funded institutes, they should be able to obtain the highest scientific quality possible, because otherwise the taxpayers' money would be wasted. In research-based policy reports, value judgements and policy goals should at least be made transparent, because in reality, they are unavoidable. At the same time, policymakers need and want value-based, one-sided advice from renowned scientists. To meet this need, legitimate forms of value-based policy advice must be found as well.

1.2   The case of economics

The general problems discussed above apply to economics as well, and they are even exacerbated by specific properties of this discipline. First, economics deals with a very complex system – the economy – which is extremely difficult to analyse. And just as the climate is difficult to predict (Sarewitz 2004), so forecasts, which are biased by hidden value judgements, contain very real dangers. As a result, recommendations for political action informed by hidden (personal) political agendas are a common problem in the field of economic policy research and advice.

Another key problem arises from the fact that economics, as a science, of course has no monopoly on providing advice on economic policy, economic aspects of other policy problems or other policy arenas (see also the outlook section). For example, legal scholars and political scientists give advice on almost all policy fields. And consultants, who mimic research-based advice, are present in all arenas. This results in pressure to provide advice that is not based on the best kind of economic research possible. Perhaps even more important, the competition between scientific disciplines in the policy advisory market creates the problem that representatives of the respective disciplines try to say the same things, i.e. give the same advice, because they believe that unanimous advice given by one discipline is more likely to be accepted by decision-makers than a chorus of divergent advice. Due to this strategy, two problems arise.

First, when a discipline tries to speak with a single voice, the mainstream of that discipline becomes stronger and stronger. A strong mainstream will become blind to new kinds of problems. Second, economists in particular believe that they can win the competition with other disciplines in the field of policy advice by giving simple and loud advice, and especially by repeating simple messages – which necessarily contain hidden values and goals – as often as possible. For example, one common statement often heard from economists, 'It is certain that we must reduce the tax burden', contains a host of assumptions, values, and political goals within the term *must*. Economists often assume that the government can survive on less money because government expenditures are already too high. Unequivocal statements about *musts* pretend a sound knowledge of the potential side-effects – for example, that taxation discourages gainful employment. But very often, this knowledge is not very solid: in the case at hand, still very little is known about the effects of high taxation on the labour supply, especially of males.

In other words, economists and economics as a discipline do not have a *theory of communication*. Thus, when academic economists (and the same seems to be true for other scientific disciplines) communicate in the public sphere, they do so based on very simple ideas about good communication. Empirically it has been shown that most economists believe that they must formulate their ideas in very simple terms for the general public – that otherwise, nobody would listen to them and their often unpopular messages. So economists repeatedly advocate, for example, reducing tax rates and privatising government services. And when doing so, they not only remain silent about the weak empirical evidence they have about the impact of their proposals; they also very often mix scientific arguments (about impacts) with political statements (which they should make as citizens, but not as scientists).

Many economists have clear personal ideas about the aims a government should try to achieve. The worst thing they can do, of course, is to use their scientific advice as a vehicle for covertly promoting personal agendas. But working openly to persuade politicians of the merit of their specific agendas is not much better. For example, if economists argue in favour of reducing public expenditures because this would increase freedom in society, this is not a good way of giving advice. Politicians do not like this kind of advice: they are the specialists in the field of values and objectives, and economics as a science is not focused on values per se. Now, because most economists have no experience (as citizens) with politics, they are in fact not very successful in persuading politicians to adopt certain values and goals. One side-effect of such efforts at persuasion is that the economists' findings are discredited in the eyes of politicians. As a result of their bad reputation in the policy arena, economists' research insights are often not taken into account by politicians or governments. Thus, before seeking research-based policy advice, policymakers should first attempt to answer the following questions:

- Which problems need *research-based* advice, and which problems do not?
- Which aspects of the problem can be analysed by the policymaker's staff (for example, research units within government ministries)?[2]
- Which aspects should be analysed by commissioning researchers?
- Which aspects should be analysed by independent research institutes (independent advisers)?
- Might an ad hoc commission be necessary to stimulate the political decision-making process? Should the members of such a commission participate in their capacity as scientists or in their capacity as citizens?

Given the basic problem of hidden agendas, quality control in the field of research-based policy advice, and especially in economic and social policy, must pursue two goals:

- ensure the best possible scientific quality of statements about the future state of the world and about the impacts of policy programmes; and
- disclose hidden goals in statements by scientists and foster open discussion of political goals.

---

[2] Possibly provided by researchers who are not on the tenure track common within ministries, where *research careers* normally culminate in a permanent position as civil servant.

2   The *leading institutes* for economic research in Germany

In Germany, there exists a system of think-tanks on economic research financed by the federal and state governments.[3] These institutes are financed through the Leibniz Association (WGL). As of 2009, they are (in alphabetical order): German Institute for Economic Research (DIW Berlin), ifo Institute for Economic Research (*Information und Forschung*, Munich), Kiel Institute for the World Economy (IfW, Kiel), Halle Institute for Economic Research (IWH, Halle), Rheinisch-Westfälisches Institute for Economic Research (RWI Essen), and the Centre for European Economic Research (ZEW, Mannheim).[4]

These institutes have the aim of providing independent, public advice based on the highest possible research quality standards. All these institutes were founded in the early to mid-twentieth century to promote empirical economic research, which at that time was underdeveloped at the German universities. Since the very beginning, there has been a pronounced division of labour between the university economics departments and the institutes that conduct empirical economic research (see Tooze 1999, 2001).

Since its inception after World War II, Germany's system of *leading research-based economic think-tanks* (führende Wirtschaftsforschungsinstitute) has tried to tackle the problem of hidden value judgements and hidden policy agendas by fostering competition between institutes. When this system was established, the idea was that the different institutes would take differing perspectives, based on different assumptions and theories, value judgements, and policy goals ('institutional plurality') (Postlep and Wagner 1998). Moreover, it was assumed that by means of competition between the institutes, scientific quality would be ensured as well.

---

[3] In the classification developed by Wilhelm von Humboldt (and published around 1810), they belong to a class of institutes situated outside the university and the Academy of Sciences that he calls 'inanimate institutes' (leblose Institute) or 'support institutes' (Hilfsinstiute) (Humboldt 1810: 454). The experiments and studies they conduct are not 'pure' basic research but support the Academy and the university. He gives the example of medical and biological collections (anatomische und zootomische Theater). Although the institutes are 'inanimate', they belong to the system of research (höheren wissenschaftlichen Anstalten), but are under the direct supervision of the government (unmittelbar unter Aufsicht des Staates). The author is grateful to Wolfgang Rohe (then Wissenschaftsrat/German Council on Science and Humanities) who pointed him to the quotes and the respective paper by Wilhelm von Humboldt (after a stimulating presentation to the Wissenschaftsrat by Peter Weingart (2006) on policy advice).

[4] Up to 2005, ZEW was not a member of the WGL; ZEW replaced the Hamburg Institute of International Economics (HWWA, Hamburg) which was closed – for quality reasons – on 31 December 2006.

For these research institutes, the potential problem of hidden values or private political agendas in research-based policy advice is tackled by promoting competition between the institutes and debates in the general public. The hope is that by means of public discussions, value judgements and (private) policy goals will be disclosed. Whether or not this strategy has really been successful remains to be studied, but it is certain that the individual institutes cannot promote concrete proposals for reform without discussion. Competition between the institutes is really a system of checks and balances.

Against the background of the problems of value-ladenness of the discipline and the political ambitions of economists, the quality of research at Germany's leading economic research institutes, and the ability of the system to disclose hidden values and goals came under scrutiny starting in the early 1980s. The German Council on Science and Humanities (Wissenschaftsrat) was instructed to evaluate the system of 'leading economic research institutes' (see Hoffmann and Wagner 1998). At the end of this process, which took about six years, recommendations were published (see Wissenschaftsrat 1998, 2002) and stricter quality controls were implemented by the institutes' funding bodies (the federal and state governments) (see Schmidt 2006; Ketzler and Zimmermann 2009).

This evaluation process not only detected scientific quality problems within the institutes due to their insufficient integration into the scholarly community of university economists (Wissenschaftsrat 1998); it also identified quality problems throughout the entire German economics community, which was not adequately integrated into the global community of economists (Wissenschaftsrat 2002). In particular, the evaluation found that empirical research, which is of utmost importance for forecasting and policy analysis, was underdeveloped at German universities. As a result, one could say that whereas the economic research institutes suffered from a lack of theory,[5] the universities suffered from a lack of empirical research. To make things even worse, both systems were not communicating enough with each other – and all of them were not communicating enough with economists abroad (especially with the economics mainstream in the Anglo-American world).

This is not the place to describe the scientific improvements that have been made in the economics departments of German (and European) universities in recent years, nor to discuss the problems of an economic

---

[5] They were truly *inanimate* in Humboldt's sense (1810) (see n 3 above).

science whose mainstream is based on narrow assumptions about the rationality of economic agents. In this chapter, the mainstream is accepted as the benchmark for good scientific quality in economic science.

Given the importance of demand in determining how scientific policy advice is received and how it takes effect, research-based advice cannot be improved just by improving the scientific quality of the advisers. To improve the impact of the advice, it is crucial to increase awareness and knowledge of the issues among both the general public and decision-makers.

3   An example: the German Institute for Economic Research (DIW Berlin)

In this section, measures for quality assurance within and between the leading economic research institutes are discussed using the example of the German Institute for Economic Research (DIW Berlin). The rationale for this choice is simply the fact that the author of this contribution is affiliated with DIW Berlin, since 1989, as director of the German Socio-Economic Panel Study (SOEP).[6]

The German Institute for Economic Research (DIW[7] Berlin) is one of the six leading economic research institutes in Germany. It is an independent, non-profit academic institution which is involved in economic and social policy advice and, since about 2000, in basic research in applied economics.[8] DIW Berlin was originally founded in 1925 as the Institute for Business Cycle Research (Tooze 1999, 2001) and was later renamed the German Institute for Economic Research. Current economic and structural data, forecasts and advice as well as services in the area of quantitative economics are provided to decision-makers and to the broader public. The institute's research findings provide a basis for the exchange of ideas among experts and other relevant groups.

---

[6] The SOEP-group based at DIW Berlin is responsible for a multi-disciplinary longitudinal study. Thus, the author is not involved substantially in economic policy advice given by the institute itself. When he became a university professor in 1992 at Ruhr University in Bochum, he continued to work on a part-time basis for SOEP. Since 1997 he has held a joint appointment with DIW Berlin and a university: from 1997–2002 with the European University Viadrina in Frankfurt (Oder) and since 2002 with the Berlin University of Technology (TUB).

[7] DIW stands for Deutsches Institut für Wirtschaftsforschung.

[8] Before 2000 just one group at the DIW was dealing with basic research (but not mainly in the field of economics), the German Socio-Economic Panel (SOEP) study, which was and is led by the author of this article.

In the mid-1990s, the Wissenschaftsrat's evaluation of DIW Berlin uncovered problems in the scientific quality of the institute's work.[9] There, as at all of the other five institutes, only a few papers were being published in refereed journals.[10] Thus, the policy advice was lacking a sound scientific basis. However, the evaluation also brought to light that this problem was not only the result of the institute's own failings, but also of misguided government supervision, which placed too much emphasis on direct policy advice and too little on sound research.

After the evaluation, the goals set by the government and the Leibniz Association (WGL)[11] were changed to focus more on basic research (while still conducting applied research, which is necessary for policy advice) and – as an indicator of successful sound research – on publications in refereed journals. Before 2000, the main publication outlet was the *Weekly Report* (*Wochenbericht*), which was edited in-house. Since 2000, DIW Berlin has been committed to conducting applied economic research recognised by the international scientific community[12] and to providing, on this basis, research-based policy advice to national, European, and international policymakers, the business community, and the general public.

The basic idea of quality control at DIW Berlin is that the quality of policy advice is ensured best by publications in peer-reviewed journals (see Wissenschaftsrat 2007). So, ideally, all policy advice should be based on published and peer-reviewed findings. In order to ensure this, all of the researchers at DIW Berlin are required to publish in peer reviewed journals. Moreover, only publications in journals listed in the Social Science Citation Index (SSCI), the Science Citation Index (SCI), the index for Arts and Humanities (A&H) and the Computational Statistics (CompStat) index are counted. Already the papers selected for publishing in the DIW Berlin *Discussion Paper*, a preprint series, must have a good chance of being accepted by such a journal. Thus, all manuscripts submitted to the discussion paper series are reviewed by staff members, who evaluate them on this basis.

---

[9] The site visit took place in 1996; the report was published in 1998.

[10] Moreover, most of the publications in refereed journals were authored by a project group outside the regular departments: the SOEP Group.

[11] The WGL is the *umbrella organisation* of about eighty non-university research institutions (in all fields) in Germany.

[12] Since then, a broad range of external *Research Professors* and *Research Affiliates* have been coming to DIW Berlin to conduct research alongside the institute's regular staff. Research Professors and Affiliates cooperate for a specific time, perform cross-sectional tasks, manage scientific surveys (such as thesis projects, dissertations), and provide an important stimulus to the institute's work.

In other words, the DIW's reaction to the Wissenschaftsrat's critique was not to hire a small contingent of top researchers that would publish a huge number of papers to make up for the rest of the staff, who would continue to focus on policy advice, and not publish in peer-reviewed journals. DIW Berlin chose another strategy: it tried to lift all researchers up to a level that allowed them to do basic research (in applied fields) and to publish in established peer-reviewed journals.[13]

However, the government and the general public often cannot wait for peer-reviewed results. So the DIW implemented an internal peer review system for policy advisory reports. A very strict internal review system for the *Weekly Report* (*Wochenbericht*) has been in place since its inception, but it makes a huge difference whether fellow researchers have experience publishing in peer-reviewed journals are the reviewers for the *Wochenbericht* (as is now the case) or if the reviewers have no experience in high-level scholarly publishing (as was the case before).

Even an internal referee system is sometimes not fast enough to meet the need for quick responses for a public debate. Sometimes journalists want a spontaneous statement on an issue that was never discussed before, either in the political arena or in the scientific community. An example is the demand for estimates about the economic impact of events like the 9/11 catastrophe.

So the rule is that only staff members who have already published high-quality papers in their field of expertise should talk about that (and only that) field in public. High-quality papers may include peer-reviewed policy reports, peer-reviewed Discussion Papers, Wochenberichte, or, in the best-case scenario, papers in SCI/SSCI-listed journals. The heads of the six research departments of DIW Berlin decide about the rights (and the duties) of staff members to release public statements and to interact with journalists. The communications department has the task of coordinating the responsibilities of the departments for different fields. The president has the right to talk about any of the institute's research fields in public.

However, because total *ex-ante* quality control of public statements is not really feasible, the best concept of quality control over policy advice is the concept of *quality assurance by selecting the right staff members*.

---

[13] An analysis done by Ketzler and Zimmermann (2009) shows that all the leading institutes are becoming more successful in giving policy advice on a sound scientific basis. Whereas in 2000, none of the institutes had more than 20 per cent of their researchers publishing in high-visibility refereed journals, in 2005, almost 50 per cent of the scientific staff of the best institute (DIW Berlin) were publishing in such journals.

This is very much the principle that is applied by the best research universities when they grant tenure. They do not necessarily evaluate their faculty by counting *ex-post* publications and third-party funds; instead, they ensure top research and teaching quality by selecting promising faculty members (see Frey and Osterloh 2006).

Because an institute cannot survive without a strong research reputation,[14] the idea of *quality control of policy advice by scientific reputation* can work – but only if the whole scientific community agrees on the same goals. In the case of economics, it is important that empirical research has a strong reputation. This was not entirely the case in Germany up to the 1990s. After the Wissenschaftsrat's comprehensive evaluation of the field of economics in Germany, the discipline changed its aims and priorities. Empirical research counts now more than ever (Schmidt 2007) and the research infrastructure for doing empirical research is undergoing significant improvements (KVI 2001; Solga and Wagner 2007).

4   Conclusions and outlook

The publicly funded *leading institutes for economic research* are better prepared than ever to fulfil their role as economic think tanks providing research-based policy advice. Empirical research in economics is stronger than ever, and more capable than ever of offering a sound basis for policy advice. And the institutes under supervision of the Leibniz Association (WGL) are working hard to build and strengthen their scientific foundations. The main instruments of quality control are (1) the selection of promising researchers who will be able to provide solid scientific input to policy advice and (2) publications in peer-reviewed journals. But the problem of the hidden political agendas that could be pursued by individual institutes cannot exclusively be controlled by internal quality measures within each institute. In order to overcome this danger, competition among the institutes in the public debate remains a key *quality measure*.

The institutes, on the other hand, (or their directors and staff) can pursue clandestine political goals and promote hidden values because the disclosure of values and goals is difficult when a discipline is dominated by its mainstream. And this is especially the case when this mainstream believes that the general public and politicians cannot understand anything but the most simplistic statements. Simplicity mostly implies short statements, that usually contain implicit values and goals. If this situation coincides with a dominant mainstream, the

---

[14] Which an older professor can do, at least as an individual.

competition between the institutes will not work because every single institute will convey the same values and goals to the general public. This problem can only be overcome through competition between different disciplines dealing with the same problem.

So it is important that, for example, not only economists give advice about the tax system, but also lawyers, sociologists and psychologists. For the public, conflicting advice can be puzzling, but there is no better measure for the disclosure of hidden value statements and the political goals of scientists and institutes. Thus, a chaotic chorus of different policy recommendations – which may seem at first to discredit science and research in the public eye – actually has a genuinely positive value. The general public (and politicians and governments) should accept that research-based policy advice must be *chaotic* whenever value judgements and political aims play a major role (as it is the case with most issues of economic and social policy).

But one problem, already discussed in section 1, remains. The general public, politicians and decision-makers do not just want research-based economic advice. They also want scientists and researchers to partici-pate in setting the agenda (by contributing new issues), and they want economic research institutes to play a role in day-to-day debates on economic policy and economic aspects of other policy fields. These aims frequently imply policy advice on a very weak scientific basis. Moreover: although it is not the role of research institutes, politicians ask them for confidential advice about the values and aims they may want to promote and achieve.

For example: in the public debate on tax reform, politicians do not just want demonstrations of the effects of different tax schemes. Often, policymakers, and even the general public, want advice about the *goals* that a particular reform ought to achieve. Ultimately, decision-makers often want a rather partisan kind of advice. This desire is extremely valuable for individual politicians, and in some cases ultimately for society as well, but it undermines the scientific basis of the advice. Because this problem is unavoidable, publicly funded think tanks – which for very good reasons are not allowed to give partisan advice – should not be the only ones in a society.

Privately funded think tanks that are free to give partisan advice are necessary, too. These kinds of *biased* partisan think tanks are well known abroad (for example in the USA), but not in Germany.

If publicly funded (economic) think tanks have to ignore particular value systems and political aims, then the political parties and other organisations (like employer associations, trade unions, etc.) need to found their own think tanks based on their specific values and aims.

Up to now, only an Employer Association and the Association of Trade Unions are running small economic think tanks: the Institute of the German Industry (iw Cologne) and the Macroeconomic Policy Institute (IMK Düsseldorf).

It is an interesting question whether we should have fewer publicly funded, non-partisan, research-based economic institutes in Germany and more partisan, but research-based think tanks. The major parties have foundations promoting political education, but currently do not run their own research institutes or think tanks. They should understand the problems this situation entails and consider founding non-independent economic institutes and think tanks.

REFERENCES

Frank, Robert H., Gilovich, Thomas and Regan, Dennis T. 1993. 'Does studying economics inhibit cooperation?', *The Journal of Economic Perspectives* 7/2: 159–71.

Frey, Bruno S. and Osterloh, Margit 2006. *Evaluations: Hidden Costs, Questionable Benefits, and Superior Alternatives*, Working Paper No. 302 of the Institute for Empirical Research in Economics, Zurich: University of Zurich.

Frey, Bruno S. and Meier, Stephan 2005. 'Selfish and indoctrinated economists?', *European Journal of Law and Economics* 19: 165–71.

Hoffmann, Lutz and Wagner, Gert G. 1998. 'Die Rolle der empirischen Wirtschaftsforschung für die Politikberatung', *Wirtschaftsdienst* 78/3: 185–92.

Humboldt, Wilhelm von 1810. *Über die innere und äußere Organisation der höheren wissenschaftlichen Anstalten in Berlin. Wilhelm von Humboldt Ausgewählte Schriften – Herausgegeben von Theodor Kappstein*, Berlin 1917: Borngräber.

Kaube, Jürgen 2006. 'Die Öffentlichkeit der Wissenschaft', *Max Planck Forschung* 3: 15–18.

Ketzler, Rolf and Zimmermann, Klaus F. 2009. 'Publications: German economic research institutes on track', *Scientometrics* 80/1: 231–52.

KVI (Commission for the Improvement of the Statistical Infrastructure) 2001. 'Summary report of the commission set up by the federal ministry of education and research (Germany) to improve the statistical infrastructure in cooperation with the scientific community and official statistics', *Schmollers Jahrbuch* 121/3: 443–68.

Postlep, Rolf-Dieter and Wagner, Gert G. 1998. 'Zur Ökonomik grundfinanzierter wirtschafts- und sozialwissenschaftlicher Forschung', *Jahrbücher für Nationalökonomie und Statistik* 217/3: 345–58.

Sarewitz, Daniel 2004. 'How science makes environmental controversies worse', *Environmental Science & Policy* 7: 385–403.

Schmidt, Christoph 2006. 'Fokus, Fokus, Fokus? Zur Rolle der außeruniversitären Wirtschafsforschungsinstitute', *Allgemeines Statistisches Archiv* 90: 617–22.

Schmidt, Christoph 2007. *Policy Evaluation and Economic Policy Advice*, IZA Discussion Paper 2700, Bonn.

Solga, Heike and Wagner, Gert G. 2007. 'A modern statistical infrastructure for excellent research and policy advice – Report on the German council for social and economic data during its first period in office (2004–2006)', *Schmollers Jahrbuch* 127/2: 315–20.

Tooze, Adam 1999. 'Economic statistics and the Weimar state: The Reich's statistical office and the institute for business-cycle research, 1924–1933', *Economic History Review* LII.

Tooze, Adam 2001. *Statistics and the German State 1900–1945: The Making of Modern Economic Knowledge*, Cambridge University Press.

Weingart, Peter 1999. 'Scientific expertise and political accountability: Paradoxes of science in politics', *Science and Public Policy* 26/3: 151–61.

Weingart, Peter 2006. 'Providing policy advice is an academic duty', *Humboldt Kosmos* 87: 8–11.

Wissenschaftsrat 1998. *Wirtschaftsforschungsinstitute der Blauen Liste in den alten Ländern – Allgemeine Gesichtspunkte* (Drs. 3320/98), Berlin.

Wissenschaftsrat 2002. 'Empfehlungen des Wissenschaftsrat zur Stärkung der wirtschaftswissenschaftlichen Forschung an den Hochschulen', *Schmollers Jahrbuch* 122/4: 635–51.

Wissenschaftsrat 2007. 'Kriterien des Ausschusses Ressortforschung für die Begutachtung von Bundeseinrichtungen mit FuE-Aufgaben' (Drs. 7693–07), Berlin.

12 Quality control and the link between science and regulation from a national and EU administrator's perspective

Geoffrey Podger[1]

Introduction

This chapter has to be read against the background of the last five posts of the author spread over fifteen years. I became particularly involved in issues surrounding the scientific input in policy in 1991 when I took over responsibility for health promotion in the UK, and a key issue for us was whether science was properly taken into account in policymaking or whether it was excessively *values driven*. The issues we were dealing with included alcohol consumption, drug taking and issues including AIDS surrounding sexual behaviour. Subsequently, in 1996, I moved across to the Ministry of Agriculture in the UK taking responsibility for both scientific assessment and risk management. My career continued in this field with the creation of the independent Food Standards Agency, whose Chief Executive I became and, in 2004, I was chosen as Executive Director of the European Food Standards Agency, being then responsible for only risk assessment. Both these bodies were the direct result of the BSE crisis – a subject to which I will return. Finally, since the end of November 2006 I have been the Chief Executive of the British Health and Safety Executive which is responsible for both avoiding accidents in the workplace and promoting occupational health and has both scientific and regulatory responsibilities.

The theory

In theory, of course, there is no great problem regarding quality control and the link between science and regulation. The best scientists produce the best science, the regulators conscientiously base their rules upon it taking account of relevant non-scientific factors and – Bob's your uncle – the deal is sealed. In reality, however, the possibility of shipwreck lurks at each stage of the voyage, and the transfer between the completed risk

---

[1] The views expressed are strictly personal.

assessment and the risk managers is particularly hazardous. Hence I propose to examine the problems of risk assessment, the issues relating to the transfer to risk management and, finally, the inherent difficulties with the risk management process of regulation.

The perils of risk assessment

Put very crudely, risk assessment for most regulatory issues consist of bringing together relevant experts, getting them to examine the expert work already undertaken in the area and then asking them to conclude, if possible in quantitative terms, as to their assessment of the risk. Would that it were so simple!

In recent years, not least because of the sensitivity of issues, be they nuclear power or GM food, there has been a strong tendency to question closely how panel experts were chosen. This has usually been accompanied by a welter of accusations that the experts chosen were biased ab initio and not fit people to *sit in judgement*. Certainly all the institutions I have worked for were scrupulously careful to avoid experts, however good, of whom such criticisms might legitimately be made. EFSA, for example, responded in very great and public detail to personal attacks on individual members of its GMO panel, and I have to say the views of the Board, which are publicly available, fully reflected my own confidence in their good faith.

The modern tendency to attack experts on unjustified grounds should not, however, in my view, lead us to believe that there is not an inherent problem in the choice of experts. Science, like other disciplines, tends to proceed by the formation of schools of thought accepted or challenged by each generation. Should the challenge succeed, a new school of thought is formed reflecting the work of the challenge and the process continues. We should never, of course, conclude from this that all scientific positions are essentially transitory and cannot be regarded with any degree of certainty but equally we would be unwise to believe that the possibility of a change in view does not exist – *never say never* as the saying goes. Thus we have an inherent difficulty in that risk assessors cannot guarantee absolute certainty in their assessments, but regulators and political authorities, faced with relentless media pressure, have often felt naked without such assurances and potentially driven towards what in scientific terms would be over compensatory measures for a particular risk. This has manifested itself in issues of real difficulty: The original scientific view of the likelihood that BSE would infect humans was that this was very unlikely. Given what was known at the time, this was a very reasonable view but subsequent events showed it to be wrong.

Conversely, the UK has seen large-scale controversies as to whether mattresses cause cot deaths or whether certain vaccines are harmful to children, where the original scientific view has been much disputed and there have been considerable shifts in public behaviour but the original scientific view is generally now accepted. Hence we have a problem in that whilst acting on what we know – or believe we know on best authority – is certainly, in my view, the best way forward, there will always be uncertainties and an occasional dramatic change of expert view as happened with BSE.

We should not, however, in my view, become over depressed by the discovery, if that is what it is, that scientific knowledge is inherently sub-optimal. The real lesson of BSE, particularly in the UK, is not that the population cannot accept scientific doubt but rather that they do not care to be given assurances with 100 per cent confidence in one week, only to be told the opposite the next. Hence a key part of the communication of risk assessments has to be a willingness to communicate doubt but in a way which the receiver of the message can accept as reasonable. In my own experience this is much less of a Herculean task than it may appear: People are quite prepared to function with large elements of uncertainty in their daily lives and very often seek no more than the assurance that the best estimation that can be made has been made. Once our expert panels or committees have been appointed, we are, however, by no means out of the woods regarding the quality of our risk assessments. Particular problems which need to be carefully considered include:

1. whether the question asked admits of a scientific answer or even if it does, whatever that answer will actually be of any use to the regulator asking the question;
2. wherever there are a prior issue of methodology or approach to be considered;
3. whether there is a need for further research before the question can be answered;
4. wherever there is reason to doubt the data submitted by an applicant under an approvals process.

The first question is, if anything, one of the most fundamental challenges to good science leading to good regulation. When EFSA was first established, I well remember the incredulity of our Commission colleagues that we should presume to argue about the questions given to us. Yet over time, Commission colleagues became quite as enthusiastic as we were for a process of dialogue over the question asked to make sure that what was being asked was eventually going to lead to conclusions which were scientifically meaningful and would be useful. Issues of methodology and approach are key to forming conclusions and for those reasons should be fought over hard by the experts involved. Otherwise there is a serious risk, as has for example been argued to be the case in relation to nutrition expert committees, that the results of any study will follow directly from the names of those appointed to study it given their allegiance to particular ways of data interpretation.

Certainly more generally at EFSA we obliged our external experts to declare not merely financial but also intellectual interests, not because the latter were in any way a disqualification but simply because it was essential that there should be an element of expert challenge.

The issue of the need for further research often bedevils risk assessment. Clearly it is desirable for assessors to indicate if they wish a particular experiment to be conducted (as for example could easily be done in relation to BSE by feeding species with contaminated feed). At the same time it is important that the possible need or desirability for new research does not prevent scientific advice coming forward on present knowledge with all the caveats as to the uncertainties. Of course, if present knowledge is genuinely inadequate to permit of any conclusions, this should be stated. It is, however, important not to delay decision-making merely because the knowledge base could be reinforced.

Finally, a controversy much in recent evidence has been that of whether independent scientists advising risk managers should accept data provided by companies seeking scientific acceptance of a particular product. The key issue to me would seem to be not who funds the data collection but whether there is reason to challenge that it has been produced accurately to proper scientific standards.

There is little reason why the taxpayer should be expected to fund replication of studies undertaken by an applicant unless there is real doubt as to its integrity. I have never seen evidence for this proposition and it was clear at EFSA that GM food data for example, which became the casus belli in our area, could be and was already challenged by our experts, and that much of the data was in fact supplied to companies by reputable third parties. We should also remember that human medicines are approved on the basis of company submitted data – what evidence is there that this actually causes a problem?

Transfer between risk assessors and risk managers

The transfer of the output of the risk assessors to the risk managers is again not without problems. Risk managers clearly have to take account of factors which risk assessors can ignore. Some may be quantitative or at least quantifiable whereas others are more subjective or qualitative. In the quantitative field, it is clearly proper that the consequence of potential risk management measures should be costed in order to allow for some kind of risk benefit analysis. In my own experience such costings are inherently difficult and subject to rather less independent rigour than scientific risk assessment.

The source for such costings is often industry which will tend to inflate or deflate costs according to whether or not they wish to proceed. Costs produced will also tend to be gross rather than net with the result that the cost benefits of a risk management proposal will often be ignored. Thus, for example, those representing the agriculture sector have in the past resisted additional food safety measures on grounds of cost without recognising the increased profits to be derived from a range of products becoming more acceptable and more valuable to the consumers as a result. Conversely, large businesses may be influenced to underestimate the cost of risk management measures if they perceive that the overall effect of a proposed regulation may be to raise a higher barrier to market entry and thus provide a commercial advantage to those, like themselves, already achieved in a particular sector.

These issues become ever more important when one considers the inputs to the qualitative issues for risk managers. Public opinion, for example, is notoriously difficult to assess. Anti-GM campaigners have continually sought to argue that there are high levels of public concern about GM food. Yet bodies like the UK Food Standards Agency have found little evidence that the public links GM food amongst its concerns unless prompted to do so by the questioner.

The issue becomes even more complex when stakeholder dialogue is used to determine, or at least advise, on difficult risk management issues. I should say at the offset that I am myself a strong advocate of stakeholder dialogue as a means of allowing strongly held views to be represented, and to establish whether a greater degree of common ground between the *warring parties* may not exist than was immediately obvious. A good example of this would be the successive review of BSE control measures in the UK held again by UK FSA where the whole range of opinion from farmers, to scientists, to the relatives of those who had died from variant CJD (Creutzfeld–Jakob disease) were represented. Here were genuine shifts of opinions as a result of stakeholders being able to interact directly with the scientists who were advising: The farmers were convinced of the dangers of prematurely relaxing control measures whilst both the relatives of the vCJD and consumers did come to accept that by then very low levels of risk could and should be tolerated.

Nevertheless, we should certainly not take the view that stakeholder consultation is without risks or that it invariably lends to greater acceptance of the best science or a willingness to act on it. In particular, organisations representing a single point of view are likely to use any offer of their involvement as an opportunity for publicising their own position rather than being prepared to reconsider their views in the light of other arguments, including those of the scientists. They are more or less obliged to do this if they are to maintain their *raison d'être*, but the effect of their participation can often then be to simply increase the level of public disquiet and misunderstanding and thus to make a rational and proportionate decision at the political level less likely.

There is also, in my view, a serious danger that defamatory attacks on scientists who refuse to bow to group pressure will ultimately mean that fewer and fewer of the best scientists will be prepared to engage in public debate at all, and the field will simply be left to their less authoritive but more publicity seeking colleagues.

None of this, however, should be taken as a plea to leave the formulation of risk management measures to scientists alone. I strongly agree that they should be involved, not least to prevent misinterpretation of their own results by risk managers whether or not innocently motivated. However, we equally have to accept that risk assessors will often have a slight prejudice in favour of excessive action in relation to their own subject area, as evidenced by the repeated views of nutritionists that we should price confectionary *out of the market*, of public health specialists that we should cease drinking alcohol and of toxicologists who believe that life can and should be made *carcinogen free*.

The interface between politicians and risk managers

As we all know, it is precisely at moments of apparent crisis that it is most difficult for scientific messages to be communicated effectively at the political level. This is not surprising given that such events are normally accompanied by

1. high levels of media coverage;
2. high emotional feelings (particularly where deaths) have occurred;
3. virulent political opposition to a ruling politician's position;
4. a desire to find people to blame;
5. a demand for absolute guarantees that the incident will not recur.

Faced with the kind of pressures listed above, there is a severe limit as to what help can be offered by science and its exponents to politicians. Cold reason does not resonate well in emotional situations; science is not a tool essentially to place blame and scientific recognition of uncertainties is such that there can rarely be an absolute guarantee of non-recurrence. It is hardly surprising that in these circumstances the politicians may find the scientist's contribution less than helpful. Although their worlds overlap, they are not the same. This was vividly brought home to me when looking after food safety in the UK and an incident came to light of meat being on sale from animals wrongly fed from a preheated mix which contained human excrement.

Whilst the scientist was quite happy to declare the food safe provided proper assurances could be given to the length and temperature of the heat treatment, the minister concerned found it unbelievable that he should be expected to announce that such food was safe on the grounds that people would first not find this an emotionally convincing proposition. Both, of course, were correct!

It is equally important, in my view, that the responsibilities of scientists and politicians do not become confused. On more than one occasion in my last post when appearing before the European Parliament, I was challenged as to how I could say that EFSA was an independent body and how, in any case, could this be desirable. I always made clear that my position was that we in EFSA gave the best scientific advice we could, independent of political influence, and that subsequently it was for politicians to decide how they wished to act. To do otherwise is, if unintentionally, to subvert democracy, and I think that it is ultimately for politicians to balance the *apples and pears* of complex issues (e.g. risk vs. cost), to judge the claims of rival stakeholders and to conclude on the great intangibles such as ethical issues, public acceptability and the level of protection to take against uncertainty.

Conclusion: the way forward

In this chapter I have not hesitated to make clear the difficulties for politicians and scientists alike in maintaining the integrity of scientific advice in the handling of contentious real world issues. It would, however, be wrong to maintain that there are not a number of steps we can take which will preserve better, if not perfectly, the quality of scientific advice without encroaching on territory and decisions that are properly the politician's. Let me outline the main ones.

At the risk of seeming trite it is clear that transparency both of process and outcome is helpful to the proper presentation of science and its use and acceptance at the political level. Throughout the EU and beyond, much has been done to bring about this end. Clearly part of gaining public and political confidence in scientific risk assessment is if the process has gained acceptance by scientific peers or at least by a reputable majority, recognising that there will always be those with *axes to grind*. This can be achieved by having scientific committees composed of reputable experts, by (where time allows) a willingness to consult on conclusions and, above all else, publishing in full conclusions and the studies on which they are based to allow for critical and informed comment. Countries, including my own, which have been faced with real difficulty in relation to credibility have gone further by including, for example, consumer representatives in scientific committees and by encouraging them to meet in public. Others, no less reputable, have set their forces against precisely such measures and indeed I have successively run organisations (EFSA and FSA) which took up these varying positions. The unifying factor, however, was the desire to ensure transparency of outcome and approach and it seems to me that this is the fundamental assurance that politicians both deserve and need public credibility.

The second very important point for political acceptance of science is that scientists should not give advice which goes beyond their competence. This, in my view, embraces not only the issue I have already discussed of covering doubt and uncertainty, but also of not pretending or appearing to pretend that science resolves issues which are desperately important but of a non-scientific nature. To take an obvious example, we may believe – and I do – that the evidence shows clearly that GM food is as safe as its conventional equivalent. It does not, however, follow that those who object per se to GM food for whatever reason should thereby be obliged to eat it. Society has to decide this kind of issue as to what level of choice should be made available by law and what can be left to the market. This has to be resolved on non-scientific grounds because it is a non-scientific question. By the same token, debates on nuclear energy have to distinguish between scientific debate on how the technology can be safely regulated and broader non-scientific issues surrounding both public acceptability of nuclear power and indeed, in this instance, its relative life-cycle cost.

The final point I would make is that if scientists wish to win a greater acceptability and use of their expertise at the political level, they have to be willing to accept that the manner of its communication is important in itself and is not simply a subset of the substance of the advice. At EFSA and elsewhere I have myself been involved in a continuing dialogue with scientific experts as to how we can provide advice which is at least intelligible to intelligent and interested lay people. Otherwise there is a serious risk that important information is effectively obscured by the manner of its expression. This is not simply an inevitable consequence of the complexity of an issue, although that can be all or part of the explanation, it may be that there is a conscious or subconscious desire amongst risk assessors and risk managers to obscure difficult issues and prevent proper public recognition and debate. To take an example known to all of you, can one really believe that the present nutrition labelling requirements of the EU are actually understood by ordinary people (who are after all the intended users) or have we historically seen a connivance by experts and the relevant business interests to provide information which is precise, scientifically accurate and generally unintelligible. So there is still much to do. Nevertheless, my own view is optimistic. Much has been achieved in recent years and, as I hope this chapter has indicated, much more still could be achieved in making maximum use of scientific advice at the political level for all our benefit. As Goethe famously wrote, 'Immer streben ist das Leben' and here as elsewhere there is much striving to do!

13 Science into policy: The European Environment Agency

*Sven Dammann and David Gee**

Providing environmental information and framing the discourse – the EEA's tasks and institutional settings

The European Environment Agency (EEA) is a specialised agency of the European Union (EU), dedicated to supporting sustainable development and to helping achieve significant and measurable improvements in Europe's environment, through the provision of timely, targeted, relevant and reliable information on the environment (EEA 2004). Main clients of the Agency's indicator- and case study-based assessments are the European Commission, the European Parliament, the Council of the European Union – especially through the EU-presidencies – and the thirty-two member states of the EEA (membership of the EEA is also open to countries that are not among the twenty-seven member states of the EU). Its seat is in the Danish capital Copenhagen.

The EEA currently has an annual budget of circa €40 million and approximately 180 staff members.

The EEA has been operational since 1994.[1] Its founding regulation's Article 1 (EEC 1990) defines its role as follows:

To achieve the aims of environmental protection and improvement laid down by the Treaty and by successive Community action programmes on the environment, the objective [of the EEA] shall be to provide the Community and the Member States with:

- objective, reliable and comparable information at European level enabling them to take the requisite measures to protect the environment, to assess the results of such measures and to ensure that the public is properly informed about the state of the environment,
- to that end, the necessary technical and scientific support . . .

---

* The views expressed by Sven Dammann are personal and not those of the European Economic and Social Committee or the European Commission. There are no conflicts of interest for either author.

[1] Thus almost twenty-five years after the creation of many *national* environmental advisory bodies (see Susan Owen's chapter in this book, Chapter 5).

For the purposes of achieving the objective set out in Article 1, the tasks of the Agency shall be:

- to help ensure that environmental data at European level are comparable and, if necessary, to encourage by appropriate means improved harmonization of methods of measurement ...
- to provide uniform assessment criteria for environmental data to be applied in all Member States ...
- to stimulate the development and application of environmental forecasting techniques so that adequate preventive measures can be taken in good time ...
- to stimulate the development of methods of assessing the cost of damage to the environment and the costs of environmental preventive, protection and restoration policies (EEC 1990: Articles 1 and 2).

It is noteworthy that the founding document explicitly entrusts the EEA with the task of providing not only data and information about the present and future states of the environment, but also data necessary for the *framing* of policy issues and the identification and evaluation of environmental measures and legislation (EEC 1990: Article 2.II).

The EEA does not carry out research itself. Accordingly, essential elements of its work are

- to maintain extensive networks with sources of environmental data and information such as the environmental agencies of the member states and the research communities;
- to organise the regular gathering of harmonised environmental data and, based on these data;
- to generate transnational state-of-the-environment reports suitable for use in policymaking.

The Agency has three main target audiences, each with specific needs:

1. the public: here, the challenge is to turn the data and information into messages that are comprehensible to laypersons;
2. policymakers in the European Commission, the European Parliament, the European Council and in the member states, working with the identification, implementation and effectiveness of EU-legislation and policies;
3. experts in the scientific sphere, interested both in aggregated data and in more specific information such as a time-series of data for a certain river or catchment area or an urban agglomeration.

The Agency sees its role as the main provider of environmental information at the EU-level throughout the whole policy cycle of:

1. problem framing and identification;
2. policy response;
3. implementation of policy measures;
4. environmental and health impact assessment and monitoring; and
5. evaluating the effectiveness of the policies.

Key for assuring reliable, credible and targeted environmental reporting: the European Environment Information and Observation Network (EIONET), the Management Board and the Scientific Committee

Three institutional elements are key to assure the reliability and credibility of the EEA outputs:

1. the European Environment Information and Observation Network (EIONET) assures a reliable stream of data from quality assured sources;
2. the Scientific Committee's advice provides assurance that the EEA's work complies with criteria and concerns of the scientific community; and
3. the Management Board's oversight ensures that the EEA's work meets the needs of the policymakers and the public in the member states and the EU institutions.

The European Environment Information and Observation Network (EIONET) is crucial for the credibility of the EEA outputs, as it organises the passing of 'information for environmental policy from official scientific sources through officially controlled channels in comparable units and formats ... which is to render them reliable, objective and comparable' (Waterton and Wynne 2004).

The EIONET[2] is established by the EEA founding regulation as a network of national organisations and experts dealing with environmental informational services. Important elements of the EIONET are:

- National Focal Points (NFP; typically national environment agencies or environment ministries in the member states): they coordinate national networks and assist in communicating the EEA information to end users in the member states;
- National Reference Centres (NRC): national organisations and experts nominated by the EEA member states to work with the EEA in specific thematic areas;

[2] See http://eionet.europa.eu/

- European Topic Centres (ETC): consortia of institutions across EEA member states dealing with a specific environmental topic (water, terrestrial environment, resource and waste management, air and climate change, nature and biodiversity).

Other important contributors are European and international organisations, such as the European Statistical Office (Eurostat) and the Joint Research Centre (JRC) of the European Commission, with whom the EEA has agreements on data transfer and cooperation in the areas of resource accounting, chemicals, environment and health, soil and forestry, the Organisation for Economic Co-operation and Development (OECD), the United Nations Environment Programme (UNEP) and Food and Agriculture Organization (FAO), and the World Health Organization (WHO).

The Management Board determines the overall direction of the EEA. It comprises thirty-two representatives of the EEA's Member States, two representatives of the European Commission (DG Environment and DG Research) and two representatives of the European Parliament, thus giving the main users of the EEA's products an important say on the Agency's work programme. Though it contrasts with the concept of an advisory body's complete independence in the determination of its work content (see Chapter 5, Susan Owens' chapter on the UK Royal Commission on Environmental Pollution), the Management Board is a core element of the necessary 'interaction of scientists with policymakers' and 'knowledge auditor' (see De Wit, Chapter 8). Enshrined in the governance structure of the Agency, it has in practice been key to assuring the quality of the EEA products in terms of relevance, timing and targetedness. It has achieved this without compromising the Agency's independence with regard to data collection and publication. At one of their very first meetings the Management Board underlined the essential importance for the credibility and legitimacy of the EEA that data should be assembled by scientific experts according to uniform criteria established by the Agency experts. The Board stressed that this should not be altered or suppressed for political reasons, and resolved that the information published by the Agency should be published on the sole authority of the Executive director and his/her staff and should not be subject to amendment for political reasons by the Management Board or any member of it.

The Management Board also approves the appointments of the EEA's *Scientific Committee*, which assists the EEA in providing scientific advice and delivering professional opinion on any scientific matter in the areas of work undertaken by the Agency. It is composed of twenty independent scientists from the EEA member states, covering a variety of environmental fields. The members are identified through an open selection process and appointed for a four-year term, renewable once.

Quality was key to establish the EEA as a credible actor

The EEA has never had to face a credibility crisis such as the one the Netherlands Environmental Assessment Agency was confronted with due to its non-transparent handling of scientific uncertainty (Van der Sluijs 2002; see also his contribution to this book, Chapter 14). On the contrary, it has established itself as an important, if not *the* most important authority with regard to assessing the European environment and European environmental policies. Key to obtaining this position was the compliance of EEA products with the three quality-attributes of:

- *saliency* (reflecting whether an actor perceives the assessment to be addressing questions relevant to their policy or behavioural choices);
- *credibility* (reflecting whether an actor perceives the assessment's arguments to meet standards of scientific plausibility and technical adequacy); and
- *legitimacy* (reflecting whether an actor perceives the assessment as unbiased and meeting standards of political fairness).

(Identified in the *Global Environmental Assessment Project* (Clark *et al.* 2002) as determinants for the influence of assessments.)

The report *The European Environment – State and Outlook 2005* (EEA 2005b), a core product of the Agency, provides a good illustration of how *saliency, credibility* and *legitimacy* are obtained in practice. As a new feature the 2005 report contained the 'Country scorecards', a direct comparison of member states' performance with regard to a core set of environmental indicators such as *greenhouse gas emissions per capita/per GDP, energy consumption per capita/per GDP* or *share of renewables in electricity*. This politically sensitive, comparative display was obviously extremely salient and highly relevant to key policies on climate change and their implementation. But how was credibility and legitimacy to be achieved?

The above-mentioned fact that data is assembled by scientific experts according to uniform criteria established by the Agency experts, and that neither data nor published information is altered or suppressed for political reasons, was the first essential for credibility and legitimacy.

Having said this, it is important that the Agency should work closely with the prime sources of information in the member states. The outlook was therefore 'developed in a process of extensive consultation with the member states and, in particular, with the experts on environmental reporting within those countries . . .' (EEA 2005b: 501). The EEA ensured 'that the scorecard has legitimacy with its member states by using a consultative approach to develop the methodology; [and by using] only Core set indicators with the highest quality of validated data' (EEA 2005b: 505).

The countries were additionally invited to contribute their own voice to the overall assessment and interpretation of the scorecard results as part of the country analysis section. This section provided an opportunity for countries to raise issues specific to their situation and to bring in relevant information that served to balance the scorecard results.

The upshot of this careful consultative process is that although worse-performing member states are not always happy with being ranked in direct comparison with other countries, they are sufficiently involved in the process to accept its legitimacy and have never seriously challenged the figures that have emerged and the implied comment on the effectiveness of implementation in the different member states. This process involving countries in assessments was further developed in the 2010 State of the Environment report (EEA 2010).

Two main contexts of quality: reliable data for influential assessments

The example above well illustrates two different contexts of quality of EEA products:

- In connection with the EEA's task of establishing regular flows of harmonised data from its member states on the five thematic areas, climate change, air, water, biodiversity and land use, and to transform these into indicator-based reporting *quality* is a question of establishing and maintaining a reliable production line from the acquisition of data, their numerical and graphical expression, their interpretation in response to the respective policies and their distribution and communication to the target audiences.
- In the context of the EEA's role as an organisation at the boundary between the sphere of science and the sphere of policymaking, where the agency has evolved from a mere provider of environmental information to European policymakers to being an influential voice in the environmental policy discourse, *quality* is framed in a broader way as a question of what characteristics of the EEA's products can maximise their influence, while always maintaining acceptance by the member states and the European Commission.

Quality at the level of data gathering and processing

The example above from the EEA's third state and outlook report on the European environment talks of 'indicators with the highest quality of validated data'; *quality* refers here to data-characteristics such as density, completeness, level of aggregation, representativeness for the system in question, precision and actuality; in line with the EEA's task to provide 'reliable and comparable information at European level' (EEC 1990: Article 1.2). A senior staff member of the EEA's Information and Data Service explained the difficulties of establishing a regular flow of data and how this task has evolved during the fifteen years of the EEA's existence:

10 years ago we were happy to know *what kind of data* we wanted, then we had to find the data and then we had to assess its quality, checking for example, if the level of aggregation was appropriate. Countries are not so keen on reporting on wastewater plants that emit into the open sea, to name an example, as this is politically sensitive. Providing data at an unsuitable level of aggregation can be a way to disguise shortcomings.

The EEA always provides transparent meta-information on the quality of the presented data in its reports.

Reporting obligations linked to technically often somewhat vague environmental conventions and EU environmental legislation had to be operationalised and streamlined, fixing formats and procedures of data gathering and transmission. What began in the 1990s as a one-directional flow of reporting data from the member states to the EEA is now being developed into a web-based *shared* information system that renders data equally accessible to all data network nodes. The question 'What kind of data do we want, to answer what question?' has been at the origin of the EEA's data gathering – *quality at the level of data* is embedded in the second context of quality – the provision of information to users.

Framing of quality in the context of provision of information to users

For fulfilling the EEA's mission 'to help achieve significant and measurable improvements in Europe's environment, through the provision of ... information on the environment to policy making agents and the public', the following dimensions of quality are relevant:

1. knowledge context;
2. relevance to the problem in focus;
3. reliability of the information;
4. robustness of the information;
5. timing; and
6. targetedness.

Knowledge context

The information published in EEA reports needs to be properly contextualised. The graph of a state of the environment indicator such as 'reduction of biodiversity by member states in terms of number of species becoming extinct per year', for example, needs to be explicit about the uncertainties in the measurement, about ignorance, about the extent of interpolation as well as about the possibility of surprises (for example, non-linear developments and tip-over effects when surpassing natural thresholds and triggering self-reinforcing feedback-loops). When the information concerns the state of the environment and possible political responses, it should crystalise contradictions and trade-offs of different solutions or approaches. This is, for example, relevant with regard to the future energy policy of the EU and the different strategies applied, since each of the discussed sources of energy (coal, renewables, nuclear, energy saving, biofuels, etc.) bring about their own specific consequences and uncertainties.

Many actors outside the scientific realm wish for simple information and simple policy conclusions. But it is not always possible to satisfy this wish. A knowledge-provider like the EEA has to be careful not to over-simplify and must communicate the qualities, the complexities and uncertainties of information arising from different sources, as well as multi-causal contexts. Information from mono-disciplinary discourses may be of a different quality than information that has been developed in an inter-disciplinary context that integrates multiple knowledges, including lay and local knowledge. 'When magnitude and type of error are uncertain, social choices (for example, about burdens of proof) become just as important as scientific standards' (SETAC 2002).

It is also important for the EEA to properly characterise the nature of the knowledge base from which it derives its information. The complexity of ecosystems, for example, arises partly from the role of *multiple factors* in controlling ecosystem functions. There is a great deal of knowledge about many factors taken *singly*, but much less knowledge about how these factors *interact* to control ecosystem-level processes.

Similarly, within biology, our understanding of genes has shifted from *simple* genes with a single function towards a complex pattern of many genes, each playing a small role in a lot of tasks. This underscores the importance of moving beyond reductionism to systems biology.

The quality of information provided can strongly influence the framing of the public debate and can have implications for policy options. For example, if there appears to be a plausible risk from a chemical or other agent, the question arises: is the agent *needed* (or how much is it needed) and do we want the uncontrollable uncertainties that its use may bring about? (Waterton and Wynne 2004). These are questions of values and may be reflected in the pursuing of a policy base on the precautionary principle.

The EEA has explicitly addressed the relevance of 'precaution', ignorance and uncertainty to the environmental and health impacts of chemicals and other agents in its report, *Late Lessons from Early Warning: the Precautionary Principle 1896–2000*, one of its most influential reports[3] which was translated not only into Japanese and Russian, but also turned into film documentaries and taken up in university teaching and vocational training curricula.

Relevance to the problem in focus

As scientific knowledge expands, the inter-connections between ecological and biological systems and the complexity of the systems science 'become' greater. This has implications for the *precision/relevance* and the *specificity/comprehensiveness* trade-offs in integrated assessments. The philosopher of science and founder of fuzzy set theory Lotfi A. Zadeh pointed out that: 'As the complexity of a system increases, our ability to make a precise and yet significant statement about its behaviour diminishes until a threshold is reached beyond which precision and significance (or relevance) become almost mutually exclusive characteristics' (Zadeh 1965). When providing information about complex ecological and biological systems, the Agency therefore can often only provide information that is *relevant* rather than *precise*, especially when the goal is the prevention, and not just the identification, of harm.

The characteristics of the problem in focus have implications for the relevance of the knowledge to be provided. Relevant questions are:

• Knowledge for what? – Is the problem framed appropriately to address the key policy questions? Do we have the data to answer these questions? How can we obtain the relevant data as opposed to the available data?
• Knowledge for whom? – Are risk creators or risk takers the target group? Who or what may be the victims of any harm? Future generations; far flung people; particular species or ecosystems?

---

[3] One of the report's case studies, ' "Mad cow disease" 1980s–2000: how reassurances undermined precaution', a case which let to the establishing of the European Food Safety Authority (EFSA), is also addressed in Michael D. Rogers' contribution to this book (see Chapter 7).

- At what scale and focus are measurements and monitoring appropriate to the problem? For a chaotic system, for example, the frequency of monitoring is crucial.[4]

Reliability of the information

Information provided by the EEA as the basis for policy advice must be *reliable*. The degree of reliability expected of the information, however, may vary with the context: 'What is the information for?' – is it for the identification and evaluation of a problem? Or for the reduction, elimination, or adaptation of the problem? Is the information for helping to identify potential harm or for justifying the provision of environments that will promote health, such as green spaces? And what are the costs of being wrong in acting or not acting, and who will bear those costs?

These questions are crucial for determining the strength of evidence, and therefore the quality of information needed to justify different policies. In his influential 1965 paper on association or causation in environmental health, the epidemiologist Austin Bradford Hill proposed different strengths of evidence for different purposes:

- *relatively slight* evidence – for example, to protect pregnant women and the foetus from a possibly teratogenic effect of the contraception pill;
- *fair evidence* – for example, to prevent exposure to a probable carcinogen in the workplace;
- *very strong evidence* – for example, to prohibit public smoking or to implement dietary restrictions on the public.

Other generic levels of evidence appropriate for different purposes are:

- beyond all reasonable doubt;
- reasonable certainty;
- balance of probabilities/evidence;
- strong possibility; and
- scientific suspicion of risk.

The Swedish chemical law, for example, provides for a 'science-based suspicion of risk' as sufficient for action by the regulator (to restrict a chemical substance), which can be overturned only by proof 'beyond

---

[4] De Wit underpins relevance and contextualisation as important quality criteria in his chapter of this book (see Chapter 8), making the point that without these, high scientific quality of knowledge may go along with low political applicability.

reasonable doubt' provided by the producer that the substance is 'safe' (Wahlström 1999). This illustrates nicely the idea of different strengths of evidence for different purposes as well as the placing of different burdens of proof on different actors at different parts of the process.

Robustness of the information

EEA information must also be scientifically and socially robust. The *robustness* of the science includes the nature of the knowledge available, the methods used to generate it and to what degree these are prone to error, as well as the use of the knowledge, with some uses requiring more robustness than others. These issues need to be rendered transparent to policymakers and require a 'willingness to communicate doubt', as Podger puts it in his contribution to this book (see Chapter 12). In this context, two main directions of error can occur in the environmental health sciences, for example. These errors can be false positives (i.e. asserting that A causes B when it does not) or false negatives (i.e. asserting that A does not cause B when it does). These main directions of error should be widely known, communicated to policymakers, and considered in the respective policies.

Table 13.1 displays these main directions of error for some of the commonly found methodological features of the environmental health sciences. It shows that the methods are more likely to generate false negatives than false positives, which can contribute to bad policymaking where exposures are already occurring but wrongly considered harmless due to false signals (or false interpretation of the signals) from the science world.

In the light of the above, an important conclusion of a workshop on scientific uncertainty at the *Bridging the Gap* Conference on sustainability research and sectoral integration, jointly organised by the Swedish Environmental Protection Agency, the European Commission and the EEA in 2001, was that 'improved scientific methods to achieve a more ethically acceptable and economically efficient balance between the generation of "false negatives" and "false positives" are needed' (EEA 2001). The fourteen case studies in the EEA report *Late Lessons From Early Warnings – The Precautionary Principle 1896–2000* (EEA 2001), which are all false negatives, show how a more detailed scrutinising of science for policy and a precautionary approach to policymaking can increase the chances of anticipating costly impacts, of achieving a better balance between the pros and cons of technological innovations, and of minimising the costs of unpleasant surprises. In their search for

Table 13.1 *On being wrong: environmental and health sciences and their main directions of error (Gee 2006)*

Scientific studies	Some methodological features	Main[a] directions of error – increase chances of committting a
Experimental studies (animal laboratory)	• High doses	• False positive
	• Short (in biological terms) range of doses	• False negative
	• Low genetic variability	• False negative
	• Few exposures to mixtures	• False negative
	• Few foetal-lifetime exposures	• False negative
	• High fertility strains	• False negative (developmental/ reproductive end points)
Observational studies (wildlife and humans)	• Confounders	• False positive
	• Inappropriate controls	• False positive/negative
	• Nondifferential exposure misclassification	• False negative
	• Inadequate followup	• False negative
	• Lost cases	• False negative
	• Simple models that do not reflect complexity	• False negative
	• Publication bias towards positives	• False positive
Both experimental and observational studies	• Scientific/cultural pressure to avoid false positives	• False negative
	• Low statistical power (e.g. from small studies)	• False negative
	• Use of 5% probability level to minimise chances of false positives	• False negative

[a]Some features can go either way (e.g. inappropriate controls) but most of the features mainly err in the direction shown in this table.

regulatory false positives, Hansen, Krayer von Krauss and Tickner 'found only a very limited number of true false positives' and conclude that 'fear of false positives is not a reasonable argument against future application of the precautionary principle. The concern for false positives should also be weighed against the very substantial evidence of numerous false negatives that have resulted from past practices' (Hansen *et al.* 2007). They emphasise the key point the EEA report *Late Lessons From Early Warnings* helped to document: That 'too little attention is being paid to avoiding false negatives. Regulatory decision makers often worry about taking too much precaution but do not seem to have similar worries about not taking precaution enough' (Hansen *et al.* 2007). The current global financial collapse is a recent example of a very damaging failure of financial regulators to heed the early warning signals that were available and to apply prudence instead of profligacy. *Social robustness* means that the EEA strives to assure the usefulness of its products by developing these throughout the different phases of the framing of a problem, supporting the development of policy measures and monitoring the effectiveness of these measures in close contact with the EEA's user groups. The EEA adheres to a circular and iterative model of risk analysis (in contrast to a linear model) as sketched in Figure 13.1. A formalised procedure of extended peer review, as Funtowicz and Ravetz demand it for 'postnormal conditions' where stakes and uncertainties are equally high (Funtowicz and Ravetz 1990; see also the contributions of Van der Sluijs, Petersen and Funtowicz to this book, Chapter 14), however, is not yet in place at the EEA.

Timing and scaling

A society's response to an emerging issue can be slow, especially if it is a new paradigm that causes problems for the political and economic forces that gain from the old one. For example, the scientific work of Copernicus (1473–1543, *On the Revolutions of the Celestial Spheres*, was only published in the year of his death, though he had developed his theory several decades earlier); and Galileo (1564–1642) was convicted in 1633 to house arrest for the rest of his life because he agreed with Copernicus. These are striking illustrations of how reluctant societies can be to acknowledge and to incorporate scientific evidence, especially if it is new.

More recent examples are the contesting of the risks of asbestos and passive smoking – in both cases it took decades until scientific early warnings, followed by increasingly observable impacts, finally led to policy measures. Changes in environmental systems (and, accordingly, also their scientific monitoring) very often happen at a comparatively *slow* pace that conflicts with the *fast* policy cycles of democracies and markets. In addition, effects often do not occur at the same location and at the same scale as the causes, for example the chemical pollution of the Arctic from European emissions of pollutants (EEA 2003, chemicals chapter).

The unfolding global climate change we are currently witnessing is another striking example of how difficult it apparently is for societies to react appropriately to long-term, large-scale environmental threats; and the hole in the ozone layer is another example of the remoteness in scale of the effect from the many emission sources of a pollutant.

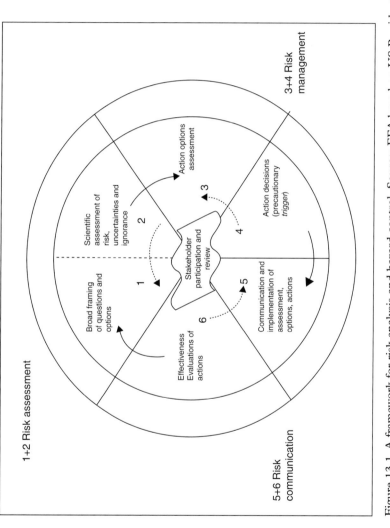

Figure 13.1 A framework for risk analysis and hazard control. Source: EEA based on US Presidential Commission on Risk (1997), Royal Commission on Environmental Pollution, UK (1998), Codex Alimentarius, 2007, National Academy of Sciences 2009.

The EEA addresses these problems of timing and scaling in different ways: for example, the Agency's *Neighbourhood-Project* provides *map-based local* environmental information (for example, on air pollution) whilst the state of the environment reports cover both the national levels (to render the different performances of the different member states comparable) and the European level. Furthermore, the agency contributes to global environmental reporting via its cooperation with the United Nations Environmental Programme.

Data-modelling produces mainly quantitative outlooks and projections such as distance-to-target evaluations or trend analyses. Drawing on both qualitative and quantitative data, the scenario project *Prelude*[5] on different long-term (thirty years from now and beyond) land-use scenarios for Europe brought together experts and stakeholders to address policy agenda setting and emerging issues. With regard to the launching of its products and activities, the EEA often benefits from working closely together with the rotating EU-presidencies to highlight certain issues as priorities during the six months of a presidency.

Targetedness

The EEA's different target audiences, comprising risk-creators as well as risk-takers and victims, policymakers, interest groups, the interested public, science and recently also the younger generation as tomorrow's decision-makers, require targeted information in formats that meet the demands of these different groups. Examples of such formats are the environmental encyclopaedia *Epaedia*,[6] a multimedia source of information that explains environmental issues and their interconnection in an easily understandable way, or the environmental online computer game *Eco-Agents*[7] for a younger audience. Other examples are two-page EEA briefings for policymakers or technical reports for experts.

Disseminating expertise in the field of quality control and quality assurance

In line with its mandate 'to provide uniform assessment criteria for environmental data' (EEC 1990: Article 2), quality control and quality assurance is not only relevant to the EEA with regard to its own products, but also with regard to products aiming at helping other actors to

---

[5] Prospective Environmental analysis of Land Use Development in Europe, http://scenarios.ewindows.eu.org/reports/fol077184.
[6] http://epaedia.eea.europa.eu.   [7] http://ecoagents.eea.europa.eu.

increase the quality of their advice to policy. The EEA's main activities in this respect are:

1. *Late lessons from Early Warnings*: in 2001, the EEA published the report *Late Lessons from Early Warnings – The Precautionary Principle 1896–2000* (EEA 2001). Based on the analysis of fourteen case studies on hazards raised by human economic activities such as the use of asbestos, certain chemicals, the depletion of fishing stock, the mad-cow disease or the ozone layer, the authors from different natural scientific disciplines as well as from the field of science-policy interface distilled twelve *lessons* on the handling of uncertainties and risk. The positive reception of the report has led to a follow-up project with further case studies, covering additional aspects such as the manipulation of science, the significance of lay-knowledge, institutional responses to long-term problems, economic implications of action and inaction, legislative responses to different bodies of evidence and implications for research for policymaking.

2. A review of the *Bradford-Hill criteria*: a joint-project of the EEA and the Imperial College in London has brought together leading epidemiologists to review the criteria for causality in epidemiology and toxicology as discussed in the famous paper by Hill (1965), to take stock of the knowledge in this field, to produce guidelines for a scientifically robust handling of causality in the environmental health sciences, and to expand the relevance of approaches to the evaluation of evidence to other environmental issues such as ecosystems, ecosystem services, and to the positive health benefits of good environments.

3. Sharing expertise in integrated environmental assessment:[8] since its foundation in 1994, the EEA has developed a unique expertise in environmental assessment that integrates[9] the different aspects of the DPSIR-indicator approach and puts the indicator-based reporting

---

[8] *Integrated* here refers to the rationale that environmental requirements cannot be dealt with detached from the societal pressures and driving forces that are the root of environmental problems but have to be inserted into other policies. Environmental reporting has to reflect this. In the case of the EEA this has led (a) to reporting on different relevant domains such as transport, land use or household consumption and (b) to reporting on the state of environmental policy integration itself, e.g. in the technical reports No 2/2005 *Environmental Policy Integration in Europe – State of Play and an Evaluation Framework* and No 5/2005 *Environmental Policy Integration in Europe – Administrative Culture and Practices.*

[9] 'The work of the EEA is built around a conceptual framework known as the DPSIR assessment framework. DPSIR stands for Driving forces, Pressures, States, Impacts and Responses. Particularly useful for policymakers, DPSIR builds on the existing OECD

and the analysis of the data into the respective policy contexts. This expertise is disseminated and shared with partners, for example, in seminars with the environmental protection agency of the USA or in the development of a training curriculum in the context of the UNEP environmental reporting project GEO.

Conclusions

From the perspective of the European Commission many of the special-ised agencies of the European Union are typically seen as a means of *outsourcing* of support or implementation tasks that exceed the adminis-trative capacities of the Commission but are deemed necessary for the Commission to fulfil its mandate in the different policy areas. Policy-making and control usually stay with the Commission.

While the Commission's Directorate General for the Environment 'had [initially] assumed that it would be possible for the Agency' to operate in that limited support role and to 'provide information without directly influencing policy' (Waterton and Wynne 2004), the EEA has managed to *emancipate* itself from such a restricted role and to establish itself as an entity substantially independent of DG Environment with a considerable influence of its own in shaping the European environmen-tal discourse. This is partly due to the fact that the EEA officials, with some support from the Management Board and the Parliament, struggled successfully to expand the agency's mandate to cover the whole policy cycle. It is also due to the Commission's own growing recognition that allowing the EEA to make policy effectiveness analysis part of the agency's mandate, and to produce cogent and powerful reports analysing key issues, actually helped to reinforce the external constituency for environmental action. It has built support for action in the Parliament, the Council, the Economic and Social Committee and amongst the wider policy community and civil society. In so doing, it has

---

model and offers a basis for analysing the inter-related factors that impact on the environment. The aim of such an approach is:

- to be able to provide information on all of the different elements in the DPSIR chain,
- to demonstrate their interconnectedness,
- to estimate the effectiveness of Responses.

During the start-up phase of the Agency, priority was largely given to the areas of Pressures, State and Impacts. Now, increasing attention is given to Driving Forces and Responses, in co-operation with the Commission services, including Eurostat. The EEA is moving towards this, and the five programme areas of the second multiannual work programme cover, to different extents, all the steps in the chain' (EEA 2005a; and available at www.eea.europa.eu/documents/brochure/brochure_reason.html).

also strengthened DG Environment's hand in advancing new measures or urging more effective enforcement, and has thus become a powerful ally and friend to the Commission (if occasionally a critical one) rather than a minor supporting actor.

This recognition and this authority is crucially due to the *quality*, in its many dimensions, of the EEA's products and work as described above. The way the agency carefully strives to maintain high levels of quality, in the context of data gathering and processing as well as in the context of the provision of information to its different user groups, the resulting high degree of *saliency, credibility* and *legitimacy* of the EEA's assessments, the extensive network by which it is linked both to science and to policy communities, as well as its acknowledged politically impartial role as a champion of the environment, have given its statements a weight that has at times exposed the inadequacy of present policies or their implementation and, though unintentionally, challenged the remits of the Commission (Waterton and Wynne 2004).

As also illustrated in Susan Owens' chapter on the UK Royal Commission on Environmental Pollution (Chapter 5), the provision of information has the potential to influence agenda setting; and *information necessary for framing policies* provided by the EEA in fulfilling its mandate (EEC 1990: Article 2.II), once in the public arena, becomes itself an agent of shaping the debate and consequently of *framing policies*. The EEA's practice to influence policy by provision of information and other *soft* mechanisms, in contrast to regulation ('regulation by information' (Majone 1997)), and to strengthen legitimacy by strong inclusion of stakeholders (Clark *et al.* 2002), is echoed by a corresponding tendency towards stronger use of *soft* mechanisms in European Union governance (EC 2001).

The EEA's compliance with quality criteria from the two different spheres of science and of policymaking have established the Agency as a *boundary organisation*[10] at the science-policy interface, i.e. an organisation that communicates, translates and sometimes mediates between the

---

[10] In accordance with Guston's definition: 'Boundary organizations attempt to solve these problems [of dual accountability] by meeting three criteria: first, they provide the opportunity and sometimes the incentives for the creation and use of boundary objects and standardized packages; second, they involve the participation of actors from both sides of the boundary, as well as professionals who serve a mediating role; third, they exist at the frontier of the two relatively different social worlds of politics and science, but they have distinct lines of accountability to each. In this third criterion, the concept of boundary organizations borrows from principal-agent theory (also known as ideal contracting), which holds that organizational relations may be understood as (a series of) delegations of authority from principals to agents within or between organizations' (Guston 2001: 400f.).

arenas of science and policy (Cash *et al.* 2003): Transforming data from the environmental scientific sphere into knowledge formats useful for actors in the policymaking sphere, and translating policy questions into knowledge generation activities in the scientific sphere, the EEA has to manage the dual accountability to science and politics. This role is also reflected in the organisational structure of the EEA, with the policy world represented in the Agency's Management Board, and the scientific world represented in its Scientific Committee.

While quality criteria in the context of data gathering and processing have been laid down in protocols for the parties involved, quality criteria in the context of the provision of information to the agency's different user groups has so far been handled somewhat more informally. Since drafting this chapter, the EEA has further demonstrated its commitment to quality by implementing a Quality Management System, based on the ISO 9000 standard. In 2008, this project had led to a draft Quality Manual and a master list of procedures (EEA 2008) to be further operationalised.[11]

Provided that it can continue to maintain and strengthen the quality of its work in the two senses discussed here, there seems every reason to suppose and hope that the EEA will continue to improve its output and strengthen its influence to the benefit of environmental policymaking, and ultimately of the European environment itself.

---

[11] It should also be noted that as an EU-body, the EEA operates under the 'Decision on code of good administrative behaviour' (OECD 1993) and a Regulation regarding public access to documents (EC 2001).

REFERENCES

Cash, David W., Clark, William C., Alcock, Frank, Dickson, Nancy M., Eckley, Noelle, Guston, David H., Jäger, Jill and Mitchell, Ronald B. 2003. *Knowledge Systems for Sustainable Development*, Proceedings of the National Academy of Sciences, USA – National Academy of Sciences.

Clark, William C., Mitchell, Ronald, Cash, David, Alcock, Frank and John F. Kennedy School of Government 2002. *Information as Influence: How Institutions Mediate the Impact of Scientific Assessments on Global Environmental Affairs*, Cambridge, MA: Harvard University Faculty Research Working Papers Series, RWP02–044.

Codex Alimentarius 2007. *Principles for Risk Analysis for Food Safety*, Rome: FAO/WHO.

EC 2001. Regulation (EC) No. 1049/2001 of the European Parliament and of the Council of 30 May 2001 regarding public access to European Parliament, Council and Commission documents, OJ L 145/43, 31 May 2001.

EEA 2001. *Late Lessons from Early Warnings: The Precautionary Principle 1896–2000*. Environmental Issues Report No. 22, Copenhagen. (Edited by: Poul Harremoës (chairman), Malcolm MacGarvin (executive editor), Andy Stirling, Brian Wynne and Jane Keys (editors), David Gee and Sofia Guedes Vaz (EEA editors).)

EEA 2003. *State of the Environment Report No 3/2003*, available at: www.eea. europa.eu/publications/environmental_assessment_report_2003_10.

EEA 2004. *The European Environment Agency – Who We Are – What We Do – How We Do It*, available at: http://org.eea.europa.eu/documents/brochure2004/ general_brochure_web-EN.pdf.

EEA 2005a. *EEA core set of indicators*, EEA Technical Report 1/2005, Copenhagen.

EEA 2005b. *The European Environment – State and Outlook*, Copenhagen.

EEA 2008. *Draft EEA Quality manual* (internal working document).

EEA 2010. *The European Environment State and Outlook Report*, Copenhagen.

EEC 1990. Regulation (EEC) No. 1210/90 of 7 May 1990 on the establishment of the European Environment Agency and the European Environment Information and Observation Network, OJ L 120, 11 May 1990, pp. 1–6.

European Commission 2001. *European Governance – A White Paper*, COM (2001) 428 final, Brussels, 25 July 2001.

Funtowicz, S.O. and Ravetz, J.R. 1990. *Uncertainty and Quality in Science for Policy*, Dordrecht: Kluwer.

Gee, David 2006. 'Late lessons from early warnings: Toward realism and precaution with endocrine-disrupting substances', *Environmental Health Perspectives* 114 (supplement 1, April 2006): 152–60.

Guston, David H. 2001. 'Boundary organizations in environmental policy and science: An introduction', *Science Technology & Human Values* 26: 399.

Hansen, Steffen Foss, Krayer von Krauss, Martin P. and Tickner, Joel A. 2007. 'Categorizing mistaken false positives in regulation of human and environmental health', *Risk Analysis* 27/1: 255–69.

Hill, Austin Bradford 1965. 'Environment and disease: Association or causation?', *Proceedings of the Royal Society of Medicine* 58: 295–300.

Majone, G. 1997. 'The new European agencies: Regulation by information', *Journal of European Public Policy* 4/2: 262–75.

National Academy of Sciences 2008. *Science and Decisions: Advancing Risk Assessment*, Washington DC.

OECD 1993. 'Core set of indicators for Environmental Performance Reviews', OJ L 267, 20 October 2000, Code of Good Administrative Behaviour, Relations with the public.

Royal Commision on Environmental Pollution 1998. *Environmental Standards*, London: Stationery Office.

SETAC (Society of Environmental Toxicology and Chemistry) 2002. *Interconnections between Human Health and Ecological Integrity.*

US Presidential Commision on Risk Assessment and Risk Management 1997. *Final Report*, Washington DC.

Van der Sluijs, J. P. 2002. 'A way out of the credibility crisis of models used in integrated environmental assessment', *Futures* 34: 133–46.

Wahlström, Bo 1999. 'The precautionary approach to chemicals management: A Swedish perspecive', in Carolyn Raffensperger and Joel A. Tickner (eds.), *Protecting Public Health and the Environment; Implementing the Precautionary Principle*, Washington DC: Island Press, pp. 51–69.

Waterton, C. and Wynne, B. 2004. 'Knowledge and political order in the European Environment Agency', in S. Jasanoff (ed.), *States of Knowledge – The Co-Production of Science and Social Order*, London and New York: Routledge, pp. 87–108.

Zadeh, Lotfi A. 1965. 'Fuzzy sets', *Information and Control* 8(3): 338–53, Academic Press Inc. (cited from Jeroen C. J. M. van den Bergh (ed.), 1999, *Handbook of Environmental and Resource Economics*, Ashgate: Edward Elgar Publishing).

14 Reflective approaches to uncertainty assessment and communication

*Jeroen P. van der Sluijs, Arthur Petersen and Silvio Funtowicz**

1 Introduction

Policy decisions in many areas involving science, including the environment and public health, are both complex and contested. Typically there are no *facts* that entail a unique correct policy. Furthermore, political decisions on these problems will need to be made before conclusive scientific evidence is available. Decision stakes are high: The impacts of *wrong* decisions based on the available limited knowledge can be huge. Actors disagree on the values that should guide the decision-making. The available knowledge bases are typically characterised by imperfect understanding (and imperfect reduction into models) of the complex systems involved. Models, scenarios and assumptions dominate assessment of these problems, and many (hidden) value loadings reside in problem frames, indicators chosen and assumptions made.

The evidence that is embodied in scientific policy advice under such *post-normal* (Funtowicz and Ravetz 1993) conditions requires quality assessment. Advice should be relevant to the policy issue, scientifically tenable and robust under societal scrutiny. Governmental and intergovernmental agencies that inform policy and the public about complex risks increasingly recognise that uncertainty and disagreement can no longer be suppressed or denied, but need to be dealt with in a transparent and effective manner. In response to emerging needs, several institutions that interface science and policy have adopted *knowledge* quality assessment approaches, where *knowledge* refers to any information that is accepted into a debate (UK Strategy Unit 2002; EPA 2003; MNP/UU 2003; IPCC 2005). One of these is the PBL Netherlands Environmental Assessment Agency (Planbureau voor de Leefomgeving or PBL in Dutch; part of which – then named MNP – was previously associated

---

* The views expressed are those of the authors and do not represent necessarily those of the European Commission.

with the National Institute for Public Health and the Environment, RIVM), a governmental agency that performs independent scientific assessments and policy evaluations. PBL has recently implemented a comprehensive, multi-disciplinary checklist approach to knowledge quality assessment, which takes into account the societal context of knowledge production, which will be discussed later on in this chapter.

Such a structured approach to knowledge quality assessment can help to achieve a better awareness of the limits of science in relation to the task of knowledge producers to provide a scientific basis for policy debate. One of the responsibilities of scientific advisers is to point out those situations in which the focus cannot primarily lie on *reducing uncertainties* but where decision-makers will have to *cope with untameable uncertainties and complexities*. This can avoid misunderstandings and undue expectations of the role and competence of science in complex environmental problems.

2   Models cannot remedy ignorance

Since the 1980s, computer models are increasingly being used in complex environmental assessments and foresight: they enable analysts to simulate reality and run several scenarios, thereby integrating knowledge from different disciplines. Applied systems analysis has become the dominant method in environmental assessment. The assumption ladenness of the models themselves, the use of models, the degree to which they can be validated or evaluated, and the transparency of models have been criticised over the years.

To give some examples, Hornberger and Spear (1981, cited in Saltelli 2002) argued that non-linear models with many parameters generally have many degrees of freedom and can be made to produce virtually any desired behaviour, often with both plausible structure and parameter values.

Oreskes *et al.* (1994) highlighted the assumption ladenness of models and argued that natural systems are never closed. They argued that earth system models can, in principle, never be *verified* or *validated*, but only *confirmed* or *corroborated*. Beven's (2002) concept of equifinality (the phenomenon that models may be non-unique in their accuracy of both reproduction observations and prediction) and Beck's (2002) closely related notion that almost all models suffer from a lack of identifiability (many combinations of values for the model's parameters may permit the model to fit the observed data more or less equally well) further emphasise the problematic nature of models and model predictions as a source of knowledge for decision-making.

Yearley (1996) argued that values and value-laden assumptions enter into the formulation of environmental issues before the *facts* are even established by science. Yearley gives examples regarding carbon dioxide, ozone destroying chemicals and biodiversity and concludes that though, at first sight, science might be thought to be clearly universal and thus incontestably applicable to global problems, in practice its universality can be deconstructed and undermined. A similar argument is made by Stirling (1999, 2001), who stresses the critical dependence of final results of risk assessment studies to the starting assumptions made.

Van der Sluijs (1997; Van der Sluijs *et al.* 1998) argued that the building of environmental assessment models inevitably involves subjective choices and value-laden assumptions. Lack of transparency with regard to these assumptions and uncertainties, and lack of reflection on how knowledge that is conditioned on these models and its assumptions differs from well-established knowledge, lead to misunderstandings in the science policy interface on the nature of this type of knowledge. There is a tendency to treat this knowledge as if it is not different from well-established knowledge. The history has many examples of scandals and loss of trust in the scientific basis for policies based on lack of understanding of the nature of knowledge stemming from model-based assessment and foresight. A classic example is the scandal of the IIASA energy scenarios in the 1980s: In a critical review of the models used for these scenarios, Keepin and Wynne (1984) concluded that: 'Despite the appearance of analytical rigour, IIASA's widely acclaimed global energy projections are highly unstable and based on informal guesswork. This results from inadequate peer review and quality control, raising questions about political bias in scientific analysis.' They made a strong case for the need to conduct a rigorous analysis of assumptions in forecasting tools used in the energy field, and the need to test the robustness and sensitivity of results. They argue strongly for an open and accessible documentation and rigorous peer review. The case led to a crisis within the institute and has triggered institutional learning towards more attention for uncertainty and quality control to regain credibility for their work with peer communities and the public.

More recently the Netherlands National Institute for Public Health and the Environment (RIVM) encountered a similar scandal: Early in 1999, H. de Kwaadsteniet, a senior statistician, accused the institute of 'lies and deceit' in their State of the Environment Reports and Environmental Outlooks. In a Dutch quality newspaper (*Trouw*) he criticised RIVM for basing their studies on the *virtual reality* of poorly validated computer models while RIVM presents these results as point values with unwarranted significant digits and without elaborating the uncertainties.

It triggered a vehement public debate on the credibility and reliability of environmental numbers and models. The case got front page and prime time coverage in the mass media over a period of several months and led to debate in the Netherlands' Parliament (Van der Sluijs 2002; Petersen 2006b). The case also triggered a learning process within the RIVM and led to the development of a guidance for uncertainty assessment and communication for the institute (see Section 3.2).

3   Reflective approaches to uncertainty

Until recently, the field of uncertainty analysis mainly evolved around mathematical methods such as sensitivity analysis and Monte Carlo techniques. These tools address quantitative dimensions of uncertainty using sophisticated algorithms (Saltelli *et al.* 2000, 2004). Although these quantitative techniques are essential in any uncertainty analysis, they can only account for what can be quantified and thus provide only a partial insight in what usually is a very complex mass of uncertainties involving technical, methodological, epistemological and societal dimensions. For the class of complex problems that we are concerned with in this chapter, it is often the case that unquantifiable uncertainties may well dominate the quantifiable ones, which implies that these techniques are of limited value for this particular class of problems.

In the school of post-normal science, several new multi-dimensional and reflective approaches to knowledge quality assessment have been developed to systematically address unquantifiable dimensions of uncertainty. We will discuss two key examples here, the NUSAP system and the aforementioned MNP Guidance for Uncertainty Assessment and Communication.

3.1   *The NUSAP system*

NUSAP is a notational system proposed by Funtowicz and Ravetz (1990), which aims to provide an analysis and diagnosis of uncertainty in the knowledge base of complex (environmental) policy problems. It captures both quantitative and qualitative dimensions of uncertainty and enables one to communicate these in a standardised and self-explanatory way. The basic idea is to qualify quantities using the five qualifiers of the NUSAP acronym: Numeral, Unit, Spread, Assessment and Pedigree.

The first qualifier is Numeral; this will usually be an ordinary number; but when appropriate it can be a more general quantity, such as the expression 'a million' (which is not the same as the number lying between 999,999 and 1,000,001). Second comes Unit, which may be of the conventional sort, but which may also contain extra information, as the date at which the unit is evaluated (most commonly with money). The middle category is Spread, which generalises from the *random error* of experiments or the *variance* of statistics. Although Spread is usually conveyed by a number (either ±, % or *factor of*), it is not an ordinary quantity, for its own inexactness is not of the same sort as that of measurements. Methods to address Spread can be statistical data analysis, sensitivity analysis or Monte Carlo analysis possibly in combination with expert elicitation.

The remaining two categories constitute the more qualitative side of the NUSAP expression. Assessment expresses evaluative judgements about the information. In the case of statistical tests, this might be the significance level; in the case of numerical estimates for policy purposes, it might be the qualifier *optimistic* or *pessimistic*. In some experimental fields, information is given with two ± terms, of which the first is the spread, or random error, and the second is the *systematic error* which must be estimated on the basis of the history of the measurement, and which corresponds to our assessment. It might be thought that the *systematic error* must always be less than the *experimental error*, or else the stated ⟨ would be meaningless or misleading. But the *systematic error* can be well estimated only in retrospect, and then it can give surprises.

Finally, there is Pedigree, which conveys an evaluative account of the production process of information, and indicates different aspects of the underpinning of the numbers and scientific status of the knowledge used. Pedigree is expressed by means of a set of pedigree criteria to assess these different aspects. Assessment of pedigree involves qualitative expert judgement. To minimise arbitrariness and subjectivity in measuring strength, a pedigree matrix is used to code qualitative expert judgments for each criterion into a discrete numeral scale from 0 (weak) to, for example, 4 (strong) with linguistic descriptions (modes) of each level on the scale. Each special sort of information has its own aspects that are key to its pedigree, so different pedigree matrices using different pedigree criteria can be used to qualify different sorts of information. Pedigree assessment can be further extended to also address societal dimensions of uncertainty, using criteria addressing different types of value loading, quality of problem frames, etc. (Corral 2000; Craye, Van der Sluijs and Funtowicz, 2005; Kloprogge, Van der Sluijs and Petersen 2005).

NUSAP provides insight on two independent properties related to uncertainty in numbers, namely spread and strength. Spread expresses inexactness whereas strength expresses the methodological and epistemological limitations of the underlying knowledge base. The two metrics can be combined in a Diagnostic Diagram. This maps strength of, for instance, model parameters and sensitivity of model outcome to spread in these model parameters. Neither spread alone nor strength alone is a sufficient measure for quality. Robustness of model output to parameter strength could be good even if parameter strength is low, if the spread in that parameter has a negligible effect on model outputs. In this situation, our ignorance of the true value of the parameter has no immediate consequences. Alternatively, model outputs can be robust against parameter spread even if its relative contribution to the total spread in the model is high provided that parameter strength is also high. In the latter case, the uncertainty in the model outcome adequately reflects the inherent irreducible uncertainty in the system represented by the model. Uncertainty then is a property of the modelled system and does not stem from imperfect knowledge on that system. Mapping components of the knowledge base in a diagnostic diagram thus reveals the weakest spots and helps in the setting of priorities for improvement.

Experiences so far, as reviewed in Van der Sluijs *et al.* (2005), have shown that the NUSAP method is applicable not only to relatively simple calculation schemes but also to complex models in a meaningful way. It is also useful to assess not only parameter uncertainty but also (model) assumptions. Especially when extended to include societal dimensions of uncertainty such as problem framing and value loadings, it promotes reflexivity and collective learning. The task of quality control in the knowledge base of complex and controversial (environmental) policy problems is a complicated one and the NUSAP method disciplines and supports this process by facilitating and structuring a creative reflexive process and in-depth review of the limitations of a given knowledge base. NUSAP makes the various dimensions of uncertainty explicit and enables a systematic and effective societal reflection on them. It provides a diagnostic tool for assessing the robustness of a given knowledge base for policymaking and promotes criticism by clients and users of all sorts, expert and lay and will thereby support extended peer review processes.

3.2   The RIVM/MNP Uncertainty Guidance

After the aforementioned De Kwaadsteniet affair in 1999, a national and international review of the Netherlands Environmental Assessment Agency (then named RIVM/MNP) was undertaken. The auditors recommended that MNP should start a project to systematically address terminology, methodology, interpretation and communication of uncertainty. Following these recommendations, MNP commissioned Utrecht University to develop a practical guidance for uncertainty assessment and communication in environmental assessment studies. This was done in

Table 14.1 *Foci and key issues in knowledge quality assessment*

Foci	Key issues
Problem framing	Other problem views; interwovenness with other problems; system boundaries; role of results in policy process; relation to previous assessments
Involvement of stakeholders	Identifying stakeholders; their views and roles; controversies; mode of involvement
Selection of indicators	Adequate backing for selection; alternative indicators; support for selection in science, society and politics
Appraisal of knowledge base	Quality required; bottlenecks in available knowledge and methods; impact of bottlenecks on quality of results
Mapping and assessing relevant uncertainties	Identification and prioritisation of key uncertainties; choice of methods to assess these; assessing robustness of conclusions
Reporting uncertainty information	Context of reporting; robustness and clarity of main messages; policy implications of uncertainty; balanced and consistent representation in progressive disclosure of uncertainty information; traceability and adequate backing

consultation with an international team of uncertainty experts. It was judged that the scope of the guidance system should extend beyond the mere quantitative assessment of uncertainties in model results per se, and should focus instead on the entire process of environmental assessment.

The RIVM/MNP Guidance for Uncertainty Assessment and Communication (Janssen *et al.* 2003, 2005; Petersen *et al.* 2003; Van der Sluijs *et al.* 2003, 2004; Petersen 2006a) aims to facilitate the process of dealing with uncertainties throughout the whole scientific assessment process (see Table 14.1). It explicitly addresses institutional aspects of knowledge development, openly deals with indeterminacy, ignorance, assumptions and value loadings. It thereby facilitates a profound societal debate and a negotiated management of risks. The Guidance is not set up as a protocol. Instead, it provides a heuristic that encourages self-evaluative systematisation and reflexivity on pitfalls in knowledge production and use. It also provides diagnostic help as to where uncertainty may occur and why. This can contribute to more conscious, explicit, argued and well-documented choices.

Following a checklist approach inspired by Risbey *et al.* (2005), the Guidance consists of a layered set of instruments (Mini-Checklist, Quickscan and Detailed Guidance) with increasing level of detail and sophistication. It can be used by practitioners as a (self-elicitation) instrument or by project managers as a guiding instrument in problem framing and project design. Using the Mini-Checklist and Quickscan Questionnaire, the analyst can flag key issues that need further consideration. Depending on what is flagged as salient, the analyst is referred to specific sections in a separate Hints & Actions document and in the Detailed Guidance. Since the number of cross-references between the documents comprising the Guidance is quite large, a publicly available interactive web application has been implemented (http://leidraad.pbl.nl). This web application also offers a prioritised to-do list of uncertainty assessment actions, and generates reports of sessions (traceability and documentation), which enables internal and external review.

In order to facilitate communication about the different types of uncertainty that arise in scientific assessments, an uncertainty typology is part of the Guidance. The typology is based on a conceptual framework that resulted from a process involving an international group of uncertainty experts most of whom participated in developing or reviewing the Guidance (Walker *et al.* 2003). Uncertainty can be classified along the following dimensions: its *location* (where it occurs), its *level* (whether it can best be characterised as statistical uncertainty, scenario uncertainty or recognised ignorance) and its *nature* (whether uncertainty primarily stems from knowledge imperfection or is a direct consequence of inherent variability). In addition, the typology distinguishes the dimensions *qualification of knowledge base* (what are weak and strong parts in the assessment) and *value-ladenness of choices* (what biases may shape the assessment). The typology is presented as a matrix. This uncertainty matrix is used as an instrument for generating an overview of where one expects the most important (policy-relevant) uncertainties to be located (the first dimension), and how these can be further characterised in terms of the other uncertainty dimensions mentioned. The matrix can be used as a scanning tool to identify areas where a more elaborate uncertainty assessment is required. The different cells in the matrix are linked to available uncertainty assessment tools suitable for tackling that particular uncertainty type. These tools are described in a Tool Catalogue that aims to assist the analyst in choosing appropriate methods.

The Tool Catalogue provides practical (*how to*) information on state-of-the-art quantitative and qualitative uncertainty assessment techniques, including sensitivity analysis, NUSAP (Funtowicz and Ravetz 1990; Van der Sluijs *et al.* 2005), expert elicitation, scenario analysis, and model quality assistance (Risbey *et al.* 2005). A brief description of each tool is given along with its goals, strengths and limitations, required resources, as well as guidelines for its use and warnings for typical pitfalls. It is supplemented by references to handbooks, software, example case studies, web resources and experts. The tool catalogue is a *living document* available on the web, to which new tools can be added.

4 Conclusion

Complex environmental problems have characteristics that require a post-normal science approach in which uncertainty, assumptions and value loadings are subject to explicit and systematic analysis and communication. For this class of problems, knowledge quality assessment should be at the heart of the science-society interface, in order to promote a better awareness of the limits of science in relation to the task of knowledge producers to provide a scientific basis for policy debate. In combination with a widening in focus from *reducing uncertainties* to *coping with untameable uncertainties and complexities*, this can help to avoid misunderstandings and undue expectations of the role and competence of science in complex environmental problems.

Tools and approaches for knowledge quality assessment such as NUSAP and the checklist based Guidance for Uncertainty Assessment and Communication of PBL Netherlands Environmental Assessment Agency, have now been developed, tested and made available. NUSAP helps to systematically assess the technical, methodological and epistemic uncertainties in knowledge claims and helps to focus research efforts on the potentially most problematic parameters and assumptions in models, identifying at the same time specific weaknesses and biases in the knowledge base.

PBL's Uncertainty Guidance structures the tasks of uncertainty management, promotes reflection and forces deliberate choice on how uncertainties are handled. It helps to avoid pitfalls in the assessment and communication of uncertainty.

Similar to a patient information leaflet alerting the patient to risks and unsuitable uses of a medicine, knowledge quality assessment enables the delivery of policy-relevant quantitative information together with the essential warnings on its limitations and pitfalls. It thereby promotes the responsible and effective use of the information in policy processes.

REFERENCES

Beck, B. 2002. 'Model evaluation and performance', in A.H. El-Shaarawi and W.W. Piegorsch (eds.), *Encyclopedia of Environmetrics*, Vol. 3, Chichester: John Wiley & Sons, pp. 1275–9.
Beven, K. 2002. 'Towards a coherent philosophy for modelling the environment', *Proceedings of the Royal Society London A* 458(2026): 2465–84.

Corral Quintana, S.A. 2000. *Una Metodología integrada de exploración y compensión de los procesos de elaboración de políticas públicas*, Ph.D. thesis, University of La Laguna, Spain.

Craye, M., Van der Sluijs, J.P. and Funtowicz, S. 2005. 'A reflexive approach to dealing with uncertainties in environmental health risk science and policy', *International Journal for Risk Assessment and Management* 5/2: 216–36.

Funtowicz, S.O. and Ravetz, J.R. 1990. *Uncertainty and Quality in Science for Policy*, Dordrecht: Kluwer Academic Publishers.

Funtowicz, S.O. and Ravetz, J.R. 1993. 'Science for the post-normal age', *Futures* 25: 735–55.

Hornberger, G.M. and Spear, R.C. 1981. 'An approach to the preliminary analysis of environmental systems', *Journal of Environmental Management* 12: 7–18.

IPCC 2005. *Guidance Notes for Lead Authors of the IPCC Fourth Assessment Report on Addressing Uncertainties*, Geneva: Intergovernmental Panel on Climate Change.

Janssen P.H.M., Petersen, A.C., Van der Sluijs, J.P., Risbey, J.S. and Ravetz, J.R. 2003. *RIVM/MNP Guidance for Uncertainty Assessment and Communication: Quickscan Hints & Actions List*, Bilthoven, The Netherlands: RIVM/MNP. ISBN 90-6960-105-2.

Janssen, P.H.M., Petersen, A.C., Van der Sluijs, J.P., Risbey, J. and Ravetz, J.R. (2005). 'A guidance for assessing and communicating uncertainties', *Water Science and Technology* 52/6: 125–31.

Keepin, B. and Wynne, B. 1984. 'Technical analysis of IIASA energy scenarios', *Nature* 312: 691–5.

Kloprogge, P., Van der Sluijs, J.P. and Petersen, A.C. 2005. A *Method for the Analysis of Assumptions in Assessments Applied to Two Indicators in the Fifth Dutch Environmental Outlook*, Research Report. Department of Science Technology and Society, Utrecht, The Netherlands: Utrecht University.

MNP/UU 2003. *RIVM/MNP Guidance for Uncertainty Assessment and Communication*, Bilthoven: Netherlands Environmental Assessment Agency (MNP) and Utrecht:Utrecht University (UU).

Oreskes, N., Shrader-Frechette, K. and Belitz, K. 1994. 'Verification, validation, and confirmation of numerical models in the earth sciences', *Science* 263: 641–6.

Petersen, A.C. 2006a. *Simulating Nature: A Philosophical Study of Computer-Simulation Uncertainties and Their Role in Climate Science and Policy Advice*, Apeldoorn and Antwerpen, The Netherlands: Spinhuis Publishers.

Petersen, A.C. 2006b. 'Simulation uncertainty and the challenge of post-normal science', in J. Lenhard, G. Küppers and T. Shinn (eds.), *Simulation: Pragmatic Constructions of Reality*, Sociology of the Sciences Yearbook Vol. 25, Dordrecht: Springer, pp. 173–85.

Petersen, A.C., Janssen, P.H.M., Van der Sluijs, J.P., Risbey, J.S. and Ravetz, J.R. 2003. *RIVM/MNP Guidance for Uncertainty Assessment and Communication: Mini-Checklist & Quickscan Questionnaire*, Bilthoven, The Netherlands: RIVM/MNP. ISBN 90-6960-105-1.

Risbey, J., Van der Sluijs, J.P., Kloprogge, P., Ravetz, J.R., Funtowicz, S. and Corral Quintana, S. 2005. 'Application of a checklist for quality assistance in environmental modelling to an energy model', *Environmental Modeling & Assessment* 10/1: 63–79.

Saltelli, A. 2002. 'Sensitivity analysis for importance assessment', *Risk Analysis* 22/3: 579–90.

Saltelli, A., Chan, K. and Scott, E.M. (eds.) 2000. *Sensitivity Analysis,* Probability and Statistics Series, New York: John Wiley & Sons Publishers.

Saltelli, A., Tarantola, S., Campolongo, F. and Ratto, M. 2004. *Sensitivity Analysis in Practice: A Guide to Assessing Scientific Models,* New York: John Wiley & Sons Publishers.

Stirling, A. 1999. *On Science and Precaution in the Management of Technological Risk: Volume I – A Synthesis Report of Case Studies,* Seville: European Commission Institute for Prospective Technological Studies, Report number EUR 19056 EN.

Stirling A. 2001. 'Inclusive deliberation and scientific expertise: Precaution, diversity and transparency in the governance of risk', *PLA Notes* 40: 67–71.

UK Strategy Unit 2002. *Risk: Improving Government's Capability to Handle Risk and Uncertainty,* London: UK Strategy Unit, Cabinet Office.

Van der Sluijs, J.P. 1997. *Anchoring Amid Uncertainty: On the Management of Uncertainties in Risk Assessment of Anthropogenic Climate Change,* Ph.D. thesis, Utrecht, The Netherlands: Utrecht University.

Van der Sluijs, J.P. 2002. 'A way out of the credibility crisis of models used in integrated environmental assessment', *Futures* 34: 133–46.

Van der Sluijs, J.P. 2005. 'Uncertainty as a monster in the science policy interface: Four coping strategies', *Water Science and Technology* 52/6: 87–92.

Van der Sluijs J.P., Craye, M., Funtowicz, S., Kl;oprogge, P., Ravetz, J. and Risbey, J. 2005. 'Combining quantitative and qualitative measures of uncertainty in model based environmental assessment: The NUSAP system', *Risk Analysis* 25/2: 481–92.

Van der Sluijs J.P., Janssen, P.H.M., Petersen, A.C., Kloprogge, P., Risbey, J.S., Tuinstra, W. and Ravetz, J.R. 2004. *RIVM/MNP Guidance for Uncertainty Assessment and Communication: Tool Catalogue for Uncertainty Assessment,* Utrecht University & RIVM.

Van der Sluijs, J.P., Risbey, J., Kloprogge, P., Ravetz, J., Funtowicz, S., Corral Quintana, S., Guimaraes Pereira, A., De Marchi, B., Petersen, A., Janssen, P., Hoppe, R. and Huijs, S. 2003. *RIVM/MNP Guidance for Uncertainty Assessment and Communication: Detailed Guidance,* Copernicus Institute for Sustainable Development, Utrecht University, and RIVM-MNP, Utrecht, The Netherlands, available at: www.nusap.net.

Van der Sluijs J.P., van Eijndhoven, J.C.M., Shackley, S. and Wynne, B. 1998. 'Anchoring devices in science for policy, the case of consensus around climate sensitivity', *Social Studies of Science* 28/2: 291–324.

Walker, W.E., Harremoës, P., Rotmans, J., Van der Sluijs, J.P., van Asselt, M.B.A., Janssen, P. and Krayer von Krauss, M.P. 2003. 'Defining uncertainty: A conceptual basis for uncertainty management in model-based decision support', *Integrated Assessment* 4/1: 5–17.

Yearley, S. 1996. *Sociology, Environmentalism, Globalization,* London: Sage Publications.

15 Looking through the telescope – quality assurance in scientific advice to politics

Reinhard Kurth and Susanne Glasmacher

'To support politics, where science serves the maintenance of power; to avoid disturbing the political environment, where this damages the maintenance of power.' This was the answer given by Kurt Biedenkopf when asked what politics expects from science, and he meant it 'not at all cynically' (Biedenkopf 2006). With this, Biedenkopf, who was in his career not only a politician but also a scientist (law and economics) and scientific manager (including a period as high-school principal), aptly characterised the conflict of interests in which scientific advice to politics takes place.

Scientific advice to politics is a primary function of governmental research, but this is not its only function. Scientists from a wide range of fields are carrying out research in federal and state ministerial facilities to provide to their respective ministries new knowledge in their areas of expertise. Governmental research is, to the most part, applied and oriented towards developing measures, i.e. it is of a practical nature. Its findings are usually directed to providing a scientific basis for the advice given to politics. Many facilities are also trusted with sovereign duties including testing, authorisation, standardisation and risk assessment.

These responsibilities, which stem from the duty of the state to protect its citizens, are enshrined in various laws and regulations such as the Protection from Infection Law or the Equipment and Product Safety Act. Other legal norms such as the Weights and Measures Law, the Time Act or the Federal Highway Act regulate the provision of the technical infrastructure to support commerce and the population. In this way, for example, standard time (Central European time) is set for Germany by the Physikalisch-Technische Bundesanstalt (the national metrology institute providing scientific and technical services) and made available to the public. Similarly, in preparing for new legal regulations such as federal laws or EU-regulations, the ministries under whose auspices the different scientific institutions fall can at any time call upon the expert knowledge of their facilities. The institutes must therefore be state-of-the-art with regard to their science and technology, and their information must be reliable.

There are about fifty governmental research institutes at the federal level. Under the auspices of the Federal Ministry of Food, Agriculture and Consumer Protection, for example, the Friedrich-Loeffler-Institute – the Federal Research Institute for Animal Health – is once in a while in the spotlight, not least because of avian influenza. This institute provides the ministry with scientific risk assessments that serve as a basis for measures such as the compulsory confinement of poultry or further surveillance programmes. Under the auspices of the Federal Ministry of Health, the Robert Koch Institute is the central institution of the government in the area of biomedicine. Its core responsibilities are the recognition, prevention and combating of diseases, in particular infectious diseases, and the monitoring of the health situation in Germany. Of no less relevance than protection from infection is health reporting, especially the analysis of the situation with non-communicable diseases and their associated risk factors (Kurth 2006). However, health reporting, due to its rather long-term effects on health, is not generally in the public or political spotlight, an example for which is adiposity.

The relevance of scientific advice to politics becomes apparent in cases of real or perceived acute health risks, as demonstrated by events surrounding infections with anthrax, SARS or avian influenza. In such situations the public, media and politicians expect reliable advice from those responsible for public health. They expect advice upon request, as well as recommendations for preventive and protective measures. The experiences of the Robert Koch Institute in providing scientific advice to politics allows it to make the following suggestions for the practice of, and discussions about, quality assurance in advising politics.

Publications, patents and professorships versus politics, practices and popularity

The advisory process is, in the ideal situation, a collective duty of science and politics. The final decision rests ultimately with politics. Politics encompasses the parliamentary representatives of the federation, states and communities in addition to top-level executives such as ministers, secretaries of state, other political officials and, of course, the parties themselves. Kurt Biedenkopf includes a third area not normally attributed to politics: the large social organisations that have associated and mixed themselves with politics, resulting in a commingling and ultimate disintegration of allocatable responsibility (Biedenkopf 2006).

An understanding of the differences between science and politics is necessary for successfully providing advice to politics. Bernard Choi and his colleagues have elaborated these differences well (Choi et al. 2005).

It begins with language. Technical language from scientists and health professionals is difficult for non-scientists to understand. Politicians, on the other hand, often speak in a simplified and *popular* manner. Time planning is also different. For the scientist, the acquisition of specialised knowledge and expertise over a long period of time is of highest importance. For politics, adherence to a (usually tight) schedule is sometimes more important than quality. The attention span of scientists is long and the acquisition of knowledge is accumulative. In contrast, politicians devote only a small amount of their attention to a particular topic – they need information quickly to deal with an ever-changing variety of themes. The two sides differ even in their aims. Publications, patents and professorships are for the scientists of central importance while for politicians it is crisis management and public support, aims that one can summarise as politics, practices and popularity.

A range of problems arises from these differences. Scientists are frequently sceptical about whether politicians are at all able to sensibly use research findings or recommendations for measures. Politicians, in turn, are quite often sceptical about the usefulness of research. Scientists are often frustrated because politicians frequently fail to understand complex scientific results. On the other hand, politicians are frustrated because scientists often do not give quick, clear answers in an understandable language. Scientists consider themselves to be obliged to research sponsors, scientific committees and reviewers of scientific journals, whereas politicians generally answer to political parties, taxpayers and voters (Kurth 2006, Choi *et al.* 2005).

The multifarious requirements of scientific advice to politics

The requirements necessary to allow politics to substantially follow the advice of scientists are multifarious. The first of these is trust from the side of politics and the public and – from the side of science – competitive research, initiative, perseverance, networking, resources, quality-assurance, neutrality and communication skills. From these requirements it is possible to derive criteria for quality assurance in advice to politics.

The first condition for successful advice to politics is trust. The political decision-makers and the public (as the most important *customers* of the politicians) need to trust the experts and institutions. Adequate funding for experts and institutions, the motivation of scientists for creative work and, as made apparent by acute health threats that demand compliance with rules of conduct, acceptance of recommendations all depend upon this. The experiences of politicians and the public as to whether the recommendations given by an institution or expert during previous events provided solutions play a major role. Deeper-rooted attitudes in the population with regard to health risks (*German Angst*) tend to take second place in the face of real or perceived risks to personal health.

The development of trust is a lengthy process that needs to be continuously nurtured. Governmental research facilities, with their institutionalised close cooperation with politics, hold an advantage over establishments at a distance from politics, because the acting parties are, over longer periods of time, the same. The continuous liaison with a ministry simplifies, on the one hand, an understanding of the ministerial decision processes and provides quick access to the decision-makers. On the other hand, the differences between science and politics make this relationship a constant challenge.

Trust in science, especially the natural sciences, is founded on its recognition that knowledge is the result of experimental investigation and is therefore based on re-examination and on reproducible evidence. However, science is simultaneously a dynamic process, in which new data is continuously generated, shedding new light on accepted concepts. Building a consensus and formulating generalised theories to gain insight into complex scientific relationships is achieved not only through scientific publications, but also at conferences, symposia and expert meetings. Within these frameworks, it is crucial that the individual pieces of information are examined, evaluated and brought together in the discussion to establish a general opinion. Such a consensus is then accepted by the scientific community, although it is quite normal for controversial views, treated as individual opinions, to be openly expressed (Kurth 2006a).

Own research is essential

The maintenance of scientific expertise at the competitive international level demands independent, qualified and adequately financed research. After all, it is very often necessary to evaluate problems at a point in time at which the knowledge is insufficient and the situation is unclear. Governmental institutes have an antenna function: they have to recognise in good time whether risks are increasing, whether the government has to be informed and whether there is a need for action. This can be achieved through its own research and also by a continuous analysis of the international expert literature. Protecting the populace from health risks cannot wait until the danger is clearly demonstrated scientifically.

Avian influenza can serve as an example for clarification. First of all, a short overview. The avian influenza pathogen is a highly pathogenic influenza virus of the H5N1 subtype. Since the end of 2003 the virus has spread extensively in poultry farms and wild bird populations in Asia and has meanwhile reached Russia, Europe and Africa. Over 260 humans, mostly in Southeast Asia, have become infected following close contact with poultry, more than half of whom have subsequently died as a result. Virologists worldwide have for many years warned of the risk of the virus further adapting itself to humans to initiate a global influenza epidemic (pandemic), resulting in the deaths of millions and having an enormous impact on society and business. The risk of a pandemic is presently higher than in the previous decades. This risk is significantly influenced by how widespread the virus is, by its potential to adapt to humans and by the number of species the virus can infect.

In fact, with avian influenza, no serious scientist can predict whether a mutated H5N1 will really initiate the next pandemic or when a global wave of influenza will come. However, having experienced three pandemics in the last century alone, it is indisputable that the next will come in the foreseeable future and there is a great deal of evidence that H5N1 is further on its way to adapting to humans than all other avian influenza viruses presently known (Kurth 2006b; World Health Organization 2006).

Qualified researchers

One requirement for good research results and therefore for good advice to politics is qualified experts. This includes both internationally renowned scientists employed on a continuing basis and scientists employed for a short time to work on specific projects. In this regard, junior scientists are of great importance. One can expect from them a high degree of creativity, impartiality and an open-mindedness for new thoughts and methods. At the same time, the advancement of their academic qualifications demands and strengthens the cooperation with institutions of higher education. A series of highly successful research groups run by junior scientists was established – with a limit of five years – at the Robert Koch Institute at the end of the 1990s. After completion of the projects, the group leaders received offers of professorships or laboratory leaderships and, in cases of exceptional achievement and thematic relevance (e.g. influenza research), a permanent position at the Robert Koch Institute.

In addition to the junior scientists and guest scientists, the many scientific commissions that are typically based at governmental research institutes such as the Robert Koch Institute also continuously contribute external expertise. The members of the commissions are usually appointed in consultation with the expert scientific bodies, as is the case with the Pandemic Commission, which, in the event of a global wave of influenza, should advise the Robert Koch Institute on such matters that it cannot itself cover, such as questions, for example, about vaccines or communal health protection. Other commissions based at the institute such as the Standing Committee for Vaccination or the Committee on Hospital Hygiene and Prevention from Infection develop recommendations for expert groups. The Scientific Secretariats of these commissions professionally prepare the recommendations, thereby facilitating the transfer of expertise from the commissions to the institute and vice versa.

Very often, problems exist that are not highly publicised and about which politics is therefore virtually unaware and consequently does not seek advice from its experts. Active and innovative experts in such fields are especially sought after. This was the case, for example, with the suggestion by the Robert Koch Institute to carry out a large-scale Child and Adolescent Health Survey where a lack of base data about the health situation was hindering the development of evidence-based preventive measures. In the autumn of 2006, the first results of the health survey, carried out over many years with 18,000 children, were presented. This enterprise impressively demonstrates the real strength of governmental research, the ability to address topics in the long-term. This and similar projects form the indispensable basis for measures, regulations or laws.

One should not underestimate how important good working conditions are as a basic requirement for qualified and motivated scientists. This includes sufficient personnel, supplies and equipment, the relief from administrative duties by a modern, service-oriented administration, comprehensive access to the scientific literature, the freedom to attend meetings or training courses and so on. Research also shapes significantly the working atmosphere of a public institution, working against the tendency for bureaucratisation on the one hand, and increasing decisiveness and initiative on the other.

Assuring quality

The continuing maintenance of excellence requires action at all levels. The institutionalised quality assurance at the Robert Koch Institute is achieved internally via the Research Council and externally through the Scientific Committee. The Research Council plans and evaluates the directions and major foci of research and recommends to the institute leadership research topics, changes of focus, and the distribution of research funds from the institute's budget. Members include, in addition to the institute leadership, the heads of department, the research appointee, the budget appointee, the representatives of the project groups and the junior research groups, elected representatives of the scientific staff and of the technical assistants and a representative from the Ministry of Health. The Scientific Committee, in addition to the supervisory role of the ministry, acts as an external advisory and ultimately quality assurance board. It regularly comments on the professional and scientific performance of the institute, gives advice for the development of middle- and long-term goals, promotes the collaboration with state authorities and other institutions of the public health service, with scientific institutions, professional associations, societies and organisations and gives advice for optimising the organisation of the institute.

Evaluation, in addition to the regular meeting of advisory boards, is of great importance. Performance reviews should take place from time to time within the organisational units and for the institute as a whole, the latter normally by the German Science Council. The Robert Koch Institute was last evaluated in 2005 (positively) and before that in 1997. The Science Council examines predominantly the research performance and the significance of an institute in the international context as well as its resources and organisation. Its findings are subsequently published.

The presentation and discussion of results in international scientific journals, at congresses and with colleagues ensures the solidity of data and the acceptance of findings. The Robert Koch Institute promotes, for example, the quality of diagnostics by organising inter-laboratory tests and taking part in external standardisation measures. Important operational procedures are described in so-called Standard Operating Procedures, guaranteeing the reliability of processes and the reproducibility of results. In addition, an internationally recognised quality management system based on the DIN EN ISO 9000 ff and the DIN EN ISO/IEC 17025 will be introduced and established.

The credibility of statements addressing a scientific question of public interest is highly dependent upon the scientific reputation of both the presenting scientists and the research establishments in which they work. The falsification of results by individual scientists can cause immense damage to the general trust in science (e.g. events in South Korea in 2006). Ensuring the validity of new data and maintaining effective oversight of the respective fields is becoming increasingly difficult, especially against the background of the rapid pace of information gathering and the diversification in scientific disciplines. The scientific community, with its professional associations and organisations that promote science and state funding, has therefore established guidelines for Safeguarding Good Scientific Practice.[1] The Robert Koch Institute has itself published guidelines for handling scientific misconduct.[2] This requires, for example, that original data be archived for ten years and that a representative investigates evidence of misconduct and provides a yearly report to the research council. To avoid introducing inappropriate incentives, the performance and appraisal criteria for evaluations, hiring, appointments and the distribution of funds are formulated to ensure that originality and quality is always ranked above quantity.

Measures for quality assurance have, so far, not been implemented in all government research institutes. In 2005 therefore, more than a dozen government research institutes came together to form a consortium (Arbeitsgemeinschaft Ressortforschung). In addition to a stronger public presence, this consortium has dedicated itself to ensuring the quality of its scientific work. Central to this is the introduction of regular external evaluations, a measure repeatedly called for in discussions about governmental research. Many of these institutes have already been or will soon be evaluated by the German Science Council. The governmental research institutes are therefore subjected to the same scientific *control* as universities and the research establishments of other major scientific organisations. Above all, an exchange of *best practice* recommendations, for example concerning criteria for evaluating research or filling posts for junior scientists, is sought within the framework of internal quality assurance and control.[3]

Networking is essential

To competently answer scientific questions, a network between different disciplines, institutions and levels of administration must exist. For example, in the case of avian influenza, both Agricultural and Health Ministries need reliable information and interpretations thereof to decide upon precautionary measures and emergency plans for both animals and people. For this reason, virologists and epidemiologists at the Robert Koch Institute have been carrying out research into human

[1] Proposals for Safeguarding Good Scientific Practice, January, 1998, available at www.dfg.de.

[2] Grundlagen für wissenschaftliches Arbeiten und Handeln am Robert Koch-Institut: Richtlinien zur Sicherung guter wissenschaftlicher Praxis und zum Umgang mit wissenschaftlichem Fehlverhalten am Robert Koch-Institut, 1 May 2002, available at www.rki.de.

[3] Forschen – prüfen – beraten, Ressortforschungseinrichtungen als Dienstleister für Politik und Gesellschaft, ein Positionspapier, 2006, available at www.ressortforschung.de.

influenza and its spread for many years. The Friedrich Loeffler Institute has for a long time been analysing the viruses appearing in birds and swine. The close collaboration established between the institutes involved is therefore (as between politics and research) of great advantage. Information is exchanged; people get to know each other.

This facilitates the recognition of early warning signals. For example, as mentioned above, the Friedrich Loeffler Institute was regularly examining wild birds for influenza viruses long before the first cases of avian influenza appeared on Rügen. Similarly, the Robert Koch Institute was already discussing pandemic planning long before the H5N1 avian influenza began to spread through Asia, and the German states were also engaged with this topic. As a result of a resolution passed at the 74th Health Ministers Congress on 21 and 22 June 2001, the Federal Ministry of Health was asked, in collaboration with the states, to compile a National Pandemic Plan. In October 2001, a working group *Influenza Pandemic Planning* was established under the auspices of the Robert Koch Institute with experts from the federation, states and science. The working group was given the task of preparing a plan, taking into account the federal organisation of Germany and the basic responsibilities of the states and communities for carrying out measures to protect against infections and catastrophes. The plan addresses, for example, in the case of an influenza epidemic how to produce as quickly as possible enough vaccine for the entire population or whether the stockpiling of antiviral drugs is advisable. The initial draft of the pandemic plan was provided to the states in February 2004 and was debated by the responsible committees. For the publication in early 2005, suggestions from the special working group *Influenza Pandemic Plan* of the Association of the Higher State Health Authorities of the Federal States (AOLG) were integrated and joint recommendations for its implementation were formulated. The state health ministers endorsed the plan in December 2004. A few months later a plan of action followed, in which a catalogue of measures was specified. The Robert Koch Institute continues to coordinate the pandemic planning expert group that prepared the technical part of the pandemic plan and maintains the expertise for the federal and state political decision-makers.

Without networks and without the exchanges and cooperations it would be impossible to fulfil the ever-increasing responsibilities on the limited budget provided. The networking should also, of course, work with the *customers*. For the Robert Koch Institute these are primarily the Federal Ministry of Health, the health authorities and the professional community.

Scientists and institutions that have close contact with their respective governmental departments and fulfil official duties in this area can give realistic recommendations without renouncing scientific data and facts. Nevertheless, in times of budget restrictions, the more a decision's results will cost, the more difficult the decision becomes. It is then imperative, for example, to persuade a representative in a parliamentary committee of the necessity of a decision. In such situations, personal contact to the leadership of a ministry can play a major role, or contact to the opinion-making prime ministers of the Länder if the implementation is a matter for the Länder, for example with the stockpiling of antiviral drugs in the case of an influenza pandemic.

Party political neutrality

Knowledge of political affiliations and administrative and decision-making structures is, for providing advice to politics, indispensable. But when scientists adopt politically motivated positions that are not professionally supported, they lose their role as a neutral entity and run the risk of becoming exploited. A scientist may not select scientific knowledge subjectively. It is not always possible, however, to totally ignore personal core values, convictions and experiences. Furthermore, an expert is often asked to appraise a situation about which opinions even within science are divided. In such cases, the expert's own (mostly subjective) professional experience can play an essential role. One has to be aware of this and at least do the utmost to strive for objectivity and relevance and to carefully justify appraisals. On the other hand, a deliberately false interpretation given in order to justify a political decision or to serve a special interest is reprehensible. Such a scientist soon becomes known in Germany as a *Mietmaul* (one whose opinion is for sale) and does severe damage to the reputation of science.

If politicians seek advice that is clearly intended to qualify or suppress a necessary need for action, a scientist must be ready to refuse. The cooperation between science and politics can be particularly difficult in cases where religious feelings or ideologically conditioned expectations play a dominant role. Politics can also become susceptible to the pseudoscientific propositions of ideologically oriented scientists or non-governmental organisations. An example of the latter is the *Green Gene Technology* that resulted in previous years in some political decisions being made with no basis in the prevailing scientific opinion. Ministerial directives based on pseudoscience are particularly fatal. These usually reach the public and do damage to both sides: the institute whose expertise is called into question, and the ministry that tries to distort the advice.

Communication

Communication consists not only of an exchange of arguments through language, but also the exchange of non-verbal signals through gesticulation or expression. Non-verbal communication can significantly influence the perception of a statement and can unintentionally convey, for example, a low opinion of the recipient, which is hardly likely to promote one's own (consulting) interests. '*Licet ipsa neges, vultus loquitur quodcumque tegis*', in English 'Though thou thyself sayst naught, thy face speaks out whate'er thou hidest', said Seneca (Hercules on Oeta 704/5). To this is added the information processing of the brain, which selects a huge amount of information without conscious involvement and either discards it or evaluates it. Indeed, although scientists should never become psychologists, knowledge of the basics of communication certainly makes advice to politics easier.

On the one hand, communication between politics and experts must take place, as a basis for the reciprocal advisory process. Communication with the public is also essential.[4] As a result of their statutory guidelines, governmental research institutions primarily advise politics and the professional community and provide information to the press. Independent of statutory guidelines, informing the general public as far as possible about relevant health risks or providing possible sources of information should always be one of its functions. As many people as possible should have the capability, in situations of real or perceived threat, to react appropriately or to improve their own health situation. The *customer* must feel that he or she is being taken seriously and is being comprehensively informed. The term communication does, after all, stem from the Latin *communicare* for share, inform, allow to take part, do together or unite.

Target group orientation should go without saying. The different expectations and background knowledge of the audience have to be taken into account if understanding is to be promoted, whether it consists of journalists, politicians, representatives of authorities or citizens. Max Planck is reported to have said: 'A science that is not simple enough to be explained to everyone on the street isn't true.'

---

[4] World Health Organization, Outbreak Communication Guidelines, 2005, available at www.who.int.

The reliability of information provided by a federal institute must meet especially high standards. The quality of the information should therefore be assured by internal or external expertise. The information is questioned and supplemented by an intensive exchange and networking with other scientists, authorities and institutions. Authorities should not publicly contradict each other concerning important assessments if they do not wish to risk their own acceptance and trust.

Furthermore, expert opinions must have a degree of constancy. If, for example, a danger to the public at the beginning of an event is categorically ruled out, it should not be necessary to revise this opinion a few days later. Leaders or members of a public institution have to carefully consider what they can and should say if there is at that time insufficient understanding. They have to make clear where there are gaps in our knowledge and room for interpretation. To present oneself clearly and distinctly is not always easy, particularly if one's statements are of a virtually official character. Scientists from academia are in this respect more independent and can therefore sometimes be *braver*, although such statements are sometimes guided by special interests or can be totally absurd.

Due to the dense information network of the media, new developments, suspected cases or rumours rapidly become widely known. As a result, requests for information start arriving very quickly and such information should be made available as soon as possible (or even, if possible, unsolicited), preferably via the internet. The worldwide web makes it possible for a large number of people to simultaneously access a comprehensive source of information either directly or via links. The web information can be made available in a variety of ways, written or spoken or visualised with photos and animations. However, the classical conduits of information (telephone hotlines, brochures, letters, faxes) should not be ignored. Indeed, 23 million Germans over 14 years of age (36 per cent) belong to the so-called *offliners*, the non-users of the internet who profess no intention of going online. The average age of the non-user is presently 61.[5]

Professionalism through media training or courses to train experts in interview techniques should be a matter of course. Not only scientists but also other experts such as public health officers not only have to mobilise the political decision-makers but must also be able to communicate with the press and public. Professional and personal

---

[5] (N)ONLINER Atlas 2006, Publisher: TNS Infratest und Initiative D21, available at www.onliner-atlas.de.

authority, powers of judgement and decisiveness are critical factors, particularly in situations of real or perceived crisis.

How does one recognise good advice to politics?

Evidence for the quality of advice to politics can, for example, be found in the good reputation of an institution and its prominent representatives. For example, media analyses can reveal the positive or negative image of an institution in the media. Also, responses from *customers* that receive findings from a national reference centre or consultant laboratory for example, provide direct evidence and reactions from those receiving advice. A good reputation is also made evident by how often one is asked by the media, scientific community and politics to give opinions and presentations, etc.

Success in research is an indirect quality criterion that can be and should be measured to a certain point. The consortium of government research institutes mentioned above (Arbeitsgemeinschaft Ressortforschung) has therefore published *Criteria for the Evaluation of Research in the Federal Research Establishments*.[6] Quality criteria include publications in scientific journals, activity in scientific presentations, attractiveness to guest scientists, attractiveness to national and international cooperation partners, the numbers of successful Ph.D. students, postdoctoral qualifications, lectures, professorships in establishments of higher education and non-university research establishments, the amount and origin of research funding (taking into account the restrictions imposed by funding bodies on governmental research institutes), the organisation of renowned professional conferences, scientific prizes and awards, activities as a referee for research-funding bodies and research ministries, the publication of books and magazines and the scientific quality of the posts held in expert committees.

Renowned researchers are, however, not automatically suitable for providing advice to politics, a good reputation in the media does not mean simultaneous acceptance in science, good research managers are not automatically good scientists. Success in research, communication skills and administrative expertise ideally come together for successful advice to politics, and integrity and neutrality are additionally indispensable.

---

[6] Kriterien für die Bewertung der Forschung in den Ressortforschungseinrichtungen des Bundes, Working paper, discussed in the board meeting on 2 June 2005, available www. ressortforschung.de.

The influence – usually elusive – of advisory activities on political decisions is direct evidence for the quality of the advice. An example is the implemented stockpiling of antiviral drugs as recommended by the Robert Koch Institute and the Influenza Pandemic Planning Expert Group, which was preceded by many discussions at different political levels. The Health Minister Conference of the States declared on 24 February 2006: 'On the advice of the responsible research institutes, the Robert Koch Institute, the Paul Ehrlich Institute and the Friedrich Loeffler Institute, the health ministers have ... agreed ... based on the recent research data to expand the stockpiles of antiviral drugs, as presently recommended by the RKI.'[7] This decision can partly be seen to be the result of the continuous reports in the media concerning avian influenza. Such waves of media interest cannot, however, be planned or controlled. In the case of the stockpiling decision, the initial appearance of avian influenza in wild birds on 14 February 2006 in Rügen was not foreseeable in this way.

Despite the importance of scientific quality and the ability to present arguments, in the end it is the readiness of those involved in decision-making to *look through the telescope* that is decisive. This image, taken from Brecht's play *Life of Galileo*, was used by Kurt Biedenkopf in a lecture to describe the environment in which advice to politics occurs (Biedenkopf 2006). After arriving in Florence, Galileo wished to ingratiate himself with the Medici family and decided to *give* them as a present the moons of Jupiter, which he had recently discovered. This discovery also provided further evidence for the validity of Kepler's and Copernicus' observations and therefore for the heliocentric planetary system. The court sent two scientists (!) to Galileo to take a first-hand look at the *present* but this opportunity was refused by both, who declared that they first wanted an academic discourse about whether these moons could even exist. All attempts by Galileo to persuade his guests to look through the telescope were in vain. Finally, they accused Galileo of painting the moons on the lens of the telescope and left. Ultimately the Pope and the High Inquisitor insisted that Galileo withdraw his claims if he did not wish to risk life and limb. The confirmation of the Copernican System would have confronted the church with the question of how they could explain to their believers that the events described in the Bible occurred

---

[7] Sonder-GMK zur Pandemievorsorge: Erweiterung der Bund-Länder-AG zur Koordinierung der Pandemieprävention und Aufstockung bei antiviralen Medikamenten, Press release, 24 February 2006, Ministerium für Gesundheit und Soziales, Sachsen-Anhalt.

not at the centre of the universe but on an arbitrary planet – a classic conflict between scientific knowledge and the problems of maintenance of power.

Tasks and aims of the Robert Koch Institute

The Robert Koch Institute is the central federal institution responsible for disease control and prevention and is therefore the central federal reference institution for both applied and response-orientated research as well as for the Public Health Sector.
The tasks of the Robert Koch Institute comprise:

- the identification of politically important health problems and associated scientific issues;
- applied and response-orientated research to resolve these issues;
- the assessment of scientific results through analysis of current international developments in the respective scientific areas;
- informing and advising political decision-makers and the scientific sector;
- executive tasks defined by special laws, in particular with regard to protection from infection, legislation on stem cell research, and attacks using biological agents;
- the topical realisation and coordination of federal health reporting.

REFERENCES

Biedenkopf, K. 2006. 'Was erwartet die Politik von der Wissenschaft?', in *Heidelberger Akademie der Wissenschaften: Politikberatung in Deutschland*, Wiesbaden: Verlag für Sozialwissenschaften, pp. 17–32.
Choi, Bernard C.K., Pang, Tikki, Lin, Vivian, Puska, Pekka, Sherman, Gregory, Goddard, Michael, Ackland, Michael J., Sainsbury, Peter, Stachenko, Sylvie, Morrison, Howard and Clottey, Clarence 2005. 'Can scientists and policy makers work together', *Journal of Epidemiology and Community Health* 59: 632–7.
Forschen – prüfen – beraten, Ressortforschungseinrichtungen als Dienstleister für Politik und Gesellschaft, ein Positionspapier, 2006, available at: www.ressortforschung.de.
Grundlagen für wissenschaftliches Arbeiten und Handeln am Robert Koch-Institut: Richtlinien zur Sicherung guter wissenschaftlicher Praxis und zum Umgang mit wissenschaftlichem Fehlverhalten am Robert Koch-Institut, 1 May 2002, available at:www.rki.de.
Kriterien für die Bewertung der Forschung in den Ressortforschungseinrichtungen des Bundes, Working paper, discussed in the board-meeting on 2 June 2005, available at www.ressortforschung.de.
Kurth, Bärbel-Maria 2006. 'Epidemiologie und Gesundheitspolitik', *Gesundheitsforschung, Gesundheitsschutz, Bundesgesundheitsblatt* 49: 637–47.

Kurth, Reinhard 2006a. 'Managing expectations', in Ernst Schering Foundation, British Embassy Berlin, British Council (ed.), *Trust in Science – The Dialogue with Society*, Berlin.

Kurth, Reinhard 2006b. 'The risk of world wide influenza epidemic presents a national and international challenge', in *Influenza Viruses – Facts and Perspectives*, Berlin: Grosse Verlag.

(N)ONLINER Atlas 2006. Publisher: TNS Infratest und Initiative D21, www. onliner-atlas.de. Proposals for Safeguarding Good Scientific Practice, January 1998, available at www.dfg.de.

Sonder-GMK zur Pandemievorsorge: Erweiterung der Bund-Länder-AG zur Koordinierung der Pandemieprävention und Aufstockung bei antiviralen Medikamenten, Press release 24 February 2006, Ministerium für Gesundheit und Soziales, Sachsen-Anhalt.

World Health Organization 2005. *Outbreak communication guidelines 2005*, available at: www.who.int.

World Health Organization 2006. *Avian Influenza: Significance of Mutations in the H5N1 Virus*, 20 February 2006, available at: www.who.int.

16 Scientific policy advice and foreign policymaking – Stiftung Wissenschaft und Politik (SWP), the German Institute for International and Security Affairs

Volker Perthes

SWP is an independent scientific institute that conducts policy-oriented research on the basis of which it then advises the German Parliament (the Bundestag) and the federal government on foreign and security policy issues. The analyses and publications produced by SWP researchers and their participation in national and international debates on key issues help to shape positions in their respective domains. SWP's primary goals are to translate scientific knowledge to the needs of policymakers and to undertake original scientific research. The latter is often more *applied* than *basic*, even though contributions to the body of theory in international relations have been, and will be made. In order to be successful, the institute has to fulfil a double function; to respond to the needs and interests of policymakers and to stay involved in the global high-level discourse on international relations with other academics, think tankers and practitioners.

SWP is different in several ways from other federally financed scientific agencies in Germany, especially those that work for or mainly with one particular ministry[1] and which have an official advisory or even operative function regulated by law.[2] Different from many other policy fields, advice in the foreign policy realm is not so much sought for the formulation of legal texts or the evaluation of procedures and proposals, as rather for background information and interpretation, for strategy discussions and for exchanges with foreign actors, often in second-track formats. Other than in the United States, where foreign policy think tanks have a much longer tradition, there is a much stricter distinction in Germany between the *world* of politics and that of scientific policy advice: while

---

[1] One example would be the German Development Institute, Deutsches Institut für Entwicklungspolitik (DIE), which has a special relationship with the Federal Ministry for Economic Cooperation and Development.

[2] One example here is the Robert Koch Institute (RKI) that works as a federal health authority under the auspices of the Federal Ministry of Health.

think tanks in Washington often appear like administrations-in-waiting, and scholars from think tanks tend to move into government positions when a new administration takes over,[3] such career crossovers are rather unusual in Germany. The rule is still that scientific policy advisers work with any government, and that civil servants and diplomats stay on, or only change position within the administration, after a change of government.

SWP is not exclusively working for or being consulted by one particular ministry. It regards parliament with both opposition and government parliamentary groups as well as the federal government as its prime partners. Openness to both government and opposition is of particular importance to preserve the independence of an organisation that draws 90 per cent of its funding from the federal budget.[4]

In fact, SWP defines its independence in three dimensions: First, it is politically independent, or non-partisan. All parliamentary groups are represented on the SWP Board (Stiftungsrat); and members of all parties in the Bundestag are invited to seek the advice of the institute and are supplied with SWP products. Second, SWP designs its own research agenda, it is not commissioned with specific studies and does not do *research on demand* (Auftragsforschung). The institute is always prepared though to respond to requests for briefings, brainstorming for policymakers and officials in its fields of expertise, and occasionally bids for public tenders by government ministries or other official agencies that want to fund particular studies. Third, and this should go without saying for an institution that holds academic standards high, SWP is independent with regard to the results of its research: It happens that studies in their results and recommendations are not to the liking of a particular government ministry, or stand in contrast to the position of the government. Government officials and politicians have accepted that independence makes part of the quality of SWP's expertise, that a politicisation of research and policy advice may seem useful for a policy-maker in the short run, but undermines the quality and legitimacy of scientific or science-based research in the long run. The German Council of Science and Humanities (Wissenschaftsrat) has also underlined that the 'autonomy' of SWP has helped the institute to develop 'a convincing scientific profile as basis for good policy counselling' (Wissenschaftsrat 2006: 47). Corporations have sometimes more difficulties to understand

---

[3] It is noteworthy, to give but one example, that twenty-eight scholars from the Brookings Institution entered the Obama Administration in the first nine months of its existence, quite a number of them as ambassadors (including the UN and the NATO ambassador) or assistant secretaries.

[4] The budget line for SWP is part of the budget of the Chancellor's office.

and accept that SWP, in contrast to consultancies, does not do *research on demand*. The private sector is used to buying outside knowledge and expertise according to their concrete needs, and does not, in Germany, have much of a tradition of funding independent political thinking. This may explain, to some degree, why the 'independence' of think tanks is being defined somewhat differently in Germany and in the United States: US think tanks often consider themselves as independent because they do not depend on government funding. In Germany, public funding of an institution is rather seen as an element of independence, provided direct political interference is excluded by institutional means. There are exceptions on both sides: The US Institute of Peace, for example, in some respects a good US comparison to SWP, is funded by Congress.

Function and form

Quality (for SWP as for other science-based advisory institutions) has to be defined in terms of both epistemic and political robustness, i.e. with respect to academic standards as well as to the needs of the institute's main clients and partners.[5] Quality criteria are therefore not necessarily identical to those of universities or purely academic institutions but fulfil the same purpose – namely to set standards in order to guarantee academic quality and originality. Let us here leave aside that some criteria that are increasingly being used for academic rankings in universities, such as the amount of external funds gathered, the number of Ph.D. dissertations awarded, or the number of articles published in refereed journals, have themselves come under more critical scrutiny recently.

The main difference between the output of a university and that of a think tank may be the consumer – and the relevance-orientation of the latter: the entire SWP *product*, consisting of books and papers, conferences and workshops, briefings and background discussions, need to be policy-relevant. It should help policymakers to improve their knowledge on international affairs and to take decisions. But what are the functions a foreign policy think tank needs to fulfil to be seen as relevant and thus be accepted as a partner by policymakers and government officials? These are, of course, determined by or within a particular context, and might differ from country to country, but, from a German perspective, one can identify essentially five functions (see, in more detail, Perthes 2007).

---

[5] See the introductory chapter by Justus Lentsch and Peter Weingart.

First, interpretation and clarification: this is a demand particularly of parliamentarians who do not always feel well-informed by the administration. The expertise of SWP researchers is based on their own empirical analysis of a particular foreign and security issue or a region. Therein, the institute's capacity differs from journalistic know-how in that it is not event-oriented or an ad-hoc analysis but derives from in-depth theory-led research over a long period of time. Ideally, researchers also follow a multi-disciplinary approach: the complexity of many issues in the field of international relations calls for a different perspective which exceeds set categories of international law and history, culture and religion.

Second, strategic advice, or the development of practical ideas for a long-term perspective that goes beyond day-to-day politics: this is what government ministers and officials are primarily interested in. The comparative advantage of a scientific institution – as opposed to a consultancy firm – is ideally the solid theoretical and empirical base of such advice. Some ideas might be discharged as unrealistic and vanish from the political agenda for the time being – only to come back a few months or even years later. At the same time, scientific policy advisers may need to educate policymakers about the limits of scientific knowledge. Scientific advice is necessarily often based on hypotheses, and our knowledge about the concurrence of different trends and actors' behaviour is often unsecured. Good scientific policy advice will not hide this, but rather raise the awareness for uncertainties and unexpected events as one of the realities which not only foreign and security policymakers have to cope with.

Third, testing of ideas: it is important to recognise that officials and politicians often have substantial knowledge and do develop their own ideas and strategies. Researchers should see themselves as *sparring partners* of decision-makers who can discuss and intellectually test such ideas before they have to stand the practical test of national and international realities.

Fourth, an early-warning function to identify possible mistakes and unwanted developments: consequently, an institution that provides scientific policy advice must be able to develop its own methodological set of instruments, such as scenario techniques. At best, political advice or interactive policy workshops based on such forms of research can help to prevent things from going wrong in a particular policy field; or at least help policymakers be better prepared for unwelcome contingencies.

Fifth, a think tank should be and provide a location for the open and rational exchange of ideas: it should be a place where confidentiality is guaranteed and where the barrier between parties and agencies, and ideally, also between different countries and nationalities does not matter for reflections about what is necessary, useful and doable.

The market of policy advice

Even though SWP is funded by the German government, and is one of the largest and most established players on the scene, it is aware of its changing environment. In Germany and elsewhere, new actors – such as privately funded foundations and new small think tanks – are forging their way onto what has become a market for policy advice. The number of think tanks and policy institutes has increased over the last decade, including some smaller national and some much better funded international outfits that have become active in Berlin. Most of these are *non-partisan*, but still have clear political agendas. With other resources, and usually much higher interest in media coverage, these institutions are competing for the same clientele and they are sometimes both partners and competitors to a think tank like SWP, not so much for funds, but certainly for the time and attention of decision-makers.

As SWP does not organise any public events with media coverage, it sees its own comparative advantage on this market in the quality and reliability of its product. SWP papers need to fulfil the functions outlined above, as they have to be accepted both in the academic community and in the political class. They need to be scientifically viable, reliable and readable too – a fact often ignored in university publications. Researchers at SWP need to know that they have customers with little time, and that they have to provide them with relevant, sound and reliable information, and must not bore them.

SWP has been evaluated by the German Council of Science and Humanities (Wisssenschaftsrat 2006: 47) and has also commissioned evaluations of its work by independent consultants at irregular intervals. As the SWP product is rather specific, the institute tries to secure quality mainly through in-house procedures and designs. To start with, SWP commits its scholars and researchers to a *Code for Keeping Good Scientific Practice*[6] which demands, among other things, such general scientific principles as working *lege artis*, to document all results of one's research and keep primary data, to be critical with one's own results, not to ignore unwished research results (unerwünschte Ergebnisse). It also rules that 'originality and quality' have priority over quantity as criteria for performance evaluation and promotions.

---

[6] Grundsätze zur Sicherung guter wissenschaftlicher Praxis und über den Umgang mit Vorwürfen wissenschaftlichen Fehlverhaltens, Anlage zur Allgemeinen Verfahrensordnung, 9 September 2003.

Organisational measures to secure originality and quality

To guarantee the quality of research, studies and other scholarly products to be published under the SWP logo undergo a multi-level in-house discussion and peer review process: while a short paper or comment will often be triggered by events, more deep-going studies and research papers should fit into a bi-annual research framework (Orientierungs-rahmen) which in itself is the product of an analytical discussion involving all research divisions.[7] After getting the initial go-ahead by the head of the respective research division and the Director and his deputies (Institutsleitung), a researcher or group of researchers working on a new project would generally present the research design, including the guiding theoretical assumptions and methodology, basic theses, work plan, and a statement on the relevance of the project to the Forscherforum, a bi-weekly meeting with up to sixty of SWP's academic staff, for a collegial discussion which can lead to major revisions of the original design. Researchers are further encouraged to present their work to their research division while progressing on it. Once a paper is finalised, it is critically reviewed by a peer, a researcher from another of SWP's eight research divisions. The reviewer comments on the scientific validity and political relevance, the soundness of the argument, structure of the text, and factual points, probably gives some advice on how to improve the manuscript, and finally makes a recommendation to the Director about whether or not the text should be published. The author(s) may comment on the review, or rework their manuscript; following that, the head of the research division also looks at the manuscript, adds his or her own comment and recommendation, and hands it on to the Director. The Director or one of his deputies then also reviews the text, accepts or rejects it in principle, usually writing a comment of up to several pages, often asking for some or more work on the text and to view the manuscript another time before allowing it to be copy edited and published. For short, topical papers (published as SWP-Aktuell, or SWP Comments), there is a somewhat shortened procedure. For research papers (Studien), however, this review and reworking process is diligently applied, and it can be time consuming. There is obviously a trade-off here between speed and quality: some papers could be on the market earlier, if quality standards were less rigorously applied. The decision for a somewhat lengthy process, which authors occasionally find invasive and cumbersome, has been made with an eye on one of the main criteria

---

[7] The *Orientierungsrahmen* is available to the public through the SWP homepage, at www.swp-berlin.org/common/get_document.php?asset_id=5584.

for the acceptance of SWP products among policymakers, namely their reliability. SWP can simply not afford to ruin its reputation as a non-partisan, reliable source of high-quality policy-oriented analysis. Here, one sloppy paper can do more damage than the failure not to publish a timely paper on a particular subject that policymakers want to discuss at a given moment. SWP researchers, at any rate, should be able to give verbal advice when policymakers become interested in a specific issue.

External evaluation

As indicated above, SWP and its work were externally evaluated by the German Council of Science and Humanities (Wissenschaftsrat) in 2005 as part of the Council's overall evaluation of governmental research agencies.[8] SWP has occasionally commissioned consultants to evaluate particular parts of its activity (such as the library and information services), and conducted surveys asking particular SWP focus groups to give feedback on the quality of publications or events. With particular regard to the scholarly value or epistemic robustness of its work, SWP also relies on its Research Advisory Board (Forschungsbeirat), a group of twelve university professors which, as is the case in other institutions, take upon themselves to give their good advice particularly on overall research planning. Meeting twice a year, the Advisory Board takes a close look at one or two research divisions or programmes at each meeting.

Given the policy- and relevance-oriented task of SWP, some of the quantifiable standards which science organisations or universities tend to use in performance evaluations of their staff have been seen as being difficult to apply to SWP's research work. While, to give just one example, SWP scholars quite often publish in refereed journals, the idea that *refereed* automatically means high quality is not shared by the directors and the Supervisory Board – not only because the growing number of *refereed* journals seems to indicate that a real inflationary development is at work here: a numerical increase that at the same time denotes a decrease in value. Rather than relying on the number of articles published in *refereed* journals of divergent quality, SWP has developed its own list of *relevant* journals – periodicals that are of particular value for discussion in the so-called strategic community or for international debates in particular policy fields.[9]

---

[8] On the German Council of Science and Humanities, see chapter by Andreas Strucke in this book (Chapter 9).

[9] It may be more difficult, for example, to publish a piece in *Survival* (London) which is non-refereed but is managed by a quite selective editorial committee, than in a number of journals that may be refereed but may also be read by a very limited community.

Quality is eventually, without any formal procedures or clear criteria being available here, something which policymakers and government officials as the main clients of SWP, the media, or the general public judge upon. As a rule, SWP research papers are published and posted on the SWP homepage, sometimes being critically discussed in the media or in internet forums. SWP tries to hold account about how often its experts and expertise are quoted, researchers are invited to speak to parliamentary groups or committees, invited to briefings or conferences; it also holds account of the numbers of parliamentarians or officials that join workshops and other meetings at SWP. A researcher, who is invited once, and only once, to address the working group of a parliamentary group, may need to improve his or her performance. For the political robustness of the institute's work, the time and attention that policy-makers devote to SWP and its scholars is not a bad measure. Think tanks like SWP should self-critically watch developments in that respect, lest budget cuts at some point provide a much harsher statement on the relevance that policymakers attribute to their advice.

Independence and closeness

Scientific policy advice always faces a special dilemma. On the one hand, to be accepted as a constructive partner to policymakers, there needs to be trust and confidence. This requires a certain closeness to the people in charge. Only by being in touch with decision-makers in the administration and in parliament can an effective transfer of information be guaranteed. On the other hand, there is a need to keep a certain professional distance to remain independent. Only then does scientific policy advice maintain the liberty to confront decision-makers with ideas and recommendations that might seem new and unorthodox to them. Such a minimal distance is also useful on epistemological grounds: too much closeness always carries the risk of group think. Once policymakers and scientific policy advisers laud one another as 'great minds that think alike' there could be a real problem. There is always a risk of conformity, where advisers simply follow the policymakers' lead and only serve to legitimise policies in an intelligent way. Even this kind of policy advice fulfils a certain task, but it does not attain an early-warning function or that of a critical sparring partner.

Finally, scientific policy advice should and must not for its own benefit and importance make things more dramatic than they are.[10] Confronted

---

[10] The dilemma for individual researchers is that alarmism helps to increase media appearances while circumspection may look boring to media producers. See Schneckener 2006.

with the large number of international challenges – ranging from terrorism to climate change, energy issues and failing states to poverty, the return of geopolitical competition and the integration of emerging powers into the system of global governance – the need for sound, independent scientific policy advice and well-trained and qualified experts in this field will increase in any case.

REFERENCES

Perthes, Volker 2007. 'Zwischen Hofnarr und Agendasetter: Über wissenschaftliche Politikberatung in der Außen- und Sicherheitspolitik', *Internationale Politik* 62/12: 114–23.

Schneckener, Ulrich 2006. 'Die Grenzen der Terror-Forschung', *Handelsblatt* (September 2006) 6: 11.

Wissenschaftsrat 2006. *Stellungnahme zum Deutschen Institut für Internationale Politik und Sicherheit der Stiftung Wissenschaft und Politik (SWP)* (Drs. 7262–06), available at: www.wissenschaftsrat.de/download/ archiv/7262-06.pdf.

Part V

Academies of science

17 Scientific advice for policy in the United States: lessons from the National Academies and the Former Congressional Office of Technology Assessment[1]

Peter D. Blair

Introduction

The pace of science and technology advancement over the past half-century has delivered enormous benefits to societies throughout the world as well as sobering challenges associated with the role of technology in virtually every aspect of our lives. While reaping the benefits, all of society must also cope with the challenges.

Over two centuries ago as the American democracy took shape, the founding fathers of the fledgling republic worried that democracy could flourish only when the electorate and, in particular, the institutions of government serving it are well informed about the issues upon which they must decide. Today, and increasingly, as science and technology issues become more and more prevalent, prominent, complex and of far reaching impact on society, a democratic government poorly informed about such issues carries greater and greater risk in making bad policy choices with potentially significant consequences from such choices. Yet, it is also becoming increasingly more difficult for anyone, or even any one institution, to keep pace with the frontier of scientific knowledge and its impact on society. In addition, over the last quarter century, the information revolution has expanded the quantity of information accessible to government policymakers, but more information has not proved to be necessarily better information. Indeed, a fundamental problem today is not the lack of information; rather, it is how to gauge validity and usefulness within the torrent of available information and advice.

[1] This chapter is an expansion of Ahearne and Blair (2003) and includes descriptions drawn from Blair (1994, 1997a and 1997b) and the National Academies (2005a). The author greatly appreciates the advice of a number of reviewers, including John Gibbons, Christopher Hill, Jim Turner, Michael Rodemeyer, Jonathan Epstein and E. William Colglazier. Conclusions drawn in this chapter are the author's and not necessarily those of the National Academies.

How then can government policymakers acquire useful, relevant, informed, independent, authoritative and timely advice on the science and technology dimensions of the issues they face? This chapter reviews the current and evolving role of the US National Research Council (NRC) in providing advice to government as that role compares with other current sources of advice. For this book, also considered more specifically are the mechanisms of quality control in the NRC study process, again as it compares with other sources of advice, and in particular with that of the former Office of Technology Assessment (OTA)[2] with special attention to the special needs of the US Congress for science and technology advice. Also, for purposes of this chapter, the characterisations of the Academy and OTA study processes are stylised in that they are described in the ideal and most common study situations, although in both cases there were considerable variations around the specific processes presented here.

The role of the National Academies

In the US, among the most familiar sources of independent scientific and technical advice to the federal government is the group of non-government organisations sometimes referred to collectively as the National Academies, comprising the National Academy of Sciences (NAS), the National Academy of Engineering (NAE), the Institute of Medicine (IOM), and their collective *operating arm*, the National Research Council (NRC).[3] In 1863, the US Congress chartered the NAS as an independent non-profit corporation to 'whenever called upon by any department of the Government, investigate, examine, experiment, and report upon any subject of science or art'. This charter was signed into law by President Abraham Lincoln during the height of the US Civil War.

Today the NAS, NAE and IOM are prestigious and highly selective honorary societies that each elect among the most respected scientists and engineers in the world as new members to their ranks annually. The Presidents of the NAS and NAE serve *ex officio* as the Chair and Vice-Chair, respectively, of the NRC. The NRC assembles committees of experts including many academy members to provide advice in the form of study reports to executive branch agencies of government, but the US Congress also frequently mandates studies to be carried out by

---

[2] The Congressional Office of Technology Assessment (OTA) was an independent analytical support agency of the US Congress that was created in 1972 and operated from 1973–95. The authorising legislation for OTA still exists, but Congress no longer appropriates funds for its operation.

[3] More detailed descriptions can be found at the National Academies (2004) or Ahearne and Blair (2003).

the NRC.[4] NRC studies span a wide spectrum of science and technology related issues, resulting in around 250 reports[5] annually, involving nearly 10,000 volunteers serving on study committees and in the review process as well as utilising approximately 1,000 professional staff to manage and facilitate the efforts of study committees and related activities.

NRC reports are viewed widely as being valuable and credible because of the institution's longstanding reputation for providing independent, objective and non-partisan advice with high standards of scientific and technical quality. The key strengths of the NRC in providing advice to the US government rest principally on the history of convening very high quality expertise for its study committees and on the reputation for maintaining important quality control features for independence and objectivity of reports prepared by those committees. In particular, over the years as the NRC study process evolved, many checks and balances have been incorporated to ensure quality and protect the integrity of reports thereby helping to maintain public confidence in them. In 1997, many of these checks and balances, supplemented with some additional features, were codified into federal law as NRC advice to the government became subject to a new provision of the Federal Advisory Committee Act (discussed later). In short, the NRC study process is widely accepted as a high standard for independent scientific advice to government.

Key strengths of the NRC study process

These commonly cited principal strengths of the NRC study process include the following:

- Credibility. The NRC's institutional credibility is enabled in part by its association with the NAS, NAE and IOM. In addition, the process by which the NRC conducts its work is designed to ensure the results are evidence-based and tightly reasoned as well as independent from outside government agencies and congressional interests. The Academies also conduct several studies each year using their own limited endowment resources rather than those of external sponsors. These self-initiated studies often focus on topics that the Academies' leadership believes to be important but that the government may not be willing or able to sponsor on a schedule timely enough to be useful. One such

---

[4] Academy studies carried out for Congress are usually executed under contract to executive departments and agencies as directed by Congress in authorising or appropriations legislation.

[5] See the National Academy Press (2002), the National Academies (2005c), or the National Academy of Sciences (2005).

example was the 2002 study, *Making the Nation Safer: The Role of Science and Technology in Countering Terrorism*, which followed the terrorist events of September 11, 2001 in the US. Another is the 2005 report, *Rising Above the Gathering Storm: Energizing and Employing America for a Brighter Economic Future*, which puts forward recommendations for a comprehensive and coordinated federal effort to bolster US competitiveness and pre-eminence in science and technology. And most recently the 2009 study, *America's Energy Future: Technology and Transformation*, analysed the range of energy technology options most feasible to effect transformational change in the patterns of production and use of energy in the US economy that reduce carbon emissions and oil imports while supporting economic competitiveness and growth.

- Convening power. The NRC seeks to invite the 'best and the brightest' to participate in its studies and those invitations are generally accepted. Studies are carried out by groups of volunteers who are identified not only as broadly considered among the best experts on the issues to be studied, but also are determined through a well-documented process to be free of conflicts of interest, and represent a carefully balanced set of perspectives on those issues. It is widely perceived as a prestigious honour to serve on an NRC committee (despite the fact all committee members serve pro bono) and, because of the breadth of membership in the academies and the links of the organisation to the scientific and technical communities worldwide, the NRC is well-equipped to identify leading experts to serve on study committees.

- Study process and products. A highly structured process guiding NRC studies has evolved steadily over the years, but has always been and continues to be designed to maintain balance and objectivity throughout a committee's work and to produce reports considered to be both unbiased and authoritative. A key quality control feature in the process is independent peer review. After consensus is achieved by a study committee and a draft report is prepared, the NRC process requires the committee to address all of the comments from a carefully selected collection of reviewers, whose identities are not revealed to the committee until the study is publicly released. The review process is managed by a monitor appointed by the Report Review Committee, which is an independent committee of the National Academies (discussed more later).

Overview of the NRC study process

The NRC study process can be defined as a sequence of five major stages: (1) study definition, (2) committee selection, (3) committee activity (meetings, information gathering, deliberations and report preparation), (4) report review, delivery and public release, and (5) final publication and dissemination.[6]

Stage 1: study definition

Management and staff of the NRC along with members of oversight committees (known as boards) appointed by the Chair of the NRC are responsible for oversight of specific segments of the overall NRC study portfolio. There are approximately fifty such boards or similar standing bodies in the NRC organisation, such as the Board on Energy and Environmental Systems or the Board on Life Sciences. These groups interact with sponsors to define the specific set of questions to be addressed by a prospective study resulting in a formal 'statement of task' (SOT) as well as the anticipated duration and cost of the proposed study. The SOT defines and bounds the scope of a prospective study and serves as the basis for determining the expertise and the balance of perspectives needed on the committee that will be recruited to carry out the study. In addition, the SOT serves as a fundamental point of departure for subsequent independent peer review of the draft report prepared by the study committee.

The SOT, and the accompanying detailed plan for executing the committee's work, and the project budget are all reviewed and approved or revised by the Executive Committee of the NRC Governing Board (GBEC) comprised of elected and appointed officials of the NAS, NAE and IOM. This review can result in changes to the proposed SOT and work plan and, on occasion, results in turning down proposed studies that the institution, after consideration, believes are inappropriately framed or not within the charter of the National Research Council. Following GBEC approval and execution of a contract (or grant)[7] specifically for that study with the agency sponsor, work begins on the study itself.

Stage 2: committee selection

Members of NRC study committees are formally appointed by the Chair of the NRC. Committee members serve without compensation except

---

[6] Much of this description is adapted from the National Academies (2005a). More detailed descriptions of the NRC study process include National Research Council (1998, 2000 and 2005).

[7] Costs for NRC studies sponsored by government agencies are covered and accounted for via specific contracts for each study individually. For a variety of reasons (discussed later in this chapter) the NRC has been reluctant to operate under a more centralised funding mechanism with the government, such as an annual appropriation from Congress.

for reimbursement of expenses associated with attending meetings. The selection of appropriate committee members for an NRC study, both the individuals selected and the composition of the group as a whole, is key to the credibility and authority often associated with NRC reports. A great deal of research by NRC staff and management takes place prior to appointment of a committee in order to identify the strongest possible candidates.

NRC committee members serve as individual experts, not as representatives of organisations or interest groups. They are initially appointed provisionally and a committee is not finally approved until a discussion of the committee's composition and balance is held at the first meeting where any issues regarding potential conflicts of interest or balance of perspectives represented on the committee that are raised in that discussion or by the public[8] are investigated and addressed. This discussion and follow-up consideration by NRC management sometimes results in changes to the committee membership. The goal of this process of analysing the prospective committee's composition and balance is to ensure that committees meet the following criteria:

- An appropriate range of expertise for the task. Committees are designed to include experts with the specific expertise and experience needed to address the study's SOT. One of the strengths of the NRC is the tradition of bringing together recognised experts from diverse disciplines and backgrounds who might not otherwise collaborate. These diverse groups are encouraged to conceive of new ways of thinking about problems.
- A balance of perspectives. While ensuring that the right expertise is represented on the committee is essential, it is not alone sufficient for an effective committee on most NRC studies. It is also important to evaluate the overall composition of the committee in terms of a diversity and balance of experiences and perspectives. The goal is to ensure that the most important points of view, in the NRC's judgement, are reasonably balanced so that the committee can carry out its charge objectively and credibly.
- Screened for conflicts of interest. All provisional committee members are screened in writing and in a confidential group discussion regarding possible conflicts of interest. For this purpose, a conflict of interest focuses on financial or other interest which conflicts

---

[8] Provisional committee membership is posted on the National Academies internet website for a period of twenty days prior to the first meeting of the committee and the public is invited to provide comments on the committee composition and balance of perspectives.

with the service of the individual on the committee because it could significantly impair the individual's objectivity or could create an unfair competitive advantage for any person or organisation. In particular, the term conflict of interest in the NRC study context means something more than individual bias. There must be an interest, ordinarily financial, that could be directly affected by the work of the committee. Except in very rare situations where the NRC determines that a conflict of interest is unavoidable and promptly and publicly discloses the conflict of interest, no individual can be appointed to serve (or continue to serve) on a committee of the institution used in the development of reports if the individual has a conflict of interest that is relevant to the charge of the study committee. Many potential conflicts of interest or biases, as opposed to real conflicts as defined above, are balanced by different viewpoints represented by other members of the provisional committee. Studies involving regulation or specific government programme oversight involve additional scrutiny for addressing potential conflicts of interest responding to concerns similar to those expressed in the chapter by Podger in this book (Chapter 12).

• Other considerations. Membership in the three academies (NAS, NAE and IOM) and previous involvement in NRC studies are taken into account in committee selection. The inclusion of women, ethnic minorities, and young professionals are important as well, and additional factors such as geographic diversity and a diversity of institutional affiliations are also considered.

The specific steps in the committee selection and approval process are as follows: (1) academy staff solicit an extensive number of suggestions for potential committee members from a wide range of sources; (2) a recommended slate of nominees is put forward for approval through several levels within the NRC management, with the provisional slate ultimately approved by the NRC Chair; (3) the provisional committee member list is posted for public comment on the National Academies internet site and members are asked to complete background information and conflict of interest disclosure forms, which are subsequently reviewed by academy management and staff;[9] and then (4) a discussion of the committee's overall balance and potential conflicts of interest is held at the first committee meeting; (5) any conflicts of

---

[9] The NRC conflict of interest disclosure process (National Research Council 2003) is often cited as a high standard for documenting independence and objectivity in science and technology advisory bodies; see, e.g., US Office of Management and Budget (2005).

interest or issues of committee balance and expertise are investigated; and, if necessary, (6) changes to the committee are proposed and finalised before the committee is formally approved; finally, (7) committee members continue to be screened for conflicts of interest throughout the duration of the committee's work.

Stage 3: committee activity

Study committees typically gather information through: (1) meetings that are open to the public and that are announced in advance through the National Academies internet site; (2) the submission of information by outside parties; (3) reviews of the scientific literature (and other sources as relevant); and (4) the investigations of the committee members and staff. In all cases, efforts are made to solicit input from individuals who have been directly involved in, or who have special knowledge of, the problem under consideration. In accordance with federal law and with few exceptions, information-gathering meetings of the committee are open to the public.

Any written materials provided to the committee by individuals who are not officials, agents or employees of the National Academies are maintained in a Public Access File that is available to the public for examination. The committee deliberates in meetings closed to the public in order to develop draft findings and recommendations free from outside influences.[10] The public is provided with brief summaries of these meetings that include the list of committee members present (posted on the Academy's internet site), but all analyses carried out by the committee itself and drafts of the report remain confidential. Occasionally academy studies employ consultants to provide supplemental analyses to support the staff and committee's work although this is typically not a major component of most studies.

NRC committees assume authorship of the study report, although in practice who actually drafts the report varies considerably. For example, in many cases the appointed committee members draft much of the text at all stages of a report; in other cases committee members critique drafts prepared by staff; and often collaborative combinations of committee and staff authorship produce successive drafts.

[10] Most groups created by the US government to provide advice operate under regulations pursuant to the Federal Advisory Committee Act (FACA), which does not permit, for example, such groups to operate without government officials present or in meetings not open to the public (along with many other requirements). The NRC operates under a special provision of FACA (section 15) that permits closed committee meetings. Section 15 of FACA is included for reference as Appendix A to this chapter.

Stage 4: report review

As a final check on the quality and objectivity of an NRC study, all reports undergo a rigorous, independent external review by experts whose comments are provided anonymously to committee members. The NRC recruits independent experts with a range of views and perspectives to review and comment on the draft committee report.

The NRC's report review process is structured to ensure that a report addresses its approved study charge and does not exceed it;[11] that the findings are supported by the scientific evidence and that concluding arguments are presented clearly; that the exposition and organisation of the report are effective; and that the report is impartial and objective. Each committee is required to respond to, but need not (necessarily) agree with reviewer comments in a detailed *response to review* document that is examined by one or two independent report review *monitors* responsible for ensuring that the report review criteria have been satisfied. After all committee members and appropriate academy officials have approved the final report, it is transmitted to the sponsor of the study (usually a government agency) and subsequently released to the public. Sponsors are not provided an opportunity to suggest changes in reports. The names and affiliations of the report reviewers are made public and included in the report when it is released.

Stage 5: publication and dissemination

NRC reports are sometimes delivered and released to the public in the final published form, but more frequently are delivered and publicly released in a pre-publication draft format, and subsequently edited and produced in a final published form some time later. Press briefings, congressional and executive agency briefings, and other dissemination activities are common for many NRC studies.

Special challenges for NRC study processes

Over the years the NRC process has proved consistently to be a very strong model for providing independent and authoritative advice to government. Like any process designed to serve many needs, however,

---

[11] This is, in part, necessary because study statements of task are contractually defined and, hence, sometimes result in committee's frustration at not being permitted to exceed the statement of task if the committee feels an expansion of the scope is warranted. It is generally considered the role of the institutional governance structures to ensure that a study's statement of task is properly framed.

it is not perfectly tuned to serve all the needs of all parts of government that need science and technology advice. The most commonly cited issues and challenges associated with the NRC study process are the following:

- Cost. It is often perceived to be expensive to commission an NRC study, even though committee members are volunteers whose time is contributed pro bono (except for travel expenses). At least in part this perception is due to the fact that a separate contract is negotiated for each individual study – unlike the central funding for US federal agency advisory committees. The overhead cost for the NRC is necessarily substantial, partly because many of the staff supporting studies are professionals who manage the activities of standing boards and committees as well as study committees and partly because supporting the infrastructure necessary to maintain access to key sources of volunteers, including the governance structures of the National Academies, must be maintained. In general, the cost of an NRC study is perhaps somewhat higher than that of a comparable effort carried out by a university or nonprofit think tank and somewhat less than that of a commercial management consulting firm.

- Timeliness. The NRC study process, which includes commissioning and contracting for the study, selecting and convening a study committee, arranging subsequent meetings among busy experts who are often in high demand and serving on a volunteer basis, and navigating a report through peer review, editing, production and release takes time. The average (with a very wide variance) duration of an NRC study is about eighteen months, but can be longer, especially for controversial topics. Congressionally mandated studies involve additional complications as well (discussed below). It should also be noted, however, that studies can also be carried out quite rapidly given an important national need. The report, *Making the Nation Safer*, noted above, was completed in six months. Another widely cited study, *Climate Change Science*, was completed in one month and the 2005 report, *Rising Above the Gathering Storm*, also noted earlier, was completed in six months.

- Sources of sponsorship. Most NRC studies are commissioned and paid for by federal agencies through contracts (at least one per study undertaken and sometimes many contracts per study from multiple agencies). Studies are funded from other sources as well (sometimes in addition to federal agency sponsorship), such as foundations or even limited sponsorship from private sector sponsors or even states.

Studies mandated by Congress also require the additional hurdle of enacting a federal law directing an agency to contract with the NRC. On the one hand, the practice of negotiating studies individually, whether there are multiple sponsors or not, is beneficial in that it can help ensure that the studies the NRC undertakes are relevant and important. Also the diversity of financial sponsorship for a large portfolio of studies from many executive agencies (see Figure 17.1) helps assure independence, especially by minimising the dependence of the NRC's financial support on any one federal source. On the other hand, it often takes six to nine months through a government procurement process to initiate an NRC study even after a mandated study has been enacted in law (or included in the legislative report language accompanying passage of the law). For those studies mandated by Congress, yet an additional delay often results from the time needed to implement the legislation. While it has been sometimes suggested that the Academies consider requesting an annual appropriation of funds from Congress (probably executed as a so-called task order contract with a relevant federal agency) to facilitate improved administrative efficiency in carrying out studies (e.g. reducing the time for securing individual contracts for studies), the Academies' leadership has historically been unwilling to consider this option, since such an arrangement could lead to compromises in institutional independence.

- Committee authorship. NRC study committees of experts, widely considered to be a key strength of the NRC study approach, include widely respected individuals from academia, industry and essentially all groups relevant to the study committee's charge. However, the volunteer committee of experts as authors of the report can also sometimes be a weakness. For example, NRC committees are made up of distinguished volunteers who have many other responsibilities in their professional lives. Without careful oversight by the committee chair and sometimes NRC management, committee members with the most at stake in a study or perhaps with the most available time to commit to the effort could have a disproportionate influence over a study's deliberations and outcomes. This is why the NRC places such a high priority on recruiting strong chairs, providing experienced professional support staff in managing committees, and executing rigorous procedures for identifying and addressing potential bias and conflicts of interest of prospective committee members. Committee members who attempt to abuse their responsibilities as committee members can be removed while a study is under way.

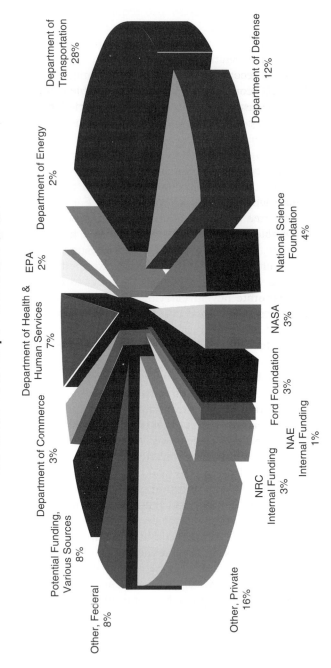

PROGRAMME SUPPORT BY SOURCE FOR FY2009
Estimated Total Expenditures of $279.4 milllion

Department of Transportation 28%

Department of Energy 2%

Department of Defense 12%

EPA 2%

Department of Health & Human Services 7%

National Science Foundation 4%

Department of Commerce 3%

NASA 3%

Potential Funding, Various Sources 8%

Ford Foundation 3%

Other, Feceral 8%

NRC Internal Funding 3%

NAE Internal Funding 1%

Other, Private 16%

Figure 17.1 Programme support by source for FY2009

A current gap in advice matched to congressional needs

As just outlined, the NRC study process is well developed and serves one important need of Congress – providing an authoritative recommendation from widely recognised experts on a specific course of action. In particular, NRC committees are usually assembled with the intention of achieving consensus recommendations supported by evidence and subject to rigorous peer review. In a very controversial subject area with scientific and other uncertainties, if a broad set of perspectives are included in the study committee a consensus might be difficult to achieve, particularly if the purpose is to include all possible scientific and other perspectives on a problem or if complex policy considerations are involved. This is why the NRC places a high priority on an appropriately balanced committee and a rigorous information-gathering phase of a committee's work, where such perspectives can be heard and considered by the committee.[12]

Since the historical focus of the NRC process has been on delivering consensus-based advice, the process as it has evolved is less well equipped to elaborate on the broader context of an issue and inform the policy debate with careful and objective analysis of the policy consequences of alternative courses of action, especially those that may involve value judgements and social or economic trade-offs beyond the scope of technical analysis. Such issues of scale and scope are also addressed in the chapter by Dammann and Gee in this book (see Chapter 13). This observation of the challenges associated with providing authoritative advice in such a context is more or less consistent with the concerns expressed in the chapter by Jasanoff, also in this book (see Chapter 2). Consequently, it has been less common for the NRC to assemble committees charged with identifying and evaluating the pros and cons of a range of alternative policy options, although such committees are sometimes created and it would certainly be possible to develop such a study process to be used more widely at the NRC.

Both types of analysis just described are important to congressional deliberation depending upon the circumstances. With the closure of the former OTA, organisations focused on the latter type of analysis, either performed by a disinterested analytical organisation within the Congress itself or readily accessible to the Congress from an external organisation,

[12] While NRC study committees strive by design to produce consensus findings and recommendations, academy policies and procedures do provide for publishing dissenting views when consensus cannot be achieved.

do not currently exist and may at some point need to be reconstructed, perhaps involving the National Academies in some way.

Example: the future of the US electric power system

As an example illustrating the analysis gap just noted, consider the case where the US Congress may be interested in the future of the electric power system following a major blackout. The salient issues could be posed in two alternative ways:

- One type of study would be to seek an authoritative set of recommendations for making the power system more secure and reliable. In such a study, the well-established NRC approach would be to assemble a committee of widely recognised experts. The committee would review what is known about the power system and currently expected paths of continued development and then prepare specific engineering, technology and operational recommendations about how to improve system reliability and performance. Indeed, such a study was recently completed at the NRC sponsored by the US Department of Homeland Security.
- In another type of study, Congress might be interested in exploring the technical as well as societal, environmental, economic, regulatory or other broad implications of alternative scenarios of evolution of the nation's electric utility industry, perhaps once again precipitated by a blackout widely perceived, correctly or not, to be the result of deregulation. Not only technical, but also political, economic, social, environmental and probably many other kinds of trade-offs and value judgements are involved in characterising a series of scenarios for the future structure of the industry, ranging from moving towards a national centrally controlled electric supply grid to fully deregulating wholesale and retail electricity segments of the industry.

In the latter case a definitive set of consensus recommendations is not the objective, and the collection of stakeholders and experts necessary to carefully identify and explore these alternatives would be considerably different than for the study committee structured to reach fact-based, tightly reasoned consensus recommendations based on scientific evidence and on specific technical issues. Rather, the objective would be to articulate the implications of alternative scenarios and accompanying policy decisions, usually at a higher level of abstraction than the former case.

In short, and perhaps at the risk of being somewhat simplistic, the first type of analysis is designed *to illuminate the scientific and technical aspects of a problem to help direct a specific course of action* while, in the second case, the analysis is designed principally *to inform the debate, including perspectives that may go beyond science and engineering.* Both types of analysis are very important to congressional deliberations. The contrasts between these two types of analysis are discussed below in a more detailed comparison of the NRC process with that of the former OTA. As noted above, the fact that the NRC process does not now generally accommodate this second form of advice does not mean that it could not; the NRC often considers and implements changes in its processes in response to government needs, although going beyond the tradition of fact-based studies with a science and technology focus to more policy-oriented studies could pose risks to the NRC's credibility so such changes would have to be implemented very carefully.

Real-time advice: a continuing imperative

As a case in point of the evolution of NRC processes, the horrific terrorist events of September 11, 2001 in the US spurred widespread interest in finding ways to contribute to the understanding of the science and technology dimensions of homeland security and countering terrorism. Specifically, many government agencies expressed urgent needs for immediate advice in these areas. In response, the NRC experimented with using its convening power to assemble small groups of experts who then provided advice as individuals, rather than as a group constituting an NRC committee. Such real-time advice, which does not result in a written report and does not carry the imprimatur of the NRC process (especially the quality control aspects of committee deliberation and independent peer review of a written report) does not constitute formal advice of the Academy to government. It has, however, provided a new means of satisfying a real government need, i.e. providing timely input to policymakers and other organisations, including, as an example, a standing arrangement with the Government Accountability Office (GAO), an agency of the Congress, discussed further below.

Additional congressional needs vary widely, including such deliverables as (1) *instant education* on a complex science and technology issue, (2) *translations* of authoritative technical reports to more readable and understandable language tuned to the needs of policymakers with very broad responsibilities, (3) summaries of landmark authoritative reports, and (4) updates or adaptations of existing reports and information to current needs, and (5) readily available and trusted expert consultants on call to help with quick turnaround questions and interpretations of complex technical information. Some of these capabilities are accessible to the Congress to varying degrees through the Congressional Research Service, but others, especially (1) and (5) are not currently generally available to the Congress, at least in any organised or readily accessible way by an organisation directly accountable to Congress.

Collaboration and the GAO experiment

In an experiment referenced above to test the feasibility of developing a technology assessment capability in another congressional support agency, the Government Accountability Office (GAO), a first-of-a-kind GAO technology assessment report on biometric technologies was released in 2002.[13] While the NRC was not involved in developing this assessment, it was asked to use its contacts to assist the GAO in identifying individuals with the proper expertise. In retrospect, there are a number of shortcomings in the approach adopted by the GAO in carrying out its first attempt at a technology assessment, most notably the lack of a substantive and accountable peer review process, but the experiment was more successful than many anticipated and the GAO seems receptive to incorporating improvements suggested by a group commissioned to review the GAO approach (see Fri, Morgan and Stiles 2002). In particular, the group identified a number of significant organisational challenges that it felt were necessary to refine the GAO approach, which could then possibly evolve into a more mature technology assessment capability within the legislative branch of government. The GAO technology assessment experiment is continuing at a modest scale of one to two assessments annually on selected topics, but the agency's ultimate capability to fill the gap in technology assessment at the scale and scope necessary for the Congress remains uncertain.

The NRC's modest role in this GAO experiment, by convening groups of experts to talk with GAO study teams, appears to have been one of the successful features of this approach and may constitute one way in which the NRC can contribute to a renewed technology assessment capability within the legislative branch, whether it would be in assisting GAO or another organisation, such as a reconfigured OTA, in addition to its more traditional response to congressionally mandated requests for assistance. The NRC's relationship with GAO also includes,

[13] Since 1996 members of Congress at various times have proposed experiments to fill the perceived gap in science and technology advice in the wake of closure of the OTA, including attempts to simply resurrect the agency; see Jones (2004) and Knezo (2005). One such experiment that has come to pass is the creation of a *pilot* technology assessment capability in the Government Accountability Office, a support agency of the Congress. The first such assessment (GAO 2002) was released in November 2002.

more generally, a standing arrangement to assemble experts to talk with GAO staff on a specific set of technical issues relevant to ongoing GAO studies. Such a mechanism provides the GAO, or whatever other organisation evolves, a degree of access to the National Academies' considerable network of technical experts.

The former Office of Technology Assessment

The GAO experiment was designed to help fill the gap in science and technology advice for congressional needs left by closure of OTA. By comparison and contrast with the NRC study process, the OTA study process used an authoritative committee of volunteers as an advisory panel rather than in the role of assuming authorship of the study itself. The study report was, instead, produced by professional staff subject to external review. On one hand, this approach permitted easier regulation of the role of the committee, particularly if achieving a consensus in a broad controversial area was unlikely, but, on the other hand, such a practice also sacrificed the authoritativeness of the best and brightest volunteer experts identified as authors of the report, an important feature of the NRC process.

Because the former OTA panels were advisory, and not the report's authors, the necessity of reaching a consensus was seldom an issue. Indeed, OTA was prohibited in its enabling legislation from making specific recommendations, so the panel was created to try to collect the views of all important stakeholders rather than to try to produce consensus recommendations. This sometimes resulted in a frustrating experience for panelists serving on OTA advisory panels who were eager to offer specific recommendations. Instead, OTA project teams sought to analyse and articulate the consequences of alternative courses of action and elaborate on the context of a problem without coming to consensus recommendations on a specific course of action, which would be difficult anyway with a diverse group with points of view that prevented consensus on many controversial issues. In the later years of the agency's existence, OTA reports included more and more specific *findings* as a carefully developed alternative to recommendations.

If required to deliver a consensus set of recommendations, even if it were permitted under the enabling legislation, the former OTA model would likely be unworkable for controversial subjects with many opposing points of view. Nonetheless, the type of study undertaken by the former OTA was an important input to congressional deliberation and it has not yet been reproduced in the Legislative Branch agencies or elsewhere, including the NRC. The Academies could probably carry out more such studies but that would likely require some significant changes in its study procedures to accommodate such studies as indicated above and in more detail below.

OTA's organisational structure

OTA operated under congressional authorisation provided in the Technology Assessment Act of 1972 and funds were appropriated in 1973 to begin operations in 1974 with a handful of staff that grew to 200 in the later years of the agency's existence. The staff structure included a core permanent staff of 143 that was supplemented with temporary staff recruited to meet the needs of current assessments. Both permanent and temporary staff included professionals from many disciplines, over half with Ph.D.s. OTA produced on average thirty-two reports per year over its history and fifty-one reports per year in the last three years of its existence.[14]

The key organisational elements created in OTA's enabling statute were: (1) the Technology Assessment Board (TAB) composed of members of both chambers of the US Congress, the House of Representatives and Senate; (2) a Technology Assessment Advisory Council (TAAC), composed primarily of private citizens appointed by TAB; and (3) the Office of the Director, which oversaw day-to-day operations of the agency.

- Technology Assessment Board. TAB was the central organisational element articulated in OTA's enabling statute with its composition unique among the legislative support agencies.[15] TAB was a twelve-member governing board of OTA, with six members of the Senate and six of the House of Representatives, divided equally between the two dominant US political parties. The principal responsibilities of TAB were to appoint the Director, to authorise the initiation of assessments requested by congressional committees, to approve the budget authority associated with those assessments, and finally to authorise delivery of assessment reports to requesting committees and the public by certifying that OTA has carried out its assessment process faithfully, i.e. that

---

[14] The entire collection of OTA assessments delivered during the agency's history (1972–95) is preserved electronically and available at www.wws.princeton.edu/ota/ and on a CD-ROM collection (Office of Technology Assessment 1996).

[15] During OTA's existence, there were four congressional analytical support agencies: the Library of Congress's Congressional Research Service (CRS), the General Accounting Office (GAO) (GAO's name was changed to the Government Accountability Office in 2004), and the Congressional Budget Office (CBO). CRS, GAO and CBO remain in operation today.

OTA had considered all the relevant stakeholder interests and issues and undergone extensive external review. OTA received an annual budget appropriation from Congress allocated to OTA's support operations and among OTA active projects as authorised by TAB.

- Technology Assessment Advisory Council. TAAC was essentially OTA's outside visiting committee. It was appointed by TAB and met periodically to review the overall direction of the agency and carry out more detailed reviews of the agency's programme activities.
- Office of the Director. The OTA Director was responsible for day-to-day operations, hiring and management of staff, interaction with TAB and TAAC, and strategic planning for as well as organisation of the agency.

OTA's process of technology assessment[16]

As noted above, OTA generally undertook assessments at the request of the Chairs of congressional committees. Typical OTA assessments took eighteen to twenty-four months to complete and cost on the order of $500,000 (1996 dollars) in direct costs (although indirect costs essentially doubled the total cost).[17] OTA assessments seldom offered specific recommendations. Rather, as noted earlier, they articulated policy options and the consequences of alternative options.

A great deal of effort went into defining the scope of an assessment once it was requested by a committee Chair. Since OTA frequently received many more requests than it could accommodate, the project directors often consulted with other congressional committees of jurisdiction and interest as well as with the TAB informally to help establish study priorities fairly. Once a general study scope was established, a proposal was prepared for formal consideration by TAB and, if approved, the assessment commenced. The portfolio of assessments addressed a broad range of subjects on the congressional agenda, such as energy and environmental technology issues, proliferation of weapons of mass destruction, global telecommunications policy, biological pest control and health care reform. The key elements of an assessment typically were the following:

- a comprehensive advisory panel of technical experts and relevant stakeholders;
- a core OTA project team including an experienced project director;

[16] OTA's assessment process is documented widely in the literature, including Guston (2003), Bimber (1996), and many others.
[17] As noted earlier, OTA delivered on average fifty-one reports per year during the last three years of the agency's existence.

- contractors and consultants selected to support major analytical tasks;
- in-house research efforts by the project team;
- workshops convened with additional experts and stakeholders to obtain the most current information possible;
- extensive review and comment of draft reports by external technical experts and stakeholder interests; and
- delivery of reports through congressional hearings, briefings, and public release, and often considerable follow-up consultation with requesting congressional committees of jurisdiction and interest.

OTA advisory panels were an important feature of OTA's assessment process. They helped refine the project scope, identified additional relevant resources and perspectives on the issues being addressed, and provided the core of extensive peer review. The advisory panel was central, but OTA took responsibility for the final product. The agency did not seek consensus from the panel because most often if there were a possible consensus decision or course of action, OTA probably wouldn't have been asked to do the study in the first place. The principal final product of an OTA assessment was a report, along with summaries, report briefs, personal briefings for members and committees, commercial publishers' reprints, and in the final years of the agency's existence electronic delivery of these products over the internet and via Capitol Hill's local area network.

At the highest level of abstraction, the OTA assessment process is similar to the NRC study process in that it can also be defined in terms of a sequence of five major stages similar to those of the NRC process.[18] However, each stage has significant differences in their details compared with the corresponding stages in the NRC process. The stages to the OTA process were the following: (1) project selection; (2) project planning and preparation; (3) project execution: data collection, analysis, and report preparation; (4) report review, delivery and publication; and (5) report dissemination, use and follow-up activities.

Stage 1: project selection

OTA worked principally for the committees of the US Congress, and, hence, projects were generally initiated as a result of inquiries from congressional committee staff ultimately resulting in formal letters of

---

[18] In terms of scale and scope of policy problems addressed, the OTA process is similar to that of the Royal Society described in the chapter by Collins (see Chapter 18) or of the European Academies Science Advisory Council discussed by Fears and ter Meulen (see Chapter 19).

request from committee Chairs and ranking members (and often from more than one committee of jurisdiction or interest). Projects could also on occasion be initiated at the request of TAB or by the OTA Director with TAB's approval, although such studies were rare. In practice, OTA staff became what many congressional committees and members referred to as shared staff for standing House and Senate Committees and, hence, studies were often initiated as a result of ongoing interaction between congressional committee staff and OTA staff.

A great deal of preliminary work often went into the planning for a new OTA assessment. Usually this work involved preliminary data collection and literature research, including reviewing relevant legislative history, congressional committee hearings and reports, and reports from other congressional agencies (Congressional Budget Office, Congressional Research Service, and GAO), all to help frame the issues for the project proposal and work plan. The major product at this stage in the assessment process was a proposal which first was approved internally by the OTA Director for consideration by TAB for review and approval. The proposal included a detailed work plan and budget proposal, and, if approved by TAB, resources would be set aside out of OTA's annual appropriation to carry out the assessment.

Stage 2: project planning and preparation

Following TAB approval, a project team of two to six professional staff was appointed. Usually the project director was a permanent staff member with experience in prior OTA assessments supplemented with additional senior and junior staff members who were either permanent staff or rotational (temporary) staff recruited for specialised skills needed to carry out the assessment. Overall, the research and writing of OTA assessments was principally conducted by a staff of about 200, of which two-thirds were the professional research staff. In the early 1990s, among the research staff, 88 per cent had advanced degrees, 58 per cent with Ph.D.s, primarily in the physical, life, and social sciences, economics and engineering. About 40 per cent of the research staff were temporary appointments of professionals recruited specifically to staff ongoing assessments (I myself came to OTA under such an arrangement). For specific information or analysis, OTA also contracted with key individuals or organisations. Contractors analysed data, conducted case studies, and otherwise provided expertise to complement staff capability.

The project team assembled a slate of nominees for the project's advisory panel by defining the major stakeholder interests in the issues to be addressed, the important science and technology expertise relevant to the assessment, and other interests as necessary to capture a very broad range of perspectives on the study scope. The advisory panel slate was submitted for approval through OTA management and ultimately approved by OTA's Director, often with revisions or additions to the originally proposed slate. The project team organised and commissioned the portfolio of contractor support tasks, assigned internal analysis tasks, information gathering workshops, and other activities as specified in the work plan.

Stage 3: execution: data collection, analysis and report preparation

Carrying out the assessment itself was typically organised around meetings of the project's advisory panel. The panel's principal responsibility was to ensure that reports were objective, fair and authoritative by helping to shape studies in the early stages by suggesting alternative approaches, reviewing documents throughout the course of the assessment and critiquing reports at the final stages. The panels typically met three times during a study, initially to help frame the study, second as an opportunity to effect mid-course corrections and, finally, as the point of departure for the initial and perhaps most important part of peer review of the draft report.

In addition to the advisory panel, many others assisted with OTA assessments through participation in technical workshops, provision of background information, and review of documents. Commissioned contractor reports, invited papers contributed to workshops, internal working papers prepared by professional staff, and interaction with parallel studies on-going in other organisations all helped shape the body of information considered as the staff began to prepare the assessment report. In all, nearly 5,000 outside panellists and workshop participants came to OTA annually to help OTA in its work.

The role of contractors in an OTA assessment evolved considerably over the agency's history. In the early years commissioning external contracts were perhaps the dominant part of a study. Over the years as the agency's professional staff developed and became much more attuned to congressional needs, contractors were used less, but were often an important part of an OTA assessment.

Stage 4: report review, delivery and public release

OTA placed a very high premium on clearly written reports that effectively communicated very complex topics to congressional staff and members and to the public. This involved writing reports specifically tuned to congressional needs, such as language suitable for and relevant to broad policy discussions, extensive examples, and illustrative anecdotes helpful for framing policy debates. Also, as noted earlier, no attempt was made to develop a consensus among panel members; in fact, a wide diversity of views was sought. OTA retained full responsibility for the content and conclusions of each report. OTA draft assessment reports went through extensive formal review and revision conducted by OTA staff and outside experts. Some outside reviewers examined portions of the report while others the entire report and the total number of reviewers involved often exceeded 100 individuals.

Accompanying a final draft report for consideration by the Director was a *response to review* memorandum prepared by the project director that reviewed all comments received on the draft report and how they were dealt with in producing the final draft report. Upon the Director's approval of the final draft assessment report and its response-to-review, copies of the final report were sent to TAB for its review and authorisation for publication. If approved by TAB, published reports were then forwarded to the requesting committee or committees, summaries and one-page report briefs were sent to all Members of Congress, and then the report was released to the public. OTA assessments were published by the Government Printing Office and were frequently reprinted by commercial publishers.

Stage 5: dissemination, use and follow-up

Upon delivery of a published OTA assessment report to sponsors and public release, frequently congressional hearings and briefings followed. Reports were disseminated widely to the relevant policy communities, and frequently OTA staff prepared publications based on the report for peer reviewed journals or other publications. OTA reports were often reprinted by commercial publishers (as a government-produced document, OTA reports carried no copyright restrictions except for attribution), and in the final years of the agency's existence electronic delivery over the internet and via Capitol Hill's local area network became standard practice. Finally, senior OTA staff involved in the effort often became subject-matter experts called upon frequently by congressional staff and members as legislative initiatives were considered in the subject area addressed by the assessment. As noted earlier, many congressional offices and members often referred to OTA project teams as shared staff experts in science and technology supporting congressional committee staffs where such expertise was often scarce.

The NRC and OTA study processes compared

Some of the differences between the NRC and OTA study processes as they relate to studies requested by Congress have already been noted and in some ways the processes are more similar than they are different (see Figure 17.2). Both involve a carefully bounded and defined scope of work culminating in a formal study request, usually in the form of a letter or congressional legislation. In both cases the scope of work is formally documented with a proposal and work plan, although in the case of the NRC the proposal takes the form both of an internal study prospectus to be approved by the NRC Governing Board[19] as well as an external contract proposal to formalise the funding sources with the sponsoring federal agencies (or sometimes other organisations). In the OTA case, the TAB authorised approval of expenditures for the study against the agency's annual appropriation. The mechanism of project funding is one of the fundamental differences between the two approaches (discussed more below), but there are many other differences as well.

Role of volunteer committee

The role, purpose and even composition of study committees in the NRC case and advisory panels in the OTA case are quite different in several respects, some of which were noted above. In the NRC case, the committee assumes authorship of the report while in the OTA case the committee is advisory to professional staff who draft the report. The quality of the study in the NRC case is much more dependent upon the quality of the committee recruited to carry it out, which explains why considerable effort is spent on recruiting high quality committees for NRC studies. Such was the case for recruiting OTA advisory panels as well, but the success of the study was relatively less dependent on the role of the advisory panel.

The quality of the staff project team was the dominant consideration in the OTA case. As noted above, members serve pro bono on NRC committees while in the OTA case a modest honorarium for service by advisory panel members was occasionally provided. NRC committees are generally recruited with the intention of coming to a consensus regarding findings, conclusions and recommendations included in the committee's report. In the OTA case, the goal was instead to have all legitimate

---

[19] Technically, this approval is delegated by the Governing Board (which meets quarterly) to its Executive Committee (which meets monthly).

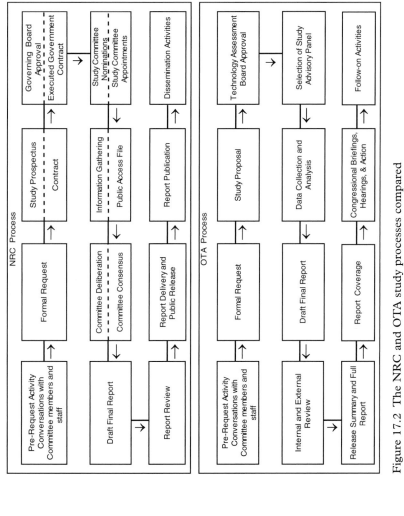

Figure 17.2 The NRC and OTA study processes compared

interests in the policy area under study represented on the advisory panel with no expectation of reaching a consensus view. Finally, because in the NRC case the committee assumed authorship of the report, elaborate institutional procedures for avoiding conflicts of interest are a high priority. In the OTA case, since the goal of the advisory committee was to include all legitimate interests, conflicts of interest were essentially encouraged, although carefully balanced in the panel composition.

Role of the professional staff

As a consequence of the differing roles and structure of NRC committees versus OTA advisory panels, the roles of the professional staff in the study process are generally quite different as well. In the NRC case, the principal responsibilities of the staff are to plan, organise and structure the study, initiate selection of the study committee membership, and facilitate the committee's work, including ensuring adherence to the policies and procedures established for NRC studies.[20] However, as noted above, even though NRC committees assume authorship of the study report, in practice draft reports for the committee's critique and consensus are produced in a variety of ways, and frequently involve committee member drafting, committees critiquing drafts prepared by staff, and collaborative combinations of committee and staff authorship. In the OTA case, the professional staff members planned and managed the assessment, and took responsibility for the report as the study authors. Finally, OTA staff were also Legislative Branch government employees with frequent day-to-day interaction with congressional staff and members before, during and after completion of OTA assessments.

Requests to initiate studies

Most congressionally requested NRC studies require that the study be mandated in law or specified in a legislative report accompanying the law when passed by Congress. Otherwise it is unlikely that the relevant executive agency would be willing to provide the funding to support the study. On rare occasions, letters of request from Members of Congress led to studies funded by internal resources of the National Academies. In the OTA case by far most studies were requested by Chairs and

---

[20] In practice the degree to which the NRC staff members are involved in drafting a committee report varies widely. In some studies staff members become very actively involved in the substance of the committee's work while in others staff principally facilitate the committee's work.

Ranking Members of standing committees of either or both chambers of the Congress, although studies were sometimes also mandated in law (although still subject to approval by TAB). OTA's statute provided for self-initiated studies approved by TAB but, as the agency matured and demands from Committees to initiate studies exceeded the agency's capacity, OTA seldom exercised its option to carry out self-initiated assessments.

Funding of studies

Most NRC studies are funded by executive agencies through a sole-source (non-competitive) contract or grant or in some cases an individual task negotiated as part of a task order contract. Sometimes funds for congressionally mandated studies are provided in appropriations legislation. Often, though, mandated studies are specified in authorising legislation or report language accompanying legislation and agencies may or may not choose to make funds available to carry out the study. In the OTA case, funds for virtually all studies were drawn from the agency's annual budget appropriation for the agency's operations and were allocated when the study proposal was approved by TAB.

Government oversight of policies and procedures

As an independent, private, non-profit organisation, many of the same laws that apply to such organisations apply to the National Academies, especially those related to, for example, employment practices or contracting and financial auditing requirements. In addition, special additional policies apply, such as section 15 of the Federal Advisory Committee Act (see Appendix A) and several Presidential Executive Orders[21] applicable to the National Academies charter and mission. So, while there are many government oversight mechanisms that apply to specific individual academy policies and procedures, there is no direct overall oversight relationship with the government.

By contrast, as a congressional agency, OTA had many fewer operational government oversight mechanisms while the agency had three direct oversight mechanisms within the Congress itself: (1) TAB, which was ultimately responsible for managing the agency; (2) the Senate and House Appropriations Committees where OTA's annual operating budget was established as part of the Legislative Branch appropriations

---

[21] The NRC was included formally under the charter of the NAS with a Presidential Executive order signed by Woodrow Wilson in 1918 and reaffirmed and revised in 1956 and 1993 (see Executive Office of the President 1993).

process; and (3) standing committees of the House and Senate (Senate Committee on Governmental Affairs and the House Committee on Science) with responsibility for oversight of OTA's authorising statute.[22]

Government oversight of study scope

As noted above the mechanism for controlling a study's scope for an NRC study is the contract or grant with a federal executive agency responsible for the funds to sponsor the study. Sometimes differences between congressional expectations, as articulated in the legislative language mandating the study, and the contract language with the designated executive agency can be difficult to resolve to the satisfaction of all concerns. In the OTA case the mechanism for controlling the study scope was ultimately the responsibility of TAB.

Report peer review mechanisms

NRC reports are subjected to an independent and anonymous peer review process. That is, the study committee is obliged to respond to comments from peer reviewers whose identity is unknown to the committee until after the report is published. Reviewers are selected through a process overseen by the executive offices of the NRC's major programme divisions and the Report Review Committee (RRC), which is a National Academies committee independent of all involved in preparation of the study report. Judgement of the adequacy of a committee's response to review is managed by the RRC. Typically ten to twelve reviewers, but often many more, provide detailed comments on the draft report. In the OTA case, while there were as many as 100 reviewers engaged in reviewing parts or all of a draft OTA report, the reviewers were generally selected by the OTA project team but often supplemented with reviewers selected by senior OTA management. The OTA project director drafted the response to review subject to the approval of senior OTA management and ultimately, OTA's Director and TAB.

Nature of reports

As noted above, NRC reports are usually designed to yield consensus findings, conclusions and recommendations from an authoritative

---

[22] Technically, OTA's authorising statute, the Technology Assessment Act of 1972 (U.S. Code, Title 2, Chapter 15, Sections 471–481), was never repealed by Congress so the agency does not exist only because funds are no longer appropriated for its operations.

committee regarding a specific course of action. OTA reports generally did not include specific recommendations but, rather, were designed to articulate the consequences of alternative options without selecting a preferred option, although, as noted earlier, in the later years of the agency's existence OTA reports included more and more specific findings as a carefully developed alternative to recommendations. It is perhaps important to note that in neither of the NRC or OTA cases is the intention of the study report to produce new technical understanding. Indeed, in both cases the intent is to collect and make understandable to broader audiences, particularly policymakers, established perspectives on the current understanding of the issue(s) under study.

Report delivery and dissemination

In most cases, dissemination of NRC reports is limited to delivery to executive agency sponsors and relevant congressional committees and released to the public through the National Academies Press (NAP) and made available on the National Academies internet site. Often the report is initially released in a pre-publication draft format in order to effect as timely as possible delivery of the information to the sponsoring agency and the public. The final printed report, including editorial but no substantive changes to the report content, follows later as published by the NAP and made available on the academy internet site. The National Academies holds the copyright on the report and the NAP offers copies of most reports for sale to the public and all reports available without charge on the academy internet site. Occasionally, the committee chair and some committee members participate in agency or congressional briefings of the report or provide testimony for congressional hearings. OTA reports, along with accompanying summaries and report briefs, were widely distributed upon public release and were available for sale through the Superintendent of Documents (Government Printing Office) and made available without charge on the agency's internet site. OTA staff frequently provided congressional briefings and testimony and occasionally executive agency briefings as well as often preparing papers and summaries based on the report for the peer reviewed literature.

Follow-up activities

For the most part, when NRC reports are delivered to sponsors and publicly released, the committee's work is largely over, except for dissemination activities noted above. Occasionally committees are re-convened for follow-up studies or committees are empanelled in the first place with the intention of producing a series of reports, such as an annual review of a federal Research and Development (R&D) programme over a period of years. In the OTA case, initial report dissemination activities were similar to the NRC routine, but with much more focus on the congressional audience, as one might expect. However, it was also very common for smaller scale follow-up background papers on topics included in the assessment to be requested by congressional committees. In addition, OTA staff members were consulted frequently by congressional committee staff on an ongoing basis in areas where OTA assessments had been completed, often for many years following the completion of a major assessment.

Conclusions

The reputation of the National Academies as a trusted source of advice for government on science and technology issues is due not only to the quality of expertise the NRC is able to involve in its work but also to the highly structured process guiding NRC studies that has evolved steadily over many years. The goal of this process, which includes many features of quality control and assurance relating both the process by which the advice is generated and the report documenting that advice, is to maintain balance and objectivity throughout a committee's work and to produce reports considered to be both unbiased and authoritative.

The National Academies have enjoyed a longstanding and effective working relationship with Congress on even the most controversial issues. There are, no doubt, many characteristics of that relationship that could be improved, both to perform the traditional NRC role more effectively and to provide some opportunities to expand that role. However, effective science advice in the unique policymaking environment of the Congress is a complex undertaking (see Smith and Stine 2003). There are a variety of options for filling the gap in analysis capabilities left in the wake of the closure of OTA, some of which might involve the National Academies (see Morgan and Peha 2003).

Many features of the OTA assessment process were similar to those used currently by the NRC, but as outlined in this chapter, there are fundamental differences as well. The OTA process was well suited to a broad policy context, paralleling that of congressional deliberation, where the questions involve the relationship of science and technology to broader economic, environmental, social and other policy issues where many legitimate courses of policy action are possible and any consensus view with all stakeholder views represented is most unlikely.[23]

As an example of this contrast between the two approaches (illustrated also by the electric utility industry case described earlier), consider the case of federal policy on fuel economy regulation of automobiles. In the early 1990s, both the OTA and the NRC were asked to consider the subject of improving automotive fuel economy and, more specifically, the feasibility of increasing fuel economy standards to achieve better fuel efficiency in the nation's auto fleet. The OTA report elaborates on the various trade-offs associated with raising standards versus alternative policy mechanisms for achieving automotive improved fuel economy (OTA 1991). The NRC study (1992) much more specifically comes to conclusions regarding the technical feasibility of various proposed standards and provides a specific recommendation on a particular set of standards that, in the opinion of the committee, is technically feasible while having minimal or at least acceptable market disruption. The NRC deliverable required that a committee of experts reach a consensus and the recommendations are widely considered authoritative. The OTA study could seek consensus on facts and analysis (although the process did not require it because the panel of experts was advisory), but it did not come to specific recommendations regarding the standards, partly because the agency's charter precluded coming to a specific recommendation in the first place and partly because the advisory panel was assembled with the broadest range of stakeholders and would likely not have been able to reach consensus anyway.

OTA-like features emerging in the NRC study process

It is interesting to note that in 2002 the NRC issued a new report on fuel economy standards (NRC 2002) where alternative mechanisms for achieving improved US automotive fuel economy were addressed, moving in the direction of an OTA assessment, although by far the most referenced portions of that report remain the identification and evaluation of the technical potential for improving fuel economy. In another more recent case, the academy's report, *Rising Above the Gathering Storm: Energizing and Employing America for a Brighter Economic Future,* (NRC 2005), is very similar in scope to an OTA assessment with the

---

[23] The reasons congressional leadership gave for closing OTA in 1995 were not so much related to the quality of the advice the agency provided to Congress but to the timeliness of its delivery; see Walker (2001) and Dawson (2001).

added benefits of a highly prestigious committee identified as authors of the report and very specific recommendations offered.

Although not carrying the 100-year-old imprimatur of the National Academies, OTA's reports developed a reputation for being authoritative as well, but OTA's strength was more, as the late Congressman George Brown, once Chair of the TAB and of the House Science and Technology Committee, put it, a 'defense against the dumb' by elaborating on the context of an issue and informing the debate with careful analysis of the consequences of alternative courses of action without coming to a recommendation of a specific course of action, which often involved value judgements and trade-offs beyond the scope of the OTA analysis.

As noted throughout this chapter, both types of analysis just described are important to congressional deliberation depending upon the circumstances, but with the closure of the former OTA, the latter type of analysis neither exists within the Congress itself nor is readily accessible to the Congress. The *OTA style* of analysis could be very useful for many executive agency needs as well.

Some OTA-like features have evolved over time with NRC studies. For example, the IOM[24] as well as other NRC programme units now often hire staff for new studies who are recognised experts themselves in a particular area to work on studies and who consequently take a more active role than was the previous custom in drafting the committee report. This method can increase the already high cost of doing NRC studies, but it has the benefit of increasing the capacity of the study committee to assemble background information efficiently, both as a basis for deliberation and for providing background documentation for the report that would likely not have been included. That is, the report now has more information that can be used both to inform the ultimate decision of the sponsor and to help rationalise the recommendations of the study committee in a more comprehensive manner. Additional OTA-like features are certainly possible at the NRC, and in some cases such features are already being introduced, but many internal and external control issues outlined in this chapter would have to be resolved for the NRC to incorporate many features of the role OTA played on Capitol Hill.

Alternatively, as possible options for filling the gap left by the closure of OTA are considered by the Congress, including simply reconstructing the office itself, it is likely that the functioning of such an office would in

---

[24] The IOM administers a collection of programme activities that operate under NRC policies and procedures, although formally they are not part of the NRC.

some ways be quite different from the OTA historical experience. For example, modern communication capabilities would enable broader engagement and collaboration with outside groups in organising the agency's work (including perhaps with the NRC) and in expanding the accessibility of the agency's work more broadly in the Congress than was possible when OTA closed in 1995. One conclusion is clear, however. In the US, at least, the need for useful, relevant, informed, independent, authoritative and timely advice on the science and technology issues to the Congress is becoming more and more noticeable as the role of science and technology increasingly influences, in often complex ways, virtually all aspects of the issues the Congress addresses.

Appendix A: Section 15 as amended of the Federal Advisory Committee Act (Public Law 105–153, 105th Congress, approved 17 December 1997)

(a) In General.– An agency may not use any advice or recommendation provided by the National Academy of Sciences or National Academy of Public Administration that was developed by use of a committee created by that academy under an agreement with an agency, unless –
   (1) the committee was not subject to any actual management or control by an agency or an officer of the Federal Government;
   (2) in the case of a committee created after the date of enactment of the *Federal Advisory Committee Act* Amendments of 1997, the membership of the committee was appointed in accordance with the requirements described in subsection (b)(1); and
   (3) in developing the advice or recommendation, the academy complied with –
      (A) subsection (b)(2) through (6), in the case of any advice or recommendation provided by the National Academy of Sciences; or
      (B) subsection (b)(2) and (5), in the case of any advice or recommendation provided by the National Academy of Public Administration.
(b) Requirements – The requirements referred to in subsection (a) are as follows:
   (1) The Academy shall determine and provide public notice of the names and brief biographies of individuals that the Academy appoints or intends to appoint to serve on the committee. The Academy shall determine and provide a reasonable opportunity for the public to comment on such appointments before they are made or, if the Academy determines such prior comment is

not practicable, in the period immediately following the appointments. The Academy shall make its best efforts to ensure that (A) no individual appointed to serve on the committee has a conflict of interest that is relevant to the functions to be performed, unless such conflict is promptly and publicly disclosed and the Academy determines that the conflict is unavoidable, (B) the committee membership is fairly balanced as determined by the Academy to be appropriate for the functions to be performed, and (C) the final report of the Academy will be the result of the Academy's independent judgement. The Academy shall require that individuals that the Academy appoints or intends to appoint to serve on the committee inform the Academy of the individual's conflicts of interest that are relevant to the functions to be performed.

(2) The Academy shall determine and provide public notice of committee meetings that will be open to the public.

(3) The Academy shall ensure that meetings of the committee to gather data from individuals who are not officials, agents, or employees of the Academy are open to the public, unless the Academy determines that a meeting would disclose matters described in section 552(b) of title 5, United States Code. The Academy shall make available to the public, at reasonable charge if appropriate, written materials presented to the committee by individuals who are not officials, agents, or employees of the Academy, unless the Academy determines that making material available would disclose matters described in that section.

(4) The Academy shall make available to the public as soon as practicable, at reasonable charge if appropriate, a brief summary of any committee meeting that is not a data gathering meeting, unless the Academy determines that the summary would disclose matters described in section 552(b) of title 5, United States Code. The summary shall identify the committee members present, the topics discussed, materials made available to the committee, and such other matters that the Academy determines should be included.

(5) The Academy shall make available to the public its final report, at reasonable charge if appropriate, unless the Academy determines that the report would disclose matters described in section 552(b) of title 5, United States Code. If the Academy determines that the report would disclose matters described in that section, the Academy shall make public an abbreviated version of the report that does not disclose those matters.

(6) After publication of the final report, the Academy shall make publicly available the names of the principal reviewers who reviewed the report in draft form and who are not officials, agents, or employees of the Academy.

(c) Regulations – The Administrator of General Services may issue regulations implementing this section.

(Note on Prior Provisions: A prior section 15 of the Federal Advisory Committee Act was renumbered section 16 by Pub. L. 105–153.)

Accompanying Legislative Report

Section 3 of Pub. L. 105–153 provided that: 'Not later than 1 year after the date of the enactment of this Act [Dec. 17, 1997], the Administrator of General Services shall submit a report to the Congress on the implementation of and compliance with the amendments made by this Act [enacting this section, amending section 3 of Pub. L. 92–463, set out in this Appendix, and redesignating former section 15 of Pub. L. 92–463, set out in this Appendix, as section 16].'

REFERENCES

Ahearne, John F. and Blair, Peter D. 2003. 'Expanded use of the national academies', in Morgan and Peha (eds.), *Science and Technology Advice for Congress*, Washington DC: RFF Press, Ch. 8, pp. 118–33 and Appendix 2, pp. 191–207.

Bimber, Bruce 1996. *The Politics of Expertise in Congress: The Rise and Fall of the Office of Technology Assessment*, Albany, NY: SUNY Press.

Blair, Peter D. 1994. 'Technology assessment: Current trends and the myth of a formula', First Meeting of the International Association of Technology Assessment and Forecasting Institutions, Bergen, Norway, 2 May 1994, available at: www.princeton.edu/~ota/ns20/blair_f.html.

Blair, Peter D. 1997a. 'The evolving role of government in science and technology', *The Bridge*, 27/3 (Fall 1997): 4–12, Washington, DC: The National Academy of Engineering, available at: www.nae.edu/nae/bridgecom.nsf/weblinks/NAEW-4NHM9J?.

Blair, Peter D. 1997b. 'Examining our science and technology enterprise', *American Scientist* 8/1: 74 (January/February).

Dawson, Jim 2001. 'Legislation to revive OTA focuses on science advice to congress', *Physics Today* 54/10: 24 (October), available at: link.aip.org/link/abstract/PHTOAD/v54/i10/p24/s1.

Executive Office of the President 1993. Presidential Executive Order 12832 (George H. Bush), *Amendments Relation to the National Research Council*, 19 January 1993, which amended Executive Order 10668 (Dwight D. Eisenhower), *National Research Council, May 10, 1956 and Executive*

Order 2859 (Woodrow Wilson), *National Research Council*, 10 May 1956, available at: www7.nationalacademies.org/ocga/PolicyDocuments.asp.

Fri, Robert W., Granger Morgan (chair), M., Stiles, William A. (Skip) 2002. 'An external evaluation of the GAO's assessment of technologies for border control', 18 October 2002.

Government Accountability Office (GAO) 2002. *Technology Assessment: Using Biometrics for Border Security*, GAO-03–174, November 2002, available at: www.gao.gov/new.items/d03174.pdf.

Guston, David 2003. 'Insights from the office of technology assessment and other assessment experiences', in Morgan and Peha (eds.), *Science and Technology Advice for Congress*, Washington, DC: RFF Press, Ch. 4, pp. 77–89.

Jones, Richard M. 2004. 'House rejects Rep. Holt amendment to establish OTA-capability', FYI: *The AIP Bulletin of Science Policy News* 116, 31 August 2004, available at: www.aip.org/fyi/2004/116.html.

Knezo, Genevieve J. 2005. 'Technology assessment in congress: History and legislative options', *Congressional Research Service*, Order Code RS21586, 20 May 2005, available at: www.fas.org/sgp/crs/misc/RS21586.pdf.

Morgan, M. Granger and Peha, John M. (eds.) 2003. *Science and Technology Advice for Congress*, Washington, DC: RFF Press.

National Research Council (NRC) 1998. *The National Academies: A Unique National Resource*, Office of News and Public Information.

National Research Council (NRC) 2000. *Roles of the Committee Chair*, available at: www7.nationalacademies.org/committees_chair_roles/index.html.

National Research Council (NRC) 2002. *Effectiveness and Impact of Corporate Average Fuel Economy (CAFE) Standards*, Washington, DC: The National Academies Press, available at: www.nap.edu/catalog.php?record_id=10172.

National Research Council (NRC) 2003. *Policy and Procedures on Committee Composition and Balance and Conflicts of Interest for Committees Used in the Development of Reports*, May 2003, available at: www.nationalacademies.org/coi/index.html.

National Research Council (NRC) 2005. *Rising Above the Gathering Storm: Energizing and Employing America for a Brighter Economic Future*, Washington, DC: The National Academies Press, available at: http://books.nap.edu/catalog/11463.html.

Office of Technology Assessment (OTA) 1991. *Improving Automobile Fuel Economy: New Standards, New Approaches*, OTA-E-504, NTIS order #PB92–115989, 1991, available at: www.princeton.edu/~ota/disk1/1991/9125_n.html.

Office of Technology Assessment (OTA) 1996. *OTA Legacy*, CD-ROM Collection (Vols. 1–5), GPO Stock No. 052–003–01457–2, Washington, DC: US Govt. Printing Office, available also at: www.wws.princeton.edu/ota/.

Smith, Bruce L.R. and Stine, Jeffrey K. 2003. 'Technical advice for Congress: Past trends and present obstacles', in Morgan and Peha (eds.), Ch. 2, pp. 23–52.

The National Academies 2004. *2004 Report to Congress*, available at: www.nationalacademies.org/annualreport/.

The National Academies 2005a. *The National Academies Study Process: Ensuring Independent, Objective Advice*, available at: www.nationalacademies.org/ studyprocess/index.html.

The National Academies 2005b. *Getting to Know the Committee Process*, Office of News and Public Information.

The National Academies 2005c. *Making a Difference: Selected Studies from The National Academies*, available at: www.nationalacademies.org/publications/ Making_A_Difference.pdf.

The National Academies Press 2002. *Complete Catalog of Books and Periodicals, 2002* (NRC reports are now indexed and available at: www. nationalacademies.org or www.nap.edu).

The National Academy of Sciences 2005. *The National Academies In Focus*, published three times annually, available at: www.infocusmagazine.org.

US Office of Management and Budget 2005. *Final Information Quality Bulletin for Peer Review*, 16 December 2006, available at: www.whitehouse.gov/omb/ inforeg_infopoltech/.

Walker, Robert S. 2001. 'OTA reconsidered', *Issues in Science and Technology*, 17/3 (Spring), available at: www.issues.org/17.3/forum.htm.

18   Quality control in scientific policy advice: the experience of the Royal Society

Peter Collins

1   Introduction

Academies around the world are increasingly in the business of giving advice to policymakers. They do this in order to influence policy outcomes. Quality management in this context is therefore about ensuring that influence is actually achieved. It is not primarily, or at least not only, about avoiding factual error. Avoiding factual error is, of course, a prerequisite for a national science academy that seeks to embody the cream of the nation's science. But there's more to influencing policy than that.

Quality management has to embrace process as much as final output, since process is a key determinant of credibility and credibility, in turn, is central to influence. Particularly on issues that arouse public interest, public perceptions about the credibility of the adviser affect how readily the policymaker can embrace the advice being offered. Credibility depends both on the overall reputation of the organisation and on how the particular project is carried out. In the current climate in Western democracies there is a premium on openness (including consultation with a range of stakeholders) and transparency. This may be challenging for an academy more used to technical debate with experts. It is not always easy for an intrinsically elite body also to be inclusive and accessible.

There is a tendency to think of science policy work in terms of writing reports. Writing a report is a good discipline in that it forces the authors to reach, and to justify, a shared position, and a written report allows that position to be transmitted to others without distortion. Whether it is an effective way of influencing policy depends, at a minimum, on whether the target audience reads it. Since many senior policymakers will not be tempted to invest hours in reading a major report, it is clear that generating the report has to be seen as part of a package of activities focused on influencing the issue in question.

So the approach to quality management has to cover the package as a whole, not just the formal written output, and all stages from inception onwards. This requires alertness to the many different factors that determine success in influencing policy. This chapter outlines how the Royal Society addresses this challenge.

2 Project definition

In policy advice as in scientific research, the prize goes to the person who gets the right question. So we put a great deal of effort into defining the parameters of the issue we are seeking to influence. This is particularly true for self-initiated projects, where we are, in effect, seeking to set the policy agenda; but it is also true for projects that respond to requests from others. There is a direct correlation between that preparatory effort and the eventual success of the project.

We have developed guidelines to steer the process of defining a project, in the form of a set of questions. These are summarised below. No project is allowed to proceed until these questions have been explored at a level of detail commensurate with the scale and complexity of the project.

- What policy question is the project addressing? Why does that question merit the attention of a national academy of science?
- What are the main project deliverables – survey, report, joint meeting, open conference, etc.? Why is the particular deliverable the best way to influence the target customer?
- How will the project take forward the Society's corporate objectives as defined in the current Business Plan? Does the question fit in with the current range of advice work? If not, is there a case for expanding that range?
- Is the question such that objective scientific evidence is relevant? If so, are we likely to be able to secure access to that evidence and use it, for example, in a published report?
- Who owns (or should own) the question at a policy level? What might they do differently as a result of the project? Could a scientific analysis have any impact on these *customers*? What is the evidence that they are indeed interested in the question as formulated?
- Who are the other stakeholders in the issue (e.g. people who are or who think they are affected by the issue)? What do we know about what they see as the crucial aspects of the issue? Do the proposed terms of reference accommodate their concerns?
- Have all relevant parts of the Society been consulted (e.g. those dealing with public communication, international relations or the media – not just the policy advice group)?

- What external factors affect the timing of the project (i.e. must it be completed by a certain time in order to have maximum impact, and can we do anything useful within that schedule)? What foreseeable factors might interfere with the schedule? What happens to the value of the project if there is a delay?[1]
- What work is already being done by others in this area? Would an intervention by the Society have particular impact that stands out from the competition?
- Is there a case for doing the project (i) in collaboration with another academy, (ii) at the European rather than national level, (iii) at the global level?

Once developed, a project proposal has to be approved by the Director of Science Policy, the Executive Secretary and the Council of the Society or a Vice-President acting on behalf of Council.

3   Carrying out the project

Our approach to carrying out projects has evolved over time and is intended to maximise both scientific rigour and public credibility – two criteria central to achieving influence on the policy process.

3.1   Project teams

Once a project has been agreed, the next quality management issue is to assemble the best group to carry it out. We are able to draw not only on the Fellows of the Society but also on many other experts – despite operating a strictly volunteer culture. This willingness of numerous experts to give freely of their time and skill is the linchpin of our policy work, and without it we could accomplish nothing. We put considerable thought into assembling a strong, balanced group covering the full set of experience needed for the project. This may include philosophers, economists and social scientists as well as natural scientists.[2] All act in

---

[1] Timeliness is obviously critical: the project has to be relevant at the time it is completed, not just when it begins. It can be a real challenge to see far enough ahead to meet this criterion, especially in the absence of an external event (e.g. a meeting of the G8 heads of governments) to provide a framework. One has to remain alert throughout the project to unexpected events that can disrupt the initial calculations about timing.

[2] For example, our April 2003 report *Keeping science open: the effects of intellectual property policy on the conduct of science* was prepared by a group that included two legal experts; the November 2002 report *Economic instruments for the reduction of carbon dioxide emissions* included two economists and a social scientist; and the July 2002 project *Infectious diseases in livestock* included a farmer, two vets and members of three public interest groups.

their individual capacities; other than when collaborating with another organisation, we generally do not include formal representatives of interest groups or government employees.

Selection of the Chair of the project group is key. The person should have sufficient understanding of the underpinning science, but does not have to be an expert in it. If there are several competing viewpoints among experts, it can be advantageous for the Chair not to be associated with any one of them. The Chair also has to be able to deal with media interest in the project (with help from the Media Office) and to represent the Society in other external forums. Our practice is that Chairs of policy groups should be Fellows of the Society, but it is common that the majority of members are drawn from outside the Fellowship.

Membership of project groups is normally subject to approval by, at least, the relevant Vice-President. We take care to balance competing views – for example, to avoid selecting for scientific orthodoxy in areas where scientifically plausible minority views exist – and to avoid appointing members with strong vested interests. The group as a whole must have the highest scientific expertise in the issue under review.

Policy groups are supported by professional staff from the Society's policy team. The division of labour between the staff and the group members varies from one project to another, but typically the staff will be responsible for: collecting and sifting evidence; developing and maintaining links with policymakers and other customers; liaison with the Society's Media Office; ensuring appropriate levels of openness and transparency; some aspects of drafting and editing; and the programme of dissemination and follow-up work. A substantial project may be supported by a manager and a policy officer, who will run the project on a day-to-day basis. The manager will report to a project director (normally the Section Head), who provides an overall steer and ensures appropriate liaison with other parts of the Society (including the relevant Vice-President) and external parties. The staff generally have a scientific training sufficient to engage with an explanation of the subject and describe it at the right level for the target audience.

3.2   Evidence

The Society's policy advice is always grounded in factual evidence, and a major part of any project is assembling that evidence. Much of it comes, of course, from the knowledge of the expert project group members and their familiarity with the published literature, but much of it is also solicited during the course of the project via a public call for evidence and via meetings to enable relevant parties to talk directly to the group.[3] These can include a wide range of stakeholders, not simply technical experts, and are an important means of enabling us to take account of public concerns on, for example, ethical aspects of the issue.[4] Indeed, the consultation can extend to aspects of the terms of reference, to allow comment on how we are interpreting the issue.[5]

Such consultation ensures that the project team can base its work on the fullest practicable range of knowledge, and that it is aware of at least some of the wider context into which its advice will be placed. It also gives all interested parties a stake in the project. This can be reinforced by publishing the evidence received, for example on the web or on a CD included with the printed report.[6]

3.3   Openness, transparency, independence

The public call for evidence makes a project open. Transparency is the process of enabling those interested to follow the progress of the project. So we announce, normally by press release, the launch of new projects[7] and publish the terms of reference and membership of project groups on the web; we may publish periodic progress reports on projects that are attracting strong public interest; we will always publish all reports, self-initiated or not, on the web[8] and nearly always also in paper form.

To respond to media interest, we will identify spokespersons – including the Chair of the project group – and provide media training to support them in engaging with journalists. Willingness to engage with the media is part of our commitment to transparency. An open and transparent process also serves to stimulate public discussion of the

---

[3] To increase transparency, these evidence meetings may occasionally be held in public, as we did for example in the July 2002 project *Infectious diseases in livestock* where we held an open meeting in Cumbria to solicit input from communities most affected by the foot and mouth outbreak.

[4] The Society's Science in Society team plays an important role developing our approach to public engagement, and, for example, helped organise public meetings for *Digital healthcare: the impact of information and communication technology on health and healthcare* (December 2006) and *Personalised medicines: Hopes and realities* (September 2005).

[5] The outstanding example here is the July 2004 project *Nanoscience and nanotechnologies: opportunities and uncertainties*.

[6] Examples are the July 2002 project *Infectious diseases in livestock* and the July 2004 project *Nanoscience and nanotechnologies: opportunities and uncertainties*. When publishing evidence, it is prudent to ensure that it does not include personal information or defamatory comments that could leave us open to legal action.

[7] For major, self-initiated projects; it would be superfluous to announce that we were planning to submit evidence to, for example, a public parliamentary inquiry.

[8] All reports mentioned here can be found at http://royalsociety.org/.

issue being addressed, which can help to shape the climate of opinion into which the eventual report is released. For example, we published submitted evidence as our nanotechnologies project progressed, and this helped to develop a more informed audience by the time the final report appeared.

Transparency is part of demonstrating that we are operating independently of political or commercial interest. Our independence is vital to our influence, especially when giving advice about controversial issues. Even on those occasions when we accept a contract from government to advise on a specific issue, we will ensure that the terms of reference are appropriate to a scientific body; we will insist that we alone decide who is on the project group and how the project is carried out; and we publish the outcome. Demonstrable independence not only increases our credibility with the public, but also increases the value of our advice to the policymakers.

3.4   Review

All reports have to be approved by the Society's Council before publication. At one level this is simply the established practice of peer review, which can often add considerably to the value of a report. At another level it is the process by which the work of an expert group becomes the view of the Royal Society. The twenty-one elected members of Council are the Society's trustees and are therefore empowered to determine, on behalf of the Fellowship as a whole, what the Society does. Their imprimatur is the prerequisite for a statement to be issued in the Society's name.

Council appoints small panels to review each policy statement or report and advise it on suitability for publication. Panels may typically have four members, of whom two may be members of Council and two drawn from a wider pool, including non-scientists where appropriate. The panels advise Council about the report, and may discuss proposed modifications to the project group. Decisions about publication are then taken at the bi-monthly meetings of Council, or in cases of urgency by a Vice-President acting on behalf of Council between meetings.

The role of the panels is not to replicate the scientific expertise of the project group but to examine whether the report has addressed the terms of reference, whether its conclusions are consistent with the evidence presented, whether its recommendations are appropriate and whether the form of the report is suited to its target audience. The members of the review panel are identified in the published report.

For small or rapid projects the whole review process may be done on behalf of Council by a Vice-President, especially in areas that have already been subject to discussion by Council, but the principles are the same.

4   Making an impact

Approval by Council of the output (e.g. a written report) marks the end not of the project but simply of the first phase. The next phase is dissemination (making sure the message reaches its target) and follow-up (making sure the target heeds the message). Dissemination in some form can start during the project, for example by holding closed or open meetings to collect evidence or to secure feedback on emerging findings.[9]

It is obvious that reports must be written at a level accessible to their target audience if there is to be any point disseminating them. This includes length, scientific complexity and linguistic complexity. All reports must have a summary accessible to the non-specialist; this may be printed separately as well as appearing in the main report.

How dissemination is done will depend on individual circumstances. Possibilities include publication (with embargoed advance copies to key people); press conferences and/or press briefings; briefings for parliamentarians and other decision-makers; extensive targeted mailings of summary versions; articles placed in relevant publications, including the national and scientific press; meetings with ministers and other targets; and seminars. Displays of free material (especially short glossy versions of reports) easily accessible to visitors to the Royal Society building are an important outlet. All this needs to be properly resourced, with the cost (time and money) built into the project from the outset.

The Society usually seeks widespread media coverage of its science policy projects in order to inform and stimulate public debate. Media coverage also raises the profile of the Society's advice to government and other policymakers – a Minister may be more likely to take a direct interest in the contents of a Society report if he or she has heard or read about it in the news, and parliamentarians are more likely to raise questions about how the government intends to respond to the Society if media coverage has stimulated interest among constituents.

---

[9] In our May 2001 project on *The health effects of depleted uranium*, for example, we held a public meeting aimed at war veterans and their representatives to expose and discuss our emerging conclusions.

The effort invested in later follow-up will depend on the circumstances. The assumption is that if we care enough to do the project in the first place we will continue to care after the first phase is complete. At the least, when we respond to an external consultation we will check whether our advice has been taken on board and, usually, comment on the outcome. It is also important to revisit completed projects periodically to consider whether more needs to be done – applauding where recommendations have been implemented, highlighting where they have not, and checking whether the Society's position needs updating.

When the project is finally complete, the project manager will write a brief report for internal use, commenting on lessons learned and, if possible, measures for judging success.

5 Conclusion

It is clear that quality management is much more than reviewing the draft output of a project. It starts with having a clear view of what one is trying to achieve – i.e. in this instance, bringing scientific insight to bear on an area of policy and thus influencing the development of that policy – and then focuses on ensuring that all aspects of the process are targeted on delivering that goal. So the main challenge is that this approach to quality should permeate the project at every step.

The process described here has evolved with experience and will, no doubt, continue to evolve. As the Society's policy activities grow in scale, for example, we may have to revisit the Council review procedure to keep the pressure on individual Council members to acceptable levels. Increasing success in influencing policy brings with it increasing exposure to attack from campaigning groups with opposing views, on such issues as GM plants, nuclear power or climate change, and hence an increasing need to make sure that our processes are sufficiently robust. The attributes of credibility may change in response to wider developments in society. Demands for rapid response can pose particular challenges for a membership organisation. What will remain central to the quality of our work – to our success in influencing policy – is a clear understanding of what we stand for and a clear view, both generically and with each project, of what we are trying to achieve.

19 European Academies Science Advisory Council (EASAC)

Robin Fears and Volker ter Meulen

Introduction: contribution of science to European policy-making

Different countries vary in the way that scientific advice is used by public policymakers (Weingart and Lentsch 2006). Governments often constitute and manage their own scientific advisory bodies as a function of the executive arm of government. This internal function has been increasingly complemented by the independent activity of national academies of science helping their national governments access science (Collins and Lindberg 2002). In member states of the EU, many academies have developed an effective relationship with national governments in advising on the scientific dimension in policymaking. Until recently, the development of an analogous relationship at the EU level (with the European Commission, Parliament and Council of Ministers) has been more challenging, although academies recognised that the scope of their advisory functions needed to extend to cover the European level and that their effectiveness could be maximised by collective activity. Several different bodies have now come into being within a relatively short period to offer scientific advice at the EU level (Fayl and Kyriakou 2002) in addition to those actually created by the EU institutions, indicating 'how widespread is the perception that alongside their official policy-advice structures, the main organs of the European Union need independent advice about science' (Collins and Lindberg 2002). Rogers in Chapter 7 and Podger in Chapter 12 of the present book provide examples of the challenges faced and the criteria used when EU policymakers take account of scientific advice.

As noted by the European Commission in its Communication *On the Collection and Use of Expertise by the Commission* (2002), the interplay between policymakers, experts, interested parties and the public at large is a crucial part of policymaking, and attention has to be focused not just on policy outcome but also on the process followed. The European Commission identifies core principles for this process: (i) soliciting high quality advice; (ii) being open in seeking and acting on expert advice; and (iii) ensuring that the methods for collecting and using advice are effective and proportionate. Comparable principles should underpin the activities of those acting to deliver advice.

EASAC

1   Organisational characteristics

EASAC – the European Academies Science Advisory Council – is formed by the national science academies of the EU member states to enable them to collaborate with each other in providing advice to European policymakers. EASAC represents a mechanism for the collective voice of European science to be heard.

EASAC covers all scientific and technical disciplines; it is funded by the member academies and by contract with interested bodies. EASAC seeks to be distinctive, compared to many other organisations (lobbyists, consultants, special interest groups) trying to influence the decision-making bodies of the EU, in providing advice that is expert, authoritative and relevant, and vigorously independent of economic or political interests.

The council sets the overall strategic direction and has twenty-five individual members – highly experienced scientists nominated, one each, by the national science academies of every EU member state that has one, the Academia Europaea and ALLEA (see Box 1).

Council is supported by EASAC steering committees in strategic areas of science, whose role is to horizon-scan, advise Council on potential projects and to help build relationships with opinion-leaders and policy-makers. Other operating procedures of the Council also ensure the relevance of EASAC work. For example, the twice-yearly EASAC Council meeting is usually hosted by the academy whose government will be providing the Presidency of the European Council during the following year, thus ensuring that EASAC members meet with the national officials responsible for progressing their Presidency priorities for science.

2   Goals

EASAC draws on the membership and networks of the academies to access the best of European science (see Box 2).

EASAC carries out self-funded projects but is also available to provide advice as required in response to requests from the European Institutions. Previous activities have included reviews of draft documents,

---

Box 1: EASAC members[1]

Current members of EASAC Bureau:
President:
Sir Brian Heap

Vice-Presidents:
Sven Kullander, Royal Swedish Academy of Sciences
Jos Van der Meer, Royal Netherlands Academy of Arts and Sciences
Josef Palinkas, Hungarian Academy of Sciences

Past-President:
Volker ter Meulen, German Academy of Sciences, Leopoldina

Other members of Council, nominated by:
Institute of Spain
ALLEA
Estonian Academy of Sciences
Royal Society, UK
Royal Danish Academy of Sciences and Letters
Austrian Academy of Sciences
Polish Academy of Sciences
Academy of Athens
Academy of Sciences of the Czech Republic
Academia das Ciencias de Lisboa
Academie des Sciences, France
Lithuanian Academy of Sciences
Royal Flemish Academy of Sciences, Letters and Fine Arts of Belgium
Latvian Academy of Sciences
Slovak Academy of Science
Academia Nazionale dei Lincei, Italy
Finnish Academies of Sciences and Letters
Bulgarian Academy of Sciences
Royal Irish Academy
Slovenian Academy of Sciences and Arts

---

briefing papers on the scientific aspects of topical issues, foresight events and workshops in advance of major debates or decisions.

EASAC agrees the initiation of individual projects, appoints members of working groups, reviews draft outputs and approves material for publication and dissemination. Project working groups are established to carry out specific tasks and their expert members, selected from all member states, give their time free of charge. Since its inception, EASAC

---

[1] See www.easac.eu for further details.

Box 2: EASAC mission and vision (see Collins and Lindberg 2002 for details).

The mission of EASAC is 'building science into policy' at the EU level by providing independent, credible, expert advice about the scientific aspects of public policy issues to those who make, or influence, policy for the EU.

The vision of EASAC is that it will be recognised by EU policymakers as the source of reliable, timely advice that reflects the best that the European scientific community can deliver. EASAC aims to be known for its expertise both in science and in the business of providing policy advice, and to be understood to be thorough in its investigations, disinterested in its recommendations and transparent in its processes.

---

has tackled a wide range of scientific issues in the areas of the environment and biodiversity, plant sciences, energy, bioscience, medicine and public health and R&D funding. In the present chapter, we draw on our specific experience from a series of projects on infectious disease (major reports were published by EASAC in 2005, 2006, 2007, 2008, 2009 and all are available at www.easac.eu)[2] and general experience with EASAC over the last five years. Each project results in a published report and accompanying press release (translated, where necessary, by individual academies). The report serves as a resource for follow-up and engagement with the European Institutions and other stakeholders – activities have included a launch meeting at the European Parliament and ongoing individual discussions with policymakers in the European Commission and Council of Ministers' secretariat, industrialists and scientists.

It is widely agreed internationally that health policies do not reflect the research evidence to the extent that in theory they could (Hanney *et al.* 2003). European countries have a long history of achievement in the biosciences, health care and public health with a tradition of incorporating the results of scientific progress in policy and professional practice. But the routes for offering scientific advice have often been fragmented and lacking in transparency.[3] It is important to address this heterogeneity in effort because there are many common challenges for EU countries at the interface of science and health policy with regard to: (i) those issues that can in principle be handled at a national level but are similar

---

[2] Projects were chaired by Volker ter Meulen with secretariat provided by Robin Fears.
[3] For example, in the area of public health policy, at least 200 organisations were reported to be active in EU countries (Health Council of the Netherlands 2006).

for many countries and, so, can be more efficiently analysed at the European level; and (ii) those issues that are transnational in themselves and require European level analysis and resolution. In addition to this objective to communicate evidence-based messages to international audiences, EASAC has a second responsibility – to share best practice to help individual academies develop their expertise and resources to deploy at the national level.

In reflecting on EASAC expertise and capability, we endorse the view from the US National Academies of Science who concluded that science advice is not so much a body of information as a procedure (the attributes of science advice are discussed in further detail by Blair in Chapter 17 of the present book and are also subject to the emerging principles reviewed by Jasanoff in Chapter 2). Science advice as a mechanism utilises the processes of the scientific culture, relying on peer review and the establishment of consensus, with explicit exposure of areas of uncertainty; broadly serving as a link between the scientific community and decision-makers.

Principles for quality and determinants of usefulness

EASAC quality criteria are based on the quality functions embodied in the parent academies and derived from their experience in contributing scientific advice at the national level. EASAC functions primarily as a coordinating mechanism for the academies rather than as a self-contained body.

Sound science is fundamental to the work of EASAC but, in itself, is insufficient to ensure quality. Broadly, and as further discussed by Lentsch and Weingart in the introductory chapter to this book, the necessary quality criteria can be distinguished in terms of scientific quality (the nature of the evidence and its integration across fields), interactive quality (the nature of the EASAC working procedures and competence of participants) and communicative quality (the flexible capability to prepare audiences, promote diffusion of outputs and catalyse ongoing dialogue). The key attributes for EASAC in this quality continuum are to be:

- *expert and authoritative* – robust, comprehensive scientific excellence based on expertise in the relevant sciences and consolidation across disciplines;
- *independent* – from government and vested interests as regards choice of projects and experts and working methods but inclusive with regard to engaging with other interested parties;

- *open and transparent* – at all stages once a project is agreed;
- *relevant and timely* – aiming to deliver longer-term perspectives but familiar with current policy development priorities and able to respond to policymaker needs (while retaining independence in operation); credible in creating realistic expectations about what can be delivered;
- *comprehensible and effective in dissemination* – at the EU and member state levels; usability of outputs requires good understanding of whether individual matters are EU or national competency.

Procedures for quality control and assurance

Quality criteria are embedded at every stage of the EASAC process, from choice of projects through to the conduct of the Working Group and dissemination activities. Our assumption is that advice can only really be judged good quality if it is used.

The EASAC secretariat was originally based at the Royal Society in the UK but since 2010 is at the German Academy of Sciences Leopoldina. The principal routine steps in the EASAC process are modelled on academy practice (discussed in detail by Collins in Chapter 18) and can be demarcated as follows.

1   Selection of project and initial definition of remit

(a) In considering whether a new project is an appropriate EASAC priority, Council applies a standard framework of evaluation to ask: What policy issues are addressed and why do they merit attention by EASAC? Is objective scientific evidence relevant to the resolution of these issues? What aspects of the issues are of current interest to EU policymakers and what might they do differently as a result of EASAC activity? Who else is working in this area and why might EASAC intervention have particular impact? Why should a project be started now?

(b) Scoping work is done to prepare for Council discussion in order to establish that a project can meet the EASAC quality criteria. This scoping work may build on previous academy activity at the national level.

(c) Defining the project remit must take account of EU audience expectations in terms of what is relevant for them, and this will often require early discussion of issues with EU policymakers.

(d) If a project proposal can satisfy the Council quality evaluation framework, there must also be sufficient EASAC resources available to ensure quality outputs. It may be necessary for Council to make hard choices in deciding priorities.

2   *Constituting the expert working group*

(a) It is the responsibility of the Council academies to nominate the Chairman and members of the working group, chosen according to their level of expertise and field, to provide a scientifically balanced, authoritative, multi-disciplinary team. Participants do not necessarily have to be fellows of any academy and can be chosen from the private as well as public research sector.

(b) At the first working group meeting, participants confirm the project scope, individual roles and responsibilities, timetable and outputs. Members participate in an individual capacity rather than as representing organisations, although some will have useful links to other relevant bodies that will help EASAC to avoid duplicating what has already been done well elsewhere and will facilitate critical review.

(c) Working group members are asked to make a declaration of their relevant interests at the outset. EASAC does not aim to exclude those who have manageable vested interests but, rather, to be aware of any relevant factors in individual participation so as not to jeopardise the quality of the eventual advice.

3   *External call for evidence*

Publication (on www.easac.eu) of the project terms of reference serves as the basis for an open call for evidence. Drawing on expertise in the working group to identify interested parties provides other direct contacts to invite evidence.

4   *Drafting report*

(a) Drafting is an iterative process, with scientific support from the secretariat, bringing together data and perspectives contributed by the Working Group and from external submissions of evidence (when the secretariat in conjunction with working group members is responsible for assessing quality). There is a collective responsibility to clarify and agree what is known and where there is still uncertainty. Most of the information used is already publicly available (preferably peer reviewed or otherwise endorsed by professional bodies) but the working group may itself generate new evidence and analysis.

(b) The working group will usually meet collectively on two or more occasions to review the evidence and discuss interpretation and conclusions; email-based interaction will continue throughout the life of the project.

(c) The working group will identify where gaps in the information available require further inquiry, perhaps recommending future work by others to strengthen the evidence base. Draft discussion points may be reviewed by other experts – on a restricted basis – on the invitation of the Chairman of the working group. The working group is expected to reach consensus on the final report (and permit their names to be published in association with it) although minority views can be recorded.

5   *Report review and dissemination*

(a) On completion of the draft report by the working group, EASAC appoints an independent expert peer review group with standard evaluation criteria. Does the report accomplish the original remit of the project? Are the conclusions and recommendations supported by the offered evidence and analysis? Are uncertainties in the evidence recognised? Are the facts and data handled competently? Does the report avoid special pleading? Are the style, tone and format of the report effective in distinguishing and communicating the key messages? Are the recommendations tractable, with a clear understanding of how they can be taken forward?

(b) The independent review groups provide their expert feedback to Council and there will usually be a phase of clarification with the working group (mediated by the Chairman) to address issues raised and reach an agreed version of the report. When the peer review process is satisfactorily completed, EASAC officers formally approve the report for publication (as hard copy and on the EASAC website). Council will also review and agree a strategy for dissemination and engagement with target audiences at the EU level. Follow-up work may involve supporting the initiation of activity in the area by other bodies (which can be viewed as a recognition of the quality of the EASAC work).

(c) The primary audiences for EASAC outputs are at the EU level but care is taken to address the global dimensions where appropriate (for example, relevant issues for developing countries or for international centres of research excellence). EASAC outputs are also designed to clarify what is relevant for EU policy and what is a member state responsibility under subsidiarity, so that the outputs are *fit for purpose*. This is particularly important in health policy where some issues require EU action but others do not. Moreover, the analysis may have been derived from a mix of evidence available from the different experiences in member states – the different contexts in which science has been applied – and this diversity of experience may suggest alternative policy options for those health issues which are a common challenge at the EU level.

6   *Dealing with uncertainties and controversial science*

The EASAC approach can be characterised as an ongoing process of inquiry, debate and verification. This continues after publication of outputs, by soliciting wide feedback and supporting continuing discussion. The phase following publication – which may in turn lead to new EASAC work – is a critical part of the continuing exploration of related issues, clarification of points of contention and reduction in uncertainty. While the science may sometimes be uncertain and the policy area controversial, what should always be clear is that EASAC processes have been conducted with rigour, respect and responsibility.[4]

Lessons drawn from EASAC experience in infectious diseases

EASAC is still a relatively young organisation and its officers encourage a culture of mutual learning. Several specific points can be emphasised from our experience.

1   *Responsibility for quality control*

The role to support quality assurance is shared among the working group Chairman and secretariat (while also capitalising on the strengths of the working group) and EASAC Council, its officers, secretariat and review panel members.

2   *Understanding the various audiences*

EASAC outputs have value as a resource of reasoned scholarship to the national academies and to other European stakeholders as well as to the EU institutions of Commission, Parliament and Council of Ministers.

---

[4] Attributes in the UK Ethical Code for Scientists (cited in Weingart and Lentsch 2006).

In order to capitalise on the quality of the EASAC outputs, it is important to be clear as to the relevance of recommendations for different audiences and to ensure that there are appropriate strategic engagement procedures – actively involving the individual academies in the dissemination phase as well as in project construction and conduct. EASAC needs to do more to understand and measure its impact at the different levels.

3   Sustained commitment increases credibility

As EASAC developed its expertise and visibility in the specific area of infectious diseases, it became progressively easier to build contact with the relevant policymakers and with scientific and industry bodies, attracting an increasing volume of external evidence. In consequence, more effective projects could be designed – because we can capitalise on early interchange with opinion leaders to identify issues and evidence, and our outputs reflect the broader evidence base.

4   Policymaker receptivity

The scientific community can influence policy in various ways – by effecting change to policy regimens but also by strengthening the intellectual environment, for example by broadening the horizon for policy issues thinking. It has been important for EASAC to differentiate its policy advice activities from lobbying and campaigning but experience teaches that those who contribute advice are most successful when cultivating a longer-term relationship with policymakers. Context is paramount, however, and there is often a window of opportunity for advising on policy.

In considering the interfaces between the scientific and policymaking communities, the conceived role of policymaker as receptor of research (Hanney *et al.* 2003) is helpful in ensuring that science advice is usable by being relevant, by being presented effectively, and to a policymaking system that is willing and capable of absorbing the advice.

5   Funding support to ensure provision of quality advice

The diverse examples of science policy advice described in this book are funded in various ways and it is important that the plurality in sources of support is maintained and, preferably, expanded. The development of the European Commission-funded Framework Programme 7 Health Theme allows more funding for research to provide evidence for policymakers.

This will be highly welcome in helping to create a systematic resource that EASAC and others can compete to use in generating high quality science advice.

REFERENCES

Collins, P. and Lindberg, U. 2002. 'Independent science advice in the EU', *The IPTS Report*, December 4–7.

EASAC 2005. *Infectious Diseases – Importance of Co-ordinated Activity in Europe*, London: The Royal Society.

EASAC 2006. *Vaccines: Innovation and Human Health*, London: The Royal Society.

EASAC 2007. *Tackling Antimicrobial Resistance*, London: The Royal Society.

EASAC 2008. *Combating the Threat of Zoonotic Infections*, London: The Royal Society.

EASAC 2009. *Drug-resistant Tuberculosis: Challenges, Consequences and Strategies for Control*, London: The Royal Society.

European Commission 2002. *On the Collection and Use of Expertise by the Commission: Principles and Guidelines*, COM(2002) 713 final.

Fayl, G. and Kyriakou, D. 2002. 'Voluntary interdisciplinary trans-national networks in an enlarged Europe', *The IPTS Report*, December 2–3.

Hanney, S.R., Gonzalez-Block, M.A., Buxton, M.J. and Kogan, M. 2003. 'The utilisation of health research in policy-making: concepts, examples and methods of assessment', *BioMed Central*, available at: www.health-policy-systems.com/content/1/1/2 (last accessed 7 April 2010).

Health Council of the Netherlands 2006. *Science Advice on Public Health at National and European Level*, available at: www.healthcouncil.nl.

Weingart, P. and Lentsch, J. (eds.) 2006. *Standards and 'Best Practices' of Scientific Policy Advice – A Roundtable Discussion with Sir David King*, Berlin: Berlin-Brandenburgische Akademie der Wissenschaften.

20 Quality control in the advisory process: towards an institutional design for robust science advice

Justus Lentsch and Peter Weingart[1]

Introduction: towards an organisational approach to science advising

In order to improve the quality of science advising and make a claim about appropriate institutional design, we first will have to understand the meaning of science advice and how it is actually practised. In the following we will derive a few very general lessons to be learned from the case narratives assembled in this book.

We started with the contention that the business of science advising has developed into a professional domain of its own. This runs contrary to a still widely shared assumption, that scientific advising is nothing else than the application of scientific knowledge to public policy problems. According to this view, there is a 'fully objective, independent and impartial domain of technoscience that experts can tap into' – the only challenge being to ensure that they do so with integrity (Wynne *et al.* 2007: 77). In fact, the relationship to the academic domain is quite complex and has to be carefully managed.[2] The provision of a particular kind of expertise-based services or 'serviceable truths' is constitutive for the professional domain of science advising (Jasanoff 1990). Following Jasanoff, activities and outputs of scientific advisory organisations must not be conflated with academic science and its products (such as scientific publications). In fact, it is expertise – not science proper – that informs regulation and policy-making, i.e. the ability to generate, synthesise, transform and assess knowledge pertaining to particular policy problems – independently from

---

[1] The views expressed are those of the authors and strictly personal.

[2] In science and technology studies (STS) this has been conceptualised as *boundary work*, activities of constructing, negotiating and defending the boundaries that demarcate science from politics (Jasanoff 1990; Gieryn 1983, 1995; Owens). However, advisory bodies not only delineate the boundaries between science and politics, but proactively manage them, i.e. are involved in a process of hybridisation, through which the production of knowledge and the production of policy become inextricably intertwined (Owens) – a process that has been also described as the 'co-production' of science and politics (Jasanoff 2004) or as 'coordination work' (Bijker, Bal and Hendriks 2009).

whether it is of interest to the scientific community. The territory of expertise is 'subject to neither purely scientific nor wholly political rules of the game' (Jasanoff).[3] Science and politics, instead, are 'inextricably interconnected' (Pielke 2007: 79). Therefore, the realm on which science advice builds has to be 'mapped, explored and better understood as a prelude to solving the problem of quality control' (Jasanoff). The question of quality in scientific advisory processes thus points our attention to the mechanisms that integrate normative and cognitive concerns on each level: the advisory body, the body of knowledge, and on the level of the individual expert (see Jasanoff).

As we have already pointed out, science advising constitutes a professional domain of its own, guided by its own standards, norms and institutions and represented in organisations of a particular kind.[4] Although this seems to be obvious, it is easily overlooked that advisory organisations have to be distinguished (and often distinguish themselves!) from scientific organisations such as universities or dedicated research organisations. Scientific advisory bodies belong to a particular kind of intermediary organisation situated between the scientific domain and the world of politics.[5] In this book we have characterised a scientific advisory organisation by the following characteristics (cf also Weingart and Lentsch 2008: 48):

- it is an institutionalised (or statutory) body;
- it performs its internal operations independently, i.e. free from external influences, particularly from its clients;
- its activities are grounded in or based upon scientific expertise;[6]
- its mandate essentially comprises to advise the legislative or the executive, i.e. the government or governmental departments, on science-related policy issues.

With regard to the question of quality we distinguish two notions of robustness: first, *epistemic robustness* that pertains to the quality of knowledge and, second, *political robustness* that refers to aspects of responsiveness and political legitimacy. The criterion of robustness focuses not so much on the one single best option given the current state of knowledge, but rather at identifying strategies whose 'most satisfactory outcomes

---

[3] All references to chapters in this book are just to the author(s). All others are specified.

[4] An analysis of the practice of policy advising in terms of the sociology of professions is given in Buchholz 2008.

[5] David Guston has characterised these kinds of organisations as 'boundary organisations' (for a case study on advisory organisations, see Guston 2005).

[6] Hence, scientific advisory bodies have to be distinguished, on the one hand, from organisations that do political counselling and, on the other hand, from representative or deliberative structures such as stakeholder fora, citizens' conferences or round tables.

Table 20.1 *Dimensions of quality*

	Epistemic robustness	Political robustness
Substantive aspects	Reliability; relevance; direction of error	Outcome
Procedural aspects	Quality assurance: quality assurance of input data; treatment of uncertainty and values; accounting for biases; integrating widest possible range of epistemic perspectives	Mandate; organisational trustworthiness and legitimacy

occur in the largest range of future contingencies' (Mitchell 2009: 93). This kind of assessment will focus on the limits and on the points where expertise-based policy options may fail. Moreover, whereas the discussion often focuses on substantive or output-oriented aspects, we propose to acknowledge the importance of procedural aspects and criteria as well. This leads to a four-dimension framework or *quality-matrix* (see Table 20.1).

The different chapters of this book each look at a particular model organisation. The focus thereby is on institutional mechanisms. Whereas in the introductory chapter we suggested a typology of advisory organisations, we will now focus on the institutional mechanisms by which science advice or *serviceable truths* are constructed. That is, we will look inside the organisations rather than at the role they play as actors in the policy process. In particular, we will ask how the procedural and substantive norms of epistemic and political robustness are set into practice via organisational routines and mechanisms within different institutional arrangements.[7] With regard to the question of institutional design, the case studies show that the main challenge is to achieve a functionally appropriate balance between (scholarly and professional) independence on the one hand, and responsiveness to the norms and requirements of the political process on the other. Obviously advisory organisations can have very different mandates and functions and thus aim at producing and delivering very different outputs, products or services. Therefore, there will not be *the* one standard solution or uniform blueprint for resolving the question of appropriate institutional design. However, at least two issues will have to be addressed:

---

[7] Bijker *et al.* (2009) went even a step further as they undertook a detailed ethnographic field study of the social practices within the Health Council, an advisory body to the Netherlands' government.

First, advisory organisations have different mandates and, accordingly, aim at different outputs as well as perform different functions in the policy process. Before trying to improve the performance and the institutional design of an advisory organisation, the various outputs advisory organisations are aiming at must be systematised. That means, the spectrum of *serviceable truths* they produce and the quality criteria they have to meet has to be mapped.

Second, when approaching the quality question from an organisation theoretical point of view, one should give an account of the core aspects that should guide the organisation of advisory activities. Adapted to the particular circumstances it should provide the basis for the institutional design, i.e. the internal procedures and institutional mechanisms putting the above-mentioned norms into practice.[8] In the following we will give a synthesis of the main institutional mechanisms and procedures across all chapters along the lines of the different stages or phases of an advisory process: (1) the preparatory phase (framing and project definition; institutionalisation and committee selection, etc.); (2) the working phase or the execution of the advisory project; and (3) the final phase or the *making of an impact* (encompassing activities such as publication, staging of the report, utilisation, etc.).

Preparatory phase: setting the stage of the advisory project

The main task in the preliminary phase of an advisory project is to prepare the stage, using Goffman's theatre metaphor, and to delineate the front-stage from the back-stage.[9]

Lesson I: Do not give advice without a mandate: clarify the mandate of an advisory organisation and its official role in the policy process

The mandate is constitutive for an advisory body as a formal organisation. It defines the basic *terms of contract*, the relationship to the client as well as to the different publics (i.e. those who are concerned with the advisory body by communication, information and decision) and, last but not least,

---

[8] The US American NRC has evaluated the United Nations' System of Science Advice along similar lines (NRC 2002).

[9] In his *Science on Stage* Stephen Hilgartner (2000: 6) alludes to the dramatic techniques science advisers use to 'enact' the basis of their authority as experts. According to Hilgartner, who borrows his theatre metaphor from the works of Erving Goffman, a 'theatrical perspective' offers new insights into how credibility is being produced in advisory settings. In order to elucidate the dramaturgical aspects of scientific advisory processes, we will take up the theatre metaphor as well.

determines the advisory body's formal or official function in the policy process. Many advisory bodies have a legal basis or are at least recognised by law, such as the German Research Institutes, the Netherlands' Advisory Councils or the European Agencies. The US American National Academy (NAS) has the legal status of a non-profit, private charity, but operates under a congressional charter of 1863.[10] It is chartered to investigate, examine, experiment and report upon any subject of science or art whenever called upon by any department of the government.

However, mandates can be very different in nature: (a) an advisory body may have a fairly general mandate (to advise upon any issue in a policy field such as the UK Royal Commission on Environmental Pollution); or (b) it may derive its advisory function from a specific and particular assignment, limited in scope and timeframe (typical for blue ribbon commissions or standing commissions in fields like risk assessment and standard-setting); in addition, (c) the advisory relation may also be governed by directive or control-and-command structures (typical for internal governmental advisory bodies such as the German Research Institutes); and, finally, (d) an organisation may advise in partial fulfilment of duties that come along with the status of a profession that its constituent enjoys.[11] Examples range from Academies (such as the Royal Society that has been granted professional independence and academic freedom by a Royal Charter in 1660) to bodies like the International Commission on Radiation Protection (ICRP) whose parent is the International Society of Radiology, a professional society committed to radiation measurement and standard-setting (Streffer).

With regard to its official role in the policy process, advisory bodies can be characterised, first, with regard to their distance from decision-making and second, whether it is about using expertise to broaden (or to narrow) the range of choices available to decision-makers.[12]

Lesson II: Getting to know when scientific advice is needed and providing it if and only if it is actually needed

'The prize', as Peter Collins remarks, goes to the one who poses the right question. Therefore, framing the question and defining the parameters

---

[10] In some countries the regime of expertise is governed by (constitutional) law – the most prominent provision being the US Federal Advisory Committee Act (see Brown 2009). But also in the Netherlands' advisory committees are regulated by constitutional law.

[11] Although these organisations may not be mandated specifically to give advice to government, one can argue that their role and their societal recognition as professional organisations imply a general mandate to communicate scientific knowledge to governments and the public.

[12] See, e.g., Pielke 2007, and Ezrahi 1980.

of an issue right at the outset is of vital importance for any advisory project. Processes pertaining to the early identification of topics are sometimes institutionalised in the form of *horizon scanning*, *foresight* or *forward look* procedures. Some of the German Governmental Research Institutes, for instance, have such an *antenna function*. In fulfilment of this function they devote a considerable amount of their research capacities to monitoring the policy field, reviewing the expert literature and to conduct research that is high-risk but not necessarily highly rewarded by the academic community (see Kurth and Glasmacher). The American National Academies, to take up another example, maintain about fifty *oversight committees*. These committees are appointed by the chair of the National Research Council and are responsible for oversight of specific segments of the overall portfolio of the Academy (Blair). The Royal Society has specific departments staffed with a considerable number of science policy analysts who support the council in picking up the right issues. The role of the staff consists in monitoring and analysing trends and developments in key policy areas as well as in relevant scientific fields.

Topics for advisory projects do not just appear from nowhere but have to be searched and identified systematically. Identifying the right topics early on requires close interaction between the advisory organisation, its clients and stakeholders. The UK Royal Commission, for instance, consults the environment ministry and other government departments on the choice of topics for investigation. The other side of the coin is to provide advice if and only if it is actually needed. In order to maintain the credibility, there should be reasons obvious to everyone why the project merits attention by the advisory organisation, whether it is actually the right one to ask (Collins; Wagner).

Lesson III: Define the project and state the task explicitly and clearly

For the success of an advisory project it is important to state the advisory task clearly and to reach a shared and mutually agreed upon definition of the advisory project – one that is sufficiently well-defined, neither too narrow nor too broad. It has to be clear on which issues advice is sought. This is not achieved easily because policy problems first have to be made amenable to science advice. Therefore, a final definition of an advisory project will not be given at the beginning of a project but results itself from a process of consultation between the advisory body and those who seek the advice.

The project definition not only determines the *terms of contract* in the advisory relation, i.e. the rights, responsibilities and legitimate expectations. It also provides the point of reference against which the adviser and those advised can position themselves front-stage as social actors in regard to their respective publics, namely as the one who decides and the one who knows.[13] However, it is essential that the project definition leaves enough space to manoeuvre to each side: in order to be legitimate, the result of an advisory process must not be known at the outset. This entails a political risk for the client whom the project addresses, as it is not clear at the outset whether the result will serve his immediate political interests. Also, authoritative advice exerts a certain binding force that may narrow the range of decision-making. In order to enhance the likelihood that the advice is recognised, a good project definition leaves options for the client to cope with the political risks its result may entail.

Similar considerations hold for the advisory body: The project definition should leave enough freedom for the advisory body to position itself as a disinterested actor who performs his activities in professional and scholarly independence and solely in the pursuit of the public good. Does this mean that an advisory body should not take position in a public debate or controversy? Quite the contrary: depending on its mandate, it can very well serve as a trustee of science-related public interests or as a 'knowledge broker' (Owens). In this function it may legitimately engage in a public debate, but should do this in the framework of disinterestedness and scholarly as well as professional independence, thereby carefully recognising the different responsibilities of science and politics, respectively. Particularly in fiercely debated policy issues, such as energy or climate policy, it is essential that the process of project definition allows the advisory body to distance itself from attempts to draw it into a political struggle. Finally, a mutually agreed upon project definition enhances the commitment on both sides and thus minimises the likelihood that the advice will remain without any effect.

The choice of an issue and the way it is framed (and by whom) suggests which aspects, values, interests or perspectives are deemed relevant and how a putative answer may look. In problem definition and framing political and epistemic aspects are entangled. Thus, it is neither solely a political activity nor one that should be left to the advisory body alone, but instead involves processes of mutual coordination and negotiation (Bijker, Bal and Hendriks 2009: 68f.). In order to maintain epistemic robustness, the project definition should keep the

---

[13] Bijker *et al.* (2009: ch. 3) arrive at a similar conclusion.

path of inquiry open to a certain extent and, at the same time, assure the salience and relevance of the project, i.e. enhance the political robustness of the results. One of the major challenges at the beginning of every advisory process is to transform a complex and probably not even well-defined request into a specific advisory project that is manageable and accessible to science-based reasoning and still yields a relevant and salient output. A pragmatic avenue to deal with this issue and to maintain the above-mentioned flexibility is the adjustment of the project definition during the preliminary phase (Feuer and Maranto 2010: 267). In any case should the advisory body have a certain degree of freedom of interpretation of its task?

What does this mean in terms of institutional mechanisms? First of all, there is a direct correlation between the preparatory effort and the eventual success of the project (Collins). Therefore, identifying the right topic and defining the project are the first steps to be taken in an advisory project. In many cases, respective processes are institutionalised, with varying degrees of freedom for negotiation and interpretative flexibility.

As mentioned earlier, in many cases, the process of topic choice is institutionalised and results in a formal written project prospectus or a formal letter of request or task. The Royal Society and the EASAC, for instance, have developed guidelines and a questionnaire to steer the process of defining a project (Collins; Fears and ter Meulen). No project is given a green light that has not been explored at a certain level of detail and that does not meet a standard framework of evaluation. Such a proposal should define the aims, the scope, the expertise needed, possible stakeholders and interests affected, and it should give reasons why the project merits attention by the organisation and whether the body is the right one to ask and is equipped to address the issue appropriately (Collins; Fears and ter Meulen). Finally, a statement of task should contain a tentative work plan and a budget proposal.

Such a 'statement of task' can also serve as a point of departure for subsequent review of the draft report (Blair). On the basis of such proposal the governing bodies of the advisory organisation formally decide whether to start an advisory process or not. Particularly if projects have a broad scope and require considerable resources, a great deal of preliminary planning and research goes into this proposal.

With regard to questions of legitimacy, it is important that an advisory project is reviewed and formally approved by the organisation. At the Royal Society, for instance, a proposal for an advisory project has to be approved by the Director of Science Policy, the Executive Secretary and the Council of the Society or a Vice-President acting on behalf of Council (Collins). The same holds for the NAS, where all projects (and the accompanying work plans) are reviewed and, based on the review, approved, revised or even rejected by the Executive Committee of the National Research Council's Governing Board, if the council believes that the project is inappropriately framed or not within the charter of the National Academies (Blair).

Lesson IV: Separate advice and representation. Select members only on the basis of their expertise or the epistemic perspective they have on the policy problem

The second important quality issue in the preliminary phase of an advisory process pertains to questions of membership, i.e. the criteria, rules and procedures that guide the identification and recruitment of members. As scientific advisory processes have to be distinguished from stakeholder consultations or other kinds of social fora, members should be selected on the basis of their expertise.[14] However, this raises further questions: What is the best group to carry out the project? How can it be assembled? Which disciplines and scientific schools are relevant and how should they be balanced? Should members act in their individual capacities or as representatives of particular societal, professional or institutional interests or perspectives? Who should chair the group? Who appoints the members? Should members be paid? How should unavoidable conflicts of financial (but also of intellectual) interests be dealt with?

According to Sheila Jasanoff, three aspects are constitutive for an advisory organisation and have to be balanced: the assembled expertise, the experts, and the body as a social entity. Thus, an answer to the question of how to organise the selection process (and according to which criteria) requires an answer on three levels: on the level of expertise we have to ask which is relevant and according to which criteria it should be selected. With respect to the experts the question concerns the role which the individual expert should play in the organisation. This includes a screening for conflicts of interests, i.e. whether candidates have commercial interests or are affiliated to a political party or to a non-profit organisation that has a stake in the matter. Many organisations have explicit Conflict of Interest (CoI) Rules and require a written and published statement when indicated.

---

[14] However, that does not mean that stakeholders, professionals, knowledgeable lay persons, etc., cannot significantly contribute to an advisory process. But one should be very careful about how to integrate stakeholders and how to solicit their special expertise. If they are integrated, this should not be because they represent a certain group but rather because they may contribute a particular epistemic perspective grounded in their experience and relevant to the issue at stake.

Finally, on the level of the advisory body the pertinent issue is which organisational provisions are taken so that the body or the group assembled to carry out the project actually function as a unified social actor. There will be no simple solution to this 'three body problem'. But this should not prevent us from having a look at institutional mechanisms by which advisory bodies try to grapple with such challenges.

For an advisory organisation to be credible and authoritative in the eyes of the public, a transparent and carefully designed process of team-formation is essential. Therefore, this process is often formalised. Its very constitution decides upon whether the body is actually equipped to carry out the advisory project. This entails questions such as: Who is responsible for the recruiting? According to which criteria should members be recruited? Who chairs the committee? What role does the staff (and the committee secretary in particular) have? In many organisations the above-mentioned project prospectus or letter of request serves as a basis for identifying and balancing the expertise considered necessary as well as for selecting the experts. The examples assembled in this book show that this process (and criteria) should be as transparent as possible.

Coming to the question of member selection, the committee chair (in the case of collegial bodies) plays a key role. Perhaps to our surprise, we find that it is not so much the special expertise that makes a good chair. Of course, the chair should have a sufficient understanding of the underlying science. Furthermore, an advisory body as a whole should represent the highest expertise and range of relevant perspectives. But particularly in cases where there are competing viewpoints amongst the members, it may be helpful if the chair is not associated with any one of them (Collins). The chair instead is responsible for facilitating and managing the process. Therefore, it is recommended that the process is chaired by a person who has a high general competence in and a comprehensive overview over the field but is not confined to a specialist's perspective. He has to be able to raise questions and make suggestions that are unlikely to emerge from a specialised discussion (see also NRC 2002: 16). Finally, the chair represents the advisory body to the external world. That is why organisations such as the Royal Society appoint as chairs only fellows whereas ordinary committee members are selected on the basis of their expertise only – regardless whether they are fellows or not.

Lesson V: Include a broad range of relevant perspectives in an appropriate balance

Another major task in team formation concerns questions of the balance between multiple disciplinary and other relevant perspectives. Often a great deal of preparatory work is required to identify the pertinent expertise and the experts. As the examples of the NAS and the Royal Society illustrate, professional staff can play quite an important role in soliciting suggestions for potential members.

As Sheila Jasanoff argues, the composition of an advisory body resembles different conceptions of objectivity. One can select members according to the expertise they have accumulated (as is the case in the US), or whether they represent a particular institutional perspective or interest (as is the case in German advisory organisations concerned with standard setting or risk assessment), or, finally, whether they are prone to discern the public good. The Royal Commission on Environmental Pollution, for instance, can be better understood as a committee of experts than as an expert committee (Owens).

Focusing on the two dimensions of expertise and the expert, the question of selection is often framed as a dichotomy between professional competence on the one hand, and the representation of political, national or other partial interests (this is taken as the rationale to giving demographic criteria or geographical/national distribution some significance, as it is the case with the ICRP).[15]

Moreover, there are different mechanisms to select the members: they can be appointed by a public authority such as the chancellor or the Queen, or they can be nominated (e.g. by relevant institutions). A further distinctive feature is whether members serve in their individual capacity, i.e. are appointed in personal capacity, or whether they represent a particular perspective or interest. The Royal Society, for instance, painstakingly attempts to balance competing views and to avoid appointing members with strong vested interests (Collins).

Features like overall expertise or committee balance do not primarily refer to the individual members but rather to the composition of the committee as a collective. Therefore, in addition to the nominations of the individual members, the slate of potential nominees is sometimes subject to review as well (e.g. Blair, Collins).

To sum up, the preparatory phase to a large extent decides upon the success of an ensuing advisory process. In order to meet the two criteria of epistemic and political robustness, an advisory body has to position itself as a particular kind of social actor, namely, one that acts in professional as well as in scholarly independence and one that is authoritative and credible in the sense that it is legitimised and competent to address the issue at hand. With regard to quality issues, the challenge thereby is

---

[15] Instead, expert selection should be better understood in terms of professional, social or political perspectives (Brown 2006).

to balance autonomy and independence on the one hand, and responsiveness to the requirements of the political process on the other. The main institutional mechanisms we have identified for the preparatory phase concern: (i) clarification of the mandate; (ii) formulation of a proposal or project outline to achieve a project definition that translates a public policy problem into a project that is amenable to *scientific* advice and nevertheless still relevant to the advisory body's publics; and (iii) establishment of a transparent selection process.

Work phase: carrying out the advisory project

As we have seen, when an advisory project finally starts, much work has already been done in order to prepare the stage. This preparatory work 'holds a promise' (Bijker, Bal and Hendriks 2009: 102), namely to present publics and policymakers with 'serviceable truths' (Jasanoff 1990). For the public authority of science advice it is essential to uphold this view front-stage. However, in fact, science's ability to do this is severely weakened and stressed (Jasanoff). The main quality issue in the final working phase is thus to integrate normative and cognitive demands and to effectively bridge between science and politics.

To answer the question which institutional mechanisms are involved in the construction of serviceable truths, and how they operate and according to which general principles, in the following we will consider three cross-cutting issues in the working phase. First, we will address questions related to information and data gathering. Second, we will have a look at how scepticism and deliberation is organised.[16] Finally, we will consider certain quality controls in the strict sense of the word.

Lesson VI: Be as open and transparent about the information input and knowledge base as possible

A key aspect to science advice is its knowledge base. However, as we have learned, in general, there will be no *facts* or a given evidence

---

[16] With regard to these first two aspects, it will turn out that openness and transparency on the one hand, and confidentiality on the other, present two sides of the same coin. These two demands will have to be reconciled in the advisory process. This lesson may surprise those who are inclined to think that transparency and disclosure of information provide the key to good governance. However, transparency will make institutions more trustworthy, if it puts those whose trust should be increased into the position to judge matters or the performance of an organisation for themselves, or to follow, check, or challenge the information disclosed (O'Neill 2006). As the example of nutrition labelling shows, a difficult issue can easily be obscured and public recognition prevented by providing information which is precise, scientifically accurate and yet generally unintelligible (Podger).

base that entail a unique correct policy, to start with (Sarewitz; Sluijs, Petersen and Funtowicz). Scientific information that is accepted as input into advisory process instead is often characterised by insufficient under-standing, uncertainties, knowledge gaps, values choices or incommen-surability between different data sets, etc. In response to emerging needs, several institutions that interface science and policy, such as advisory organisations, have adopted *knowledge* quality assessment approaches (Sluijs, Petersen and Funtowicz). One approach, discussed by Sluijs *et al.* is the so-called NUSAP-scheme, a five-dimensional notational system proposed by Funtowicz and Ravetz (1990) for the analysis and diagnosis of uncertainty in the knowledge base of complex (environmental) policy problems. According to Sluijs *et al.*, one of the basic qualifiers of knowledge input is 'pedigree', an evaluative account of the production process and the scientific status of the information used. This entails questions like who has produced or funded the data, whether the information is peer reviewed, etc. As the case narratives in this book suggest, an advisory organisation is well advised to manage and handle the issue of knowledge input as transparently as possible (and also point to the gaps in the information available and resulting research needs).

There is a huge variety of different information sources, ranging from a review of the published scientific as well as of so-called *grey* literature,[17] written and oral evidence to public meetings and hearings. In addition, some advisory organisations, the Royal Society and the European Acad-emies Science Advisory Council, for instance, publicly call for evidence. Public calls have the advantage that they make a project open and that they give all interested parties a stake in the project; this effect can be reinforced by publishing the evidence received (e.g. on the website or as an appendix to the advisory report) (Collins). In many fields, science advice has to rely on externally supplied data, environmental, economic, surveys or data on the toxicity of chemicals.[18] Management and review of data requires a professional staff that should be given independence. An even more far reaching proposal is to institutionally separate the

[17] For several reasons *grey* literature in many cases presents an invaluable source for scientific information, on issues or from regions where no *certified* scientific literature exists. However, it has to be handled with great care, as the recent quarrel about the International Panel on Climate Change shows. On radiobiology and grey science, see Shrader-Frechette 2005.

[18] The debate on issues of data ownership or the funding effect has been fiercely debated with regard to pharmaceuticals, biomedical science and risk assessment (see, e.g., Krimsky 2006). It is a big issue in the debate about REACH, the new European Community regulation in chemicals. However, similar concerns can be raised with regard to economical or environmental data.

collection of data from the advisory process – and to regard (statistical) data collection as a public good (see Den Butter on the Dutch *Polder Model* or Podger on the role of data in risk assessment on the European level).[19] In order to ensure highest transparency, the NAS maintains any written material provided by individuals who are not officials, agents or employees of the National Academies in a 'public access file' that is available to the public for examination (Blair). Networking and scientific exchange, of course, is essential for any advisory process. Consultations, whether held in private or as public expert or stakeholder consultations, ensure that the project team can base its work on a broad range of knowledge. And they have the side-effect that the project team becomes aware of the wider normative and cognitive contexts into which its advice is situated (Collins). In any case, the advisory body should be as open and transparent about the sources of information and their status as possible.

Lesson VII: Keep deliberative processes confidential and shield them from external influences

With regard to confidentiality, it is important to distinguish between the requirements for information input and knowledge-base on the one hand, and the deliberative process within the advisory organisation on the other. It is crucial for epistemic robustness to organise and manage scepticism in accordance with decision rules that ensure that a final and targeted result (mostly an advisory report) is achieved within limited time. The members of the advisory organisation must be able to step outside the dominant discourse, scrutinise taken-for-granted assumptions, constantly test ideas and stimulate mutual learning (Owens). Moreover, 'hobby horses' of individual members may become rationalised in the process of deliberation (Owens). Therefore, experts and their deliberations should be protected by a *safety zone* from external attempts to influence their work (Wagner and Steinzor 2006: 286).

Finally, it is often unavoidable to include experts who, due to their professional background or training, have a conflict of interest (i.e. personal gain or loss depending on the outcome) or bias (i.e. unpublished preferences influencing the outcome or opinion). Therefore, organised scepticism and open deliberation within the body is a key.

The case narratives demonstrate that at least two aspects are central to the management and organisation of scepticism. First, deliberation does not simply happen but rather has to be staged and facilitated. In order to

---

[19] The issue of data collection is also central to the work of institutes like the Robert Koch Institute (Kurth and Glasmacher) or the Economic Research Institutes in Germany.

further a debate, it may be fruitful to mobilise expertise by means of organised dispute (see also Bijker, Bal and Hendriks 2009: 77). In this process the role of the chair (in collaboration with the head of staff or scientific secretary) is crucial: his function is to mobilise the expertise of the individual members and confront them with each other to advance the debate (Bijker, Bal and Hendriks 2009: 77). Second, the examples demonstrate nearly unanimously that confidentiality of the internal deliberations is central to an open, rational and critical exchange of ideas (Feuer and Maranto 2010: 267). Appropriate levels of openness and transparency can be ensured by publishing brief summaries of the meetings, for instance. However, in order to prevent politicisation and to maintain the authority – and the integrity! – of the body and its members, it is essential that internal drafts, personalised minutes and individual opinions of the members remain confidential.

Lesson IX: The draft report (or whatever advisory product) should be subject to independent and extended *peer review according to predetermined criteria*

Before we can approach the quality question further, we have to introduce a basic distinction: at one level quality control of a draft report equals – notwithstanding all differences – the established practice of peer review (see below); but at quite another level quality control of review pertains also to the process by which the work of an advisory or expert committee becomes the view of the organisation (see Collins). Academies often call this procedure 'nostrification', the formal process by which a point of view becomes adopted by the organisation. This happens in a formal process by which a report or other advisory product is approved by the advisory body's governing board, council or presidency. That a report is formally approved is essential if the body is expected to speak with one voice, i.e. with its full authority, and for the advisory body to maintain its organisational credibility.[20]

The former aspect pertains to the function of peer review in the advisory setting, i.e. to ensure quality. However, as we have learned, the issue of quality control in scientific policy advice is neither a straightforward nor even a well-defined task. As has been argued at length, in

---

[20] Note, unanimous approval does not exclude minority opinions! Some organisations, like the Royal Society, have both lines of publications: publications on behalf of the organisation and publications where the organisation serves as general editor but the members of the committee and/or the professional staff take responsibility as a collective of authors for the single report.

contexts like the regulatory domain the concept of 'peer review' often means different things to different audiences (Jasanoff 1985, 1990). Peer review and the issue of quality control constitute an arena of *boundary work*; conflicts about the jurisdictional claims of the various parties involved.

However, we do not want to open Pandora's box and discuss the perils of peer review in general at this point. For the sake of the argument, we will focus on a few basic points: First of all, in an advisory setting quality controls often fulfil completely different functions than does peer review in academia: neither do quality controls in an advisory setting serve as an entry ticket to the scientific discourse, nor do they function as a mechanism for the distribution of reputation (by means of admission to a prestigious journal). Criteria used by prestigious journals (such as originality, etc.) for the acceptance of articles often prove counterproductive in the advisory setting. The reason is that they favour methodologies or lines of research that do not bear on the public policy problems at issue or are prone to certain directions of error. Both will give rise to inadvertent consequences for the overall outcome of the advisory process and the decisions or regulations based upon the advice (see Dammann and Gee). The established criteria of scientific quality alone will have to be amended and complemented by criteria that are more appropriate to the advisory context (we have alluded to such criteria in terms of epistemic robustness).[21]

However, if there are such differences between peer review in academia and review processes in advisory processes, how do the latter function and what role do they play in regard to the quality issue? Obviously, it makes no sense to replicate the scientific expertise of the committee or the advisory body; instead review processes in advisory settings should focus on the following aspects (e.g. Den Butter; Blair; Collins; Fears and ter Meulen; Perthes):

- whether the advisory product addresses the terms of reference;
- whether the conclusions are consistent with the evidence presented;
- whether the recommendations are appropriate to the request and tractable;
- whether uncertainties, *unknown unknowns* and risks are taken into account and communicated appropriately;[22]

---

[21] A general overview is given in Lentsch 2008.

[22] In fact, risk communication should be an essential component of advisory activities. See Podger. For a comprehensive overview over risk communication, see Renn 2008: ch. 7.

- whether feedback has sufficiently been incorporated (and independence preserved);
- whether the form of the advice is suited to reach its intended audience;
- whether the advice is impartial.

Putting these criteria into practice, has certain ramifications. First, nearly all advisory organisations presented in this book have formulated explicit peer review guidelines, most of them conforming to the above-mentioned criteria. Second, in academia peer review means the practice of evaluating scholarly papers by fellow professionals who are experts in the very same field in order to select them for publication – a practice that has been extended to the evaluation of grant proposals, etc. As this practice in its pure form is not appropriate to the advisory setting for several reasons many advisory organisations have modified it accordingly. Whereas criteria of traditional peer review focus on products, a good performance on the second set of criteria depends on procedural issues and the institutional set-up of the process of policy preparation (Den Butter).

Most of them appoint a separate review board for each advisory project (Collins; Blair; Fears and ter Meulen). As the focus is on questions of appropriateness, relevance, blind spots, perspectives missing, uncertainties and bias, reviewers are often drawn from a wider pool, extending beyond fellow professionals and including a broad range of complementary perspectives and of non-scientists where appropriate (see, e.g., Collins; Blair).[23] Sometimes the review board is appointed right at the beginning of an advisory project and maintains a kind of supervisory function throughout the whole process. The lines of accountability of such a review board can be organised differently: it may comment directly to the group carrying out the advisory project, but it may also advise the body's overall governing authority, such as council, presidency or board of trustees. In order to increase transparency, the NAS, for instance, in addition makes the names and the affiliations of the referees public. Notwithstanding whether it agrees with the criticism should the group carrying out the advisory project be requested to respond to the comments of the review board, preferably in a separate document? This document may be examined again in order to ensure that the review guidelines and

---

[23] Silvio Funtowicz and Jerome Ravetz have characterised such procedures that extend the pool of reviewers and include the perspective of stakeholders as *extended* peer review procedures (see Funtowicz and Ravetz 1990).

criteria have been met (Blair). Last, but not least, stakeholders and, particularly, sponsors of a request for advice must not be allowed to suggest any changes.[24]

Making an impact: staging the output

Final approval of the output (e.g. an advisory report) does not mark the end, but the beginning of the final phase of an advisory project (Collins). Starting with the publication of a report, this phase usually entails dissemination work 'making sure the message reaches its target' (Collins) and follow-up work 'making sure the target heeds the message' (Collins).

However, as important as this phase is, under any circumstances the fine line between dissemination and communication activities on the one hand, and methods of public affairs such as lobbying and campaigning should be carefully observed! Otherwise, this would easily put the outcome of the whole process and even the status of the advisory body at risk.

> *Lesson X: Making sure that the advice reaches its target!*
> *Any report should be published within an appropriate*
> *timeframe and in a targeted format.*

In order to realise an effect, an advice has to be carefully staged and launched. First of all, any advice given should be published. Publication is vital in order to maintain legitimacy and credibility. The publication of the results should be in an appropriate and targeted format (or probably even in different formats addressing different audiences) as well as within an appropriate timeframe. In some cases it may be appropriate to first make the advisory product (e.g. a report) available to clients, sponsors or exclusive target-groups such as the press in a pre-publication format, probably with a ban on publication. This gives the addressees enough time to prepare for an answer and thereby will increase the likelihood that the advice is taken on board. Moreover, timing and using windows of opportunity and public attention are very important aspects to an effective staging. Finally, additional dissemination activities, like

---

[24] The EEA's rules of procedure, for instance, ensure that information published by the Agency is published on the sole authority of the Executive Director and is not subject to amendment for political or reasons by the Management Board (Dammann and Gee).

press-conferences, side-letters to ministry officials, briefings of executive agencies or government departments, may be recommended (Blair). These activities give additional opportunity to highlight certain aspects of the advice.[25]

The second, and perhaps even more important aspect, is choosing a publication format (or different formats) targeted to the intended audience(s); usual formats are reports, short and pronounced policy papers or websites. Very important is a careful wording and framing.[26] A report should be accompanied by a brief summary that is easily comprehensible to non-specialists.

Lesson XI: Making sure that the targeted audience will attend to the advice!

The final phase in an advisory project comprises follow-up work, 'making sure the target heeds the message' (Collins). Usually an advisory body has no official channel for promoting its product once the work is released. Moreover, for reasons of impartiality and in order not to risk its status, an advisory body should be very careful about interfering with the communication and reception of the report in the public; instead it may be better advised to keep a low profile (Bijker, Bal and Hendriks 2009: 134). As the experiences show, advisory processes are most successful when cultivating a longer-term relationship with policymakers (Fears and ter Meulen; Owens). However, there are but a few things that can be done in order to help the message reach its target. The most effective one is to require a formal governmental response or formal statement of reaction (as is the case with the Royal Commission; Owens). However, such a requirement puts much pressure on the sponsors of a request for advice and therefore should be regulated in the mandate. Less demanding is to monitor the implementation, check whether the advice has been taken on board and publicly comment on the outcome (Collins; Stucke).

Finally, an important part of the follow-up work will take place informally and through networking activities of the members and staff. Often

---

[25] The Netherlands Health Council, for instance, has a newsletter with a specially designed yellow appendix which, in some cases, contains the main messages. Whereas usually appendices are ignored, the special formatting calls the readers attention to this section (Bijker, Bal and Hendriks 2009: 114).

[26] Susan Owens impressively analyses in her chapter on the Royal Commission how this has contributed to a remarkable long-term impact in some cases.

members and staff are invited to lecture and discuss the results at scientific conferences, stakeholder events or other occasions (Blair; Collins; Fears and ter Meulen; Streffer). In this way, staff involved may become subject-matter experts who are frequently called upon as other similar issues are considered (Blair). The advisory project may trigger an informal process of building up an epistemic community around an issue that may prove very effective in the long run.

Lesson XII: Promote organisational learning

Last, but not least, the examples show that those advisory bodies that promote internal *organisational learning* from past experiences are most effective in advising and influencing policymaking:[27] the Royal Society, for instance, frequently revisits completed projects for necessary updating in the light of new evidence (Collins). Learning from experience and, hence, redetermination and adjustment are essential to a robust approach to knowledge (Oreskes). Organisational learning can also be furthered by a written internal report on the advisory project of the secretary or head of staff to the governing board or council when the project is finally complete, thereby commenting on lessons learned and, if possible, measures for judging success (Collins).

Incidents like the international controversy about the institutional reform of the Intergovernmental Panel on Climate Change in early 2010 demonstrate that the advisory process is fragile, particularly when conducted under intense public scrutiny. This highlights that the legitimacy, public credibility and the reliability of advisory organisations are to a large extent a question of finding an appropriate institutional design, one that balances requirements of epistemic and political robustness. However, there is no uniform solution or blueprint. Hopefully, the case narratives assembled in this book and the general lessons drawn from them can serve as a resource to evaluate and improve the institutional design of scientific advisory organisations.

---

[27] We do not want to enter the debate about organisational learning and whether this notion makes sense at all. Instead, we just want to point the attention to a particular kind of steady and persistent behavioural changes that result from procedural knowledge, past experiences, and performances of the organisation in the advisory process and that are concerned with the basic precepts of the organisation. Factors that promote this kind of organisational change pertain to reflexive mechanisms in the governance and communication structures. For a framework, see, e.g., Siebenhüner 2002.

REFERENCES

Bijker, Wiebe E., Bal, Roland and Hendriks, Ruud 2009. *The Paradox of Scientific Authority: The Role of Scientific Advice in Democracies*, Cambridge, MA: MIT Press.

Brown, Mark B. 2006. 'Fairly balanced: The politics of representation on government advisory committees', *Political Research Quarterly* 61/4: 547–60.

Brown, Mark B. 2009. 'Federal Advisory Committees in the United States: A Survey of the Political and Administrative Landscape', in Justus Lentsch and Peter Weingart (eds.), *Scientific Advice to Policy Making: International Comparison*, Opladen & Farmington Hills: Barbara Budrich Publishers.

Buchholz, Kai 2008. *Professionalisierung der wissenschaftlichen Politikberatung? Interaktions- und professionssoziologische Perspektiven*, Bielefeld: Transcript.

Ezrahi, Yaron 1980. 'Utopian and pragmatic rationalism: The political context of scientific advice', *Minerva* 18: 111–31.

Feuer, Michael J. and Maranto, Christina J. 2010. 'Science advice as procedural rationality: reflections on the National Research Council', *Minerva* 48: 259–75.

Funtowicz, S.O. and Ravetz, J.R. 1990. *Uncertainty and Quality in Science for Policy*, Dordrecht: Kluwer Academic Publishers.

Gieryn, Thomas F. 1983. 'Boundary-work and the demarcation of science from non-science: Strains and interests in professional ideologies of scientists', *American Sociological Review* 48: 781–95.

Gieryn, Thomas F. 1995. 'Boundaries of science', in S. Jasanoff, G.E. Markle, J.C. Petersen and T. Pinch (eds.), *Handbook of Science and Technology Studies*, Thousand Oaks, London and New Delhi: Sage, pp. 393–443.

Guston, David H. 2005. 'Institutional design for socially robust knowledge: The national toxicology program's report on carcinogens', in Sabine Maasen and Peter Weingart (eds.), *Democratization of Expertise? Exploring Novel Forms of Scientific Advice in Political Decision-Making*, Dordrecht: Springer, pp. 63–80.

Hilgartner, Stephen 2000. *Science on Stage: Expert Advice as Public Drama*, Stanford University Press.

Jasanoff, Sheila 1985. 'Peer review in the regulatory process', *Science, Technology, & Human Values* 10/3: 20–32.

Jasanoff, Sheila 1990. *The Fifth Branch: Science Advisers as Policymakers*, Cambridge, MA: Harvard University Press.

Jasanoff, Sheila 2004. 'The idiom of co-production', in Sheila Jasanoff (ed.), *States of Knowledge: The Co-Production of Science and Social Order*, London: Routledge, pp. 1–12.

Krimsky, Sheldon 2006. 'Publication bias, data ownership, and the funding effect in science: Threats to the integrity of biomedical research', in Wendy Wagner and Rena Steinzor (eds.), *Rescuing Science from Politics: Regulation and the Distortion of Scientific Research*, Cambridge University Press, pp. 61–85.

Lentsch, Justus 2008. 'Qualitätssicherung in der wissenschaftlichen Politikberatung', in Stephan Böchler and Rainer Schützeichel (eds.), *Politikberatung*, Stuttgart: Lucius & Lucius, pp. 194–216.

Mitchell, Sandra D. 2009. *Unsimple Truths: Science, Complexity, and Policy*, University of Chicago Press.

National Research Council (NRC) 2002. *Knowledge and Diplomacy: Science Advice in the United Nations System*, Washington DC: National Academies Press.

O'Neill, Sarah 2006. 'Transparency and the ethics of communication', *British Academy Lectures* 125: 75–90.

Pielke, Roger S., Jr. 2007. *The Honest Broker: Making Sense of Science in Policy and Politics*, Cambridge University Press.

Renn, Ortwin 2008. *Risk Governance: Coping With Uncertainty in a Complex World*, London: Earthscan, Sterling.

Shrader-Frechette, Kristin 2005. 'Radiobiology and gray science: Flaws in landmark new radiation protections', *Science and Engineering Ethics* 11/2: 167–9.

Siebenhüner, Bernd 2002. 'How do scientific assessments learn? Part I: Conceptual framework and case-study of the IPCC', *Environmental Science & Policy* 5: 411–20.

Wagner, Wendy and Steinzor, Rena 2006. 'Conclusion: The imperatives of the principles', in Wendy Wagner and Rena Steinzor (eds.), *Rescuing Science from Politics: Regulation and the Distortion of Scientific Research*, Cambridge University Press, pp. 281–98.

Weingart, Peter and Lentsch, Justus 2008. *Wissen – Beraten – Entscheiden. Form und Funktion wissenschaftlicher Politikberatung in Deutschland*, Weilerswist: Velbrück.

Wynne, Brian, Felt, Ulrike, Eduarda Gonçalves, Maria, Jasanoff, Sheila, Jepsen, Maria, Joly, Pierre-Benoît, Konopasek, Zdenck *et al.* 2007. *Taking European Knowledge Society Seriously*, Brussels: European Commission.

Index